Why Nietzsche Still?

Why Nietzsche Still?

Reflections on Drama, Culture, and Politics

Edited by
Alan D. Schrift

UNIVERSITY OF CALIFORNIA PRESS
Berkeley · Los Angeles · London

University of California Press
Berkeley and Los Angeles, California

University of California Press, Ltd.
London, England

© 2000 by the Regents of the University
of California

Library of Congress Cataloging-in-Publication Data

Why Nietzsche still? : reflections on drama, culture,
   politics / edited by Alan D. Schrift
        p.   cm.
      Includes bibliographical references and index.
      ISBN 0-520-21851-5 (alk. paper).—
      ISBN 0-520-21852-3 (alk paper)
      1. Nietzsche, Friedrich Wilhelm, 1844–1900.
   I. Schrift, Alan D., 1955–
   B3317.W456   2000
   193—dc21   99-31466
                                            CIP

Manufactured in the United States of America

08   07   06   05   04   03   02   01   00   99
10   9   8   7   6   5   4   3   2   1

Even now one is ashamed of resting, and prolonged reflection almost gives people a bad conscience. One thinks with a watch in one's hand, even as one eats one's midday meal while reading the latest news of the stock market; one lives as if one always "might miss out on something." "Rather do anything than nothing": this principle, too, is merely a string to throttle all culture and good taste. Just as all forms are visibly perishing by the haste of the workers, the feeling for form itself, the ear and eye for the melody of movements are also perishing. The proof of this may be found in the universal demand for *gross obviousness* in all those situations in which human beings wish to be honest with one another for once—in their associations with friends, women, relatives, children, teachers, pupils, leaders, and princes: One no longer has time or energy for ceremonies, for being obliging in an indirect way, for *esprit* in conversation, and for any *otium* at all. Living in a constant chase after gain compels people to expend their spirit to the point of exhaustion in continual pretense and overreaching and anticipating others. Virtue has come to consist of doing something in less time than someone else. Hours in which honesty is *permitted* have become rare, and when they arrive one is tired and does not only want to "let oneself go" but actually wishes to *stretch out* as long and wide and ungainly as one happens to be. This is how people now write *letters,* and the style and spirit of letters will always be the true "sign of the times."

If sociability and the arts still offer any delight, it is the kind of delight that slaves, weary of their work, devise for themselves. How frugal our educated—and uneducated—people have become regarding "joy"! How they are becoming increasingly suspicious of all joy! More and more, *work* enlists all good conscience on its side; the desire for joy already calls itself a "need to recuperate" and is beginning to be ashamed of itself. "One owes it to one's health"—that is what people say when they are caught on an excursion into the country. Soon we may well reach the point where people can no longer give in to the desire for a *vita contemplativa* (that is, taking a walk with ideas and friends) without self-contempt and a bad conscience.

Friedrich Nietzsche, The Gay Science

Contents

Acknowledgments

Although the structure of this collection has evolved over the past few years, its origins can be traced to a session called "Nietzsche and the Dramas of Culture" that I organized for the 1996 meeting of the International Association for Philosophy and Literature (IAPL), held at George Mason University. At that session, earlier versions of the chapters by Debra Bergoffen, Dan Conway, Duncan Large, Jeff Nealon, Gary Shapiro, and me were presented, and the points of intersection among the overlapping themes addressed by our respective papers made it clear to me that we already had the core of what I hoped would grow into an exciting and provocative collection of essays. I would here like to thank the participants of that IAPL session for their essays and their support as this volume came together. I would also like to thank the other authors included here who accepted my invitation to contribute to a collection that I believe represents well the dynamic character of contemporary English-language Nietzsche scholarship. Thanks are also due to Hugh A. Silverman, Executive Director of the International Association for Philosophy and Literature, and Wayne Froman and John Burt Foster, Jr., organizers of the IAPL meeting at George Mason, for their willingness to relinquish the rights to the essays we presented in 1996. I would also like to acknowledge Stanford University Press for permission to reprint a chapter from Judith Butler's *The Psychic Life of Power* © 1997 by the Board of Trustees of the Leland Stanford Junior University; Dr. Francesco Buranelli and the Direzione Generale of the Monumenti

Musei e Gallerie Pontificie for permission to print a reproduction of Raphael's *Transfiguration;* and the Artists Rights Society for permission to print a reproduction of Magritte's *"Les Deux Mystères."*

Edward Dimendberg was the editor at the University of California Press who first encouraged me to submit my manuscript to California, and his enthusiasm for the project is gratefully acknowledged, as is the assistance of Cindy Fulton and Laura Pasquale.

I have benefited from the assistance and advice of several people at Grinnell College, whose contributions I want to acknowledge here. My colleagues Johanna Meehan and Cannon Schmitt read parts of the manuscript, and I have profited from their comments and suggestions. Much of the manuscript was prepared by Helyn Wohlwend, whose skill, attention to detail, patience, and willingness to do whatever needed to be done are greatly appreciated. Several of my students have helped to proofread and check references. First and foremost is Hannah Lobel, whose diligent and attentive reading of the entire manuscript caught more than a few errors that might otherwise have gone undetected. Susanna Drake, André Darlington, Jennifer Johnson, Claire Pirkle, Sarah Reimer, and Gregg Whitworth have all performed various tasks that have helped in the production of this volume. I have also benefited from the financial support of the Trustees of Grinnell College and the Grinnell College Grant Board, under the direction of Deans Charles Duke and James Swartz.

My work, and my life, continue to be supported by friends and family. To all, and most especially to Jill, Joan, and Leonard, my heartfelt thanks for your encouragement and love.

Alan D. Schrift
Grinnell, Iowa
September 1998

Abbreviations

References to Nietzsche's writings appear parenthetically using the standard English title acronyms indicated below. Unless noted otherwise, Roman numerals denote the volume number of a set of collected works or a standard subdivision within a single work in which the sections are not numbered consecutively (e.g., *On the Genealogy of Morals*), Arabic numerals denote the section number rather than the page number, and "P" denotes Nietzsche's prefaces.

References to the *Kritische Studienausgabe* (*KSA*) appear with volume number followed by the fragment number. For example, the abbreviation "*KSA* 2:4[78]" refers to volume 2, fragment 4[78].

References to *Briefwechsel: Kritische Gesamtausgabe* (*KGB*) appear with volume number followed by the page number.

References to *Friedrich Nietzsche: Frühe Schriften* (*FS*) appear with volume number followed by the page number.

References to "Homer's Contest" appear followed by page number in the Cambridge University Press edition.

References to *Thus Spoke Zarathustra* give the part number and chapter title, for example, (*Z:*3 "The Convalescent").

References to *Twilight of the Idols* and *Ecce Homo* give abbreviated chapter title and section number, for example, (*TI* "Ancients" 3) or (*EH* "Books" BGE:2).

AC   *The Antichrist.* Translated by R. J. Hollingdale. Middlesex, England: Penguin Books, 1968.

AOM *Assorted Opinions and Maxims. Human, All-Too-Human. Volume Two.* Translated by R. J. Hollingdale. Cambridge: Cambridge University Press, 1986.

BGE *Beyond Good and Evil.* Translated by Walter Kaufmann. New York: Random House, 1966.

BT   *The Birth of Tragedy.* Translated by Walter Kaufmann. New York: Random House, 1967.

CW   *The Case of Wagner.* Translated by Walter Kaufmann. New York: Random House, 1967.

D   *Daybreak.* Translated by R. J. Hollingdale. Cambridge: Cambridge University Press, 1982.

EH   *Ecce Homo* ["Wise," "Clever," "Books," "Destiny"]. Translated by Walter Kaufmann. New York: Random House, 1967.

FS   *Friedrich Nietzsche: Frühe Schriften.* 5 vols. Edited by Hans Joachim Mette, Karl Schlechta, and Carl Koch. Munich: Beck, 1994.

GM   *On the Genealogy of Morals.* Translated by Walter Kaufmann. New York: Random House, 1967.

GS   *The Gay Science.* Translated by Walter Kaufmann. New York: Random House, 1974.

HC   "Homer's Contest." Translated by Carol Diethe in *On the Genealogy of Morals.* Edited by Keith Ansell-Pearson. Cambridge: Cambridge University Press, 1994.

HH   *Human, All-Too-Human. Volume One.* Translated by R. J. Hollingdale. Cambridge: Cambridge University Press, 1986.

HL   *On the Use and Disadvantage of History for Life.* Translated by Richard T. Gray. Stanford: Stanford University Press, 1995.

KGB *Briefwechsel: Kritische Gesamtausgabe.* Edited by Giorgio Colli and Mazzino Montinari. Berlin: Walter de Gruyter, 1975.

KSA   *Sämtliche Werke. Kritische Studienausgabe.* Edited by Giorgio Colli and Mazzino Montinari. Berlin: Walter de Gruyter, 1980.

TI   *Twilight of the Idols* ["Maxims," "Socrates," "Reason," "World," "Morality," "Errors," "Improvers," "Germans," "Skirmishes," "Ancients," "Hammer"]. Translated by R. J. Hollingdale. Middlesex, England: Penguin Books, 1968. Translated by Duncan Large. Oxford: Oxford University Press, 1998.

WDB   *Werke in drei Bänden.* Edited by Karl Schlechta. Munich: Carl Hanser, 1954–56.

WP   *The Will to Power.* Translated by Walter Kaufmann and R. J. Hollingdale. New York: Random House, 1968.

WS   *The Wanderer and His Shadow. Human, All-Too-Human. Volume Two.* Translated by R. J. Hollingdale. Cambridge: Cambridge University Press, 1986.

Z   *Thus Spoke Zarathustra.* Translated by Walter Kaufmann. New York: Viking Press, 1967.

Introduction

Why Nietzsche Still?

Alan D. Schrift

A nature such as Nietzsche's had to suffer our present ills
more than a generation in advance. What he had to go
through alone and misunderstand, thousands suffer today.

Herman Hesse, preface to Steppenwolf

In 1981 the interdisciplinary journal *boundary 2: a journal of postmodern literature and culture* published a special double issue with the
provocative title "Why Nietzsche Now?" In the preface to the subsequent republication of the issue in book form, the issue's editor, Daniel
T. O'Hara, confronted the question of "why one would edit a collection
of critical essays on the renewed impact of Nietzsche's influence in modern American culture." [1] O'Hara's answer was relatively straightforward: it was, he wrote, "simply a fact of life in the disciplines of philosophy, cultural history, religious studies and literary theory in America"
that Nietzsche was an omnipresent influence. O'Hara went on to isolate
what he took to be the three major forms taken by the "postmodern appropriation of Nietzsche": the hermeneutical/philosophical strain that
followed from Heidegger's destructive hermeneutics, the deconstructive
strain inspired by Derrida, and the archaeological or genealogical strain
informed by Foucault's "genealogy of power in the scientific discourses
of modern knowledge." [2] Whether taken in isolation or blended together,
these strains of American critical theory are inspired by Nietzsche's recent appearance as "a post-structuralist strategist of textual power and
diagnostician of decadence." [3] While Nietzsche appears "as the linguistic pathologist of the diverse signs of nihilism which are constitutive of
the entire tradition of Western culture," O'Hara qualified this tradition
in an interesting way, namely, as the tradition that runs "from the age of

the Greeks to that of the Vietnam-era student revolutionaries and their current heirs in the academic and critical communities."[4]

O'Hara here gestures to a motif—the contemporary relevance of Nietzsche's critical perspective—that allows him to frame the essays in his collection as disparate answers to the question, "why Nietzsche now?" But O'Hara is by no means alone in adopting this gesture in his preface. In fact, if there is a unitary theme in the plethora of recent, and not so recent, anthologies of essays on Nietzsche, it is precisely that of Nietzsche's continuing relevance. David B. Allison, whose influential 1977 collection, *The New Nietzsche: Contemporary Styles of Interpretation,* was largely responsible for first bringing the poststructuralist French readings of Nietzsche to the attention of the English-speaking audience, likewise noted the timeliness of Nietzsche's work. Framing his collection as inspired by Heidegger's groundbreaking attempt to take Nietzsche seriously as a thinker, Allison noted that Nietzsche now appears "as one of the underlying figures of our own intellectual epoch." In the end, what Allison suggests is that the importance of Heidegger's reading of Nietzsche lies, in part, in showing that "what remains to be considered within Nietzsche's own thought somehow stands as a model for the tasks and decisions of the present generation," decisions concerning "the very validity of our contemporary forms of intelligibility."[5]

Tracy B. Strong and Michael Allen Gillespie take a similar tack in their 1988 collection, *Nietzsche's New Seas: Explorations in Philosophy, Aesthetics, and Politics.* Noting the pertinence of Nietzsche's claim to a posthumous birth, they write that "one might say that he has been reborn again and again as different generations of commentators repeatedly thought they had uncovered his true meaning."[6] They go on to comment that the most recent rebirth of this "most protean of protean thinkers" is different, however. For in his most recent incarnation, "Nietzsche no longer appears primarily as the prophet and purveyor of nihilism but as the thinker who marks a kind of ending to, or at least a rift in, the continuity of the West. He plumbs the depths of nihilism and in that exploration opens a way out of the abyss to a new and different way of thinking and being."[7] While focusing on how Nietzsche's style informs the content of his works, the essays Strong and Gillespie collect represent what they regard to be "a fair sampling of the various contemporary approaches to Nietzsche that seek to describe the course that Nietzsche charts for humanity, this course toward new seas, toward new ways of seeing and thinking that transcend the traditional distinctions of philosophy, aesthetics, and politics."[8]

Paul Patton closes his introduction to *Nietzsche, Feminism and Political Theory* (1993) in much the same way. Noting that Nietzsche's work was admired in the 1890s by anarchists, socialists, and feminists, he views our own epoch as one close to that for which Nietzsche considered he wrote. His collection is thus concerned with "the long-term effects of the crisis of modern cultural identity that [Nietzsche] diagnosed under the name nihilism." [9] As modern social and political theory have come to question traditional notions of selfhood, sexual difference, rationality, and agency, as traditional assumptions concerning the modern ideals of justice and political equality are being challenged, Patton closes his introduction with the suggestion that the reason Nietzsche's philosophy has at last become timely is because it already charted some of the directions "postmodern ethical and political thought might follow." [10]

From this brief survey, we can see that Nietzsche's fortunes have changed considerably from the time when the first of the English-language anthologies of essays on Nietzsche, Robert C. Solomon's *Nietzsche: A Collection of Critical Essays*, appeared in 1973. Solomon felt it necessary to introduce his wide-ranging sampler of perspectives on Nietzsche by commenting on the need to separate Nietzsche's thought from his biography as he "attempted to portray Nietzsche as a philosopher, a thinker occupied with philosophical problems of justification, value, science and knowledge, truth and God." [11] Today no such apologia is needed, as Nietzsche's legitimacy as a major intellectual force is no longer questioned. Instead, introductions to new collections of essays feel compelled to explain the need for presenting yet *another* Nietzsche anthology.

It is in response to this felt need that I wish to recall the motif of the contemporary relevance of Nietzsche's critical perspective with my own title: "Why Nietzsche Still?" For I think there is an important difference to be noted with the appearance of this collection, namely, that in the past few years there have been claims made, first in Germany, then in France, then in the United States, to the effect that Nietzsche's time has passed, that his perspectives are no longer pertinent in a *post*-postmodern world. [12] The essays collected here, all but one of which were written for this volume, will, I hope, answer definitively this charge of Nietzsche's critical irrelevance. For as they demonstrate, whether at the aesthetic, cultural, psychological, or political level, there are important perspectives to draw from Nietzsche as we struggle to frame these critical issues for a new millennium. They also demonstrate that these perspectives are being drawn, developed, and applied from a wide range of disciplinary and interdisciplinary frameworks throughout the English-speaking academic world, as the contributors find themselves working in departments of comparative literature, English, German, philosophy, political science, political theory, rhetoric, and women's studies.

Throughout his life Nietzsche reflected on questions of both drama and culture, and he reflected as well on the drama(s) *of* culture. As the diverse perspectives put forward in this volume show, his thought retains its relevance as a critical focus for analyzing the ongoing and contemporary dramas of culture as these dramas inform and influence what today we frame as "political." My goal has been to produce a collection that accomplishes three things: elucidate the multifaceted nature of Nietzsche's reflections; demonstrate Nietzsche's relevance for contemporary reflection on the dramas of culture as we approach the end of the second and beginning of the third millennium; and show the range of innovative and exciting Nietzsche scholarship that is being carried out across the humanities and social sciences in the English-speaking world. Toward that end, the contributors to this volume all, in one way or another, are less interested in getting Nietzsche "right" than in showing his continuing pertinence. For, as William E. Connolly has so nicely put it, the point "is not to offer the true account of the true Nietzsche hiding behind a series of masks, but to construct a post-Nietzscheanism one is willing to endorse and enact." [13]

While each chapter addresses in some way Nietzsche's comments on drama, culture, and politics, each directs these comments toward issues whose impact extends to the forefront of contemporary theoretical and political debate. The volume is divided into three parts. The first deals most directly with drama and dramatic themes. In the opening chapter, "Oedipal Dramas," Debra B. Bergoffen develops the affinities between Nietzschean transvaluation and Lacanian psychoanalysis as each rewrites the drama of Oedipus. While Lacan went further than Freud in unraveling the logic of sacrifice, Bergoffen argues that he too remains tied to this logic in his account of both the individual and the cultural psyches. Nietzsche, however, does not begin with the Oedipal paradigm and thus is clearer than either Freud or Lacan on the necessity of overcoming the sacrificial logic that animates the psyche of "modern man." Although Bergoffen is skeptical about whether Nietzsche succeeded in overcoming this logic, she takes from his invocation of woman as life and truth a motive for turning away from "the destiny of the father and the son" and toward "the genealogy of the mother and the daughter." To do so opens the space for an alternative future that, Bergoffen concludes, might allow us to get "beyond the current humanist/anti-humanist entanglements with the logic of sacrifice."

Daniel W. Conway, in "Odysseus Bound?" reads Nietzsche's late writings as akin to Odysseus's desire to experience the sirens' song: both seek to push themselves to the limit to see if they can survive the transfigurative experience that this limit would provoke. For Nietzsche, Conway suggests, this limit experience was the decadence that he identified with modernity and Christian morality. While Nietzsche saw himself as the noble warrior in mortal combat with decadence, Conway reads Nietzsche's self-presentation as in fact embodying the very decadence and *ressentiment* that his critique of modernity rallied against. Whether Nietzsche was aware of what he was doing, whether he self-consciously exposed his succumbing to decadence to serve as a cautionary tale to those who would follow him, Conway leaves an open question. What is not an open question, Conway argues, is that such an authorial strategy was the only way Nietzsche's project could have succeeded, for his self-exposure as a poster child of decadence ironically prompts his readers to carry on his project of the self-overcoming of Christian morality beyond what Nietzsche himself could have achieved.

Duncan Large, in "Nietzsche's Shakespearean Figures," surveys the wide range of references to Shakespeare throughout Nietzsche's writings as he examines how Nietzsche the dramatizing philosopher re-creates Shakespeare the philosophizing dramatist in his own image. As Nietzsche's own views evolved, so did his figuration of Shakespeare, and Large shows Nietzsche putting forward a "series of shifting identifications"—of "Shakespeare" *in* his characters, of "Shakespeare" *as* "Bacon," and of Nietzsche *with* Shakespeare. Ultimately, concludes Large, "it is because Bacon-Shakespeare is revealed as a lover of masks that Nietzsche, the lover of masks, can use Bacon-Shakespeare himself as . . . a mask, another 'metaphor' for 'Nietzsche.'" In so doing, Nietzsche's Shakespeare—as philosopher, psychologist, and antichrist—displays a "poetics of subterfuge" in which the drama of identity is played out, a drama that leads Large to suggest as answer to the question "who is Nietzsche's Shakespeare?": "one of the stations of the cross on Nietzsche's way to becoming himself, 'the crucified one.'"

The drama of identity as a process of transformation and transfiguration is at issue in David B. Allison's "Musical Psychodramatics: Ecstasis in Nietzsche." Throughout his life, Nietzsche attributed a transfigurative power to the experience of ecstasy. Although Nietzsche saw the possibility for ecstatic transformation in politics, art, myth, and religion, the field in which he most consistently located the transfigurative agency of ecstasy was music. In his examination of Nietzsche's account of musical ecstasis, Allison moves the analysis of Nietzsche's views on art to a new terrain, that of contemporary neuroscientific research. While many have reflected on Nietzsche's remarks on the relationships between art and physiology,[14] Allison brings Nietzsche's comments on dissonance as "the primordial phenomenon of Dionysian art" into contact with psychoacoustical research on the "auditory resolution of dissonance." Insofar as dissonance may stimulate the production of endorphins, Allison suggests the provocative hypothesis that Nietzsche, in the context of his neoromantic account of music, may in fact have been previewing current cognitive research on the production of endorphins that raise "what was largely an automatic, relatively homeostatic response to auditory stimuli into an intensely pleasurable experience: ecstasy."

Gary Shapiro, in " 'This Is Not a Christ': Nietzsche, Foucault, and the Genealogy of Vision," also addresses the senses as he examines Nietzsche's and Foucault's engagements with visual art and visual culture. Responding to the general view that Foucault and other twentieth-century thinkers denounce the primacy accorded to vision by the Western philosophical tradition, Shapiro argues that in Foucault we find not a denunciation but a rethinking of the visual that, like Nietzsche, theorizes the visual in relation to the linguistic. Juxtaposing Nietzsche's comments on Raphael's *Transfiguration* with Foucault's discussions of Magritte, Velázquez, and pop art, Shapiro demonstrates that Nietzsche's recurrent optical metaphors, like Foucault's recurrent panoptical imagery, should preclude the all-too-easy charge of linguistic reductionism often leveled against many thinkers in the twentieth century who take their inspiration from Nietzsche. Instead, Shapiro suggests that in our current cultural turn away from literacy and toward the visual, "a critical theory of our visual culture can learn from the Nietzschean attempt to counter the Cyclops eye with the hundred-eyed Argus of a perspectivism sensitive to the genealogy and archaeology of vision."

In the final chapter of part 1, "Zarathustrian Millennialism before the Millennium: From Bely to Yeats to Malraux," John Burt Foster, Jr., explores the tension between decadence and renewal in Zarathustrian millennialism as it has been appropriated and represented within the works of three twentieth-century authors. Foster begins by examining the Russian novelist Andrey Bely and the Anglo-Irish poet William Butler Yeats, both of whom wrote major millennial works that were heavily influenced by Nietzsche. He then moves to André Malraux, arguing that Malraux's *The Walnut Trees of Altenburg,* an unfinished novel written during the German occupation of France, sums up his response to Zarathustra. While millennial deferral is already obvious in this book, Malraux introduces yet another deferral and redefinition when he reprints key passages from *The Walnut Trees* in his autobiographical writings of the late sixties and early seventies, near the end of his close involvement with de Gaulle. At the heart of this trajectory, Foster claims, is a nexus of questions about the nature of art, global culture, and French identity at a time of dissolving boundaries and metamorphic change. Malraux's case, he concludes, suggests that Zarathustrian millennialism leads ultimately to a crisis-laden sense of *permanent* millennialism.

The chapters in part 1 focus on drama and art; those in part 2 examine more explicitly the link between drama and culture as various dramatic images from Nietzsche offer the authors the opportunity to reflect on contemporary cultural forms and forces. Judith Butler's "Circuits of Bad Conscience: Nietzsche and Freud" offers a reading of the reflexivity of internalization at the origin of bad conscience in Nietzsche's *On the Genealogy of Morals* and Freud's *Civilization and Its Discontents.* In both Nietzsche and Freud, conscience operates as a force that turns back on itself. This turning is not unmotivated, however; rather, Butler shows Nietzsche and Freud sharing a circular account of the operation of conscience that displays the process of internalization (*Verinnerlichung*) in terms of forces of social regulation that act on the psyche while at the same time participating in the formation of the psyche. Although the subject has a passionate attachment to the psyche so formed, the subject is not condemned to repeat this act of self-formation "in exactly the same way." Instead, Butler concludes that the subversive subject can engage in a short circuiting of the regulatory powers that act on it in ways that allow "a *postmoral* gesture toward a less regular freedom, one that from the perspective of a less codifiable set of values calls into question the values of [the hegemonic] morality."

In "Dramatis Personae: Nietzsche, Culture, and Human Types," David Owen and Aaron Ridley examine Nietzsche's conception of philosophy in terms of what they call his "therapeutic ambitions." Challenging the view that Nietzsche offers his account of various racial, ethnic, and national human types as matters of empirical, scientific fact that would justify some sort of naturalized hierarchy of subtypes of humanity, they argue that Nietzsche uses human types to express various cultural relations. Only if we view Nietzsche's account of human types as not based in biology but as offering exemplars of various *rapports à soi* can we make sense of Nietzsche's self-understanding as a cultural physician and articulate proponent of the classical understanding of philosophy as medicine for the soul. And such an understanding, they argue, is essential for recognizing and appreciating the role Nietzsche sought to play with his diagnosis, prescription, and prognosis for "modern man."

Alphonso Lingis, in "Satyrs and Centaurs: Miscegenation and the Master Race," displays some of the problems that develop from the sort of reading Owen and Ridley caution against as he reflects on the central distinction Nietzsche introduces into the study of cultures, namely, the distinction between plebeian and aristocratic cultures, between servile and noble morality. Nietzsche draws this distinction on the basis of what Lingis claims to be questionable biological concepts ("herd instinct" vs. "solitary instinct") and a positivistic account of animality. Drawing instead on more recent biological notions of the relationship between an animal and its ecosystem, Lingis rejects the Nietzschean view of life as a drive for ever more power, and he offers a provocative alternative to Nietzsche's biologistic distinction between noble and base cultures through a phenomenological distinction between the moral community and the exotic exception, a distinction that itself draws on contemporary biological notions of symbiosis.

In "Nietzsche and the Problem of the Actor, " Paul Patton takes as his point of departure a remark from Nietzsche's *The Gay Science,* section 361: "The problem of the actor has troubled me for the longest time." Patton explores Nietzsche's reasons for regarding the actor self as a problem and the relevance of this problem for contemporary questions about social role and agency. Like others in this collection, Patton finds Nietzsche's comments on the actor provocatively prescient; twentieth-century developments in the technology of the image, Patton argues, have led increasingly to the public sphere in modern social life coming to take the form of an electronic stage under conditions according to which, especially as concerns the political stage, seeming is being. While the modern self is aware of the arbitrary and contingent character of the roles one has assumed, one is no less committed to some of those roles. Nietzsche's concerns about the self becoming a "mere actor" thus serve as an important caution, as Patton concludes that our task is "to have an artistic relation to oneself and yet to avoid becoming a mere actor with no commitment other than the faith in one's ability to assume any given role."

Alan D. Schrift, in "Nietzsche's Contest: Nietzsche and the Culture Wars," begins by examining Nietzsche's text as the site of several polemical dramas in twentieth-century European philosophy. From here Schrift suggests that the Nietzschean critiques of both identity and nationalism can be helpful in developing a critical response to the "culture wars" and the identity politics that have encouraged ethnic nationalisms in Eastern Europe and Africa. He argues that Nietzsche's critique of anti-Semitism as an outgrowth of nationalism provides tools for criticizing a politics of national or ethnic identity in favor of the cosmopolitan ideal of producing "the strongest possible European mixed race" (*HH* 475). Similarly, the Nietzschean critique of dogmatism, grounded as it is on a perspectivist position that calls for multiplying points of view and avoiding fixed and rigid posturings, can accommodate a notion of radical contingency that seems to be both theoretically desirable and pragmatically necessary for many recent theorists who have explored the possibilities for democratic politics within a differential and agonistic public space. Schrift concludes that we might still attend to Nietzsche's remarks on democracy and the Homeric competitions as we look to a new century with strategies for avoiding a recurrence of those undemocratic confrontations that have plagued this past century.

In part 3 the question of politics takes center stage, as the authors use Nietzsche's genealogy of *ressentiment* to examine the implications of cultural analyses inspired by Nietzsche for contemporary political theory and political realities. In "Nietzsche for Politics," Wendy Brown challenges the traditional modernist approach to the relations between theory and politics as one of either identity or application. Instead, she suggests that by viewing theory and practice as operating with quite different, and conflicting, impulses and aims, a usefully agonistic relation between them might be established. Nietzsche becomes useful for politics precisely when we separate his value for political thinking from his putative political positions and values. That is, when we consider how the disruptive function of genealogy provides a source of political critique, we can see that although Nietzsche himself might have been unsympathetic to democracy, his theory promotes the ongoing contestation required for the continuation of democratic political practices. Exploring the possibility that democratic politics—"the most untheoretical of all political forms"—paradoxically *requires* theory, Brown thus concludes that democracy requires a nondemocratic, Nietzschean element if it is to succeed in producing a dynamic egalitarian order.

Dana R. Villa, in "Democratizing the *Agon*: Nietzsche, Arendt, and the Agonistic Tendency in Recent Political Theory," examines Hannah Arendt's appropriation of Nietzsche in the context of challenging those political theorists (Wolin, Connolly, Honig, Mouffe) who have made use of Nietzsche in their articulation of democracy as, in the words of Seyla Benhabib, a political sphere of "incessant contestation." [15] While these agonistic political theorists tend to criticize Arendt for not following Nietzsche further, Villa argues that "her reading of Greek political experience, along with her appreciation of the lessons of Socrates and Kant, made her acutely aware of the need to set limits, both institutional and characterological, to the *agon* that *is* political life." Her agonism, like Nietzsche's, is individualistic, but, unlike Nietzsche's, it is not particularly expressive. The result, for Villa, is an impersonal agonism that exercises greater caution because it takes greater risks, setting limits and qualifications to the agonistic ethos so as to avoid the unbridled conflicts that accompany interest-driven decision making. Arendt's tension between the individual and the impersonal, Villa suggests, may in fact take difference more seriously than those contemporary political theorists who, while following Nietzsche, may find it difficult to call for "agonistic respect" for those differing views that seek to eliminate or otherwise fundamentally challenge democratic assumptions concerning the public good.

In "'A Nietzschean Breed': Feminism, Victimology, *Ressentiment*," Rebecca Stringer examines the discourses of feminist victimology—the view that "women are victims of power, where power is understood *exclusively* as man's capacity to dominate"—in both the popular press and academic feminist political theory. While accepting that feminism is, in some sense, a reactive political project—reacting to patriarchal power relations and seeking to redistribute power according to non-patriarchal relations—Stringer argues that both academic and popular feminist critiques of feminist victimology move too quickly in assuming that victimology is inextricably conjoined with *ressentiment* and that *ressentiment* is necessarily a bad thing. Rather than reject *ressentiment tout court*, or reject Nietzsche for his rejection of feminist *ressentiment*, Stringer suggests that feminism might do well to rehabilitate the notion of *ressentiment* by exploring how it provides conditions for the possibility of creative affirmation. To this end, she proposes following Nietzsche in thinking of "*ressentiment* not so much as an eradicable 'state' in which certain aspects of feminism are presently caught but as the condition of possibility for an ongoing and creative process through which feminism is formed and earns the capacity to form itself."

In the final chapter, "Performing Resentment: White Male Anger; or, 'Lack' and Nietzschean Political Theory," Jeffrey T. Nealon offers a Nietzschean reading of one of the performative subjects in contemporary American political discourse: the "angry white male." While these subjects fashion themselves as Nietzschean "birds of prey," Nealon argues that they present themselves more often as acting out the resentment of the *Genealogy*'s "little lambs." Drawing on Jean-Luc Nancy's notion that "anger is the political sentiment par excellence,"[16] Nealon reflects on how a Nietzsche-inspired liberal political theorist like Judith Butler or William Connolly might attempt to reframe the dynamic of lack that today motivates, albeit for different reasons and toward different ends, both conservative and radical accounts of subjectivity. He concludes by suggesting that escaping this dynamic of lack might prompt a "properly political anger of transformation," one that could be called on to challenge the current tide of resentful diatribes against those framed within current talk show rhetoric as "the other."

Nietzsche predicted his fate; he knew that one day his name would "be associated with the memory of something tremendous—a crisis without equal on earth, the most profound collision of conscience, a decision that was conjured up *against* everything that had been believed, demanded, hallowed so far" (*EH* "Destiny" 1). It is on this basis that Nietzsche makes his claims to untimeliness, to a destinal status, and to a posthumous birth (see *AC* "Foreword"; *EH* "Books" 1). But within this appeal to his own futurity, there is little claim to a millennial status. Unlike his Nazi epigones, who predicted a thousand-year Reich, and unlike the lies of millennia that have heretofore passed as the highest truths and values (see *EH* "Destiny" 1), Nietzsche seemed to think that his futurity was centennial—it was the next century that was to be his. In *Ecce Homo*, he invited his readers to imagine a future that is *our* present: "Let us look ahead a century; let us suppose that my attempt to assassinate two millennia of antinature and desecration of humanity were to succeed" (*EH* "Books" BT:4). While Nietzsche's supposition of success has been less than perhaps he had hoped, there is nevertheless a sense in which he has succeeded, for there are few thinkers whose influence has exceeded Nietzsche's over the last decades of the twentieth century. And as this volume shows, Nietzsche still has a great deal to say to those of his readers whose thought takes the form of what Foucault called "an ontology of ourselves, an ontology of the present"[17] as they develop critical responses to that present and the future that will follow it.

NOTES

1. Daniel T. O'Hara, ed., *Why Nietzsche Now?* (Bloomington: Indiana University Press, 1985), vii.

2. Ibid., viii.

3. Ibid.

4. Ibid., vii–viii.

5. David B. Allison, preface to *The New Nietzsche: Contemporary Styles of Interpretation,* ed. David B. Allison (New York: Dell, 1977), ix.

6. Tracy B. Strong and Michael Allen Gillespie, introduction to *Nietzsche's New Seas: Explorations in Philosophy, Aesthetics, and Politics,* ed. Tracy B. Strong and Michael Allen Gillespie (Chicago: University of Chicago Press, 1988), 1.

7. Ibid.

8. Ibid., 9.

9. Paul Patton, introduction to *Nietzsche, Feminism and Political Theory,* ed. Paul Patton (London and New York: Routledge, 1993), xii.

10. Ibid., xiii.

11. Robert C. Solomon, introduction to *Nietzsche: A Collection of Critical Essays,* ed. Robert C. Solomon (New York: Anchor / Doubleday, 1973), 1.

12. See, e.g., Luc Ferry and Alain Renaut, *Why We Are Not Nietzscheans,* trans. Robert de Loaiza (Chicago: University of Chicago Press, 1997).

13. William E. Connolly, *Identity / Difference: Democratic Negotiations of Political Paradox* (Ithaca: Cornell University Press, 1991), 197.

14. See, e.g., *KSA* 13:16[75]: "The fundament of all aesthetics is given [in these two principles]: that aesthetic values rest on biological values, that aesthetic pleasures are biological pleasures [*das Fundament aller Aesthetik abgiebt: daß die aesthetischen Werthe auf biologischen Werthen ruhen, daß die aesthetischen Wohlgefühle biologische Wohlgefühle sind*]." Much of Heidegger's first Nietzsche lecture, "The Will to Power as Art," explores Nietzsche's projected "physiology of art."

15. Seyla Benhabib, "The Democratic Moment and the Problem of Difference," in *Democracy and Difference,* ed. Seyla Benhabib (Princeton: Princeton University Press, 1996), 9.

16. Jean-Luc Nancy, "The Compearance: From the Existence of 'Communism' to the Community of 'Existence,'" trans. Tracy B. Strong, *Political Theory* 20, no. 3 (1992): 375.

17. Michel Foucault, *Dit et écrits* (Paris: Gallimard, 1994), 4:687. See also Foucault's "What Is Enlightenment?" where he discusses genealogy in terms of its being a "critical ontology of ourselves . . . conceived as an attitude, an ethos, a philosophical life in which the critique of what we are is at one and the same time the historical analysis of the limits that are imposed on us and an experiment with the possibility of going beyond them" (trans. Catherine Porter, in *The Foucault Reader,* ed. Paul Rabinow [New York: Pantheon Books, 1984], 50).

PART ONE

Drama

CHAPTER I

Oedipal Dramas

Debra B. Bergoffen

Nietzsche and Freud measured us against the Greeks. The Greeks, Freud said, were fundamentally different from us in the way they assumed their sexuality. Greek men were expected to be bisexual. Modern men are expected to abhor their homosexual desires. We value the aim, object, and individuating and reproductive functions of the "mature" sexual instinct. The Greeks valued the bisexual, polymorphous excess of the instinct itself. Noting this difference between the Greeks' relationship to Eros and ours, Freud rejects the idea that our understanding of the relationship between the instinct and its object reflects the natural order of things. He does not, however, suggest that we should either return to the Greek way or reorder our relationship to the instinct and its object. Given the teleologies of biology and the demands of the species, we must, he said, renounce our bisexual tendencies, adopt a heterosexual identity, and accept the normalcy of foreplay but not the fetish. In these appeals to maturity and normalcy, Freud established his position as a modern and aligned psychoanalysis with the logic of sacrifice. In situating his/our desire against the backdrop of another desire, however, Freud not only showed us how the logic of sacrifice works, he also, despite insisting that this logic was necessary and universal, demonstrated its contingency and particularity.[1]

Remembering this particularity was Nietzsche's virtue. He insisted on the necessity of perspectivism. He knew that his thinking was European, not universal (see *HL* 9). He read Europe's relationship to Eros as ascetic, a nihilistic attack on the excessive body by those who could only endure life by degrading it (*GM* III). He saw Europe's ascetic ideal as a particular but not exhaustive way of playing out our Greek heritage and recommended that we burrow back to the Greeks to recover the difference between us. Unlike Freud, who saw no reason to take up the difference of Greek desire, Nietzsche recommended that we pursue this difference to remark our destiny.

The Greeks, Nietzsche said, looked into the Dionysian abyss. In awe of its terror they invoked the god Apollo and made it beautiful. Knowing that truth does not bring happiness, they opted for the *jouissance* of the dream, the image, the superficial form (*BT* 1, 3). They did not (at least not until Socrates) mistake their Apollonian creations for truths. Remembering Dionysus, they spoke of fate, chance, and destiny rather than of teleology and the requirements of the species. Where we live on Messianic hopes and in Resurrection expectations, the Greeks created tragedy.

In marking the distance between the ancients and the moderns, Freud and Nietzsche remembered that as different we are tethered. The Greeks, they told us, stand at the beginning of a lineage that we still inhabit. We are their heirs, and as their heirs they are our destiny. That destiny, Freud said, is singular but universal. It is the line of Oedipus, the incest taboo and the desires of the unconscious. That destiny, Nietzsche said, is neither singular nor universal. We have so far taken up but one line of our Greek heritage, the line of Socrates, the logos and the idea that happiness comes to those who know. For Freud, in understanding ourselves as the heirs of the Greeks (read Oedipus) we access the recesses of the dynamic unconscious and the workings of repression. For Nietzsche, in understanding ourselves as the heirs of the Greeks (read Socrates) we access the source of our *ressentiment* and the ascetic ideal. For Freud, there is no escape from the Greek tragedy of Oedipus. For Nietzsche, Socrates is neither the first nor the last Greek word.

Between Nietzsche and Freud and their diagnostic of the psyche and culture of the Western world there lies the question of humanism. That Freud is often associated with the humanist tradition and that Nietzsche is often identified as an antihumanist can be understood, I think, if we understand their divergent understanding of the Greeks. Discerning these differences, we discover that in refusing to read Nietzsche for fear of finding that his discoveries had already been made, Freud harbored misguided anxieties. Nietzsche's thought was profoundly different from his. In pointing to the differences between these two thinkers who are often aligned with each other, however, I am not so much interested in examining the mistake of reading Freud as an echo of Nietzsche as in determining the stakes of the current humanism/antihumanism debates.

As currently framed, this dispute assumes that humanism is a singular way of thinking a unique cluster of ideas. Antihumanism is depicted as an exposé of the violence of this way of thinking and is offered as an antidote to its poison. I think this formulation of the humanist tradition and of the relationship between humanism and antihumanism is mistaken. It presumes that there is a radical break between humanist and antihumanist thought and assumes that the humanist tradition is monolithic. And so if I begin with the difference between Nietzsche and Freud to indicate the differences between humanism and antihumanism, it is to get to Lacan, who alerts us to the logic of sacrifice that links antihumanism to humanism and thus teaches us to be suspicious of the current ways of formulating the humanist/antihumanist quarrel.

Beginning with Freud and Nietzsche to set the parameters of this quarrel and moving to the man who in calling himself a rereader of Freud the humanist identified himself as an antihumanist, we see that the relationship between humanism and antihumanism is more tangled than clear cut. What we also need to see, and what I will begin to work through here, is that the matter of untangling the relationship between humanism and antihumanism is a matter of delineating the logic of sacrifice that contaminates both of these modes of thought. It is a matter of asking about the possibilities of dislocating this logic from its place in contemporary life.

With these beginnings I propose the following thesis: The drama of Oedipus, as appropriated by the psychoanalytic tradition, embodies the logic of sacrifice. Lacan went further than Freud in deciphering the workings of this logic, but Lacan and Freud do not evade this logic in their own accounts of the dynamics of our individual and cultural psyche. With Nietzsche things are different. He does not begin with the paradigm of Oedipus and is therefore clearer about the workings of Oedipal man's sacrificial logic and the need to overcome it/him. Whether he succeeds in this overcoming is not, however, certain. Invoking, as Nietzsche did, the women named life and truth may not be enough. We may need to do what Nietzsche did not do, turn from the destiny of the father and the son to the genealogy of the mother and the daughter.

FREUD

As Freud reads the Oedipal tragedy, it speaks of the universality and necessity of the logic of sacrifice. The son must remake his desire in accordance with the demand of the father to find a home for it / himself within the family and the larger human community. Bowing to the threat of the father, the son consents to give up the mother on the condition that she be returned to him as the wife. (Lacan exposes the way in which an Oedipal culture legitimates violence by calling this threat the law of the Father and establishing this law as the door through which we must all pass in our entry into the symbolic.) The father will be obeyed on the condition that he ultimately consents to being replaced. The son will sacrifice his desire to the father. The father will sacrifice his place to the son. The mother's desire will be sacrificed to the genealogy of the father and the son.

Freud tells us that Oedipus is the tragedy of the son's refusal to renounce his impossible desire. If we attend to the text, however, we discover that Freud forgets to tell us that what sets Oedipus's destiny is his father's refusal to grant his son what every father must grant every son—recognition of the generational fact that in the end the son will take his place. It is this father's impossible refusal that sets this son's impossible desire loose. This father believes that abandoning his son will save him (the father) from the fate of finitude. His infinite desire betrays him. The son returns.

Noting Freud's forgetfulness regarding the father prepares us for Lacan's attention to the other thing Freud forgets—the Sphinx. Preoccupied as he is with the desire of the son for the mother, a desire the son consciously flees, Freud neglects the woman of the son's conscious desire—the Sphinx. Here another taboo is at work, the taboo of knowledge. Here the taboo is openly broken and in being broken saves the city (for a time) and brings Oedipus happiness (so it seems). Father and son are not so different. Both would rather challenge oracles (read conditions of finitude) than submit to them / it.

We do not fully appreciate the drama of Oedipus if we confine it to the parameters of the family romance. The myth of Oedipus concerns the law and the city. It is a personal tragedy that is also and necessarily a political disaster. It concerns matters of love and justice. Oedipus is not any Greek citizen; he is the son of a king who becomes a king. Jocasta is a woman of royal blood. Freud is clear regarding this essential relationship between the erotics of the family and the structure of the law.

The resolution of the Oedipus complex, he tells us, repeats an archaic political event, and it is the repetition of this event in the family scene that guarantees the social order.

Given the way Freud tells the story of our social and political origins, we would do well to remember that the desires of the bedroom are linked to those of the war room. Violence between men concerns women. The Greek drama and Freud's myth render women passive. Jocasta must obey her husband's order to destroy her son and must accept the son as her husband when he returns. The women of the primal horde do not participate in the rebellion of the sons. Their position after the revolution remains unchanged. They remain objects of male desire. Though positioned as the passive object of the law in the Greek and Freudian myths, as objects of desire the women exercise their power from a distance. They set the stage for the son's rebellion and set the terms of their subsequent desire. As the sons' envy of the father's exclusive rights to the women precipitates the primal crime that ends the politics of tyranny, the brothers' jealousy of each other establishes the law of equal sexual access that inaugurates the politics of mutual recognition and democratic rights (for men).

Played in its intimate and public registers, the drama of Oedipus may be heard as a drama of desire and finitude. It speaks of the desire to be infinite and of the particular ways in which our culture, the culture of Oedipal man, resigns us to the conditions of finitude. It teaches us that the temptations to transgress the limits of our finitude are pervasive and suggests that these temptations may have something to do with the way in which we have structured our desire; for the myth of Oedipus makes it clear that we experience our finitude as a threat to our desire and therefore resent it. From Freud's point of view, this resentment is inherent in the human condition. From Nietzsche's perspective, this resentment is a symptom of a particular form of life. As a symptom of one form of life rather than a condition of life itself, it can be overcome. Reading Nietzsche with Freud and Lacan, I see resentment as a symptom of Oedipal man. Privileging Nietzsche, I see this symptom genealogically rather than psychoanalytically and ask about its overcoming.

LACAN

Lacan is on to Oedipus. Ultimately it is not the mother he wants, it is happiness; and the route to happiness is not through the woman-mother but through the woman-Sphinx / truth. It is not the unconscious desire for the mother that blinds Oedipus, it is the conscious desire to know that destroys him. It is here in the pursuit of happiness as truth that we remain Oedipus's heirs, trapped in the labyrinth of violence that is the legacy of the ascetic ideal. On to Oedipus, Lacan warns us against the fate of an Oedipal culture, our culture, that refuses to accept the dialectic of the sovereign and forbidden truth/good and sets itself the task of securing happiness by objectifying the good and pursuing it as the truth of the master/mastery.[2] The issue for Lacan as for Freud was sublimation; but where for Freud sublimation meant science or art, for Lacan it meant subordinating science to art.

In *The Ethics of Psychoanalysis* Lacan tells us that the scientific project that dominates the West is a sign of the blindest of passions—the Oedipal desire to know.[3] As a scientist practicing the science of psychoanalysis, however, Lacan places himself in the unique position of the one not misled by the Oedipal desire. In turning his attention to this passion that is "far from having said its last word," Lacan alerts us to the fact that working through the question of science is an ethical task insofar as it concerns the future of our desire; for we, like Oedipus, are obstinate in our loyalty to truth, and we, like Oedipus, do not see that in linking science/knowledge with happiness we situate ourselves in an impossible relationship to the Thing.

According to Lacan, we are symbolic subjects. We become subjects by entering the symbolic order and exist as subjects by living within the signifying chain. To enter the symbolic order we must sever our link to the maternal Thing; to live within the signifying chain we must practice sublimation, embrace symbolic substitutes for the Thing.[4] We must accept the truth of our desire: the Thing can be circled, it cannot be had. As Oedipal subjects, we refuse this truth. We are not satisfied with this circling or these substitutes. We want the Thing. Deciding that science can deliver what it promises, an adequate presentation of the Thing, we pursue it. We decide that art, the symbolic order that would rather circle the Thing than make impossible promises, cannot bring us happiness. We relegate art to the margins of discourse and culture. But here is the irony. This pursuit of science, far from fulfilling the desire to know, works against itself. It cannot deliver what it promises. At the heart of its promise is a refusal to recognize the meaning of our desire. In refusing to confront the Thing as unrepresentable, in insisting on its power to reveal It, science forecloses the Thing. It condemns us to the return of the repressed.[5] There is nothing abstract about this return. Slavoj Žižek identifies it with the ecological crisis and Chernobyl and insists that we understand these crises / this return in terms of the relationship of science to the Thing. From his Lacanian point of view, these phenomena demand that we rethink the assumptions of the scientific symbolic and begin drafting a future science that addresses the real as that which eludes us. This science would direct its attention to elaborating rules of contingency, rules that recognize the limits of rules and that acknowledge the limits of our access to the Thing.[6]

Art challenges contemporary science's foreclosure of the Thing. Instead of following the scientific strategy of appropriating (or of claiming to be able to appropriate) the unrepresentable Thing, it validates the Thing in its unrepresentability and organizes itself around this unrepresentability. It values the signifier as a signifier that signifies without representing and in this way acknowledges the limits of the symbolic; for in announcing the truth of the signifying but nonrepresentative signifier, the artistic symbolic shatters the illusion of the identity of the signified and the signifier. Instead of foreclosing the truth of the unrepresentable Thing, it directs us toward the Thing in its unrepresentability.[7]

Lacan expresses our double relationship to the Thing by referring to it as the sovereign and forbidden good. As the sovereign good, the Thing lures our desire with the promise of fulfillment. As the forbidden good, the Thing destroys those who, taken in by the lure, demand fulfillment. Referring to the Thing as the forbidden and sovereign good is Lacan's way of teaching us to accept the cut of subjectivity as we pursue the promises of sublimation. The West, Lacan says, must learn to value the promise and forgo the demand.

As a critique of Oedipal culture, however, Lacan's thought remains caught within it. For if his analysis of the (m)other as the sovereign and forbidden good saves her from the violence of Bacon / science, for whom / which rape is a legitimate route to happiness, he reassumes the role of Oedipus and returns to destroy the mother in his analysis of the phallus as the privileged signifier. In his turn to the phallus, Lacan's antihumanist critique of the ego and exposé of the sordid relationship between the humanist pursuit of happiness and the impossible desire of / for mastery is undermined. The humanist logic of sacrifice returns. In the end, as Luce Irigaray has so eloquently shown, the fathers of psychoanalysis cannot acknowledge another desire / the desire of the other.[8]

When he follows the logic of the Thing, Lacan describes the signifying chain as anchored in the unrepresentable. So long as he follows this logic of the Thing, we can say, I think, that though he does not avoid the psychoanalytic logic of sacrifice when it comes to the Thing as the mother, he does avoid it when it comes to the Thing as the sovereign and forbidden good; for in identifying the Thing as both sovereign and forbidden, he protects it from the utilitarian calculus that is embedded in the project of happiness.

Lacan does not, however, always follow the logic of the Thing. More often than not, he gets caught up in the logic of the phallus. Where the logic of the Thing evades the logic of sacrifice figured as happiness, the logic of the phallus brings us back to the logic of sacrifice that grounds the Oedipal drama; for though Lacan claims that the phallus is not the penis and that both men and women are equally castrated, he cannot sustain these claims against the sedimentations of language. The phallus is historically situated, and as historically situated it is sexed. As sexed, it cannot be called upon to anchor a nonsacrificial symbolic order; for as sexed, it legitimates the desire of the penis and justifies the murder of the mother.[9] We see how this works if we retell the Oedipus story according to Lacan's paradigms of the imaginary and the symbolic.

According to Lacan, woman is given a place in the symbolic order so long as she takes up the function of the mother. As mother, her role in the family romance is to recognize the Name of the Father. As mother, woman grounds the phallic order. It is on her authority that the child recognizes the relationship between the father, the phallus, and the law. It is from her direction that the child passes from the imaginary to the symbolic. It is by her word that the Name of the Father is empowered to efface the presence of the mother. In assigning her this place in the Oedipal triangle, Lacan establishes the following condition of the possibility of the symbolic: woman must disappear into the image of the mother; the image of the mother must efface itself in the Name of the Father. According to this formula, Freud is correct. Civilization is grounded in an act of violence. But he is also wrong. The primal crime is not the murder of the father but the destruction first of the woman and then of the mother.[10] Further, the primal crime is not the necessary root of all civilization. It is the source of a specific Oedipal symbolic order committed to the logic of sacrifice.

NIETZSCHE

Referring to himself as having been born posthumously and as the son of a living mother and a dead father, Nietzsche gives himself a forked genealogy (*EH* "Wise" 1). He identifies himself as a doppelgänger (*EH* "Wise" 3). This recognition of doubling may explain how/why Nietzsche gets beyond the Freudian and Lacanian way of framing the humanist/antihumanist quarrel. It may explain how he expunges the logic of sacrifice from his thought. Perhaps Nietzsche's sense of himself as doubled is his way of rethinking the relationship between Dionysus and Apollo. Perhaps he goes further in inaugurating a way of thinking that forsakes the violence of humanism because he begins with the phenomenon of Greek tragedy rather than with the particular tragedy of Oedipus. Perhaps he did not get caught by Oedipus because he already knew the world was a fable. Either way, when Nietzsche confronts the abyss that Lacan calls the Thing, he does not use the phallus to circle it. He wonders whether truth might be a woman (*BGE* P) (and in this way reveals his Oedipal lineage), but unlike the heirs of Oedipus who approach the woman truth as a riddle to be mastered or as an origin to be simultaneously recognized and silenced, Nietzsche identifies himself as a lover of riddles. If he begins by accepting the advice of the old woman and taking the whip to women, he soon determines that his whip has no effect and decides that he would rather dance, laugh, and play the fool than imitate the clumsy attempts at seduction of the dogmatic philosopher (*Z*:3 "The Other Dancing Song").

Aligned with Lacan in identifying the Real object of our desire as the absolutely inaccessible Object, Nietzsche, confronting the nothingness at the heart of our desire, declares the death of God and reveals the abyss. Attributing this death of God at least in part to scientific discourse and declaring that the death of God is also and necessarily the death of science, Nietzsche tells us that we will have to invent new ways of living our impossible desires; we will, he says, have to invent new games (*GS* 125). Nietzsche's game begins with the suppositions that truth is a woman and that the world is a fable. With these suppositions, given the traditional configurations of woman as fickle, elusive, and unstable and given the traditional accounts of the fable as a juvenile, inadequate, and irrational mode of discourse, Nietzsche acknowledges the Thing as sovereign (the sublime object of our desire) and forbidden (that which forever and necessarily evades our grasp).

Those who take Nietzsche to be a nihilist mistakenly read his supposing truth were a woman and the world is a fable as marks of a doctrine of relativism rather than as the premises of a perspectivism. The usual move of those who would save Nietzsche from the charge of nihilism is to claim that there are criteria of truth at work in Nietzsche's thought—the criteria of life, or of distance, or of nobility, for example. I, like those who would save Nietzsche from the charge of nihilism, do not read Nietzsche as a nihilist. I do not try to save him from the charge of nihilism, however; for to save him from the charge of nihilism is to accept the paradigm of truth that makes the charge in the first place. Once we accept this paradigm we can only affirm Nietzsche by finding a non-nihilistic anchor for his thought. Finding no anchors for Nietzsche's thought and finding his supposing truth were a woman and the world a fable decisive in this regard (if truth is a woman and the world a fable, anchors of thought are impossible), I find that within a paradigm of thought that insists on anchors, Nietzsche is and must be a nihilist. If by a nihilist, however, we mean someone who abandons the notion of truth or who claims that all truths/values are equally meaningless or only meaningful in an arbitrary way, then Nietzsche is not a nihilist. He is not a nihilist because he establishes a paradigm of truth that renders the concept of nihilism in the above senses inoperative.[11] Abandoning the Oedipal notion of truth that identifies truth as that which answers the riddle of the Sphinx, Nietzsche opts for a concept of truth that identifies truth with the riddle rather than with its answer. In taking this option Nietzsche is not claiming that the riddle cannot be solved—Oedipus did give the right answer—but that it ought not be solved. Listening to Nietzsche, we learn that solving the riddle will not resolve our desire.

Another way to look at it is this: the Oedipal paradigm assumes that our desire seeks satisfaction and that it can be satisfied. It assumes that the proper object of our desire is truth because it presumes that desire pursues its own end, fulfillment. It claims that truth fulfills our desire and concludes that as the fulfillment of our desire, truth brings happiness. Nietzsche's assumptions are different. They are Greek in the Freudian sense; for Nietzsche values the desire rather than its fulfillment. For him, the death of God and the abyss are liberatory; for now that there is nothing to cage the play of desire, we are not engaged by the logic of sacrifice. Socrates can take up singing. Nietzsche's truth as Sphinx, woman, and riddle announces the truth of our desire—it wants life, not fulfillment. To live it must have aims that are unfulfillable. It is sustained by impossible objects and riddles, not by submission to a symbolic order grounded in the violence of the law of the Father. There are, according to Nietzsche, two types of impossible objects: the impossible object God the Father and the impossible object the abyss. To date Western culture has opted for the impossible object God. Nietzsche asks us to experiment with the other impossible object, the abyss. In Nietzsche's experiment the discourse that promises to deliver desire's object, the modern scientific symbolic, is called to task for making an impossible promise and for compromising our desire. Called to task for serving God rather than our desire, Nietzsche calls on science to serve life and its desire. He calls for a gay science—a science that understands its truths as experiments, that appreciates the distance between Oedipal truth and happiness, and that creates a symbolic order that respects the sovereignty of the Thing by valuing the circle around it rather than the line to it. Hence the eternal recurrence and the supposition that the world is a fable and that truth is a woman.

What is especially interesting about Nietzsche's supposing that truth is a woman is the way he deals with it / her. Unlike Oedipal men who have, like Bacon, also made this claim, Nietzsche does not use it to authorize rape. Neither does he, like Freud, wonder what women want and then speak of / for their desire. Nietzsche preserves the otherness of the women truth and life. He never claims to occupy the feminine position. He wonders about it, and wondering about it he speaks to and with women, not as or for them. With these moves, Nietzsche abandons the privilege of the phallus. He neither claims that having the penis means having the phallus nor assumes that there is a phallus to be had. We see that Nietzsche does not claim to have the phallus once we understand that he refuses to identify thought and being (the world; i.e., our thought of the world, the only world there is, Nietzsche says, is a fable) and abandons the project of representation (as a fable, the world, as expressive of our desire, represents nothing).

We see that Nietzsche disputes the very idea of the phallus by noting that there are two women—not one—who claim to be the phallus. These women contest each other. They are jealous of each other. They cannot, however, refute each other. As the only example in Nietzsche's work of the comradery of worthy enemies, these women's claims to the phallus disrupt the very idea of the phallus. They refuse the idea of the phallic (m)other. Rather than pursue the Lacanian route of allowing the phallus to circulate as the impossible object of our desire, Nietzsche queers the phallus, and abandons the Oedipal idea that we need the lure of a complete object to sustain our desire. Stepping outside the Oedipal regime, Nietzsche calls on us to orient our desire around the abyss, the hole between the drive and its object, and to embrace the innocence of becoming. He calls on us to affirm the drive rather than the object and teaches us to value the gap that sustains the drive's production of objects.

Calling the world a fable and calling on the women truth and life, Nietzsche seems to ask us to live our desire as innocent rather than as impossible and seems to toss the phallic crutch aside. With these moves, he articulates an antihumanism that seems to step out of the circle of the logic of sacrifice. But why do I say "seems"? Why my hesitation in placing Nietzsche outside the Oedipal scene? My "perhaps" comes to this: if Nietzsche supposed that truth was a woman and the world was a fable, he also supposed that woman loved a warrior and that it was as truth that she awaited the warrior's (but not the dogmatic philosopher's) seduction. This fable sounds too familiar. The phallus, it seems, is not easily abandoned. It has its own routes of return.

If, like Nietzsche, I too look forward to another history, one that gets beyond the current humanist/antihumanist entanglements with the logic of sacrifice, I do not take Nietzsche as my only guide. Taking Nietzsche's course and mindful of the lessons of perspectivism, I suggest that we return to the Greeks to measure the distance between us and to retrieve the traces of another order. From our current perspective, this other order is either a polymorphous or a Dionysian disorder. From a Freudian-Lacanian perspective, this disorder requires the ordering of Oedipus. From Nietzsche's perspective, it requires the intervention of the god Apollo. However, given the effects of these Oedipal orderings and the ways in which Apollonian orderings have yet to evade the sacrificial logic of patriarchal politics, I suggest that when and if we decide to invoke the God Apollo we remember that he was a twin and that this beautiful young man is tied to Diana, a woman identified as a virgin and a hunter but linked with women and their birthing bodies and invoked as the goddess of the young. I suggest that instead of continuing to insert ourselves in the genealogy of the impossible infinite demand of the Greek father who casts out his son, we take up the genealogy of Demeter, the Greek mother who rescues the stolen daughter in the name of a love that speaks of her infinite longing for the child of her flesh.

Finally, I suggest that we investigate the ways in which our reading of the myth of Oedipus is not necessarily the Greek way. We ought not assume that in appropriating the myth of Oedipus to the myths of the Oedipus complex, the revolt of the sons against the father, and the law of civilization, we are repeating the desires of the Greeks. Page du Bois, for example, tells us that the tragedy of Oedipus was not taken by the Greeks to be a tragedy of the son's desire of/for the mother but a tragedy of the twice-plowed woman's body. She tells us that the Oedipal tragedy concerns the mother's autonomy, the troubled relationship between male and female, and the fear of being estranged from the earth. The Greeks, she says, did not experience this tragedy as remarking the incestuous and castrating desires of the men.[12] Du Bois's reading of the Greek tragedy of Oedipus as a tragedy that records a crisis in the ideology of sexual difference suggests that if we follow Nietzsche in his unphallic return to the Greeks, we will not recover the instinct in its innocence of becoming but discover what Irigaray discovered—that the instinct itself is doubled, that it seeks otherness, not truth. Discovering this, we will learn, perhaps, to listen to the women truth and life with different ears and will learn, perhaps, to create new fables.

NOTES

1. Sigmund Freud, *Three Essays on the Theory of Sexuality,* trans. James Strachey (New York: Basic Books, 1962).

2. Jacques Lacan, "Aggressivity in Psychoanalysis," in *Ecrits,* trans. Alan Sheridan (New York: W. W. Norton, 1977).

3. Jacques Lacan, "The Moral Goals of Psychoanalysis," in *The Seminar of Jacques Lacan: The Ethics of Psychoanalysis 1959–1960,* trans. Dennis Porter (New York: W. W. Norton, 1986).

4. Ibid., "The Death Drive."

5. Ibid., "Das Ding," "Das Ding II," "The Object and the Thing," "On Creation *Ex Nihilo.*"

6. Slavoj Žižek, *Looking Awry: An Introduction to Jacques Lacan through Popular Culture* (Cambridge, Mass.: MIT Press, 1992), 34–39.

7. Lacan, *The Ethics of Psychoanalysis,* "Marginal Comments."

8. Luce Irigaray, "The Blind Spot in an Old Dream of Symmetry," in *Speculum of the Other Woman,* trans. Gillian C. Gill (Ithaca: Cornell University Press, 1985).

9. For a fuller account of this, see my "Queering the Phallus," in *Disseminating Lacan,* ed. David Pettigrew and François Raffoul (Albany: SUNY Press, 1996).

10. Luce Irigaray, "Chapter X," in *Elemental Passions,* trans. Joanne Collie and Judith Still (New York: Routledge, 1992).

11. For a more detailed analysis, see my "Nietzsche's Madman: Perspectivism with Nihilism," in *Nietzsche as Postmodernist,* ed. Clayton Koelb (Albany: SUNY Press, 1990).

12. Page du Bois, *Sowing the Body: Psychoanalysis and Ancient Representations of Women* (Chicago: University of Chicago Press, 1988), 69–74.

CHAPTER 2

Odysseus Bound?

Daniel W. Conway

But I with my sharp sword cut into small bits a great round
cake of wax, and kneaded it with my strong hands, and soon
the wax grew warm, forced by the strong pressure and the
rays of the lord Helios Hyperion. Then I anointed with this
[wax] the ears of all my comrades in turn; and they bound me
in the ship hand and foot, upright in the step of the mast, and
made the ropes fast at the ends to the mast itself; and themselves sitting down smote the grey sea with their oars.

Homer, The Odyssey

I am still waiting for a philosophical *physician* in the
exceptional sense of that word—one who has to pursue the
problem of the total health of a people, time, race or of
humanity—to muster the courage to push my suspicion to
its limits and to risk the proposition: what was at stake in all
philosophizing hitherto was not at all "truth" but something
else—let us say, health, future, growth, power, life.

Friedrich Nietzsche, The Gay Science

How clever was Herr Nietzsche? Clever enough to equate morality with
diet (*EH* "Clever" 1), apparently, and to prefer the lusty naturalism of
Rossini to the constipated gravity of "German music" (*EH* "Clever" 7).[1]
Clever enough to husband the depleted vitality and dwindling creativity
at his disposal, never striving "for *honors,* for *women,* [or] for *money*"
(*EH* "Clever" 9). Clever enough to attend carefully to the "small things
which are generally considered matters of complete indifference" (*EH*
"Clever" 10), to the quotidian nuances of nutrition, place, climate and
recreation (*EH* "Clever" 8). Clever enough, in the end, to have become

what he was, by following his "formula for greatness in a human being": *amor fati* (*EH* "Clever" 10).

This testimony to Nietzsche's cleverness is drawn, however, from an exceedingly dubious source: his ersatz autobiography, *Ecce Homo*. Although this bristling little book yields a wealth of insights into Nietzsche's life and career, its aspirations to hagiography should pique the suspicions of even his most adoring readers. This is an author, after all, who has already suggested that "modern men" could not "stand a *true* autobiography," for they could not "endure a single truth 'about man'" (*GM* III:19). Remarking on the reluctance of modern readers to see their heroes and villains as they really are, he asks, "What prudent man would write a single honest word about himself today? He would have to be a member of the Order of Holy Foolhardiness to do so" (*GM* III:19). In light of such remarks, we are obliged to approach Nietzsche's autobiography with heightened suspicions of his honesty. Indeed, unless we are prepared to take his feckless (or prudent) word for it, we must look elsewhere to gauge the true range and depth of his abiding cleverness.

A successor psychologist, Sigmund Freud, reportedly opined that "[Nietzsche] had a more penetrating knowledge of himself than any other man who ever lived or was ever likely to live." [2] This platitude certainly concurs with Nietzsche's familiar account of himself, but it also dodges the pragmatic question of determining the precise depths to which his "penetrating" self-knowledge actually reached. Did he achieve a level of self-knowledge commensurate with his general knowledge of human psychology? Was he sufficiently apprised of his own failings — his decadence, resentment, romanticism, anxiety of influence, and so on — that he was able to arrange for their preemptive neutralization?

Let us grant that Nietzsche's understanding of decadence is, as he insists, both unprecedented and unrivaled. "In questions of *décadence*," he may very well be "the highest authority on earth" (letter to Malwida von Meysenbug, 18 October 1888; *KGB* III/5:452). But how familiar was he with the particular manifestations and eruptions of his own decay? How exacting was he in applying his general diagnosis of modernity to his own psychic disarray? He knew, for example, that decadence typically expresses itself in symptoms unknown and unimaginable to the agents in question, who generally stand in the worst possible position to detect and interpret the signs of their own decay. He also knew that decadence characteristically manifests itself in various delusions of grandeur, such as the perception of oneself standing "between two millennia"[3] or the conviction that one can manage the effects of one's own decay. This impressive fund of general knowledge corroborates his claim to authority in all matters of decadence, but it does not yet suggest an intimate familiarity with the specific facts of *his* condition. Our guiding question thus stands: To what extent was Nietzsche able to subsume his own erratic life under the general theory of decadence that he advances?

Nietzsche was not as clever as his most loyal readers tend to suggest. He did not possess sufficient self-knowledge to close the circle of his thought and complete his critical project.[4] Nor did he finally attain the panoptic standpoint he disallows to other thinkers. Most important, he succeeded neither in resisting the philosopher's temptation to exempt himself from his own blanket diagnoses nor in defending the exemption he surreptitiously issued to himself. Having exposed the recidivistic error to which all philosophers naturally fall prey, he was powerless to resist this error in his own right. Like all previous systems of thought, Nietzsche's philosophy "creates the world in its own image; it cannot do otherwise" (*BGE* 9).

The fatal flaw of all philosophers and psychologists hitherto, he announces, lies in their common failure to forge the final, self-referential link in the concatenation of their own pet insights. Philosophers are all "advocates who resent that name, and for the most part even wily spokesmen for their prejudices" (*BGE* 5). Nietzsche presents no exception to this general truth, despite his occasional protestations to the contrary. He may have been more successful than his predecessors in applying his signature insights to his own situation, but in the end he too fails to subject himself to the withering critical gaze he trains on others. Having told us that all philosophers "tyrannically" excuse themselves from their own critical inquisitions, that the presumption of philosophers constitutes "the most spiritual will to power" (*BGE* 9), he promptly corroborates this claim by issuing himself an exemption from his otherwise inclusive diagnosis of modernity. Precisely *because* he is decadent, he perversely insists, he has taken the measure of his age (*EH* "Wise" 1).

At this juncture, however, it would be premature to reject Freud's assessment of Nietzsche's "penetrating" self-knowledge. He neither pursued nor claimed for himself the transparency of soul that would invite a definitive self-examination. While accounting for the genius that distinguishes himself and his fellow genealogists, he candidly remarks, "We are unknown to ourselves, we men of knowledge—and with good reason. We have never sought ourselves—how could it happen that we should ever *find* ourselves?" (*GM* P1). Reprising this curious maxim in his "autobiography," he offers to share the secret of his prodigious cleverness: "To become what one is, one must not have the faintest notion *what* one is" (*EH* "Clever" 9).

By treading this *via negativa*, Nietzsche actually joins his former nemesis, Socrates, in obeying the imperative of the Delphic oracle: *know thyself*. Like Socrates, moreover, Nietzsche embraces the oracle's pronouncement in the full force of its defining irony. He pursues self-knowledge, that is, despite his guiding insight into the futility of any such quest. The irony of the Delphic injunction, as of the twinship of the philosophers it joins, thus arises from the unattainable nature of the goal it assigns to the votaries of the oracle:

> Consequently, given the best will in the world to understand ourselves as individually as possible, "to know ourselves," each of us will always succeed in becoming conscious only of what is not individual but "average." (*GS* 354)

To obey the Delphic imperative and resolutely pursue the goal of self-knowledge, one must already understand that definitive self-knowledge is impossible to attain:

> We are necessarily strangers to ourselves, we do not comprehend ourselves, we *have* to misunderstand ourselves, for us the law "Each is furthest from himself" applies to all eternity—we are not "men of knowledge" with respect to ourselves. (*GM* P1)

Nietzsche's interpretation of the Apollonian oracle thus reveals the Dionysian wisdom encrypted within the Delphic injunction. Issued to a healthy people, for whom self-knowledge is coextensive with spontaneous self-expression, the imperative *know thyself* is otiose, if not unintelligible. Nothing comes more naturally to the representatives of a healthy people or epoch than an unquestioned, prereflective, embodied self-knowledge. It is a hallmark of healthy peoples and ages that self-knowledge never becomes an issue to be addressed, much less a lack to be filled. Issued to a decadent people or epoch, however, the Delphic imperative amounts to a sibylline joke, played by malicious gods on enfeebled mortals (*GS* 335). The stipulated need for self-knowledge points not to the possibility of actually gaining self-knowledge but to the irreversible decay that this need signifies. Anyone who *lacks* self-knowledge will most assuredly never attain it.

Socrates indirectly confirms Nietzsche's interpretation of the oracle's pronouncement when he locates his alleged "wisdom" in the knowledge that he does not know.[5] This nihilistic insight, celebrated by Socrates and Nietzsche alike, is attainable only by decadent philosophers, who pathologically call into question the unjustified, prereflective practices that define a people or an epoch. As they expertly unravel the instinctual fabric that binds their respective peoples and epochs, decadent philosophers are left clutching a single, nihilistic thread. They may know nothing else, but they at least know that they know nothing. Here, one step removed from the self-consuming wisdom of Silenus, decadent philosophers presume to pass judgment on the (meaningless) whole.

One's obedience to the imperative *know thyself* thus leads *not* to self-knowledge but to the enactment of one's inevitable self-destruction. Whereas a healthy soul "knows" itself immediately and without oracular prompting, a corrupt soul will sooner expend its residual vitality than surrender its innermost secrets. *Nosce te ipsum,* Nietzsche candidly concedes, thus constitutes "a recipe for ruin" (*EH* "Clever" 9). Is it merely a coincidence that Socrates alone pursues the oracle's gnomic pronouncement to its absurd, self-consuming conclusion, whereby he obliquely accuses his fellow Athenians of collective impiety? Or that Nietzsche, two millennia removed from the suicide of Socrates, would dare to court madness and self-destruction in order to become what he was?

For nihilists like Socrates and Nietzsche, then, the point of obeying the oracle's imperative cannot be to gain self-knowledge. Indeed, if the primary justification of the pursuit of self-knowledge were to lie in the promise of its successful attainment, then one would be foolish to engage in its pursuit. Although it is true that one might receive in the process a negative, tragic insight, this humble morsel of wisdom could never be considered an adequate justification for the pain and hardship endured. For both Nietzsche and Socrates, the real justification of the pursuit of self-knowledge lies elsewhere, in a vague anticipation of the type of person one might become in the process. Socrates thus explains that if we continue to seek that which we do not know, we will become "better men, braver and less idle"—even if we never gain knowledge of anything.[6] Nietzsche similarly insists that his own genealogical investigations contribute to the constitution of a fructifying regimen of self-overcoming, a therapeutic "technique of the self" that may enable him to explore further the undiscovered country of decadence. He remains forever unknown to himself, but his pursuit of self-knowledge nevertheless yields indirect, unanticipated benefits for his ongoing struggle with the decadence of late modernity.

The hunt for self-knowledge will always fail to turn up its elusive quarry, but it may nevertheless succeed in transforming the hunters into *signs* of the excess vitality required to participate in the sport. The quest for self-knowledge thus furnishes an effective ascetic pretext for the expenditure of residual vitality. One is still a fool for seeking self-knowledge, but one becomes a significatory—and therefore significant—fool in the process. Strictly speaking, however, even this justification remains indirect and external, for seekers of self-knowledge are unable to determine in advance the dialogic meaning of the signs they will become. To quest for self-knowledge in order to embody a *particular* sign is to confuse cause and effect.

The most that decadent philosophers can hope for from their quest for self-knowledge is to reveal themselves fully to others in the embodiment of their inexorable decay. This dialogic self-revelation is the source of Nietzsche's mitigated triumph in the "dangerous game" he plays. Although he fails to provide a definitive account of his age, he successfully transforms himself into a sign of his times. He thereby contributes to our appreciation for the governing *ethos* of his age, by bodying forth (albeit unwittingly) an incarnate critique of modernity. Although ultimately unknown to himself, he trained his successors to probe the self-referential blind spot that vitiates his critical enterprise. Regardless of its success or failure, any attempt to take the measure of Nietzsche will lead to the dissemination of his teachings.

The hard truth of Freud's insight thus lies in the tragic formulation of his appraisal of Nietzsche's "penetrating" self-knowledge. Nietzsche may have failed to attain the Promethean measure of self-understanding that would make him whole again, but his knowledge of himself nevertheless outstrips that of most mortals. His foolish pursuit of self-knowledge is doomed to failure, but it might contribute nonetheless to his readers' understanding of the age he involuntarily represents. If this is true, then how best might we describe and convey the unparalleled self-knowledge he attained?

I wish to portray Nietzsche as pursuing the sort of transfigurative limit experience that would occasion an enhancement of humankind as a whole. In many respects his pursuit of a limit experience resembles that of Odysseus, who similarly sought to advance the recognized frontiers of the human condition. Odysseus longed for an experience previously unknown to mortals: to survive the thanatonic song of the sirens. While bewitched by the sirens, he knew, any mortal would dash himself on the nearest rocks. Such a state, in which one unthinkingly craves what is most disadvantageous for oneself, is not unlike the condition Nietzsche calls "decadence." His agency bounded by a horizon of distinctly human experiences, Odysseus could not have known in advance what it would be like to hear—and survive—the song of the sirens. He could know only that he would be transfigured by the experience and that the extant complement of human perfections would be permanently expanded.

On his own, Odysseus knew, he was not equal to the limit experience he sought. He too would dash himself on the rocks if tempted by the sirens. Guided by the goddess Circe, he consequently implemented measures designed to insulate his pursuit of a transfigurative experience from his own, all-too-human limitations. He famously instructed his crew to bind him to the mast and to sail within auditory range of the sirens' lair. Having preemptively compensated for his all-too-human weaknesses, he would be free to experience the reveries of sirenic intoxication without fear of accepting their invitation to die. If his initial orders to his crew were to prevail as securely as the lashes that would soon bind him to the ship's mast, then he would need first to prepare his shipmates for the adventure that lay ahead. They must be disciplined to ignore the subsequent, countermanding orders that he knows the sirens will elicit from him. By sealing his shipmates' ears with wax, Odysseus effectively founded a community that would compensate for his own acknowledged weaknesses, a community that would not permit him to recoil from his moment of transfiguration. Once bound to the mast by his newly deafened comrades, he could neither refuse nor resist the epiphany he craved. No twinge of ambivalence would be permitted to deflect the limit experience he sought.[7] The wisdom of Odysseus, justly celebrated in the circulatory myths of Greek antiquity, thus emanates from an unflinching appraisal of his own, all-too-human limitations. As Nietzsche might say, the wisdom of Odysseus lies in his uncanny ability to turn his destiny to his advantage.

In his desire to stand between two millennia, Nietzsche resembles Odysseus before the mast. Cognizant of his own decadence, if not of its precise manifestations, Nietzsche must insulate his pursuit of a limit experience from his own, all-too-human weaknesses. Unable to confront his own decadence in its immanence and specificity, he frames a plan for enlisting others to do so for him. He thus anticipates, and potentially compensates for, the unknown effects of his own decay. He knew, for example, that he would need to recruit readers who would continue his incipient rebellion against Christian morality. Such readers, he also knew, must heroically resist the blandishments of discipleship, lest they succumb to the spell of a clever priest. Hoping to induce the self-overcoming of Christian morality, he strove to extend his formative influence into the coming millennium, at which time he would be recognized and revered as the Antichrist. To prepare himself to stand between two millennia, he thus attempted to neutralize the effects of his own decay while attracting a fellowship of anti-Christian successors.

Like Odysseus, Nietzsche is not equal to the limit experience he seeks. Having briefly tasted epiphany before, in the form of the adventitious thought of eternal recurrence (*EH* "Books" Z:1), Nietzsche understands that his conscious pursuit of transfiguration is severely jeopardized by his all-too-human weaknesses. He must enlist the help of others, and he must discipline these others to execute their original charge, despite the subsequent demands he knows he will make of them. If he is to succeed in orchestrating for himself the transfiguration he craves, then he must first seal his readers' ears to the decadent longings that emanate irrepressibly from his writings.[8] Duly trained, such readers would turn a deaf ear to the entreaties of Nietzsche's decadence, just as Odysseus's crew ignored his crazed demands to be unbound and released to his death. Guided by the divine patronage of Dionysus, Nietzsche reprises the self-neutralizing strategy of the clever Odysseus. His experiments are designed to found a community of readers who will safely transport his teachings across the "open sea" of late modernity (*GS* 343).

Like the loyal members of Odysseus's crew, Nietzsche's "perfect" readers would belay, if necessary, any subsequent orders that might divert them from their appointed course. They would heed only his original call to arms, ignoring his subsequent and inevitable wish for spineless sycophants and fawning disciples. It is no coincidence that his favorite image for his perfect readers is borrowed from Zarathustra's heartfelt address to his intrepid shipmates:

> To you, the bold searchers [*Suchern*], researchers [*Versuchern*], and whoever embarks with cunning sails on terrible seas—to you, drunk with riddles, glad of the twilight, whose soul flutes lure astray to every whirlpool, because you do not want to grope along a thread with cowardly hand; and where you can *guess,* you hate to *deduce*—to you alone I tell the riddle that I *saw,* the vision of the loneliest. (Z:3 "On the Vision and the Riddle" 1)

Here, however, the Odyssean parallel ends. Nietzsche did not enjoy the luxury of an exclusively mythic existence,[9] and his experiments have failed to reproduce the resounding success of the clever Odysseus.

Whereas Odysseus could rely confidently on his loyal, battle-tested crew, Nietzsche must count on unknown readers whom he neither trusts nor admires. While his desperate situation imbues his pursuit of a limit experience with a degree of danger unknown to Odysseus, it also seals his inevitable failure. To be sure, Nietzsche *did* eventually attain a sort of limit experience, which he described to his friend Heinrich Köselitz, under the macabre signature "The Crucified," as gloriously ecstatic: "Sing me a new song: the world is transfigured [*verklärt*] and all the heavens rejoice." [10] This transfiguration is more regularly called "madness," however, and it bears no resemblance to the calamitous limit experience he led us to expect on his behalf. Rather than deafen his perfect readers to the siren song of decadence, he now lends his voice to its ubiquitous chorus, even as he clamors for silence. In fact, if we appeal to the evaluative standards that *he* consistently invoked in his post-Zarathustrian writings, then we must pronounce him a loser in the "dangerous game" he desperately plays.

From Nietzsche's own decadent perspective, his campaign to unseat Christian morality would appear to be a failure. He has attracted all the wrong readers, and the madness that enveloped him is certainly not the limit experience he sought. Instead of the philosopher-commanders who would oversee the era of "great politics," legislating the transition to the successor age to modernity, he has sired lawgivers manqué, political bullies and thugs, and papier mâché *Übermenschen*. For every Stefan George or Thomas Mann (decadent artists in their own right), Nietzsche has inspired a legion of graffiti artists, hack playwrights, and adolescent songwriters. It would appear, then, that he cannot afford the readership he desires. His decadence enforces instinctual needs that subvert the cultivation of the perfect readers he envisions. His ingenious experiments ultimately fail to insulate his readers from his decadence. Not unlike another mad Teutonic genius of the nineteenth century, Nietzsche creates monstrous "children" whom he ultimately cannot control.

In arriving at an "objective" assessment of his influence, however, we must beware of accepting uncritically his own criteria of evaluation. Although he claimed to pursue an experience that is altogether new, which would permanently augment the complement of extant human perfections, he characteristically assessed his progress in terms of what was known and familiar to him. His diagnosis of modernity was similarly unoriginal in its Protestant anticipation of demise and apocalypse, and his hazy vision of the postmodern, tragic age to come betrays his bourgeois, romantic yearnings (letter to Köselitz, 4 January 1889; *KGB*

III / 5 : 575). Nietzsche vowed to "break history in two," but the rupture he eventually celebrates only reinforces the hegemony of the traditions from which he claims to stray. He promised to deliver "dynamite," but he has apparently attached to this dubious ordnance an interminably long fuse.

While his need for slavish readers is certainly symptomatic of decadence, his desire for masterly readers is equally so—especially insofar as it manifests a romantic anachronism. As we have seen, Nietzsche subscribes to a romance in which he would personally train an intrepid vanguard of swashbuckling warrior-genealogists. These perfect readers must complete their apprenticeship by disowning their master, only to return later as his equals and compatriots (Z:1 "On the Gift-Giving Virtue" 3). Steeled by this manly rite of initiation, they swear their unerring fealty to Nietzsche and pledge their lives to the destruction of Christianity. Regardless of how we might ultimately judge his unique rendition of this masculinist romance, his idle speculations on the likely consequences of his "explosion" are no more authoritative than Odysseus's imaginations of the sirens prior to his transfigurative experience before the mast. As his own theory of decadence expressly indicates, his discursive critique of modernity holds philosophical value only as a symptom of his own decay.

Nietzsche's apparent failure to endue his philosophy with the novelty and originality he promises should come as no surprise to his readers. Did he not teach us to beware of priests and philosophers who claim to bear "glad tidings"? Did he not warn that *anyone* who discovers a new route to the enhancement of humankind will invariably present this path as impassably strewn with obstacles and barriers, such that all would-be pilgrims are dependent on the "assistance" of the resident expert guide? In order to explore the undiscovered countries of the human soul, he sensibly insists, we must forcibly negate the colonizing influence of the philosophers who initially point the way. But what of a philosopher who stands under the name *Nietzsche?* On this point of self-reference he remains uncharacteristically silent, unable in his besetting decay to entertain for long the possibility that he too postpones the enhancement of humankind.

Nietzsche has failed to assemble the readership he sought for his war on Christianity, but his books have in fact attracted readers who are uniquely suited to toil in the twilight of the idols. He envisioned a vanguard of warrior-genealogists whom he would personally train in the arts of manly contest, but his actual readers are nook-dwelling creatures of *ressentiment,* versed in the "effeminate" arts of subterfuge, duplicity, and deception. He yearned for disciples who might tear him to shreds in a pique of maenadic possession, but he instead attracts treacherous followers who will betray him and distort his teachings to suit their own designs.[11] His readership is not what he hoped for, but it accurately reflects what his own critique of modernity would lead us to expect of any decadent philosopher. Although he would certainly disown such readers as unworthy of his legacy, he would do so only because they bear an unbearable resemblance to him. Like their reluctant "father," these readers are agents of decadence, who anachronistically expend their residual vitality in the service of heroic ideals. Following him, they advance the campaign against Christianity through the use of priestly weapons and stratagems, all the while mouthing a litany of noble pieties.

Nietzsche's irrepressible decadence might appear to compromise his confrontation with modernity, but only if we also accept without question his preferred standards for success and failure. The warrior-genealogists whom he hoped to muster would certainly be an impressive sight, especially against the blighted backdrop of late modernity. But they would also be stunningly ill equipped, much like Sophocles' Ajax, to negotiate the shades and shadows of a decadent epoch. The contestatory arena within which such heroes thrive presupposes an age or people that can afford to defend the *agon* against those scoundrels and malcontents who would change the rules of the contest in order to reward their own underhanded "virtues." Since late modernity can afford neither to stage nor to defend a heroic *agon,* Nietzsche's nascent rebellion is much better served by the shifty rogues and dissemblers who bear the unmistakable imprint of *his* decadence. They alone can summon the requisite deception and trickery to vanquish the last surviving priests of Christendom, and they alone can be counted on to consume themselves in the priestly Armageddon that will (supposedly) bring modernity to a close. Most important, they alone will betray even Nietzsche in their hateful campaign to exterminate the priestly class.

Although he could not conceive of his readers needing to trample *him* in the service of the anti-Christian rebellion he foments, he trained them to beware of all priests, especially those who, like him, strike the pose of the anti-priest. Unbeknown to Nietzsche, then, he cultivated a readership that would grant him no quarter were he to reveal himself as an obstacle to be overcome. He furthermore, and equally unwittingly, armed his successors with the priestly weapons they would need to vanquish him and all other anti-priests. So although he was unable to assess honestly the nature and effects of his own decadence, he actually compensated for this failing when training his successors. His actual readers are free to pursue his anti-Christian ends through any means necessary, including a renunciation of him and his signature teachings. Through his confrontation with modernity, that is, he inadvertently created the audience he wants rather than the audience he needs. His experiments inaugurated an intergenerational torch race, whose participants may successively illuminate the gloaming until the arrival of those who will greet the dawn of the postmodern epoch.

It may be possible, of course, and perhaps even desirable, to chart the parallel descent of alternative lineages of Nietzschean readership. Diligent genealogists may even succeed in identifying the "heroic" lineage he desired, or in locating those "perfect" readers who quietly toil in the twilight of the idols to disseminate the transformative teachings that will redeem modernity. I am concerned here to trace one particular lineage of Nietzschean readership, which I take to have descended from the mitigated, unanticipated success of his confrontation with modernity. From the perspective of this particular line of descent, his books appear to have attracted readers who continue his political project while questioning the formative influence he exerts over them. Although it would be precipitous to claim that these readers have broken free entirely of discipleship, it is undeniable that they have forged for themselves a significant critical distance from him.

Versed in the critical strategies they have learned from observing Nietzsche in action, these readers inoculate themselves against his own peculiar strain of priestly pathogenesis. These readers know that he is not to be trusted, that his enmity for the weak and misbegotten is also directed at *them*. These readers are better prepared, when the time comes, to betray even him to further the ends of the rebellion he incites. By the same token, however, the apostasy of his children is never complete. They may turn on him, denounce him, even profane his teachings, but they do so only by implementing the insights and strategies he has bequeathed to them. Indeed, the recent campaign to auscultate the idol of Nietzsche and to depose him from his exalted station as a "master of suspicion" may be the greatest testament to the power of his confrontation with modernity.[12] In the end, he may be "born posthumously" after all, in spite of himself.

Although Nietzsche's "revaluation of all values" fails to achieve the grandiose goals he set for it, it may nonetheless serve the greater ends of his erratic rebellion, albeit by means unimaginable—and unpalatable—

to him. It is entirely possible, in fact, that his actual readers, whom he would despise precisely for the decadence they have inherited from him, have already contributed to the self-overcoming of Christian morality. The pernicious moral concept of *sin,* for example, is gradually yielding its privileged place to diagnoses of sickness, addiction, and other organic dysfunctions. As a consequence, contemporary physicians of culture command ever more confidently their appointed standpoint beyond good and evil. That this transition from evil to sickness would disgust Nietzsche, that he would expose the therapist-kings of late modernity as cleverly disguised priests, tricked out in tweed, is, in the end, irrelevant. His fantasies of a heroic redemption of modernity must be treated as symptoms of, rather than solutions to, the besetting decadence of the epoch. The eventual demise of Christian morality may follow any one of a number of descensional trajectories, and his contribution to its disintegration need bear no resemblance whatsoever to the leading role he reserves for himself.

Nietzsche has in fact exerted a powerful influence on the course of twentieth-century thought, and he commands an ever-growing influence as we approach the turning of the millennium. That this influence deviates from his fantasies about it, that he has been lionized by sundry permutations of the reviled "man of *ressentiment,*" is, finally, beside the point. He has created a readership in his own decadent image, and, for better or worse, this audience will determine the fate of his anti-Christian rebellion. He may have failed to create the intrepid warrior-genealogists who would bravely escort him across the threshold of the new millennium, but this failure need not crush his incipient anti-Christian rebellion. In fact, his weakness for this hackneyed romance of male bonding may actually serve to align his political agenda with his unique historical situation.

The recent academic campaign to discredit appeals to authorial intention might discourage us from attributing to Nietzsche the conscious designs that the disposition of his current readership obliquely suggests. Some critics might argue that the experimental devices I have discerned in his writings are more properly attributed to my own unexamined readerly response. Still others might explain his enduring influence in terms of the fascination his iconoclasm holds for a decadent culture arrested in a state of protracted adolescence. Reservations about authorial intentions, especially when motivated by legitimate epistemic concerns, are salutary possessions for any careful reader. I fear, however, that the attack on authorial intention all too often manifests a latent resentment of genius itself, a contempt for aesthetic productions whose design outstrips those of ordinary mortals in originality and audacity. While it is clear that most of Nietzsche's readers could never have anticipated and compensated for the deleterious effects of their own decadence, it does not necessarily follow that Nietzsche himself was similarly limited.

If, as Freud claims, Nietzsche amassed an unprecedented wealth of self-knowledge, then perhaps we should be prepared to attribute to him authorial designs so elaborate and complex as to suggest the inspiration of genius. As I have suggested, Nietzsche may very well have known that he would quail before the transfigurative task he set for himself and that he must enlist others who would inflict on him the violence that he would, in the end, spare himself. In light of this "penetrating" self-knowledge, is it not possible that he schooled his readers in suspicion and symptomatology so that they might assist him in an attack on Christianity to which he knew he was not equal? Is it not possible that his experiments have succeeded in compensating even for those weaknesses of which he was ignorant? Is it not possible that he has cleverly sealed our ears so that we would not heed his cries of surrender to the siren song of decadence? Finally, is it simply a coincidence that his books have in fact contributed to the production of readers who continue his life's work, despite the obstacles he has planted in their path?

In the end, Freud may be right about the pioneering reaches of Nietzsche's "penetrating self-knowledge." Like the clever Odysseus, he objectively surveyed his all-too-human limitations and implemented corrective measures. He may have failed to attain the final, self-referential insight that would have completed his critique of modernity, but he presided over the training of those successors who might yet do so for him. He may have flinched from beholding himself in the full, terrifying embodiment of his decadence, but he furnished the symptomatological tools others would need to plumb the murky depths of his lacerated soul.

Nietzsche's decadence is thus responsible for the crowning irony of his life and career: It is only as a decadent, as the consummate man of *ressentiment,* that he commands anything like the power and influence he regularly claims for himself. Had he somehow succeeded in creating the audience he needed, his anti-Christian rebellion surely would have foundered. It is only insofar as he has *failed* to control his readership, attracting readers whom he summarily disowns, that his political agenda remains viable at all. If his self-engineered explosion succeeds in clearing the way for a new, tragic *agon,* it does so only because he has unwittingly tapped an abundant store of priestly resentment.[13] His rear-guard attack on the Christian priesthood succeeds not because he in-duces Christian morality to take a fatal, self-referential turn but because he trumps Saint Paul with his—and modernity's—sole remaining card: he betrays even himself in a self-consuming assault on the Christian priesthood. Only as a martyr, not as a squanderer, does he hasten the self-overcoming of Christian morality.

To all appearances, Nietzsche remained blind to the secret of his limi-ted success. Soothed by the tonic melodies of his marathon piano im-provisations, confident in his mad resolve to assassinate the political and religious leaders of Europe, he never fully confronted the reflection of his own visage in the yawning abyss of decadence. Spared a final, devastat-ing self-examination by the onset of insanity, he blissfully acceded to the station of the millennial Antichrist. Had he suspected that his exit from the labyrinth would pursue the low road, tracing clandestine paths through malodorous swamps and lowlands, tunneling through dimly lit subterranean nooks and chambers, he never could have embarked on this Hyperborean expedition.

NOTES

1. With the exception of occasional emendations, I rely throughout this chapter on Walter Kaufmann's translations/editions of Nietzsche's books for Viking Press/Random House and on R. J. Hollingdale's translations for Cam-bridge University Press.

2. Cited in Ernest Jones, *The Life and Work of Sigmund Freud* (New York: Basic Books, 1953), 2:344.

3. Nietzsche suggests this description of himself in a letter to Reinhardt von Seydlitz on 12 February 1888 (*KGB* III/5:248).

4. According to Maudemarie Clark, Nietzsche creates the world in his own image, but, unlike all previous philosophers, he does not do so self-deceptively: "Nietzsche knows perfectly well that [his doctrine of the will to power] is not the truth" (Clark, *Nietzsche on Truth and Philosophy* [Cambridge: Cambridge University Press, 1990], 240).

5. *Apology,* 21 c–e, 23 a–b. Gregory Vlastos argues that Socrates' irony shelters an implicit epistemic distinction between two species of knowledge, in *Socrates: Ironist and Moral Philosopher* (Ithaca: Cornell University Press, 1991), esp. 21–44. In contrast to Vlastos's influential interpretation, I follow Nietzsche in interpreting Socrates' claim as an unironic statement of the nihilism that de-fines his peculiar life. It is not so much, as Vlastos suggests, that Socrates knows (but lacks/refuses the analytic tools to articulate) that knowledge admits of mul-tiple dimensions as that he knows that knowledge, once acquired by decadent philosophers, is useless to effect political change. As kindred nihilists, Socrates

and Nietzsche thus understand that the Delphic imperative shelters an esoteric teaching, which is available only to those who have already gained insight into the natural cycle of growth and decay.

6. Plato, *Meno,* trans. G. M. A. Grube (Indianapolis: Hackett Press, 1976), 20, 86 b–c.

7. My understanding of Odysseus's self-neutralizing strategies is indebted to Jon Elster's lucid discussion of "binding" and "precommitting," in *Ulysses and the Sirens: Studies in Rationality and Irrationality* (Cambridge: Cambridge University Press, 1979), chap. 2.

8. Nietzsche borrows this Odyssean motif to advertise his own "strange and insane" task. Likening the allure of metaphysics to the bewitching song of the sirens, he vows to scour the "eternal basic text of *homo natura*" of all supernatural accretions:

> To translate man back into Nature; . . . to see to it that man henceforth stands before man as even today, hardened in the discipline of science, he stands before the *rest* of Nature, with intrepid Oedipus eyes and sealed Odysseus ears, deaf to the siren songs of old metaphysical bird catchers who have been piping at him all too long, "you are more, you are higher, you are of a different origin!" (*BGE* 230)

9. Alexander Nehamas maintains that Nietzsche largely succeeded in living his "life as literature": "In engaging with [Nietzsche's] works, we are not engaging with the miserable little man who wrote them but with the philosopher who emerges through them, the magnificent character these texts constitute and manifest" (Nehamas, *Nietzsche: Life as Literature* [Cambridge, Mass.: Harvard University Press, 1985], 234). Nehamas does not explain, however, *how* "the miserable little man" escapes "our" engagement with Nietzsche, or *why* we should allow "him" to do so; nor does Nehamas identify the readership that comprises the "we" to which he refers. In any event, Nietzsche himself does not restrict his focus to the "magnificent characters" who are constituted in and through literature. He insists, for example, that "a Homer would not have created an Achilles nor a Goethe a Faust if Homer had been an Achilles or Goethe a Faust" (*GM* III:4).

10. Letter to Köselitz, 4 January 1889 (*KGB* III/5:575).

11. Foucault thus maintains, "The only valid tribute to thought such as Nietzsche's is precisely to use it, to make it groan and protest. And, if the commentators say I am being unfaithful to Nietzsche, that is of absolutely no interest" ("Prison Talk," trans. Colin Gordon, in *Power / Knowledge: Selected Interviews and Other Writings 1972–1977,* ed. Colin Gordon [New York: Random House, 1980], 53–54).

12. Hence the recent appearance of *Pourquoi nous ne sommes pas nietzschéens,* ed. Alain Boyer et al. (Paris: Éditions Grasset et Fasquelle, 1991). For a sensible treatment of the recent turning away from Nietzsche by French intellectuals, see Alan D. Schrift, *Nietzsche's French Legacy: A Genealogy of Poststructuralism* (New York: Routledge, 1995), chap. 5.

13. Robert C. Solomon calls attention to the potentially productive expressions of resentment in his essay "One Hundred Years of Resentment: Nietzsche's

Genealogy of Morals," in *Nietzsche, Genealogy, Morality: Essays on Nietz-sche's "On the Genealogy of Morals,"* ed. Richard Schacht (Berkeley: University of California Press, 1994), 95–126. Solomon maintains, "An ethics of resent-ment is not just a matter of good character / bad character or good emotions and bad emotions. It is also—contra Nietzsche (and MacIntyre)—a question of justification, of the political and social context and the legitimacy of motives and emotions" (124).

CHAPTER 3

Nietzsche's Shakespearean Figures

Duncan Large

SHAKESPEARE: PHILOSOPHER, PSYCHOLOGIST, ANTICHRIST

The English, it is fair to say, did not rank among Nietzsche's "most favored nations." From the tirade against seventeenth- and eighteenth-century English philosophical empiricism in paragraph 252 of *Beyond Good and Evil* to his repeated attacks on individuals of his own age (and the movements they inspired)—Bentham and Mill, Darwin and Spencer, Dickens and George Eliot, utilitarianism and the Salvation Army—it is abundantly clear that on the whole he had scant respect for English writers and thinkers. Yet a small number do escape his censure, and preeminent among these is Shakespeare. Nietzsche discusses Shakespeare periodically throughout his philosophical career: all told, in his notes, letters, and published works he quotes from or alludes or explicitly refers to almost half the plays and a number of the sonnets.[1] He was given the standard (Schlegel-Tieck) German translations of the complete works as a Christmas present in 1861 when he was seventeen,[2] and thereafter—despite his "small English"—he acquired a thirteen-volume English edition of the plays and Thompson's *Illustrations of Shakespeare*,[3] as well as a variety of works of Shakespeare criticism.[4] He also took every opportunity to attend performances of Shakespeare plays, which by the second half of the nineteenth century had become staple fare in theaters throughout Europe.[5]

There are certain features that remain discernibly constant through-out Nietzsche's remarks on Shakespeare. First, his interest is caught above all by the psychological penetration and power of Shakespeare's character portraits, specifically those of Hamlet, Brutus, and Caesar. In November 1883 he writes his sister urging her to read Shakespeare because his plays are full of the kind of strong characters in which "our age" is so poor: "raw, hard, powerful granite-people" (*KGB* III / 1:452). When he writes "In Praise of Shakespeare" in *The Gay Science* (*GS* 98)—his longest meditation on the dramatist—his panegyric is prompted by his admiration for Shakespeare's creation Brutus, that heroic figure who had the "spiritual strength" and "independence of soul" to turn against even what he loved most, and he writes in a similar vein in *Ecce Homo:* "When I seek my highest formula for *Shakespeare* I find it always in that he conceived the type of Caesar" (*EH* "Clever" 4). Second, like Freud, who argues in *The Interpretation of Dreams* that "it can only have been the mental life of the poet that confronts us in *Hamlet,*"[6] Nietzsche plays the psychological sleuth in reading Shakespeare and is quick to extrapolate from the fictional characters to the character of the poet himself. Thus in *The Gay Science* he remarks that Brutus's speech to the poet in *Julius Caesar* IV, 3, "should be translated back into the soul of the poet who wrote it" (*GS* 98); in *Ecce Homo* he states that "the great poet creates *only* out of his own reality" (*EH* "Clever" 4; cf. *HH* 176; *D* 240, 549). Third, from his earliest notes on Shakespeare Nietzsche shows himself to be interested not simply in Shakespeare's evocative power as a dramatist but in his specifically philosophical insights too. Shakespeare was the "best reader" of Montaigne, Nietzsche maintains (*RWB* 3; cf. *KSA* 8:11[38], 11:26[42]), and he makes his dramas correspondingly thought-provoking, "full of ideas" (*HH* 176)—even at the risk of alienating the theatergoing public—although, unlike Montaigne, his philosophizing is always carried out by proxy, through the mouths of his creations, whose impassioned speeches thus serve to develop their characterizations (*KSA* 8:23[146]). The counterpole to his Brutus, the exemplary man of action, is Hamlet, the metaphysician par excellence who knows of more things in heaven and earth than are dreamt of in Horatio's more circumscribed philosophy. In *The Birth of Tragedy,* Hamlet is cast as the supreme example of "the Dionysian man" who has "looked truly into the essence of things" and thereby gained "true knowledge, an insight into the horrible truth" (*BT* 7), which is what renders all action otiose and paralyzes him. "To feel

in this way," Nietzsche will write in *Ecce Homo,* "one must be profound, abyss, philosopher" (*EH* "Clever" 4).

For Nietzsche, then, Shakespeare is an exemplary philosopher and
psychologist, but—to complete Walter Kaufmann's unholy trinity—he
is also an exemplary anti-Christian,[7] repeatedly saluted for his irreligion
(*HH* 125; *D* 76) and refusal to treat the stage as a platform for shallow
moralizing (*D* 240; *KSA* 7:9[42]): his "ethical wisdom" (*KSA* 1: p. 548)
is of a far higher order. In all these ways, Nietzsche appropriates Shakespeare as his own model, creates him in his own image: Nietzsche the
dramatizing philosopher is drawn to Shakespeare the philosophizing
dramatist. But just as Nietzsche himself changes over the course of his
philosophical career, so, inevitably, Shakespeare is ceaselessly refigured
and recontextualized: the jobbing thespian is constantly assigned new
roles in the drama of Nietzsche's own self-overcoming/self-becoming.
To paraphrase Heidegger, I want to ask the question, Who is Nietzsche's
Shakespeare?

SHAKESPEARE AND TRAGEDY

Various documents survive which attest to Nietzsche's earliest response
to Shakespeare during his schooldays at Pforta. In May 1863 he was
given the task of writing an essay, "Description of the Character of
Cassius in *Julius Caesar*" (*FS* 2:193–200), which already foreshadows
his later appreciation of the play in that he devotes the larger part of it
to a consideration of the friendship between Cassius and Brutus. During
this early period he did not need any academic prompting to devote
himself to Shakespeare, though: his papers include eight pages of hand-
written excerpts from the plays (*FS* 2:458) and a set of notes, "On
Makbeth" (*FS* 3:114–15); Gervinus's *Shakespeare* was one of his most
frequently read books in 1863 (*FS* 2:334).

Shakespeare's 300th anniversary fell the following year, and Nietzsche's class marked it by giving a public reading of *Henry IV, Part 1*,
with Nietzsche himself playing the somewhat unlikely role of Hotspur—
"not without false pathos," according to his classmate Paul Deussen.[8]
(In the light of his later barbed remarks on Wagner's overblown "histrionism" [*GS* 368; *CW* 8–9], it is amusing to think of the young Nietzsche as a ham actor.) That pathos is also evident in a poem in ten *ottava
rima* stanzas which Nietzsche penned to mark the occasion (*FS* 2:412–
14), covering in some detail the history of Shakespeare's varying for-

tunes in England after his death, from the closing of the playhouses under the Puritan regime through the Restoration with its bowdlerized,
bewigged performances to the true renaissance of Shakespeare's world
in the soul of "Garrik," which shone its morning sunlight on only the
loftiest peaks, represented by Lessing and Herder. The idolatrous final
stanza of the poem courts blasphemy, as Nietzsche evangelizes for the
resurrected Shakespeare-Christ walking once again in our midst. Already by the age of nineteen, then, Nietzsche was well versed in the vi-
cissitudes of Shakespeare reception, and his boundless admiration for
the poet—"a young eagle crowning the days of his nation's blossoming"—is patent (*FS* 2:412). These will serve as the raw materials from
which he will fashion and refashion his image of Shakespeare in the
years to follow.

It is not surprising that the greatest concentration of Nietzsche's
notes on Shakespeare should come at the time of his most intense engagement with tragic drama and its history, in his preparations for *The
Birth of Tragedy* in 1870–71. It is clear from his notebooks of this period, indeed, that throughout most of the planning stage for this work
he was intending to devote a chapter of it to the English dramatist, who
would serve as the principal bridge between the spirit of Aeschylus and
Sophocles and that of Wagner (*KSA* 7:7[120, 130], 9[122]). In the
construction of this bridge, however, Nietzsche faced a major problem,
for in proposing a theory of *The Birth of Tragedy out of the Spirit of
Music* he could hardly overlook the fact that, a few songs and masques
aside, Shakespeare's dramas do not lend themselves to being construed
as forerunners of the *Gesamtkunstwerk*. "This puts him in an awkward
position, which he deals with by almost total evasion," comments
Michael Tanner.[9] But Tanner's statement needs to be qualified, for although it is true that very little on Shakespeare remains in *The Birth
of Tragedy* (aside from the remarks on Hamlet which I have already
quoted), in Nietzsche's notebooks he goes to some lengths to appropriate Shakespeare for his project, on the one hand to envisage "Shakespearean drama as the consequence of Greek tragedy" (*KSA* 7:8[48])
and its author as "the fulfillment of Sophocles" (*KSA* 7:7[131, 134],
9[132]), on the other to bring Shakespeare and Wagner together by
stressing the ("Germanic") "musicality" of Shakespeare's writing (*KSA*
7:1[38]). He produces various attempts at a solution, each of them ingenious but ultimately unsatisfactory. He claims, for example, that it is
the "Germanic mission" to perfect the art form—music—which is the
true fulfillment of the tragic knowledge that inspired Socrates' misguided

scientific enterprise (*KSA* 7:7[174]; cf. 7[166]) and that Shakespeare stands in direct "relation" to this mission, as "'the poet of tragic knowledge' [. . .] the *music-making Socrates*" (*KSA* 7:7 [130–31]). Nietzsche constructs Shakespeare as "the adequation of the *thought* of music" (*KSA* 7:9[109]), arguing that Shakespeare fulfills what was present only in outline in Sophocles, "the birth of *thought from music*"—a process that is "really Germanic" (*KSA* 7:9[125])—and he sets up a pair of proportional relations such that Shakespeare is to ancient Greek drama what "Germanic music" (i.e., Wagner) is to ancient Greek music (*KSA* 7:9[132]). "Shakespeare as the highest *Dionysian* power guarantees the magnificent development of German music" (*KSA* 7:8[48]), we are emphatically told, and yet at the same time Nietzsche also admits that Shakespeare's theater is genealogically related to Greek "New Comedy" and that, by shedding the chorus, it has thereby *lost* the Dionysian element of the dithyramb, which has been dissipated into pure imagery (*KSA* 1: p. 515 f., 7:7[134]).

THE GERMAN "SCHÄKESPEAR"

In the end it seems Nietzsche realized such tangled sophisms were far from convincing, and he left all these remarks out of *The Birth of Tragedy* (so as at the same time to heighten the impact of his contemporary idol).[10] What is most interesting about these aborted attempts, though, is that Shakespeare nevertheless emerges from this early period as an honorary German, to be ranged alongside Bach, for example, as an embodiment of "the aboriginally German spirit [*der urgermanische Geist*]" (*KSA* 7:9[143]).

With respect to this nationalistic appropriation of Shakespeare, Nietzsche was merely following in the footsteps of a great many earlier Germanic writers over the previous century, along a well-trodden path stretching from Shakespeare's "discovery" by Hamann, Wieland, and Lessing in the mid-eighteenth century through his idolization by Herder and the Sturm und Drang movement of the 1770s to his subsequent adoption as "national writer" by the Jena romantics at the turn of the nineteenth century and canonization with the rightly acknowledged masterpieces that are the Schlegel-Tieck translations.[11] It is certainly ironic, however, that Nietzsche should reach the same end point having started from a radically different premise, for the birth of interest in Shakespeare in eighteenth-century Germany had been predicated on what was construed as the polar opposition of this "Nordic" genius to the stifling spirit of Greek tragedy (as mediated by French classicism), with its Aristotelian formalisms and its constraining unities above all.[12] By his startlingly innovative, anti-Aristotelian reconception of the birth of tragedy in ancient Greece and his championing of Wagner as the contemporary reincarnation of its spirit, Nietzsche seeks to reconcile the (Anglo-)German and the Greek, combined in opposition to the *Roman* (*KSA* 7:9[143]).

The one earlier German Shakespeare interpreter whose opinions Nietzsche takes to heart is Goethe, whose preoccupation with Shakespeare was quite as intense and sustained as his own, from the "Shakespearean" practice of his dramas *Götz von Berlichingen* (1773) and *Egmont* (1788) to his archetypal bildungsroman, *Wilhelm Meister's Apprenticeship* (1795–96), large portions of which—the fruits of Goethe's direction of Shakespeare plays in Weimar—are devoted to detailed discussions of "production values" for the hero's staging of *Hamlet*. It was Goethe's own reflections on Shakespeare that interested Nietzsche most, however: the twenty-two-year-old's address "On Shakespeare's Day" ("Zum Schäkespears Tag," 1771), which marked one of the key moments in the inception of the Sturm und Drang Shakespeare cult (the day concerned being simply the name day for William); the later essay "Shakespeare *ad infinitum!*" ("Shakespear und kein Ende!" 1813–16); and the remarks on Shakespeare attributed to him in what Nietzsche deemed "the best German book there is" (*WS* 109), Eckermann's *Conversations with Goethe*.[13] As so often in matters of literary taste, then, Nietzsche sounds a number of Goethean themes in his appreciation of Shakespeare, and indeed he quotes Goethe on several occasions, drawing on and engaging with the "Shakespeare-Bild" of his illustrious predecessor.

In general, the intensity of Nietzsche's admiration for Shakespeare as *the* preeminent modern dramatist who brooks no comparison—the heroic, isolated genius uniquely capable of creating titanic "granite-people"—matches Goethe's breathless description (in "On Shakespeare's Day") of a dramatist who surpasses even Prometheus in the "*colossal greatness*" of his characterizations.[14] Goethe praises Shakespeare's plays for liberating him from the "prison" of "regular theater," conceding that "his plots are, to speak in accordance with the common style, not plots";[15] Nietzsche will likewise welcome the "unfettering" impact of this "'great barbarian'" (*HH* 221) and praise him as "a disorderly genius" (*EH* "Clever" 3). Goethe judges Shakespeare by aesthetic rather than moral criteria, arguing, "What noble philosophers

have said of the world applies equally to Shakespeare: what we call evil
is merely the obverse of good"; [16] for Nietzsche, too, Shakespeare is
beyond good and evil: he "speaks out of a wickeder age than ours is"
(D 240) and is capable of taking *"pleasure in cruelty"* (KSA 9:11[89]),
indeed "dramatists are in general somewhat wicked men" (HH 176).
Shakespeare's mastery of psychology, which Nietzsche so admires, is a
quality Goethe highlights before him: "Shakespeare is a great psychologist," he remarks to Eckermann, "and his plays teach us how people
feel." [17] Shakespeare's Romans are "all nothing but flesh-and-blood
Englishmen, but they are certainly human beings," Goethe argues in
"Shakespeare *ad infinitum!*" [18]—a passage Nietzsche quotes with ap-
proval in the second *Untimely Meditation* (HL 5; cf. KSA 7:29[117]).
Nietzsche even echoes Goethe's argument (throughout "Shakespeare *ad
infinitum!*") that Shakespeare's plays are so cosmic they are more suited
to the page than the stage (cf. KSA 7:9[126], 8:19[47]). The volume of
Illustrations of Shakespeare which Nietzsche owned was, not coinci-
dentally, the same edition as the one Goethe acquired on its publication
in 1825: those who lament the appearance of comic-book Shakespeare
plays might be surprised to discover the interest Goethe and Nietzsche
shared in what Eckermann describes as "a highly important English
work depicting the whole of Shakespeare in engravings"! [19]

REVALUATIONS (LESAGE CONTRA SHAKESPEARE)

One of the great slogans in Goethe's address "On Shakespeare's Day" is
"Nature! Nature! Nothing so much like nature as Shakespeare's characters," [20] and here too Nietzsche initially echoes Goethe in praising
Shakespeare's "naturalism" (KSA 7:7[151], 9[85]). However, on this
point he finds Goethe's evaluation increasingly problematic and gradually distances himself from it, later admitting to finding it rather naive
and dated. In *Human, All-Too-Human,* he admits that Shakespeare's
Montaigne-inspired practice of putting maxims in the mouths of his
characters, though one that he applauds, is "counter to nature" (HH
176); he criticizes "even Goethe" for promoting the cult of Shakespeare-
as-genius (HH 162) and argues elsewhere that Goethe's admiration for
Shakespeare's supposed "naturalness" was merely a sign of the times, of
his adherence to Rousseauism (KSA 9:4[32], 13:11[312]/WP 849).
    Since Nietzsche had himself wholeheartedly endorsed Goethe's admi-
ration for Shakespeare, this move away from Goethe's appreciation can
also be read as an indirect criticism of the naïveté of his own earlier ap-

proach to Shakespeare, and indeed from the mid-1870s there are more explicit criticisms of Shakespeare in Nietzsche's writings too—in a note from 1883 he even goes so far as to call *Hamlet,* the play that had figured so prominently and so favorably in *The Birth of Tragedy,* "a *botched* work" (*KSA* 10:7[68]). In one sense this revaluation is a product of the general disillusionment with artists and their artifacts that set in after Nietzsche's break with Wagner, but in Shakespeare's case the need for a revaluation was all the more pressing given the way in which, in his notes for *The Birth of Tragedy,* Nietzsche had so unequivocally associated the English dramatist with the German composer and "the aboriginally Germanic spirit" (*KSA* 7:9[143]). After his break with Wagner in the mid-1870s, and in general his violent turn against (pan-)German nationalism in disgust at the founding of the Reich in 1871, Nietzsche could not have continued to find Shakespeare interesting and admirable had he not recast him as other than the monolithic "Urgermane," the proto-Wagner. As with Laurence Sterne, another English writer whom Nietzsche greatly admired, he initially expressed his admiration in the most forceful ways he knew, by echoing Goethe, on the one hand, and comparing the effect of Shakespeare's writings to that of Wagner's music, on the other, but after his break with Wagner this left him with the need to reassess the writer accordingly.[21] In Shakespeare's case he eventually managed to do this rather more successfully than with Sterne, but there is a transitional phase in which it is apparent that he is not sure quite how to "place" him.

This revaluation is under way as early as October-December 1876, in a note on eloquence in tragedy, where Nietzsche suddenly sets Shakespeare off against the German dramatic tradition, arguing that the latter has no place for eloquence of the kind one finds in Greek and French drama, whereas with Shakespeare "the Spanish influence which dominated the court of Elizabeth is unmistakable: the abundance of images, their *recherché* nature, is not human in a general sense, but Spanish" (*KSA* 8:19[95]). This is presumably a reference to the popularity at the Elizabethan court of Kyd's *The Spanish Tragedy,* one of the principal sources for Shakespeare's *Hamlet,* but the highlighting of this putative Spanish influence on Shakespeare is signally at odds with Nietzsche's previous presentation of him as "naturalistic" and proto-Wagnerian— in the same note, indeed, he goes on to argue that "Wagner abandons the art of eloquence entirely."

Together with Shakespeare in this same note, Nietzsche praises another writer who was notably influenced by the Spanish style (in his case Cervantes): the French novelist and dramatist Alain-René Lesage (1668–1747), author of the highly successful picaresque memoir-novel *Histoire de Gil Blas de Santillane* (1715/1724/1735). Yet the alliance between the two writers is contradicted in a terse note from late 1880 which reads simply: "I never tire of *Gil Blas:* I breathe a sigh of relief, no sentimentality, no rhetoric as in Shakespeare" (*KSA* 9:7[81]). This change of heart is illuminated by a note from the following fall in which the chain of association is extended to another non-Spanish writer who re-creates the spirit of Spain in his fictions, when Nietzsche expresses bemusement that he should be "overcome at almost regular intervals by such a longing for *Gil Blas* and the novellas of Mérimée" (*KSA* 9:15[67]; cf. 13:25[3]). Here it becomes clear, then, that Nietzsche is in the process of theorizing the dichotomy which will eventually dominate *The Case of Wagner,* between the "Mediterranean" spirit of Bizet's *Carmen* (and the Mérimée novella on which it is based) and Wagner's dourly "Germanic" music dramas, but in the earlier 1880s this dichotomy is set up using a different pair of emblems—Lesage contra Shakespeare. Nietzsche rehearses the eighteenth-century opposition between Shakespeare and the French, only his French model is of the generation after Racine and Corneille (cf. *KSA* 12:10[53]/*WP* 120), and Shakespeare has temporarily ended up on the wrong side of the evaluative divide.

The nascent "North-South divide" reappears in paragraph 77 of *The Gay Science* in the context of a discussion of artistic "vulgarity," when Nietzsche contrasts "the vulgar element in everything that gives pleasure in Southern Europe," which he does not find offensive "because there is no sense of shame and everything vulgar appears as poised and self-assured as anything noble, lovely, and passionate," with "a vulgar turn in Northern works," which "offends me unspeakably," for "here there is a sense of shame." As examples of the former he gives Italian opera and "the Spanish novel of adventure (most readily accessible for us in the French disguise of Gil Blas)"; as the only instance of the latter he gives "German music"—for which, of course, read Wagner, whom he had cited by name in the draft version of the passage (*KSA* 14: p. 248). But Shakespeare's guilt by (earlier) association is spelled out in a similar note from spring 1884, where it is he (together with Balzac—a damning comparison indeed!) who is now criticized for stooping so low as to seek to please the pit: "I can hardly stand this baseness of Shakespeare and Balzac: a smell of plebeian emotions, a metropolitan sewer-stink greets the nose everywhere" (*KSA* 11:25[123]). In book 2 of *Human,*

All-Too-Human, Nietzsche had paid Shakespeare a decidedly double-edged compliment in praising him as one who, despite being "a barbarian, that is to say erroneous and deformed from head to toe," could nevertheless "still be the greatest of poets" (*AOM* 162), and here it seems he has finally lost patience with Shakespeare's "tastelessness."

This condemnation persists until the draft stage of *Beyond Good and Evil* (*KSA* 14: p. 365), in which the 1884 note is taken up again and reworked to become paragraph 224 of the published work, although in the final version Nietzsche strikingly reverses the evaluative polarity: "the disgusting odors and the proximity of the English rabble in which Shakespeare's art and taste live we do not allow to disturb us any more than on the Chiaja of Naples, where we go our way with all our senses awake, enchanted and willing, though the sewer smells of the plebeian quarters fill the air" (*BGE* 224). Nietzsche here (and in the sixth and seventh parts of *Beyond Good and Evil* generally) is for once not setting himself at an ironic distance from his fellow Europeans, and he writes in the first-person plural: Shakespeare might have been laughed at by the age of Aeschylus, he argues, but "our" age can turn its "historical sense" to its advantage and appreciate all the better the qualities of this " 'great barbarian' " (as a more "noble" age could not). Nietzsche is finally reconciled with Shakespeare, because he has finally succeeded in reconfiguring him to his satisfaction: Shakespeare is no longer the monolithic naturalistic genius but rather "this wild abundance of colors, this medley of what is most delicate, coarsest, and most artificial"; moreover, he has been prized away from his "aboriginally Germanic" roots once and for all and endowed with a wholly new set of heterogeneous typological characteristics: he has become "Shakespeare, that amazing Spanish-Moorish-Saxon synthesis of tastes." Whereas Goethe (and Schelling and Friedrich Schlegel before him) had contrasted Shakespeare with the Spanish dramatist Calderón,[22] Nietzsche, by contrast—ten years after his earlier note—finally realigns the (Anglo-) "Saxon" Shakespeare with "the Spanish influence which dominated the court of Elizabeth" (*KSA* 8:19[95]) and adds a touch of Othello for good measure (cf. *HH* 61). He complicates Shakespeare's genealogy considerably here, then—the operative premise still being that the dramatist's creations must reflect aspects of his own personality. Shakespeare has become altogether more interesting than before, for Nietzsche introduces into his characterization that element of self-difference which allows him to be venerated as a paradigm of agonal self-struggle. In other words, in the 1880s Nietzsche no longer relies on Goethe's appreciation of Shakespeare as his prop, for instead he ranks him alongside Goethe himself and figures him as a prototypical *Übermensch*. Such an impression is confirmed by a note from summer-fall 1884: "The highest man would have the greatest multiplicity of drives, in the relatively greatest strength that can be endured. Indeed, where the plant 'man' shows himself strongest one finds instincts that *conflict* powerfully (e.g., in Shakespeare), but are controlled" (*KSA* 11:27[59]/*WP* 966).[23]

"SHAKE-N-BACON"

By the mid-1880s Shakespeare has thus been redeemed in Nietzsche's eyes, reinterpreted as a model of refinement who succeeds in lifting himself out of the mire of Rousseauistic naturalism by controlling his "barbaric" tendencies. His ability to please the plebs with comic interludes involving motley "mechanicals" and other such rustics is no longer to be regretted but marveled at, like Lesage's comic creation Gil Blas (*GS* 361): Shakespeare is realigned with the civilizing influence of "Mediterranean" culture and ascribed the true nobility which consists in mastering conflicting drives.

It is but one step beyond this position to argue that Shakespeare, like Johann Wolfgang von Goethe, actually *was* a nobleman, to move from typological to "actual" genealogy, which is precisely the move Nietzsche makes, for over the course of the 1880s, concurrently with his rehabilitation of Shakespeare, he gradually convinces himself that "Shakespeare" was but a pseudonym for his Elizabethan contemporary Lord Verulam, Francis Bacon. The association between the two grows ever closer in Nietzsche's mind: in a note from 1881 he prepares the ground when he writes of Bacon's "histrionism" (*KSA* 9:11[99]); by 1885 he is writing of "Baco and Shakespeare" (*KSA* 11:34[92]), and in 1887 of "the case of Shakespeare (provided that he really is Lord Bacon)" (*KSA* 12:9[166]/*WP* 848). But by the time of *Ecce Homo* this proviso has fallen away, and he confesses: "I feel instinctively sure and certain that Lord Bacon was the originator, the self-tormentor of this uncanniest [*unheimlichsten*] kind of literature: what do *I* care about the pitiable chatter of American shallow-pates and muddle-heads?" (*EH* "Clever" 4).[24]

The last part of this remark indicates that Nietzsche was well aware of the larger debate surrounding the authorship of "Shakespeare's" plays which continues unabated to this day, prompted by the paucity of reliable information about the playwright's life and doubts that what is

known about this apparently ill-educated and little-traveled son of a
Stratford wool merchant could possibly be squared with the quality of
the plays and poems attributed to him, their breadth of vocabulary and
range of reference. Goethe had been aware of these doubts but dismissed
the whole question as an irrelevance;[25] nevertheless, over the years a vast
number of candidates for the "real" Shakespeare have been put forward,
including most of the other leading Elizabethan playwrights (individually, or as a group), Walter Raleigh, and even Elizabeth I herself.[26] The
current favorite among the "anti-Stratfordians" is Edward de Vere, the
seventeenth earl of Oxford, but "Oxfordian" theory has been gaining
in currency only since the publication in 1920 of J. Thomas Looney's
"Shakespeare" Identified (which, incidentally, convinced Freud that
Oxford was the true author);[27] in Nietzsche's day the leading theory was
that "Shakespeare" was a front for Francis Bacon who, because of his
close association with the court, had been obliged to publish all his plays
and the majority of his poems under a pseudonym.

"Baconian" theory had been launched in the late eighteenth century,
but it rapidly gathered momentum from the mid-nineteenth century
with the publication of a succession of books, pamphlets, and magazine
articles arguing the case, preeminent among them The Philosophy of the
Plays of Shakspere Unfolded (1857) by the American expatriate intellectual Delia Bacon (no relation), who succeeded in persuading no less
a figure than Nathaniel Hawthorne to write a preface. By the 1880s
Bacon had become established as the leading anti-Stratfordian candi-
date, and his cause was given a boost by the publication in 1888—the
year in which Nietzsche wrote Ecce Homo—of The Great Cryptogram:
Francis Bacon's Cipher in the So-Called Shakespeare Plays by another
American writer, Ignatius Donnelly, who took his cue from Bacon's
documented interest in cryptology and purported to discover Bacon's
"signature" encoded across the Shakespearean oeuvre. When Nietzsche
directs his scorn at "the pitiable chatter of American shallow-pates
and muddle-heads," then, he is not, as might first appear, fending off
the arguments of American anti-Baconians, for the opposite was in
fact the case. It was American writers who were the most vociferous in
advocating the Baconian cause, and indeed most of the leading figures
in late-nineteenth-century American intellectual life professed themselves Baconians, or at least rejected the "Stratfordian" orthodoxy—
not only Hawthorne but also John Greenleaf Whittier and Oliver Wen-
dell Holmes, William and Henry James, Walt Whitman (one of whose

last poems is "Shakespere-Bacon's Cipher"), and two writers whom Nietzsche particularly admired, Ralph Waldo Emerson and Mark Twain (whose last work, *Is Shakespeare Dead?* has become one of the classics of "Baconian" literature).[28]

Nietzsche's scorn in *Ecce Homo* is directed, rather, at the pedantic and pedestrian methods of those such as Delia Bacon and Ignatius Donnelly who had sought to prove Bacon's authorship of "the Shakespeare plays" by means of textual parallels or hidden ciphers rather than simply relying on their instincts and intuition, as he did himself, to sense the cannily repressed identity of the true author returning to haunt "this uncanniest kind of literature." His attitude on this point is still the same as twelve years earlier, when he had contrasted his superior understanding of Shakespeare to that of a different set of pedants: "I believe I understand Shakespeare better than teachers of the modern English language do, even though I make mistakes. As a general rule *anyone* will understand an older author better than the philological language teacher does: how come?—Because philologists are nothing but aged grammar school boys" (*KSA* 8:19[6]).[29] Donnelly used the letters from Bacon's name to decipher the "message" "Shakst spur never writ a word of them" in *Henry IV, Part 1* (the play in which Nietzsche had acted as a schoolboy), but such methods are easily debunked, as the recent reaction to Michael Drosnin's *The Bible Code* has shown, and indeed no sooner had Donnelly's book appeared than a certain Reverend J. Nicholson published a rebuttal, *No Cipher in Shakespeare,* in which he applied Donnelly's methods to the same text to decipher the message "Master William Shakespeare writ the plays."[30] Nietzsche will have no truck with such specious caviling, or the feeble-minded literalism which inspired it, and he differs in this respect from Freud, who built up an extensive library of publications on "the Shakespeare problem" and whose interest in it, as Peter Gay convincingly demonstrates, derived from a "passion for puzzle solving," a "'greed for knowledge.'"[31]

Irrespective of the "true" answer to the authorship question, Nietzsche's identification of Shakespeare with Bacon is clearly prompted on one level by straightforward snobbery, by the belief that "nobility of soul" must actually attest to nobility of birth, and it is no accident that his favorite Bacon quotation should be a suitably patrician passage from *De Augmentis Scientiarum* (which he picked up from his reading of Schopenhauer): "The ordinary ruck has praise for the lowest virtues, admiration for the mediocre, and for the highest virtues no sense at all."[32]

But Nietzsche's subscription to the Baconian theory of Shakespearean authorship has a more worthy explanation too, for it marks the culmination of that agonal logic—the logic of the split subject, the only artistically productive kind—which we saw him beginning to sketch out in Shakespeare's case in *Beyond Good and Evil* 224. It is said that the historical Shakespeare was a small-time poacher, but Nietzsche knew—again from Schopenhauer—that Bacon was a big-time felon,[33] and the magnitude of his offense gives Nietzsche the perfect opportunity to argue that Shakespeare-Bacon's soul encompassed the greatest possible diversity of drives, that "the power for the mightiest reality of vision is not only compatible with the mightiest power for action, for the monstrous in action, for crime—*it even presupposes it*" (*EH* "Clever" 4). It is no surprise that Nietzsche should be most forthright in identifying the two writers in a text, *Ecce Homo,* which hinges to such an extent on questions of identity and authorship. He treats the name "Shakespeare" as a persona, a mask, and admires Bacon accordingly in a text in which he is so concerned to proclaim his own name as a composite of pseudonyms ("Schopenhauer," "Wagner," "Paul Rée," and the rest).[34]

The more Nietzsche identifies Shakespeare with Bacon, then, the more he himself—having become convinced, for similar reasons, that he was actually of noble (Polish) pedigree[35]—identifies with Bacon-Shakespeare and his characters. In the same paragraph of *Ecce Homo* in which he asserts the incontrovertible identity of the two Elizabethans, for example, he writes, "I know of no more heartrending reading than Shakespeare: what must a man have suffered to need to be a buffoon to this extent!" (*EH* "Clever" 4; cf. *GS* 98), while at the beginning of the last chapter he concedes, "Perhaps I am a buffoon" (*EH* "Destiny" 1).[36] In drawing a veil over his relationship with Wagner he speaks with Hamlet's famous last words (*EH* "Wise" 3), and his question "Is Hamlet *understood?*" (*EH* "Clever" 4) will modulate in the last chapter into the first-person singular and become a persistent refrain: "Have I been understood?" (cf. *KSA* 11:41[7]/*WP* 1051). Immediately after writing, of Shakespeare, that "the great poet dips *only* from his own reality" (*EH* "Clever" 4), Nietzsche tells us of his own reactions to *Thus Spoke Zarathustra,* and the paragraph concludes with a further identification, a speculation on *non*identification: "Suppose I had published my *Zarathustra* under another name—for example that of Richard Wagner—the acuteness of two thousand years would not have been sufficient for anyone to guess that the author of *Human, All-Too-Human* is the visionary of *Zarathustra.*"[37]

CONCLUSION ("THE REST IS SILENCE")

"Nietzsche's Shakespeare" is thus an intricate series of shifting identifications, for not only does he identify Shakespeare *in* his own characters, and Shakespeare *as* Bacon, but he himself also identifies more and
more intensely *with* Shakespeare. After his interest in Shakespeare is
aroused during his schooldays at Pforta, his identification with Shakespeare is initially mediated through Wagner and Goethe; latterly it is mediated through a set of implicit syllogisms: Shakespeare is a self-creating
Dionysian proto-*Übermensch* (like Goethe[38]—like Nietzsche himself,
as he would have us believe); Shakespeare *is* Hamlet, Brutus, and Caesar (as is Nietzsche). The "unmasking" of Shakespeare as Bacon opens
the way, though, to the final act in this drama of identifications, for
Nietzsche's concern is ultimately not so much with the *politics* of subterfuge that he so admires in Shakespeare's Brutus as with emulating
what one might call the *poetics* of subterfuge that he associates with
Bacon-Shakespeare himself. Ultimately it is because Bacon-Shakespeare
is revealed as a lover of masks that Nietzsche, the lover of masks, can use
Bacon-Shakespeare himself as . . . a mask, another "metaphor" for
"Nietzsche."

The mask finally drops, though, along with all Nietzsche's others, on
3 January 1889, the date on which we find his last, poignant, reference
to Shakespeare in the letter to Cosima Wagner, where his identification
with his typological forebear is by now absolute: "It is a prejudice that
I am a man. But I have often lived among men already and I know everything they can experience, from the lowest to the highest. Among Indi-
ans I was Buddha, in Greece I was Dionysus,—Alexander and Caesar
are my incarnations, as is the Shakespeare poet, Lord Bakon" (*KGB*
III / 5:573). At the end of his career he finally *becomes* Shakespeare-
Bacon, for he becomes "every name in history" (*KGB* III / 5:578) as he
is transported into the empyrean realm above and beyond them all. Indeed if one reexamines *Ecce Homo* with the benefit of this hindsight, it
is as if he marshals his various Shakespearean figures here for one final
review, outstripping them all with his hubristic hyperbole. Shakespeare
may have been the writer most attuned to Montaigne *before Nietzsche
arrived on the scene,* but, Nietzsche declares, "I have something of
Montaigne's wantonness in my spirit, who knows? perhaps also in my
body" (*EH* "Clever" 3); Shakespeare may have been, in Goethe's words,
"a great psychologist," but "out of my writings there speaks a *psychologist* who has not his equal" (*EH* "Books" 5), and the impact of Shake-

speare the "'great barbarian'" (or Bacon the monstrous criminal) pales beside that of Nietzsche himself, who is "by far the most terrible human being there has ever been" (*EH* "Destiny" 2). In sum, Shakespeare may have been "a young eagle crowning the days of his nation's blossoming" (*FS* 2:412), but Nietzsche "come[s] from heights no bird has ever soared to" (*EH* "Books" 3)—*Thus Spoke Zarathustra* is the *non plus ultra* of human creativity, and "a Goethe, a Shakespeare would not for a moment have known how to breathe in this tremendous passion and solitude" (*EH* "Books" Z:6).

Throughout his works, Nietzsche cuts a series of Shakespearean figures which culminate in the figure of Bacon-Shakespeare himself, the productive tension of whose self-difference is mirrored and magnified in Nietzsche's own case to the point where, at the moment of his Turinese apotheosis, the figures cut back, the productive tension becomes a destructive explosion, and Dionysus-Nietzsche is torn apart, Nietzsche-Hamlet falls into the abyss. Who is Nietzsche's Shakespeare? One of the stations of the cross on Nietzsche's way to becoming himself, "the crucified one."

NOTES

References to Nietzsche's published works are by volume, section, and paragraph number, and English translations are taken from the standard versions by Walter Kaufmann and R. J. Hollingdale, except for *Twilight of the Idols*, where I have used my own published version (Oxford University Press, 1998). Translations of Nietzsche's unpublished notes, letters, and juvenilia are also mine.

1. In the published works these are *Hamlet, Julius Caesar, Macbeth, A Midsummer Night's Dream, Much Ado About Nothing, Othello, Richard III, Romeo and Juliet, Timon of Athens, Troilus and Cressida*, and *Twelfth Night* (cf. *KSA* 15: p. 353). His letters show a further knowledge of *Henry IV, Part 1, The Merchant of Venice*, and *The Tempest* (cf. *KGB* "Gesamtregister" 123); in the juvenilia, *King Lear* (*FS* 2:384) and *The Taming of the Shrew* (*FS* 3:82) are also mentioned.

2. See Ronald Hayman, *Nietzsche: A Critical Life* (London: Quartet, 1981), 43, and *FS* 2:67. Nietzsche had written his mother on 3 December 1860 suggesting an edition of "Sheakspeare" as a Christmas gift for that year: "I simply must now have an edition of Sheakspeare, since a knowledge of him is part of one's general education and in the upper forms we are very often set essays on individual plays" (*KGB* I/1:133).

3. See Max Oehler, ed., *Nietzsches Bibliothek* (Weimar: Gesellschaft der Freunde des Nietzsche-Archivs, 1942), 41.

4. According to Oehler's catalog, the only work by Victor Hugo which he

owned (perhaps one should say, allowed himself to own) was a German translation of *William Shakespeare* (34); his personal library also contained a published lecture, "Shakespeare in seiner Bedeutung für die Kirche unserer Tage,"
by August Schwartzkopff (23), a copy of Stendhal's *Racine et Shakespeare* in the
original French (35), and a German edition of Emerson's two *Representative
Men* essays on Goethe and Shakespeare (40)—all heavily annotated—as well as
a three-volume German translation of Taine's *History of English Literature* (35).
He makes allusions and references to a number of other Shakespeare critics—
Gervinus (*FS* 2:334; *BT* 22; *KSA* 7:27[55]), Rapp (*KSA* 7:1[57]), Hartmann
(*KGB* II/3:234), Custine (*KSA* 11:25[52])—in addition to the remarks on
Shakespeare by Schiller (*KSA* 7:9[77]) and, as we shall see, Lessing, Herder,
Wagner, and Goethe.

   5. While still at school, for example, he mentions having attended partial
or complete performances of *The Merchant of Venice* (*KGB* I/1:94), *Julius Cae-
sar* and *A Midsummer Night's Dream* (*KGB* I/1:146), *Henry IV, Part 1* (*KGB*
I/1:283), and *Julius Caesar* again (*KGB* I/1:283). In Bonn he attended *The
Taming of the Shrew* (*FS* 3:82), in Leipzig *Hamlet* (*KGB* I/2:132 f.) and
Romeo and Juliet (*KGB* I/2:154) twice (*KGB* I/2:361).

   6. *The Standard Edition of the Complete Psychological Works of Sigmund
Freud,* ed. and trans. James Strachey, 24 vols. (London: Hogarth Press and In-
stitute of Psycho-Analysis, 1953–74), 4:265.

   7. Commenting on Sonnet 94, Kaufmann himself argues that "Shakespeare's un-Christian ideal [. . .] was also the ideal of Nietzsche" (*From Shakespeare to Existentialism: An Original Study,* 3d ed. [Princeton: Princeton University Press, 1980], 5).

   8. *Conversations with Nietzsche: A Life in the Words of His Contemporaries,* trans. David J. Parent, ed. Sander L. Gilman (New York: Oxford University Press, 1987), 14. Nietzsche's version of his performance is rather different:
"In the afternoon we read *Henry IV* in front of a large audience. I read Henry
Percy with a great deal of excitement and anger" (letter to Gustav Krug and Wilhelm Pinder, 12 June 1864, *KGB* I/1:283).

   9. Michael Tanner, *Nietzsche* (Oxford: Oxford University Press, 1994), 15;
cf. M. S. Silk and J. P. Stern, *Nietzsche on Tragedy* (Cambridge: Cambridge University Press, 1981), 280 f.

   10. He did not abandon the exercise entirely, however, and in his notes for
the fourth *Untimely Meditation* he returns to the search for parallels between
Shakespeare and Wagner, drawing on Wagner's own comments on his English
forebear (*KSA* 8:11[13, 29], 27[75]). Even as late as *Daybreak* Nietzsche is
drawing a parallel between *Macbeth* and *Tristan and Isolde* which is favorable
to both (*D* 240).

   11. The history of German Shakespeare reception has been copiously documented. Roy Pascal, *Shakespeare in Germany: 1740–1815* (New York: Octa-
gon Books, 1971 [reprint of 1st ed., 1937]), gives a good overview and includes
the major texts, although the most comprehensive edition of source material is
Hansjürgen Blinn, ed., *Shakespeare-Rezeption: Die Diskussion um Shakespeare
in Deutschland,* 2 vols. (Berlin: Schmidt, 1982–88), and the most authoritative
(if symptomatic) German monograph remains Friedrich Gundolf, *Shakespeare*

und der deutsche Geist (Berlin: Bondi, 1911). The nature of German Shakespeare translations is expertly examined by George Steiner, *After Babel: Aspects of Language and Translation,* 2d ed. (Oxford: Oxford University Press, 1992), 400–13; Simon Williams, *Shakespeare on the German Stage,* vol. 1: *1586–1914* (Cambridge: Cambridge University Press, 1990), is an excellent study of the performance history.

12. See especially Lessing's remarks on Shakespeare in his *Briefe die neueste Litteratur betreffend* and *Hamburgische Dramaturgie* (respectively, 1759 and 1768, in Pascal, *Shakespeare in Germany,* 50–52) and the essay on "Shakespear" which Herder contributed to the collection *Von deutscher Art und Kunst* (1773, in Pascal, *Shakespeare in Germany,* 75–90).

13. Goethe's relation to Shakespeare has, not surprisingly, received more critical attention than that of any other German writer. The best description of his early Shakespeare reception, and that of the other *Stürmer und Dränger,* is given by Goethe himself, in book 11 of *Dichtung und Wahrheit* (ca. 1812); the most exhaustive study is Kurt Ermann, *Goethes Shakespeare-Bild* (Tübingen: Niemeyer, 1983). In English, James Boyd tracks down references to Shakespeare in the first chapter of his *Goethe's Knowledge of English Literature* (New York: Haskell House, 1973 [reprint of 1st ed., 1932]), 1–79, although a more useful overview is Roy Pascal, "Constancy and Change in Goethe's Attitude to Shakespeare: Goethe and the Tragedies," *Publications of the English Goethe Society,* n.s. 34 (1964): 153–74.

Before the publication of translations of Shakespeare's plays had a standardizing effect, eighteenth-century German writers used a wide variety of spellings for his name (the "correct" spelling of which is in any case only a nineteenth-century convention), although even in this context Goethe is (as usual) egregious, for he not only uses a remarkably Germanized spelling, he is also inconsistent (using both "Schäkespear" and "Schäckespear" in the early address, for example). Nietzsche uses some outlandish variations during his schooldays—"*Sheagspeare*" (*FS* 1:47), "Sheakspeare" (*KGB* I/1:133; *FS* 1:250), "Sheakspere" (*FS* 2:67)—but thereafter is remarkably consistent and, two minor deviations aside (*FS* 3:338; *KGB* II/1:297), uses the accepted standard throughout the rest of his career, even in his notebooks and letters. Shakespeare's function in Nietzsche's philosophy will change dramatically, but his name will not.

14. Goethe, "Zum Schäkespears Tag," in Pascal, *Shakespeare in Germany,* 100. Nietzsche even goes further than Goethe in this respect, for Goethe's sense of Shakespeare's uniqueness was later nuanced, especially in the wake of Tieck's contextualizing editions of plays by Shakespeare and his contemporaries, *Alt-Englisches Theater* (1811) and *Shakespeare's Vorschule* (1823–29), which persuaded him of the literary merits of the Elizabethan age as a whole (cf. Ermann, *Goethes Shakespeare-Bild,* 293–353; Boyd, *Goethe's Knowledge of English Literature,* 74 f.), whereas Nietzsche makes no effort to set Shakespeare in his contemporary context, and his admiration remains correspondingly unalloyed. For Tieck's relation to Shakespeare (and Goethe), see Roger Paulin, "Das Buch über Shakespeare," in *Ludwig Tieck: A Literary Biography* (Oxford: Clarendon Press, 1986), 239–70.

15. Pascal, *Shakespeare in Germany,* 99 f.

16. Ibid., 100 f. Ursula Wertheim argues persuasively that Goethe's reference to "noble philosophers" here implies Spinoza in particular. See "Philosophische und ästhetische Aspekte in Prosastücken Goethes über Shakespeare," *Goethe-Jahrbuch,* n.s. 26 (1964): 54–76, esp. 61–65.

17. Johann Peter Eckermann, *Gespräche mit Goethe in den letzten Jahren seines Lebens,* 2 vols. (Basel: Birkhäuser, 1945), 1:168 (26 July 1826). Harold Bloom has recently developed precisely this argument in *Shakespeare: The Invention of the Human* (New York: Riverhead Books, 1998).

18. Goethe, "Shakespeare ad infinitum," in *Goethe's Literary Essays,* ed. and trans. J. E. Spingarn (New York: Harcourt, Brace, 1921), 177; cf. Eckermann, *Gespräche mit Goethe,* 1:215 (31 January 1827). The impact of *Julius Caesar* on Goethe, as on Nietzsche, was particularly strong: in 1771, at the same time as his address "On Shakespeare's Day," he began planning a *Cäsar* of his own, working on it periodically until 1775, and although he eventually abandoned the project, Shakespeare's *Julius Caesar* was the most important influence on *Egmont,* and it was also one of the Shakespeare plays produced in Weimar under Goethe's supervision. See Boyd, *Goethe's Knowledge of English Literature,* 37–44; and Nicholas Boyle, *Goethe: The Poet and the Age,* vol. 1: *The Poetry of Desire (1749–1790)* (Oxford: Clarendon Press, 1991), 105.

19. Eckermann, *Gespräche mit Goethe,* 1:156 f. (25 December 1825).

20. Pascal, *Shakespeare in Germany,* 100.

21. See my article "'The Freest Writer': Nietzsche on Sterne," *The Shandean* 7 (November 1995): 9–29.

22. For Goethe, see "Calderón's *Daughter of the Air,*" in Spingarn, *Goethe's Literary Essays,* 209; and Eckermann, *Gespräche mit Goethe,* 1:168 (26 July 1826). For Schelling and Friedrich Schlegel, see Pascal, *Shakespeare in Germany,* 33–35.

23. The passage in *Twilight of the Idols* where Nietzsche is at his most fulsome in praising Goethe—"he disciplined himself into a whole, he *created* himself" (*TI* "Skirmishes" 49)—is preceded eleven paragraphs earlier by a similar description of Julius Caesar as the "finest type" of a nature endowed with "pitiless and terrible instincts which require the maximum of authority and discipline to deal with them" (*TI* "Skirmishes" 38). As Alexander Nehamas rightly points out, "we must not assume without question that he is thinking of Caesar as a historical figure" here, since his later praise for Shakespeare on account of his having "conceived of the type of Caesar" (*EH* "Clever" 4) allows us to suspect that in *Twilight,* as elsewhere, he has Shakespeare's Caesar above all in mind (Nehamas, *Nietzsche: Life as Literature* [Cambridge, Mass.: Harvard University Press, 1985], 227).

24. It should not be overlooked that this identification of Shakespeare with Bacon also represents a rehabilitation of Bacon, who had been dismissed in paragraph 252 of *Beyond Good and Evil* as "signif[ying] an *attack* on the philosophical spirit" and the following year ranged alongside Aristotle, Descartes, and Comte as (merely) one of the "great *methodologists*" (*KSA* 12:9[61]/*WP* 468). For Nietzsche on Bacon-as-Shakespeare, see especially Bernd Magnus, Stanley Stewart, and Jean-Pierre Mileur, *Nietzsche's Case: Philosophy as/and Literature* (New York: Routledge, 1993), 61–77. Surprisingly, Laurence Lam-

pert's excellent *Nietzsche and Modern Times: A Study of Bacon, Descartes, and Nietzsche* (New Haven: Yale University Press, 1993) makes no mention of Nietzsche's Baconian theory of Shakespeare authorship.

25. See Boyd, *Goethe's Knowledge of English Literature*, 81 f.

26. An accessible and refreshingly agnostic overview of the competing candidates is John Michell, *Who Wrote Shakespeare?* (London: Thames and Hudson, 1996). Samuel Schoenbaum's chapter, "Deviations," in *Shakespeare's Lives* (Oxford: Clarendon Press, 1970), 529–629, has become the classic "Stratfordian" refutation of all such "heresies."

27. See Peter Gay, "Freud and the Man from Stratford," in *Reading Freud: Explorations and Entertainments* (New Haven: Yale University Press, 1990), 5–53; Nicholas Royle, "The Distraction of 'Freud': Literature, Psychoanalysis, and the Bacon-Shakespeare Controversy," *Oxford Literary Review* 12 (1990): 101–38; and Michell, *Who Wrote Shakespeare?* 162–67 ("Dr. Freud and Mr. Looney").

28. For the development of the Baconian hypothesis, see Michell, *Who Wrote Shakespeare?* 113–60 ("Bacon as Shakespeare"). As an explanation for the preponderance of Americans among late-nineteenth-century Baconians, Michell argues plausibly that "the movement for deciphering Shakespeare can be seen as one of the many offshoots of Spiritualism" (152), although the Baconian hypothesis continues to attract adherents and most recently, like all good controversies, the "Shakespeare authorship debate" has been flourishing on the Internet. The most prominent Baconian Websites are the Shakespeare Authorship Center of San Francisco (http://www.sirbacon.org), maintained by Lawrence Gerald; the Shakespeare Authorship Information Centre (http://users.netmatters. co.uk/itbs/saic/), maintained by Francis Carr—a "Higher Baconian" (Michell) who argues that Bacon also wrote *Don Quixote*—and "Shake-n-Bacon" (http:// fly.hiwaay.net/~paul/), maintained by Paul J. Dupuy, Jr., which gives access to the writings of one of the most prolific contemporary Baconian cryptographers, Penn Leary. The Shakespeare Oxford Society (http://www.shakespeare-oxford. com) is the best funded and most professional of the anti-Stratfordian groups, while "The Shakespeare Authorship Page" (http://www.clark.net/pub/tross/ ws/will.html), maintained by Dave Kathman and Terry Ross, is the Internet's main upholder of Stratfordian orthodoxy, "Dedicated to the Proposition that Shakespeare wrote Shakespeare."

29. The subject of this note was initially Montaigne (see *KSA* 14: p. 591). The previous year Nietzsche's French translator, Marie Baumgartner, had pointed out that he (unlike Shakespeare, as he claimed) was in fact not such a good reader of Montaigne after all, prompting the unusually humble response: "Before I idealize Montaigne, I ought at least to understand him correctly" (letter to Marie Baumgartner, 7 April 1875, *KGB* II/5:40).

30. See Graham Phillips and Martin Keatman, *The Shakespeare Conspiracy* (London: Century, 1994), 56. Even other Baconians were quick to distance themselves from Donnelly and his ilk, although in most cases the backlash came from English writers dismissive of American scholarship. See, for example, Walter Begley (writing anonymously as "A Cambridge Graduate"), *Is it Shakespeare?* (London: Murray, 1903), 7; Sir George Greenwood, introduction to

E. W. Smithson, *Baconian Essays* (London: Cecil Palmer, 1922), 24 f. The standard work demolishing Donnelly's claims is William F. Friedman and Elizabeth S. Friedman, *The Shakespeare Ciphers Examined* (Cambridge: Cambridge University Press, 1957).

31. Gay, "Freud and the Man from Stratford," 46, 49.

32. Schopenhauer quotes the passage in the original Latin (*De Augmentis Scientiarum,* VI, 3) in *The World as Will and Representation,* 2, §31 (trans. E. F. J. Payne, 2 vols. [New York: Dover, 1969], 2:391); Nietzsche quotes it (again in Latin) at *KSA* 12:10[98]/*WP* 249 and playfully misquotes it at *KSA* 8:5[83]. Despite espousing the Baconian theory of Shakespeare authorship, Nietzsche actually owned only one of Bacon's works, the *Novum Organum,* in German translation (see Oehler, *Nietzsches Bibliothek,* 17). The other Bacon quotation which he notes (*KSA* 8:16[19]) is also at second hand, from Emerson (see *KSA* 14: p. 586).

33. "Ungrateful, filled with lust for power, wicked and base, he ultimately went so far that, as Lord Chancellor and the highest judge of the realm, he frequently allowed himself to be bribed in civil actions. Impeached before his peers, he pleaded guilty, was expelled from the House of Lords, and condemned to a fine of forty thousand pounds and to imprisonment in the Tower" (*The World as Will and Representation,* 2, §19 [in Payne's translation, 2:228 f.]).

34. In a note from fall 1887, "Shakespeare?" is listed (together with "Epicurus?" Schopenhauer, Stendhal, Napoleon, "Goethe?" "Beethoven?" and Machiavelli) as one of the "posthumous people" who are "less well understood but better heard than timely ones" (*KSA* 12:9[76]), whereas in the published version of the same thought (*TI* "Maxims" 15) any doubts are dispelled and Nietzsche's only example is himself.

35. See my article "Nietzsche and the Figure of Copernicus: *Grande Fantaisie on* Polish Airs," *New Readings,* no. 2 (1996): 65–87.

36. Nietzsche also stresses, however, that he is "the *anti-ass* par excellence" (*EH* "Books" 2)—by contrast with Shakespeare's Bottom?

37. See Sarah Kofman, *Explosion I: De l' "Ecce Homo" de Nietzsche* (Paris: Galilée, 1992), 326–35; Rodolphe Gasché, "*Ecce Homo* or the Written Body," in *Looking after Nietzsche,* ed. Laurence A. Rickels (Albany: SUNY Press, 1990), 128 f. Nietzsche had in fact intended publishing *Human, All-Too-Human* under a pseudonym ("Bernhard Cron"), until his publisher insisted otherwise: see William H. Schaberg, *The Nietzsche Canon: A Publication History and Bibliography* (Chicago: University of Chicago Press, 1995), 58 f.

38. On this point, Nietzsche's description of Goethe as "a convinced realist" (*TI* "Skirmishes" 49) can be compared to his description of Bacon as "the first realist in every great sense of the word" (*EH* "Clever" 4).

CHAPTER 4

Musical Psychodramatics

Ecstasis in Nietzsche

David B. Allison

Every tissue and nerve vibrates in me. . . . I have never had
such a feeling of rapture as when listening to [the Overture to
Die Meistersinger].

Letter to Rohde, 27 October 1868

From his earliest notes to his final delusional correspondence, one is
struck by the transformative, transfigurative agency Nietzsche finds in
the notion—and in the experience—of ecstasy. In one way or another,
ecstasy will play a principal role in Nietzsche's accounts of politics, art,
myth, and religion, and it will resonate in his accounts of a joyful wisdom, the eternal return, the will to power, and the overman—lending
them an intensity with which the subject, the reader or audience, is inspired to identify.

To be ecstatic is, of course, to be eccentric—to put out of place, to be
outside, to be drawn outside oneself, out of one's wits, transported: at
once, rapture and dispossession. It has to do with transgression of limits, forms, and boundaries—of oneself, of one's own limits, and, often
enough, of imposed limits, laws, and prohibitions. Generally speaking,
the whole issue of ecstasy is marginal enough to be proscribed by authority, normalcy, and traditional orthodoxy. Derrida tells us that philosophy has always had it in for the margins.[1] He proposed—and Hegel
disposed—that philosophy always wanted to govern its other, such that
it could set its own limits. Philosophy, he says, is the only discourse that
consistently defines itself. What exceeded those stated limits simply
could not be articulated. Perhaps it could only be seen or felt, in some
most unusual manner. For Schopenhauer, this inarticulable excess was
the metaphysical "Will"—for Kant, the metaphysical "*Ding an sich.*"
For Lacan, when the margin opens up between need and demand, it is

more simply, and quite simply, *"das Ding."* Piercing the symbolic order of law and language, desire finds *das Ding* as a point, a real place, the earthly delight of desire's own saturation—speechless, a place of death for the socially constructed ego. In other words, *jouissance*—a supra-lapsarian garden, paradisiacal ecstasy.

In the post-Hegelian discourse there seems to be a renewed interest in ecstasy. Beginning with the emotional intensity of the spiritual subject in Kierkegaard through the dialectical constitution of the subject in Kojève—from the surrealists (drawing on Freud) through the work of Bataille, Foucault, and Lacan, followed by Deleuze and Guattari—ecstasy is given a rigorous psychological, that is, antimetaphysical, examination, an analysis that at the same time opens up a remarkable social-political dimension to this phenomenon.

What were formerly held to be the objects, or even the causes, of ecstatic rapture—the Passion of Jesus, hierarchies of Cherubim and Seraphim, Thrones and Principalities, choruses of Archangels and Plotinian Emanations of the Divine, not to mention the overwhelming waves of the World Will and the ineffable, ungraspable Sublime—redolent of Oscar Wilde's English foxhunters—these objects are now regarded by psychologists as psychologically causative "triggers," that is, certain occasions or events that seem to be associated with the onset of ecstatic states.[2] Some triggers are termed "inducing triggers" and others "inserted triggers," the latter of which are said to be the set of intense qualities that correspond to the lived or experienced sense of ecstasy. Inducing triggers include nature, sexual love, exercise, religion, art, poetic knowledge, recollection, and beauty—even "those short, plump little cakes called 'petites madeleines.'" Inserted triggers include experiences described in what are termed "up-words" and "up-phrases"—that is, experiences associated with sensations of flying, weightlessness, floating, rising up, and so on—as well as "contact words"—that is, experiences that include claims of union, presence, mingling, identification with totality, god, nature, spirits, peace, timelessness, perfection, eternity, knowledge, and bliss. Such feelings include loss of self, of time, of place, and of limitation and language. One likewise feels a gain of eternity, a feeling of release, a new life, another world, joy, satisfaction, salvation, perfection, mystical knowledge, and enhanced mental capacity.[3]

Now it was precisely because Nietzsche could vividly experience and undergo such ecstatic states that he came to criticize Schopenhauer's metaphysical account of the World Will, the noumenal reality, which purportedly subtended all empirical individuation and sensible representation, that is, that metaphysically real realm, which subtended and thus precluded, any possibility of its appearance, its experience.

Schopenhauer claimed that the World Will can be experienced in one unique way—namely, in music, where, he argued, the object of music is the Will. But, because experience itself belongs to the order of representation, of phenomenal reality, of appearances only, this perforce excludes by definition any experience of the noumenal. Now while this Schopenhauerian metaphysical division seems to prefigure the Nietzschean distinction between the Apollonian and Dionysian orders in *The Birth of Tragedy,* Nietzsche will in fact cast this distinction forth, not in metaphysical terms, but in exclusively psychological terms—indeed, in strikingly modern psychological terms of an entirely naturalistic, empirical order. To do this, however, Nietzsche had to explain to himself how these ecstatic states were possible, and in what they consisted. The key to his explanation was what served as a "trigger" for his own experience, and he found this in his passionate experience of music—as had Schopenhauer himself. Beginning with his drafts from 1869, he focused on the complex ecstatic experience of music, and this resulted in an unpublished work of 1871, "On Music and Words."[4] The very title suggests his early dependency on Schopenhauer, as its terms are predicated on the opposition between representation, that is, language or the language of images, and the purported object or ground of representation, music, that is, the nonimagistic Will.[5]

What complicates matters for Nietzsche is that he finds himself in the perplexing situation of trying to explain all this by trying to accommodate himself to the prevailing aesthetic models of music, all of which were hopelessly conflicted. The romantic view has music expressing every variety of emotion and feeling. Hanslick's formalist view has music expressing nothing beyond the formal properties of the composition itself—tonality, melody, harmony, rhythm, and so on. For Hanslick, music certainly does not express emotion or feeling, since music is nonintentional, and for him, at least, it surely does not express any urgings, strivings, and conflicts of a World Will. Schopenhauer's metaphysical view is championed by Wagner—and, initially, by Nietzsche. Yet at this very time Wagner himself goes on to develop a view of opera that has music become instrumental to the drama and the libretto, thus subverting the primary expressive value of music and contradicting Schopenhauer's own claims as well.[6]

Nietzsche's resolution to all this—to the competing models of romanticism, Schopenhauer, Hanslick, and Wagner One and Two—is simple and dramatic. By focusing on his own ecstatic experience of music, he undercuts each of these models, yet he leaves the so-called integrity or primacy of music intact. While the immediately preceding tradition had debated the objective status of music, according to one model or another, Nietzsche comes to realize in this early essay of 1871 the very simple truth that it is the subjective states of our experience of music that provokes our ecstatic response. Again, what is now termed its "trigger" effect. And because our ecstatic response is of such a nature that we feel positively transfigured by the experience, an experience characterized by loss of ego and by a suspension of ordinary object relations, the very distinction between subject and object becomes blurred and attenuated, if not entirely suspended. The distinction that supports ordinary intentional experience, between the objective and subjective genitive, simply does not obtain in the ecstatic state.

In addressing exactly what the object of music is, that is, the theoretical model of its subject matter, Nietzsche realizes that its object (*Gegenstand*) is given to us as the content (*Inhalt*) of our own intensely undergone aesthetic experience, our ecstatic states of dispossession. This musically charged state of ecstatic dispossession is precisely what he terms "the Dionysian state," and such a state is effectively the entire *field* of experience, shorn of simple subject-object relations. Schiller had earlier termed this state one of intense "mood" or "disposition," specifically a "musical mood" (*musikalische Stimmung*), and this had been discussed by Schopenhauer, but it is Nietzsche who really analyzes it in detail—to be followed in a strikingly similar fashion by Heidegger's account of "*Stimmung*" in *Being and Time*.

To explain the nature of this state, Nietzsche argues against the romantics (and with Hanslick) that this intense, musically ecstatic mood cannot take place on the level of feelings or sensations, because they are still bound with specific object representations. Rather, what occurs in this state of Dionysian-musical enchantment is an emotional dissociation or detachment of affective states from specific object relations. It will be this new distinction—between feelings (*Gefühle*) and emotions or affects (*Affekte*)—that will begin to emerge as an explanation for the broader phenomenon. The former do not have the power to generate the Dionysian state of dispossession because they retain their fixed association with representations. It is on the level of affect or emotion that the dissociation begins to take place. The excitement provoked by musical tonality is experienced as a fluidity of affect, in that intense emotional states lose their conventional associations and tend toward reinvesting

their objects of pleasure with more immediate, hallucinatory cathexes—
and such states involve an extreme intensification of psychic discharge,
resulting in a heightened increase of satisfaction. But to the extent in
which further intensification of psychic discharge is provoked and occurs, with its concomitant increase in pleasure, so do the states of affect become progressively freed from their associative connections, their
regular accompanying object representations, until the point of frenzy
(*Rausch*) is attained, in which case the underlying drives (*Triebe*) become
completely free-flowing, anarchic, and unbound. These deeper instinctual drives will ultimately constitute the power (*Kraft*) or force (*Macht*)
that drives the emotions themselves—and for the intense, musically aesthetic experience, they will constitute what he calls the very "sanctuary
of music." [7]

Nietzsche will often speak of these states of Dionysian excess and
frenzy as states of "drunkenness," "the horrible 'witches brew' of sen-
suality," "intoxication," and "wanton abandon," and, indeed, by the
time he composed *The Birth of Tragedy*, he begins to explain the Dionysian drives themselves by appeal to these most natural—and most extreme—states of intoxication and frenzy. This is, of course, opposed to
the other natural term by which he addresses the Apollonian drive—as
the state of dreaming. This experienced state of intense emotional intensity and dissociation, when one's drives themselves are no longer
bound—what Freud would later describe as the psychic level of primary
process formation—is precisely the Dionysian state of disindividuation
or dispossession. Thus Nietzsche would write, in a draft as early as
1869, that music is "through and through symbolic of the drives [*der
Triebe*]" and is thus "more general than any particular action" (*KSA*
7:1[49]). And, as the drives—the instinctual expressions of psychic
energy—are themselves unconscious or sublimated, their subjective
translation occurs to us as intense emotional states. The musical effect
(*musikalische Wirkung*) thus occurs on the deeper level of drives and is
in turn quickly discharged or depotentialized to become an emotional
affect (*Affektwirkung*). Or, according to a strikingly similar Freudian
vocabulary, all drives are expressed in terms of emotion and representation, and emotion—or affect—is, for Freud, the qualitative expression
of the quantity of instinctual energy, or drive. That these affective states
can be transformed, for example, through conversion, displacement,
and transformation of affect will constitute the very dynamics of tragic
drama in *The Birth of Tragedy*.

With Nietzsche's analysis of the psychological dynamics of the ecstatic state brought about by music, in the writings leading up to his "On Music and Words" essay of 1871, he then turns to consider the origin of these states in *The Birth of Tragedy*. Specifically, he will turn toward the musical origins of tragedy—what he, following Aristotle, considered to be the highest, most developed art form in classical Greek culture. Indeed, the original subtitle for *The Birth of Tragedy* was "Out of the Spirit of Music."

It is well known that Nietzsche traces out the structural components of tragic drama according to his understanding of its historical development. Basically, he identified its earliest moments with the emergence of lyric poetry and primitive folk music, where versification was intensified by musical accompaniment—specifically, by the intensely rhythmic and tonal language of flutes, pipes, drums, zithers, sackbuts, and heptagons. The intoxicating effects of these instruments on the Greek populace is sufficiently witnessed by Aristotle's strenuous rejection of them, in *The Politics*. Aristotle tells us that such music serves only the "vulgar pleasure" of the audience. "It does not express a state of character, but rather a mood of religious excitement; and it should therefore be used on those occasions when the effect to be produced on the audience is the release of emotion, and not instruction." [8] What Nietzsche finds especially significant in this musical accompaniment is the element of tonal dissonance, which manifests the forcefulness and dynamic character of the visionary's world—a Dionysian world capable of every tension, transformation, stress, intensity, and pulsion.

It is with the early Dionysian cults, and with the dithyrambic poetry of Archilochus, in particular, that the dynamics of music become focused on provoking the ecstatic states of dispossession, of disindividuation, among the fellow cult participants. The lyric poet effectively created a musical mood in his audience, inducing an emotional or affective disposition that was so all-pervasive in its intensity and generality that the poet and his audience literally become intoxicated, dispossessed. Effectively, the musical mood was intensified by the addition of Dionysian ritual and erotic imagery—with a little help from one's other friends, narcotics, wine, and stimulants—as well by the addition of the chorus, the Dionysian cult participants, who would chant and sing, lending resonance and harmony to the musical instrumentation, who would reinforce its melodic progression, and thus contribute a heightened emotionality to the music—all the while dancing, swaying rhythmically, overcome with passion.

That Nietzsche chose to focus on dissonance as "the primordial phenomenon of Dionysian art" (*BT* 24) was prescient. Dissonance presupposes the entire creative reservoir of musical elements within the tonal system—arguably, within any tonal system: tone, sonority, beat, rhythm, tempo, harmony, measure, melody, polyphony, progression, and so on. Modern cognitive science shows that, much like the visual field, which we continually stabilize and model, according to a relatively small number of visual foci, so with the auditory field, we anticipate tonal progression, chord development, and harmonic resolution—according to the cultural norms that govern the tonal scale.[9] On the twelve-tone scale, resolution usually occurs within the diatonic frame, offset by the chromatic or "dissonant" tones above that, as well as by certain minor keys. We know from his early essays that Nietzsche was familiar with Helmholtz's important work on tone sensation, which experimentally demonstrated that pleasure tends to accompany the listener's resolution of musical dissonance into consonance. Effectively, music sets up anticipations and then satisfies them. As Robert Jourdain has recently described this, the anticipation is of temporally developing patterns in tone, melody, harmony, rhythm, tempo, phrasing, and form. As Jourdain says, music is basically "a construction of a continual temporal flux, orchestrated according to precise proportions in which the listener's anticipation of tonal movement and proportion are gracefully integrated and resolved."[10] To the extent that the musical composition can continually reshape and heighten anticipation, by withholding resolution—by temporarily violating and delaying resolution—and then satisfy the more complex anticipation with a crescendo of resolution, music becomes far more "expressive" and more richly satisfying. In short, it yields great emotional satisfaction—where our experience is heightened to exceed the fulfillment of ordinary satisfaction, that is, of built-up tension and its satisfying, pleasure-giving release.[11]

Recent work in musical psychoacoustics shows that with the auditory resolution of dissonance, within the neural routings of the primary and secondary auditory cortex, the entire kinesthesic muscular system becomes subsequently engaged to help "score" or "model" or "map" these complex tonal progressions and structures onto the body itself, as a kind of sensory-motor register, so as to supplement the auditory system in attaining resolution, completion, and, thereby, satisfaction. And it is with this supplement of kinesthesic modeling (effectively, a somatic encoding)—whereby the body is moved to mimic beat, rhythm, harmony, and melody through muscular flex and contraction, that is, through bodily gesture, movement, and dance—that the higher-order neural networks in the somatosensory and motor cortex areas of the brain begin to produce endorphins. And it is precisely this production of endorphins that raises what was largely an automatic, relatively homeostatic response to auditory stimuli into an intensely pleasurable experience: ecstasy.[12] Or, as Nietzsche expressed this in 1869, the power of musical experience operates on our instinctual drives so as to provoke their discharge into highly excited emotional states, characterized by fluidity of affect and ego loss—that is to say, dispossession, disindividuation.

Reexamining the Dionysian states of frenzy (*Rausch*) some sixteen years later, Nietzsche would devote some four sections in *Twilight of the Idols* to this issue, beginning with section 8 of the chapter "Skirmishes of an Untimely Man." He says, for example, in section 10,

> In the Dionysian state [of frenzy] . . . the whole affective system [*das gesammte Affekt-System*] is excited and enhanced; so that it discharges all its means of expression at once and drives forth simultaneously the power of representation, imitation, transfiguration, transformation, and every kind of mimicking and acting. The essential feature here remains the ease of metamorphosis, the inability *not* to react (similar to certain hysterical types who also, upon any suggestion enter into *any* role). It is impossible for the Dionysian type not to understand any suggestion; he does not overlook any sign of an affect [*Zeichen des Affekts*]. . . . He enters into any skin, into any affect: he constantly transforms himself. Music, as we understand it today, is also a total excitement and a total discharge of the affects, but even so, only the remnant of a much fuller world of expression of the affects, a mere residue of the Dionysian histrionicism.

And it is at this state of charged and fluid affect that Nietzsche claims his distinctive resolution to the question of tragedy. This is the point where the Dionysian dithyramb, or the classical tragic drama, rejoins with the voice of Apollo to form the celebrated "fraternal union" between Dionysus and Apollo.

Insofar as it is a specific cult ritual, the Dionysian transformation entails a modification of the ecstatic process. One "loses" oneself and becomes an other, but only according to a certain image of deep ritual significance. The follower of Dionysus ritually reenacts a precise mythological role; that is, he ritually invokes a specific image or vision according to which he becomes other than himself in this emotional reconfiguration, this new affective cathexis or bond. In the case of the Dionysian ritual, the image extended to the excited participant is that of the Satyr.

Once the ritual dithyramb was brought to the stage as a public spectacle (i.e., during the reign of Pisistratus), the actor intervened and assumed the part of what was until then the visionary state of the Satyr chorus. Wearing the ritual mask, the actor became the figure of Dionysus himself, or that of his surrogate, the tragic hero. Nietzsche explained that "drama in the narrower sense" began here, with the introduction of the actor, as it implied a forceful distinction between the chorus and audience. The chorus itself did not require the real representation of Dionysus, because it already held Dionysus before itself as a visionary state. Representation was required only for the audience, not for the chorus. Accordingly, the function of the chorus changed radically. As Nietzsche would remark in section 8 of *The Birth of Tragedy,*

> Now the dithyrambic chorus was assigned the task of exciting the mood [*Stimmung*] of the listeners to such a Dionysian degree that, when the tragic hero appeared on the stage, they did not see the awkwardly masked human being but rather a visionary figure, born as it were from their own rapture.

Nietzsche went on to argue that the representation of the god or hero was made fully convincing to the audience by the double process of transference and condensation. Initially the audience transferred its own rapturous vision of Dionysus onto the specific representation (the actor), thereby transforming the concrete actor into the god Dionysus (or into the tragic hero, who was himself one ritual image of Dionysus): "He transferred the whole magical image of the god that was trembling before his soul to that masked figure and, as it were, dissolved its reality into the unreality of spirits" (*BT* 8). Once the transfer was made, the process of transformation could be completed by a second stage—a kind of image intensification—and this was brought about by the actor himself.

Ecstatically charged by both the chorus and the audience to a heightened state of divinity, of divine presence and authority, the actor then took it upon himself to condense this fevered excitement into the most economical form of expression: the epic pronouncement, the precise statement of Dionysian wisdom, which until the moment of his speech had been everywhere only felt. Viewed as this trembling figure, and sustained by the intoxicated chorus and the transported audience, "Dionysus no longer speaks through forces but as an epic hero, almost in the language of Homer" (*BT* 8). He now appeared dreamlike and spoke through the clairvoyant language of images. The forces struggling for expression—the frenzied music and dance, the disindividuated states of excess, joy, suffering, and abandon—all found their voice but now in the language of Apollo.

It was Sophocles and Aeschylus who intervened and invested the ritual dithyramb with the more extensive mythological content of the epic tradition. And by doing this, Nietzsche maintained, not only did they save these myths from the inevitable fate of becoming mere historical curiosities, but they gave them their highest achievement: they infused the myths with the profound significance of Dionysian wisdom. The already fading world of Homeric myth henceforth became reanimated by a far deeper and more penetrating worldview. As Nietzsche would remark, "Dionysian truth takes over the entire domain of myth as the symbolism of *its* knowledge which it makes known partly in the public cult of tragedy and partly in the secret celebrations of dramatic mysteries, but always in the old mythical garb" (*BT* 10).

Under the hand of Sophocles and Aeschylus, the old myths were retained and became strengthened; they became vehicles of Dionysian wisdom, which taught that all human suffering comes from individuation— whether this be of the individual who confronts the laws of nature, society, the gods, or fate. By the same token, this reinvigorated mythical teaching would reawaken the possibility of a social and political community. And this could only occur when the frenzied disindividuation of the Dionysian celebrant yielded and submitted to modification—when it became transformed, at the urging of the chorus, into a collective embrace, an impassioned identification by the audience with the spectacle of a common mythology, history, and destiny. All this would occur immediately, on the very stage set before them. It was an ecstatic embrace indeed.

We recall that, for Nietzsche, the "death of tragedy" comes about with Euripides' reform—his introduction of the rationally explicative prologue, his concern with clarity of personal motives and intelligible "character representation," the merging of the chorus with the actors themselves, thus effectively diminishing its role as well as eliminating the role of the accompanying musical instrumentation. The mythopoeic dimension of tragedy thus becomes reduced by the sober pronouncements of natural language, the emphasis on dramatic naturalism, and the perfectly conventional portrayal of emotions. Under the spell of the "new demon, Socrates," and in the absence of its traditionally tragic content, tragedy becomes more and more a fully conscious vehicle of rational strategy and intelligent characterization—largely a dramatized tale or narrative—that finally evolves into what Nietzsche described as "that drama which resembles a game of chess," the new Attic comedy. In the end, Nietzsche remarked, "the spectator is in general no longer conscious of the [tragic] myth, but of the vigorous truth to nature and the artist's imitative power" (*BT* 17). In replacing music and myth with dialectal argumentation, the essence of tragedy was destroyed, "since this can be interpreted only as a manifestation and projection into images of Dionysian states, as the visual symbolizing of music, as the dream-world of Dionysian intoxication" (*BT* 14).

Ultimately, Nietzsche claimed, it was too late to preserve tragic culture itself. The mythical heritage that sustained its social and political basis had been irretrievably destroyed: "What did you want, sacrilegious Euripides, when you sought to compel this dying myth to serve you once more? It died under your violent hands" (*BT* 10).

Doubtless, it was one of Nietzsche's most striking and compassionate achievements to have understood that the death of myth laid nothing at all to rest, save perhaps that which was most meaningful and valuable: for only after its effective demise does a culture begin to feel "the deep sense of an immense void"—what Nietzsche would later describe in *The Gay Science* as the breath of empty space, the ever colder and darker night, which attends the death of the old God.[13] Only in retrospect and with the lament bred from an unspeakable loss can one finally understand, Nietzsche says, "how necessary and close the fundamental connections are between art and the people, myth and custom, tragedy and the state" (*BT* 23). For the Greeks, this understanding came entirely too late to avert their decline into Alexandrine culture and political vassalage. For a period of more than five centuries, the myths that had infused tragic drama and had brought classical culture to its highest development were hardly less than the very lifeblood of Greek social and political existence. If the individual of classical Greece felt himself to be far more than an isolated subject, through his enjoyment of tragic drama, his sense of belonging was likewise acutely political. Having become who he was through the vital resources of myth and the significance it conferred on him, the individual fully assumed a political being at the same time: he shared the values, aspirations, beliefs, and concerns of those with whom he lived. Not only did he thereby find his home and familiarity in this condition, but he felt it to be more primary and praiseworthy than reason itself, a sentiment that even provoked the usually inquisitive Aristotle to exclaim, in the *Nicomachean Ethics*, "there is no need to ask why this [civic sentiment] is so."[14]

Nietzsche ended *The Birth of Tragedy* with the hope that a specifically modern culture could somehow retrieve the significance of its all but forgotten mythical heritage and fuse this with the immense resources that yet remain to be developed in music. That he once so positively located this hope for an awakened culture in the person of Richard Wagner Nietzsche quickly came to regret. But in his subsequent works Nietzsche himself would assume this task and devise his own responses to the abstract and mythless state of the modern distress.[15] By way of a new and joyful wisdom, the myth of the eternal return, and the prospect of a higher humanity, ennobled and united by the grand style, Nietzsche would time and again attempt to answer Zarathustra's bewildered exclamation, "How many new gods are yet possible?"

NOTES

1. Jacques Derrida, "Tympan," in *Margins of Philosophy,* trans. Alan Bass (Chicago: University of Chicago Press, 1982), ix–xxix.

2. Marghanita Laski, *Ecstasy: A Study of Some Secular and Religious Experiences* (Bloomington: Indiana University Press, 1961), 16.

3. Ibid. See esp. appendixes A–J, 375–533. Laski gives an interesting analysis of Nietzsche's remarks on musical ecstasy in section 1 of *The Case of Wagner,* in appendix A, 405 ff.

4. The essay is translated into English by Walter Kaufmann and is found as an appendix in Carl Dahlhaus's *Between Romanticism and Modernism: Four Studies in the Music of the Later 19th Century,* trans. Mary Whittall (Berkeley: University of California Press, 1980), 106–19, and in *KSA* 7: pp. 359–69, 185–90. For an extended analysis of this text, see David B. Allison, "Some Remarks on Nietzsche's Essay of 1871, 'On Music and Words,'" in *New Nietzsche Studies* 1 (Fall-Winter 1996): 15–41.

5. Interestingly, the title itself was given to the essay by Nietzsche's subsequent editors—perhaps reinforcing their view, the common view, that Nietzsche was indeed a rigorous Schopenhauerian. Nietzsche strongly contests this charge in his later 1886 preface to *The Birth of Tragedy.*

6. On Wagner's theoretical position at this time, see Carl Dahlhaus, "The Twofold Truth in Wagner's Aesthetics: Nietzsche's Fragment 'On Music and Words,'" in Dahlhaus, *Between Romanticism and Modernism,* 19–39.

7. Music is indeed a "sanctuary" in that it is its own world. It is a constructed, artificial world, which is immediately experienced as a completely controlled environment, engaging the emotions and structuring the reception of temporality and movement: it resolves an enormity of elements and anticipations into perfect form, beauty.

8. *The Politics of Aristotle,* bk. 8, chap. 6, trans. E. Barker (New York: Oxford University Press, 1962), 348–49.

9. In his recent volume, *Music, the Brain, and Ecstasy: How Music Captures Our Imagination* (New York: Wm. Morrow, 1997), Robert Jourdain specifies

three kinds of dissonance to be resolved by the listener: auditory critical band frequency interference and synchronicity of sound beat—both of which are complemented by overtone interactions—as well as the more complex structural element, harmonic dissonance, involving chord movement; see esp. 100–105.

10. Jourdain, *Music, the Brain, and Ecstasy,* 302–3.

11. Ibid., 312–13.

12. While the auditory cortex is densely connected to the temporal and frontal lobes of the brain, it is not so connected to the motor cortex or the somatosensory cortex (and this would seem to block the automatic engagement of the kinesthetic-motor system by the auditory system). Rather we seem to use our muscular system to represent musical patterns of tension, anticipation, impetus, movement, trajectory, contour, and so on, so as to serve as a system of notation to inscribe and remember musical patterns as they transpire temporally and thus to amplify our experience of its complexity and the satisfaction this yields. Thus musical patterns are replicated in the motor system as well as in the auditory system. In this sense, our kinesthetic system becomes a kind of resonator; the body literally permits itself to become an instrument, to be played by the music. More simply stated, perhaps, this is exactly how we "go with the flow," how we "get into" musical rhythms and harmonic cadences. And it is at this level of bodily representation that the neurons within the kinesthetic-motor system are excited and begin to discharge endorphins, further enhancing the sense of pleasure—in this case, delight, ecstasy—in our experience of music. And we become transformed. (Jourdain, *Music, the Brain, and Ecstasy,* 324–26.)

13. Aristophanes portrayed Socrates, in *The Clouds,* as teaching the criminal doctrine that "Zeus is not." In a note from the period of *BT,* Nietzsche also remarked, it "is a very ancient Germanic idea" that "all the old Gods must die . . . Sigurd, Odin, Balder" (*KSA* 7:5[57]).

14. Aristotle, *Nicomachean Ethics,* 1095b.

15. For a supplementary discussion about how Nietzsche viewed the modern crisis in culture during this period, see his work of 1873, *On the Uses and Disadvantages of History,* esp. chap. 4.

CHAPTER 5

"This Is Not a Christ"

Nietzsche, Foucault,
and the Genealogy of Vision

Gary Shapiro

I

There is nothing surprising about linking the names of Nietzsche and Foucault, something that Foucault himself frequently did. We know that the practices of archaeology and genealogy owe much to *On the Genealogy of Morals;* and in *The Order of Things* Foucault celebrates Nietzsche for being able to look beyond the epoch of "man and his doubles," thinking of the *Übermensch* as designating that which is beyond man, and for serving, along with Mallarmé, as one of the prophets of the hegemony of language in the emerging episteme of the postmodern world. Here I want to focus on other affinities, influences, or inspirations that have to do with what these thinkers saw, that is, their engagement with visual culture and visual art. Foucault is a theorist of the visual and of the complex and sometimes uncanny relations between the visual and the linguistic, a thought that is expressed gnomically in his reading of Velázquez's *Las Meninas* when he says that "the relation of painting to language is an infinite relation." [1] In addition to his essay on René Magritte, *This Is Not a Pipe,* which contains the outlines of an archaeology of Western painting, the rest of Foucault's work is full of references to the painters of madness (e.g., Bosch and Goya) and to the artists of his own time: for example, there are passages on Andy Warhol and introductions to the work of the photographer Duane Michals and the photographic painter Gerard Fromanger. [2] Foucault began a book on

Edouard Manet, which apparently would have developed the suggestion
that the artist inaugurates or exemplifies a turn within painting to the
kind of intertextuality in which pictures refer to other pictures through
the medium of the museum; this parallels the literary intertextuality
that Gustave Flaubert exemplified in *The Temptation of Saint Anthony,*
which is said to constitute a "Fantasia of the Library."[3] We can imagine
that such a work from Foucault would have put a new, archaeological
spin on ideas about museum culture and the age of technical reproduction that are associated with André Malraux and Walter Benjamin.

Beyond the explicit discussions of visual art in Foucault's writing,
there is a rather constant concern with visual scenarios and mechanisms of power, perhaps the best known being the execution scenes
and the interrogation of panoptic strategies in *Surveillance and Punishment,* but such inquiry also marks a work like *The Birth of the Clinic,*
which explores the development of the clinical gaze and sets itself the
task of "re-examin[ing] the original distribution of the visible and the
invisible."[4] This last phrase contains the formula for the critical but
implicit dialogue with Merleau-Ponty that runs through Foucault's
concern with the visual and is most evident in the chapter on *Las Meninas* in which he deploys the phenomenologist's language of the visible
and the invisible to suggest that their relation must be understood ar-
chaeologically rather than as a timeless foundation of all expression and
communication.[5]

In *Downcast Eyes: The Denigration of Vision in Twentieth-Century
French Thought,* Martin Jay claims that Foucault joins many other
twentieth-century thinkers in denouncing the traditional philosophical
primacy of vision, demoting it from the position that Plato awarded it as
"the noblest of the senses."[6] I suggest that closer attention to Foucault's
texts (as well as to those of several other writers discussed by Jay) will
show that it is more specifically a certain model of vision that Foucault
is exposing and contesting, while he develops an alternative conception.
This alternative involves both a deeply historical or archaeological account of the radical shifts in visual culture and a suggestion of the forms
that can be taken by a visual resistance to prevailing modes of display
and surveillance: we have not only the Panopticon but also Manet and
not only the photographic and video mechanisms of fixing identities but
also the styles of Magritte, Warhol, and Michals to disrupt them.[7] Foucault is not opposed to "the visual turn" that many observers, such as
W. J. T. Mitchell, have detected in recent work in the humanities; his
work is already being used to give that tendency a greater degree of his-

torical depth and has a potential for exploring issues that philosophers, literary critics, and art historians are just beginning to consider with regard to "the original distribution of the visible and the invisible."

This dimension of Foucault's work has Nietzschean sources and parallels; considering these will help to clarify the projects of both thinkers and to show how they intersect with the rethinking of visuality that is on the current intellectual agenda. It might be thought that Nietzsche, with his notoriously poor vision, has little to say about that sense; yet frequently the place of one's wound is also the source of one's genius. Let us recall that what recurs in eternal recurrence is the *Augenblick*, the moment of vision, or the twinkling of an eye. And while it is clear that the *Augenblick* is not exclusively or narrowly visual, respect for Nietzsche's writing ought to make us linger a bit with his choice of this word. It might be said, with some justice, that a German speaker does not hear the visual connotations of *Auge* and *Blick* here (as it is sometimes said that the *Hand* in Heidegger's *zuhanden* is similarly inaudible). If that is the case, the text of the chapter in *Zarathustra* called "On the Vision and the Riddle" does much to emphasize precisely that visual dimension, beginning with its title. The lighting is set rather precisely in "the deadly pallor of dusk," and the central scene, where Zarathustra confronts the dwarf who embodies the spirit of gravity, is described in terms of their contemplation of a gateway inscribed with the word *Augenblick*. And before arriving at the gateway Zarathustra challenges the dwarf to rethink the nature of vision by asking "Is not seeing itself—seeing abysses? [*Ist Sehen nicht selber—Abgründe sehen?*]" (Z:3 "On the Vision and the Riddle").[8] To consider vision as necessarily seeing abysses is to understand it as indefinitely open and complex; it is to theorize it as necessarily multiple and perspectival. Such an approach is to be sharply distinguished from the model of the fixed and totalizing gaze that haunts philosophy and common sense, and which is sometimes, with rough justice, associated with the system of rigorous perspective developed in quattrocento painting or with the optics of Descartes.[9]

I want to suggest some of the connections between Nietzsche and Foucault, and some of the implications that their work may have for the visual turn in recent critical thought, by focusing on the readings that they give of two ostensibly quite different paintings. Let us begin by considering Foucault's reading of Magritte's work *Les deux mystères* in *This Is Not a Pipe*, a painting that is one of the great emblems of surrealism. This picture, like the scene set by Nietzsche in *Zarathustra*, involves not only a vision and a riddle but also an inscription that marks a visual dis-

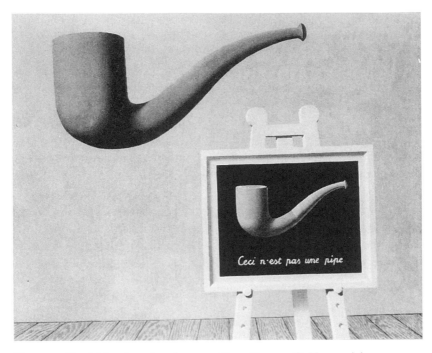

Figure 1. René Magritte, *Les deux mystères.* © 1999 C. Herscovici,
Brussels / Artists Rights Society, New York.

play. Perhaps, as Foucault suggests, this painting also provides a look
into the abyss and helps us to discover once more that all vision is seeing abysses. Foucault makes sense of this painting, providing a verbal
commentary on and counterpart to it, an *ekphrasis* as it is called in the
rhetorical and art historical traditions, in something of the spirit of
Vasari or Diderot. At the same time he is sensitive to the guideline that
he had laid down earlier, according to which

> the relation of language to painting is an infinite relation. It is not that words
> are imperfect, or that, when confronted by the visible, they prove insuperably
> inadequate. Neither can be reduced to the other's terms: it is in vain that we
> say what we see; what we see never resides in what we say.[10]

To begin tracing out the complexity of a painting that itself involves a
linguistic element, Foucault imagines that the blackboard that very os-
tentatiously offers an image of a pipe along with the inscription "*Ceci
n'est pas une pipe*" is part of a scene of instruction that itself involves
the relation between the visual and the linguistic; in his reconstruction

a teacher attempts to demonstrate the distinction between words and things by insisting that words, images, or representations are not to be confused with that which they designate, or depict, or to which they refer. The teacher is commenting, perhaps a bit clumsily, on the infinite relation of the visible and the linguistic. While this very sincere pedagogue is intoning his lesson, and in the process has found it necessary to make ever more complex and reflexive formulations that will guard at every level against the possibility of confusing words and things, another pipe or image appears, floating above what we see on the easel. As Foucault describes it:

> Negations multiply themselves, the voice is confused and choked. The baffled master lowers his extended pointer, turns his back to the board, regards the uproarious students, and does not realize that they laugh so loudly because above the blackboard and his stammered denials, a vapor has just risen, little by little taking shape and now creating, precisely and without a doubt, a pipe. "A pipe, a pipe," cry the students, stamping away while the teacher, his voice sinking ever lower, murmurs always with the same obstinacy though no one is listening, "And yet it is not a pipe." He is not mistaken.[11]

Foucault's account of how this painting achieves its effect can be explicated by and is probably indebted to Gilles Deleuze's understanding of eternal recurrence and of the simulacrum; these in turn derive from Nietzsche.[12] Let me state just a few of Foucault's explicit or implicit claims about this painting and Magritte's other work: the paintings confront us with the necessity of thinking the simulacrum, that is, the image that is a copy of a copy, an image that finally floats free of any tie to an original; this image *floats*—that is, like the simulacrum as understood by the Epicureans it has a filmy or vaporous status, as exemplified by the upper pipe; the work maintains a complex balance between language and visual image; it participates in both by virtue of being an unraveled calligram; the work sets up a series of distinctions between various actual and virtual audiences in terms of their naïveté or depth of understanding of the scene. Moreover, Foucault suggests somewhat indirectly that Nietzsche's thought of eternal recurrence is a good way of theorizing the indefinite repetition of the simulacrum and the way in which it functions without being anchored to any foundational reality.

Foucault's theorization of the simulacrum in the 1960s ought to be seen against the background of the emergence of pop art. In a stunning page on Warhol, he sketches a way of reading the repetition of images

as a way of summoning forth the "phantasm," the free-floating and infinitely replicable simulacrum.

> This is the greatness of Warhol with his canned foods, senseless accidents,
> and his series of advertising smiles: the oral and nutritional equivalents of
> those half-open lips, teeth, tomato sauce, that hygiene based on detergents;
> the equivalence of death in the cavity of an eviscerated car, at the top of a tele-
> phone pole and at the end of a wire, and between the glistening steel blue
> arms of the electric chair. . . . [I]n concentrating on this boundless monotony,
> we find the sudden illumination of multiplicity itself—with nothing at its
> center, at its highest point, or beyond it—a flickering of light that travels even
> faster than the eyes and successively lights up the moving labels and the cap-
> tive snapshots that refer to each other to eternity, without ever saying any-
> thing: suddenly, arising from the background of the old inertia of equivalences,
> the striped form of the event tears through the darkness, and the eternal
> phantasm informs that soup can, that singular and depthless face.[13]

"Nothing at its center": this can be read as saying, with Nietzsche, that
there is no center, or in Buddhist fashion as suggesting that the center is
nothingness. Perhaps it is an odd place, Warhol in Paris of the 1960s, for
a meeting between Nietzsche and the Buddha. Foucault ends *This Is Not
a Pipe* with a mantra:

> A day will come when, by means of similitude relayed indefinitely along the
> length of a series, the image itself, along with the name it bears, will lose its
> identity. Campbell, Campbell, Campbell, Campbell.[14]

II

Nietzsche's fullest exploration of an individual painting has a much
more explicit connection with a religious tradition. He offers a commentary on Raphael's *Transfiguration* in *The Birth of Tragedy*. Before rereading this text, we should recall that the *Transfiguration* occupies a
special place in Raphael's work and in the veneration of Raphael that
was practiced by figures like Vasari, Goethe, and Jacob Burckhardt. It
was Raphael's last painting, and there is a continuing dispute over exactly how complete it was at the time of his death. We know from Vasari
that it was displayed at the time of his funeral in the Pantheon. Critics
have long been divided on the question of whether and to what extent it
is a unified work and whether it marks the possibility of a new departure in Raphael's art that would lead away from classicism to a style that
tolerates greater ruptures and discontinuities. There are two distinct
scenes in the painting, based on two Gospel texts that narrate different

episodes. Some critics have found that the work does not succeed in uni-
fying these two disparate segments, but the usual verdict has been that
Raphael daringly created an unexpected and higher unity by combining
them. This was the opinion of Goethe, recorded in his *Italian Journey,*
which Nietzsche would almost certainly have read; recounting his viewing the painting with a group in Rome, he tells us,

> The quieter members of the group were annoyed to hear a repetition of the
> old criticism that it has a double action. . . . [I]t is odd that anyone should
> ever have found fault with the grand unity of this conception. . . . How, then,
> are those upper and lower parts to be separated? The two are one: below, the
> suffering part, in need of help; above, the effective, helpful part, both of them
> linked together. To express the sense of this in another way: can the connec-
> tion between the conceptual and the real be severed? [15]

It is to this painting, the most controversial work of the Italian artist
universally revered by the Germans who discovered or constructed the
Renaissance, that Nietzsche turns when he wants a visual illustration of
his new theory of art.

It is worth noting that in a book supposedly consecrated to the spirit
of music, Nietzsche has so much to say about the visual world, including the visual aspect of tragedy, something that, as he says, escapes the
"one great Cyclops eye" of Socrates. In rereading this familiar passage,
I think we can discern some of the same themes that appear in Foucault's
essay on Magritte. Nietzsche introduces this *ekphrasis* in section 4 of the
Birth, where he is describing the Apollonian form of art:

> In a symbolic painting, *Raphael,* himself one of these immortal "naive" ones,
> has represented this disempowerment [*Depotenziren*] of appearance [*Schein*]
> to the level of mere appearance, the primitive process of the naive artist and
> of Apollinian culture. In his *Transfiguration,* the lower half of the picture, with
> the possessed boy, the despairing bearers, the bewildered, terrified disciples,
> shows us the reflection of suffering, primal and eternal, the sole ground of the
> world: the "mere appearance" here is the reflection of eternal contradiction,
> the father of things. From this mere appearance arises, like ambrosial vapor
> [*Duft*], a new visionary world of mere appearances, invisible to those wrapped
> in the first appearance—a radiant floating [*Schweben*] in purest bliss, a
> serene contemplation beaming from wide-open eyes. Here we have presented
> in the highest artistic symbolism, that Apollinian world of beauty and its
> substratum, the terrible wisdom of Silenus; and intuitively we comprehend
> their necessary interdependence. Apollo, however, again appears to us as the
> apotheosis of the *principium individuationis,* in which alone is consummated
> the perpetually attained goal of the primal unity, its redemption through
> mere appearance. With his sublime gestures, he shows us how necessary is

Figure 2. Raphael, *Transfiguration*.

the entire world of suffering, that by means of it an individual may be im-
pelled to realize the redeeming vision, and then, sunk in contemplation of it,
sit quietly in his tossing bark, amid the waves. (*BT* 4)

Nietzsche had not seen this painting, other than in reproductions, at the
time that he wrote the passage, for he had not yet visited Rome. He had
probably seen Raphael's *Sistine Madonna* (on which he comments in
The Wanderer and His Shadow 73), which is in Dresden. But he would
have been acquainted with the rich tradition of Raphael worship among
the Germans, and he certainly would have been familiar with Burckhardt's paean to Raphael and to the *Transfiguration* in particular, which
is to be found in his *Cicerone,* a book that Nietzsche often praised as invaluable; and Nietzsche would have heard Burckhardt expounding such
views in lectures and conversation.[16]

What is striking in Nietzsche's *ekphrasis* is the stress on appearance
as appearance, *Schein als Schein,* which emphasizes that what we see is
illusion, shining, radiance, appearance severed from any ground. This
shining is the simulacrum, that whose nature is simply to shine or to appear. It may be that this is why Nietzsche transfigures the *Transfiguration* by identifying the floating figure as Apollo, for to name him as
Christ would be to become involved in questions of how the radiant appearance is caused by, grounded in, or expressive of some deeper principle. Raphael had made a design for the work in which God the Father
did appear in the upper level of the painting and Jesus was shown as
transfigured, but there was no scene involving the possessed boy. In this
respect the artist already begins the work of expelling the level of the
transcendent that Nietzsche observes in the painting.[17] The two levels of
the *Transfiguration* make it eminently suitable to demonstrate the way
in which Apollonian art has the capacity to represent, include, and transcend the Dionysian. Of course, it represents the Dionysian only by giving it Apollonian form; in a stricter sense we might say that the Dionysian cannot be represented but only embodied or performed.

As Burckhardt and subsequent historians of art point out, Raphael has
done something quite daring in juxtaposing two quite different scenes
from the Gospels, one in which the disciples fail to heal a possessed boy,
because their faith is not great enough; and one that precedes it narra-
tively, and is not necessarily set in the same place, in which Jesus is transfigured, accompanied by the figures of Elijah and Moses. Burckhardt is
impressed by the floating, arguing that Raphael's Christ is the first successful floating figure in Italian art and that "the form and expression of

Christ reveal one of the great secrets of art, which sometimes elude the endeavors of centuries." [18] The secret has to do with the representation of a floating and radiant being, and here Nietzsche seems to be in agreement with Burckhardt. The imagination of the believer, following the biblical text, which tells us that "his face did shine as the sun, and his raiment was white as light" (Matt. 17:2), requires a presentation of Jesus that, according to Burckhardt, "presupposes a brilliant self-contained illumination of the form, and therefore the absence of all shadow, as well as of all modeling." [19] But this is impossible and defeats the principles of painting, at least of the style that Raphael was practicing; the solution, Burckhardt adds, was for Raphael to substitute floating for this impossibility of a nonmodeled, nonshadowed figure. In other words, Raphael comes as close as possible, within the conventions of his art, to producing a figure that exemplifies *Schein als Schein*. About one hundred years later, Foucault will discern Magritte's floating pipe as playing a role that closely parallels this floating Christ.

Or is this figure indeed Christ? Nietzsche implicitly raises the question by referring to the floating apparition as Apollo, the radiant and shining god, the god of appearances and visual manifestations. Has not Nietzsche transfigured Raphael's ostensibly Christian *Transfiguration?* Keeping Magritte in mind, we might wonder whether the painting is effectively being retitled "This Is Not a Christ." Thinking about the two paintings together, along with the *ekphrases* of Nietzsche and Foucault, we might detect some uncanny affinities; we can now acknowledge the surrealist dimension in the great classicist Raphael while recognizing that Magritte may not be wholly unconcerned with religious themes. The same point could be restated from the standpoint of art history. Hans Belting, in his great study of Byzantine art, *Likeness and Presence,* demonstrates that the icon was not considered merely as the representation or likeness of the saint but as the saint's very manifestation.[20] Typically, icons were not displayed but kept under wraps and taken out only on special occasions, such as the feast day of the saint. As Italian art moved away from Byzantine thought and practice, it came to understand the image as a likeness, not a reality; or in the terms of German aesthetics, as adapted by Nietzsche, it came to a point where it was able to acknowledge and even celebrate *Schein als Schein*.

I observed earlier that Nietzsche sees the *Transfiguration* as one of the highest exemplars of Apollonian art. This is true, but it overlooks the specific context within which he makes this claim. In section 4 of the *Birth* Nietzsche is still examining the analogy between art and the dream, and he is attempting to show how this analogy illuminates the case of the naive artist. In the course of this discussion, he implies not only that the naive artist is Apollonian and inspired by dreams or dreamlike states but also that we require such art to show us what dreams are. Art is not merely a form or consequence of the dream but the first way that we have of gaining access to it. Or as Freud said a quarter of a century later, the poets and artists showed the way long before his own work of *Traumdeutung*.

The naive artist of whom Nietzsche speaks is naive in no pejorative sense; indeed Nietzsche's writings are full of praise for Raphael, who is frequently cited as a supreme artistic genius and three of whose paintings are subjects of rather detailed discussion, an honor he accords to no other painter. The naive artist, in the German aesthetic tradition that Nietzsche draws on here, must be understood in terms of Schiller's distinction of the naive and the sentimental. Schiller's simplest formulation is that the naive poet *is* nature while the sentimental poet *seeks* nature. The naive artist is there in the material, in the work itself; we might say that such artists are self-effacing, except that as they have never been the themes of their own work there is no call for effacement. The sentimental artist is concerned with his or her own feelings and responses and does not let us forget them. In considering the case of the naive artist Nietzsche generalizes considerably on Schiller's formulation; he wants to understand the artist who is enthralled by the content and structure of the dream, and apparently indifferent to his own role in it.

The dreamer whom Nietzsche imagines is so immersed in the dream that "in the midst of the illusion of the dream world and without disturbing it, he calls out to himself: 'It is a dream, I will dream on'" (*BT* 4). Today this would be called an instance of lucid dreaming, in which the dreamer chooses to prolong and explore his or her own dream; Nietzsche instead emphasizes the element of submission or acceptance in the dreamer's attitude. And he suggests that we can interpret such phenomena by following "the dream-reading Apollo," who is also the god of radiance and of painting. As Nietzsche's *ekphrasis* of Raphael implies, Apollo is not only the god who inspires such visions but is also, in this case, their subject. Reflecting on the dream, in a philosophical voice that harkens back to Schopenhauer, but is also informed by Schiller's celebration of *Schein*, Nietzsche puts forward the view that "the truly existent primal unity, eternally suffering and contradictory, also needs the rapturous vision, the pleasurable illusion, for its continuous redemption" (*BT* 4). Empirical and phenomenal reality are simply appearance or illusion in this perspective; but then the dream is "a *mere appearance of mere appearance,* hence a still higher appeasement of the primordial desire for mere appearance" (*BT* 4).

At this point Nietzsche invokes Raphael and the *Transfiguration* to explain how the artist and the painting display "the disempowering of appearance to the level of mere appearance." Without such display would we be able to grasp and comprehend the dream process or the activity of the Apollonian artist? On Nietzsche's reading, what Raphael displays is the process of naive art itself; it is still naive insofar as it is not sentimental, not concerned with the persona and feelings of Raphael himself, but it is naïveté raised to a higher level insofar as it shows us the procedure of the naive itself.

Is this meant to be a timeless pronouncement about the nature and scope of painting? Let us recall that Foucault sketches an archaeology of painting, according to which there are radical breaks between the assumptions and procedures of different epochs. From a later perspective we can see that the protocols of a painting like *Las Meninas* are not those of a van Gogh self-portrait, of a Magritte, or of a Warhol wall of Marilyns or Jackies. Velázquez, Foucault maintains, was capable of representing everything but representation. Nietzsche, as we have just seen, claims that Raphael is one of those immortal naive ones just because he does display the possibility of display. These views are not necessarily inconsistent; Foucault might very well agree that the Raphael of 1520 belongs to a different regime of visuality than the Velázquez of 1650, whom he takes to be emblematic of the dawning classical age.

In *This Is Not a Pipe* Foucault begins to sketch an archaeology of Western visual culture, distinguishing the era from roughly Giotto to the impressionists as one in which words and images are kept as distinct as possible and painting is expected to provide us with only a visual scene; this is to be distinguished both from the conventions of medieval painting and illustration that preceded it and from the crisis of representation that Foucault identifies with Kandinsky, Klee, and Magritte. This is just a sketch, and it is one that would make no distinction, so far, between Raphael and Velázquez. If we were to follow the archaeology of *The Order of Things,* however, we could reconstruct a somewhat different way of distinguishing approaches to the visual.[21] There Foucault is explicitly concerned with verbal discourses, even if he does use *Las Meninas* to illustrate the protocols of the classical age; but we might think, tentatively, of extending this archaeology to visual art. In that case, the art of the Renaissance could be seen as analogous to "the prose of the world," in which similitude and analogy are the dominant modes of thought; painting would then have goals such as linking microcosm and macrocosm. In a painting like the *Transfiguration* this might involve showing a series of connections among art, dream, possession, and divine manifestation. The art of the classical era would attempt, like *Las Meninas,* to exhibit every function and permutation of representation but would be debarred from exploring what it is that makes representation possible, a point that Foucault makes when he says that Velázquez's painting points to an ineluctable absence, an empty space in front of the painting that is hypothetically occupied, in an unstably oscillating pattern, by the viewer, the model, and the artist himself. The visual mode of modernity, in which human beings attempt to know themselves by exploring and articulating their own limits, would produce an artistic equivalent of the "analytic of finitude." Kant, Marx, and the early Heidegger, despite what seem to be vast philosophical differences, can be seen as offering different versions of what these limits are and what their consequences might be (finitude being understood diversely here as the conditions of sensibility and representation, the necessity of labor and productivity, or the fundamental structures of anxiety and being-toward-death). The art appropriate to such an episteme would be typified by the self-portrait of the meditative or anguished artist (Cézanne or van Gogh, for example) who constantly interrogates himself and the possibility of visual representation in the same gesture. (It seems to me that Foucault would see Merleau-Ponty's valorization of Cézanne's painting as an accurate way of understanding the project of modernity but as making unwarranted claims of generality insofar as it ignores what is distinctive in other artistic epochs.) If it is the emergence of language that follows the exhaustion of the analytic of finitude and the disappearance of man, then the art form that might flourish at such a time could be one that, like the work of Magritte and Warhol,

> dissociated similitude from resemblance, and brought the former into play against the latter. . . . Resemblance presupposes a primary reference that prescribes and classes. The similar develops in series that have neither beginning nor end, that can be followed in one direction as easily as in another, that obey no hierarchy, but propagate themselves from small differences and among differences.[22]

Given this sketch, there appear to be a number of connections between the epoch dominated by similitude and that in which language displaces man; both are characterized by the leading role taken by an indefinitely expansive system of structures rather than by a fixed, tabular mode of representation or by an inquiry into the limits of that being who is thought to be the condition of representation itself. From such a perspective it is possible to see how Foucault might have found Raphael to be working in a quite different epoch of visual culture than Velázquez, and how we might see the plausibility of taking works from the first and last of these eras to have some possible affinities that might escape a more conventional (and Hegelian) art history.

In any case, Nietzsche himself, after *The Birth of Tragedy*, was to mark some archaeological reservations about Raphael. One aphorism in its entirety from *Daybreak* reads,

> *Transfiguration.*—Those that suffer helplessly, those that dream confusedly, those that are entranced by things supernatural—these are the *three divisions* into which Raphael divided mankind. This is no longer how we see the world—and Raphael too would no longer *be able* to see it as he did: he would behold a whole new transfiguration. (D 8)

In a later jotting Nietzsche notes that even a great artist like Raphael was not free of Christian infection, for "finally even his transfigured Christ is a fluttering, entranced [*schwärmerisches*] little monk that he does not dare to show naked. Goethe's got it right there" (*KSA* 11:26[3]).

III

In beginning to articulate the ways in which Nietzsche and Foucault are linked as theorists of visual culture and of visual art, of *Schein* and the simulacrum, it is worth marking the fact that Foucault's first published text, *Dream, Imagination, and Existence,* is concerned with the oneiric theme that is crucial to Nietzsche's *Birth of Tragedy*. Like Nietzsche, Foucault wants to insist that the dream is not a secondary or marginal process but a primordial form of human existence. Ostensibly commenting on Ludwig Binswanger's *Dream and Existence,* Foucault criticizes Freud for having an overly textual and linguistic approach to the dream; this parallels Nietzsche's implicit criticism of Aristotle and almost the entire post-Aristotelian tradition for reducing tragedy to plot, with an accompanying demotion of music and spectacle. This is the reduction that already begins, according to *The Birth of Tragedy*, with the "one great Cyclops eye of Socrates"; Aristotle simply disagrees as to the intelligibility and the ethical meaning of tragedy once it has been so reduced. To some extent Foucault anticipates the opposition between Jacques Lacan and Jean-François Lyotard about the role of image and language in Freud's dream theory. For Lacan, Freud has a linguistic account of the dream; the images of which the dream consists are essentially, as Freud declares, a rebus, or picture puzzle that has a linguistic equivalent. According to Lyotard, it is the constant tension between language and image that characterizes the Freudian dream, and art generally.[23]

What we might call the Nietzschean or Lyotardian side of Foucault's dream book is its insistence on image and imagination; there is even a suggestion that the main literary genres can be understood in terms of typical forms of dream imagination. Against any linguistic reductionism, Foucault insists on the importance of dream space and dream landscape. Yet this most Heideggerian of Foucault's texts also deviates from Nietzsche in its account of the dreamer's position with regard to his or her own dream. For Nietzsche, in *The Birth of Tragedy,* there is something impersonal or naive about the dream and the art that both illuminates it and is derived from it. For Foucault, who is sympathetically developing a strain of Heideggerian existential phenomenology that underlies Binswanger's work, the dream is a form of *Existenz;* he writes,

> In the dream, everything says "I," even the things and the animals, even the empty space, even objects distant and strange which populate the phantasmagoria. . . . To dream is not another way of experiencing another world, it is for the dreaming subject the radical way of experiencing its own world.[24]

By the time he came to write *The Order of Things,* Foucault would doubtless have rejected the subjectivism of this formulation as part of the thought characteristic of the epoch of man, and he might have seen this kind of fascination with the dream as one manifestation of the return and retreat of the origin that displays the instability of "man and his doubles."

What is notable about this early text is that, like *The Birth of Tragedy,* it proposes to see its subject in an irreducibly visual perspective, and we can find a similar motif in Foucault's later writings, some of which are explicitly concerned with visual art. If art is, as Plato said, "a waking dream," then understanding the dream's visual dimension will yield a distinctive conception of art. This approach seems to me to provide an important corrective to some attempts to categorize Foucault as a linguistic reductionist; the same applies to many others who are considered to be poststructuralists. Such readings often proceed by citing the importance of Nietzsche for these thinkers; but I have suggested some reasons for thinking that we may be ready for a different approach to both thinkers, to their relationship, and to the way in which they theorize the relationship between the linguistic and the visual.

IV

The visual turn in cultural theory can be seen as a response to a change in culture generally. Traditional literacy, based on printed texts, is being displaced or demoted by a culture of the screen, which may be cinematic, video, or computer based. Newspaper editorials express dismay at the increased use of films in university classes ostensibly devoted to literature and at the rise of media studies, often focused on popular figures (as I write, concern is being voiced about courses on Madonna and Princess Diana). Precocious children, who once learned to read before their peers, now find themselves at the computer screen, manipulating an array of images sometimes accompanied by text; stories that were once children's classics, first read aloud and then accessible through the young reader's own efforts, are now encountered originally through video versions that the younger generation may very well assume to be the definitive ones, bearing the same relation to the text as does a contemporary film to its "novelization."

Juxtaposed with such changes in our use and deployment of the media, the musings of Nietzsche and Foucault about two paintings may seem rather quaint and inconsequential. Let me suggest, however, that these thinkers have resources that could help us in coming to terms with our rapidly changing cultural situation. Nietzsche's *ekphrasis* of Raphael occurs in the context of his analysis of ancient tragedy and his optimism (later abandoned) about the possibility of a rebirth of the tragic spirit, exemplified by Wagnerian performance. *The Birth of Tragedy* is not concerned simply with the musical dimension of the art, as music is conceived today; *mousiké* involves dance as well as melody and song. Moreover, Nietzsche is concerned with the visual dimension of tragedy and opera throughout the *Birth*. Part of the deficiency of current theater and opera, from his point of view, is its failure as vision or spectacle. Whereas Aristotle had classified *opsis* (spectacle) along with music as one of the less significant dimensions of tragedy, Nietzsche addresses a "friend" whom he imagines to reflect on his experience of contemporary performance; such a listener and spectator, he suggests, will have to acknowledge that the effect of a true musical tragedy, purely and simply, as he knows it from experience . . . [will be] as if his visual faculty [*Sehkraft*] were no longer merely a surface faculty but capable of penetrating into the interior, and as if he now saw before him, with the aid of music, the waves of the will, the conflict of motives, and the swelling flood of the passions, sensuously visible, as it were, like a multitude of vividly moving lines and figures. (*BT* 22)

Clearly, it is Wagner, as well as Aeschylus, whom Nietzsche has in mind. He is concerned with the question of how a visual culture can be invigorating or deadening, and this was a concern that outlasted his enthusiasm for one nineteenth-century composer and showman. The analysis that he offers of ancient tragedy has a specifically visual dimension and involves what is perhaps the first statement of Nietzsche's perspectivism (even if he does not yet adopt that term). Part of what renders the Greek art unique is that it involves a kind of double vision: the spectators see the actors on the raised stage, or *skené*, but at the same time they identify with the chorus in the orchestra and project themselves into the vision that these have of the same scene. On this account the viewers are virtually seeing from two places at once; they embody a multiplicity of perspectives that Nietzsche contrasts with "the one great Cyclops eye of Socrates" (*BT* 14). Nietzsche thought that he was doing more than making a discovery about the conditions and techniques of the theater of Dionysus in fifth-century Athens. We might attempt a contemporary formulation of his question. How can our media be structured so that we will not be confined to a Cyclopean vision? How can we learn to work with a multiplicity of perspectives? How, in short, can vision be reframed perspectivally?

Foucault articulates the archaeological dimension of Nietzsche's thought, including his thought of the visual, which is already implicit in *The Birth of Tragedy*. Although that book can be read as one more instance of the Sisyphean quest of modernism that is characterized by "the retreat and return of the origin," it can also be seen as a study of the massive ruptures that mark off from one another two forms of culture and their structuring presuppositions. Foucault updates Nietzsche's visual archaeology in his reflections on Magritte, pop art, and the oscillating boundary between the photographic and the painterly. He suggests that we need notions such as the simulacrum and eternal recurrence to make sense of the repetitive images on our many screens, in our museums, and now in our imaginations. Moreover, in keeping with his principle that every form of power is correlated with forms of resistance (itself a restatement and politicization of Nietzsche's teaching concerning the will[s] to power) we could look to Foucault for some suggestions about the relation between hegemonic visual regimes and the practices that resist them. These connections are not thematized explicitly in Foucault's work. Although he abandoned his project on Manet in 1968, perhaps in response to political pressures that led his thought in other directions, this does not mean that such a project would have lacked a political dimension. It might have focused on the institution of the museum and other forms of the visual canon; these have a dual nature, suggesting an official, monumental history and also offering an archive with the possibility of retrieving forgotten and neglected images of opposition. The books on surveillance and the clinical gaze are contributions to a genealogy of vision that follows some Nietzschean suggestions. This project is like *The Birth of Tragedy* in juxtaposing distinct forms of visual culture, as Nietzsche contrasted the affirmative perspectivism of tragedy with the flattening out of vision ushered in by Socrates. Foucault seeks to identify an art that resists the clinical gaze and the corpse of anatomical observation with the radical image of experienced death or decay (as in Goya), or that counters the banal and soporific repetitions of advertising and television with the disruptive simulacra of Magritte and Warhol. A critical theory of our visual culture can learn from the Nietzschean attempt to counter the Cyclops eye with the hundred-eyed Argus of a perspectivism sensitive to the genealogy and archaeology of vision.

NOTES

1. Michel Foucault, *The Order of Things: An Archaeology of the Human Sciences* (New York: Random House, 1973), 9.

2. For Bosch, van Gogh, and Goya, see *Madness and Civilization*, trans. Richard Howard (New York: New American Library, 1967), 18, 29, 224–31; on painting and death, see *The Birth of the Clinic: An Archaeology of Medical Perception*, trans. A. M. Sheridan Smith (New York: Random House, 1975), 171; on Warhol, see *Language, Counter-Memory, Practice*, trans. Donald F. Bouchard and Sherry Simon (Ithaca: Cornell University Press, 1977), 189. Foucault's essay on Duane Michals is "La Pensée, l'émotion," in *Duane Michals: Photographies de 1958–1982* (Paris: Musée d'Art Moderne de la Ville de Paris, 1982), iii–vii; the essay on Fromanger is the introduction to the catalog *Fromanger: Le désir est partout* (Paris: Galerie Jeanne Bucher, 1975), n.p. (10 pp.).

3. See the remarks on Manet in Foucault, *Language, Counter-Memory, Practice*, 92–93; see also David Macey, *The Lives of Michel Foucault* (New York: Pantheon Books, 1993), 189.

4. Foucault, *The Birth of the Clinic,* xi.

5. For some suggestive remarks about Foucault's sense of the complex relations of the discursive and the visual, see Gilles Deleuze, *Foucault,* trans. Seán Hand (Minneapolis: University of Minnesota Press, 1988), 47–70.

6. Martin Jay, *Downcast Eyes: The Denigration of Vision in Twentieth-Century French Thought* (Berkeley: University of California Press, 1993), 383–416.

7. See Gary Shapiro, "French Aesthetics: Contemporary Painting Theory," in *The Encyclopedia of Aesthetics,* ed. Michael Kelly (New York: Oxford University Press, 1998), 2:235–40, for an attempt to develop this point succinctly with regard to a number of recent French philosophers.

8. Citations from Nietzsche's works are from the translations by Walter Kaufmann.

9. See Gary Shapiro, "In the Shadows of Philosophy: Nietzsche and the Question of Vision," in *Modernity and the Hegemony of Vision,* ed. David Michael Levin (Berkeley: University of California Press, 1993), and "Nietzsche and Visuality," in *The Encyclopedia of Aesthetics,* 3:364–66.

10. Foucault, *The Order of Things,* 9.

11. Michel Foucault, *This Is Not a Pipe,* trans. James Harkness (Berkeley: University of California Press, 1983), 30.

12. Gary Shapiro, "Pipe Dreams: Eternal Recurrence and Simulacrum in Foucault's Ekphrasis of Magritte," in *Word & Image* (January-March 1997): 69–76.

13. Foucault, *Language, Counter-Memory, Practice,* 189.

14. Foucault, *This Is Not a Pipe,* 54.

15. Johann Wolfgang von Goethe, *Italian Journey,* trans. Robert R. Heitner (New York: Suhrkamp, 1989), 364.

16. Nietzsche praises Burckhardt's *Cicerone* to Carl von Gersdorff in 1872, when he hears that the latter is planning a journey to Italy: "It seems to me that one should wake up and fall asleep with the reading of Burckhardt's *Cicerone:* there are few books that can so stimulate phantasy and prepare one for the conception of the artistic" (letter of 18 October 1872 [*KGB* II/3:68]); similar enthusiasm is expressed in a card to Mathilde Maier of 6 August 1878 (*KGB* II/5:345) and in a letter of 6 July 1883 to his sister Elisabeth, to whom he had just given a new edition of the book as a birthday gift (*KGB* III/1:391).

17. Louis Marin makes this point in his sensitive and complex essay, "Transfiguration in Raphael, Stendhal, and Nietzsche," in *Nietzsche in Italy,* ed. Thomas Harrison (Saratoga, Calif.: Anima Libri, 1988), 67–76.

18. Jacob Burckhardt, *Der Cicerone* (Stuttgart: Alfred Kroner Verlag, 1964), 857; I have generally followed the translation by Mrs. A. H. Clough (London: John Murray, 1879), 145.

19. Ibid.

20. Hans Belting, *Likeness and Presence: A History of the Image before the Era of Art,* trans. Edmund Jephcott (Chicago: University of Chicago Press, 1994).

21. I have attempted to make a similar suggestion in "Art and Its Doubles: Danto, Foucault, and Their Simulacra," in *Danto and His Critics,* ed. Mark Rollins (Cambridge, Mass.: Blackwell, 1993), 129–41, esp. 137–39.

22. Foucault, *This Is Not a Pipe,* 44.

23. See Jean-François Lyotard, "The Dream-Work Does Not Think," trans. Mary Lydon, in *The Lyotard Reader,* ed. Andrew Benjamin (Cambridge, Mass.: Blackwell, 1989), 19–55.

24. Michel Foucault, "Dream, Imagination, and Existence," trans. Forrest Williams, *Review of Existential Psychology and Psychiatry* 19, no. 1 (1986): 59.

CHAPTER 6

Zarathustrian Millennialism before the Millennium

From Bely to Yeats to Malraux

John Burt Foster, Jr.

I

As we know, Nietzsche—meaning both his thought and the arguments, positions, or motifs derived from it—pervades twentieth-century culture. Not only was he a catalyst in many fields besides philosophy, but his name became a byword for the most diverse national groups and among readers at all levels of sophistication. In weighing Nietzsche's significance at the threshold of a new millennium, we need to recall this past, for in one key respect it anticipates the project of this book. Among this century's writers and artists as well as the larger public, Nietzsche has again and again been identified with a major cultural transition, even to the point of personifying the end of one epoch and the dawn of another. Crucial in promoting this image has been a vivid but at times superficial and easily misunderstood motif in Nietzsche's thought: his Zarathustrian millennialism.

This form of time-consciousness, though taken from the hero of Nietzsche's best-known book, owes little to what the author claimed was his covert idea about time in *Thus Spoke Zarathustra* and the book's real philosophical point, the doctrine of eternal recurrence. Instead, it depends on Nietzsche's special sense of Zarathustra's historical situation, which in his autobiography, *Ecce Homo,* he explains in terms of a double identity. His hero was both the ancient Persian prophet Zoroaster (from the sixth century B.C.E.) and the present-day prophet of a "new humanity," who would undo the mistakes of his predecessor. As Nietzsche puts it, "Zarathustra created this most calamitous error, morality; consequently, he must also be the first to recognize it" (*WDB* 2:1153; *EH* "Destiny" 3). What Nietzsche means by morality is open to debate, and answers have tended to vary with what his readers see as the cultural status quo; but it is easier to define the millennial outlook embedded in the idea of *two* Zarathustras. History, this ancient-and-modern mouthpiece implies, divides into long intervals of thousands of years; these periods, including most emphatically Nietzsche's own, are marked by false assumptions and weakened human potential, but they do lead to short bursts of grand, revivifying cultural change.

As the name should suggest, Zarathustrian millennialism has an ambivalent relationship with Christianity. Millennialism in the West is traditionally associated with dates like 1000 and 1666, following a number mysticism that is obviously tied to the Christian calendar. But if the original Zarathustra flourished long before Christ, Persian Zoroastrianism did funnel into Christianity (as Nietzsche himself well knew). Moreover, most readers of *Zarathustra* notice its biblical tone and language, which differ strikingly from Nietzsche's other works of the 1880s. By the same token, though this decade lacks any obvious number symbolism, *Zarathustra* (along with Nietzsche's other works) first became widely popular somewhat later, in the 1890s. Its initial reception thus coincided with the fin de siècle, whose mood of anxiety and even crisis about the impending twentieth century certainly drew on a residual calendrical mysticism. That Nietzsche himself was insane during the entire decade, then died with ominous precision in 1900, only strengthened the case for conflating Zarathustrian millennialism with this more traditional analogue.

A similar ambivalence marks the willfully provocative title of Nietzsche's last book, *The Antichrist*. In German this phrase can actually mean "the anti-Christian," and given that the main target of Nietzsche's argument is Christianity rather than Christ, he probably had this meaning in mind. But for those who stop at titles, he had apparently invoked the arrival of the Antichrist, a traditional millennial prelude to Christ's world-ending Second Coming. And indeed, we might ask, what was the basic premise behind Zarathustra's double identity, if not a secularized revaluation of such a Second Coming—a return that instead of fulfilling prophecy takes back an error?

Within a decade, therefore, Zarathustrian millennialism could look like a brilliant anticipation of the fin-de-siècle spirit. Certain Nietzschean passages seem to support this view, like this question from *Twilight of the Idols:* "Is not the nineteenth century, especially at its close, . . . a century of *decadence?*" (*WDB* 2:1025; *TI* "Skirmishes" 50). Yet even this passage voices his distinctive time-consciousness, for not just the end of the nineteenth century but the entire century has fallen victim to a "calamitous error," here given the name "decadence." In other words, Nietzsche can fairly be called a "philosopher of the fin de siècle" only if we concede a significant displacement in the term. The French word *fin* gains a starker sense of finality, an implication that basic meanings and purposes in the culture have lost their validity. "End" no longer refers just to a calendrical unit; it means the disappearance of an entire system of values, the definitive closure of certain kinds of significance. Similarly *siècle,* rather than designate a period of one hundred years, regains some of the original meaning to be found in *saeculum,* or age. In most Nietzschean contexts, after all, decadence involves much more than the late nineteenth century; it reaches back over the whole of Western culture to various religious, philosophical, and ethical founding figures near the beginning of recorded history, with his character Zarathustra as a case in point.

In this millenarian context, it becomes clear that the many recent debates about Nietzsche's modernity or postmodernity have obscured a second crucial polarity in his outlook. Alongside the analyst of decadence stands a prophet of renewal—the figure who corresponds to the other, contemporary half of Zarathustra's dual identity. Or, to use Matei Calinescu's vocabulary in *Five Faces of Modernity,* Zarathustra's millennial time-consciousness unites the logic of decadence with the aspirations of the avant-garde.[1] This Nietzschean motif thus reveals the interdependence of two distinct approaches to cultural innovation: out of a fin-de-siècle sense of decadent, dying traditions grows the avant-garde quest for new beginnings.

In the United States the best-known, though also somewhat inadvertent, expression of Zarathustrian millennialism is probably *2001: A Space Odyssey* (1968), from a screenplay by the director Stanley Kubrick and the science fiction writer Arthur C. Clarke. Both the opening credits and the final sequence of this film are accompanied by the dramatic sunrise music from Richard Strauss's *Thus Spoke Zarathustra* (1896), soon to become a favorite theme for the Apollo astronauts. This music itself derives from the end-of-century reframing of Zarathustrian millennialism, as suggested by its original subtitle, "Symphonic optimism in fin-de-siècle form, dedicated to the twentieth century,"[2] which explicitly proclaimed a dualistic time-consciousness poised between cal-endrical endings and fresh beginnings. But Kubrick and Clarke's title of course overtrumps Strauss, for it shifts this attitude ahead to the true millennium, to the point of stressing the often ignored fact that the mil-lennial year is not 2000 but 2001. Such shifts forward in the crucial boundary date, we shall see, will occur repeatedly during the dissemina-tion of Zarathustrian millennialism.

Kubrick and Clarke's distant echo of Nietzsche preserves, more-over, some of its predecessor's ambivalence. Granted, the first segment of Zarathustrian music connects with images that seem remote from traditional Christian chronology: first an unearthly cosmic "sunrise" as glimpsed from behind the moon and earth in syzygy, then a caption evoking a Darwinian "dawn of man" four million years ago. But the film's last moments leading to the Richard Strauss reprise are less clear cut. After falling through an apparent hole in space, the hero comes back to himself in a strange hotel-like room, ages rapidly to a state of utter decrepitude, then becomes a newborn baby floating against the backdrop of the solar system, looking big as the sun. That mysterious final image could be the emblem for a utopian new epoch of extrater-restrial humanity, an avant-garde goal attained only after a prior phase of decadent senescence. But then again the cosmic baby could evoke the Nativity, the ultimate reference point, after all, for the film's title.[3]

The version of Zarathustrian millennialism made famous by 2001 is, however, just one in an array of representations that, usually linked only by their reference back to Nietzsche, have appeared at different sites during the twentieth century. Traces of the motif may be found, for ex-ample, in the ideas of epochal rupture that suffuse the thought of Hei-degger, Derrida, Deleuze, or Foucault. Looking beyond this philosophi-cal constellation, however, and mainly at novelists and poets who come before it, this chapter considers the presence of Zarathustrian millenni-alism within Western literature. I shall take three telling examples from widely separated subcultures and track the motif as it moves from the 1890s to the 1940s, starting in Russia with the symbolist novelist Andrey Bely. I shall then move to Anglo-Ireland and the poet William Butler Yeats (by way of his affinities with the German novelist Thomas Mann) and end in France with André Malraux at the cusp between his careers as leftist novelist and Gaullist public figure. Whatever other meanings Nietzsche may promise as we near the millennium, his mil-lennialism itself has already provoked a long, many-faceted, and reveal-ing response.

II

The Russian fascination with Nietzsche, which goes back to 1888 and some lectures given in St. Petersburg by the influential Danish critic Georg Brandes, is poorly known except among Russian scholars. Until recently two major obstacles were the banning of Nietzsche's writings in the Soviet Union and the drastic revaluation of most literature and culture from 1880 to 1920 to reflect the policies of the Bolshevik regime. Yet at times Nietzsche himself, who liked to imagine that his Polish-sounding name betokened Slavic ancestry, gave Russia top billing among the early signs of international interest that came his way just before he went insane in 1889. "I have only *choice* natures among my admirers," he could remark in a letter, "only high placed and influential people, in St. Petersburg, in Paris, in Stockholm, in Vienna, in New York" (*WDB* 3:1344; letter to Franziska Nietzsche, 21 December 1888).

As described in Bernice Rosenthal's *Nietzsche in Russia,* this Russian connection could take a startling array of forms, ranging from *either* neo-Christianity *or* neopagan sensationalism to what is now called Nietzschean Marxism. Behind the ferment, however, the basic time mystique of the fin de siècle is obvious, for Russians from a wide spectrum of ideological and artistic positions united to interpret Nietzsche as the spokesman for an apocalyptic, almost millenarian yearning for cultural renewal. Responding to his strong sense of contemporary decadence, in other words, they realized that this diagnosis was actually a challenge—one demanding an even more intense quest for innovation. Thus the symbolist painter Vrubel, a great admirer of Nietzsche, could state in 1899: "I am, after all, a certified decadent. But this is a misunderstanding." Reference elsewhere to "the so-called decadence, which I hope will soon be recognized as a renaissance," sets the record straight.[4]

Andrey Bely's novel *Petersburg,* originally written in 1913, is a delayed but revealing expression of this Russian enthusiasm for Nietzschean millennialism. No less a writer than Vladimir Nabokov considers this book the best Russian novel of the early twentieth century, on a par with the canonical work of Joyce, Proust, and Kafka. As a precocious, intellectually well-connected young man born in 1880, Bely gained his earliest impressions of contemporary culture in the 1890s. They included a first acquaintance with Nietzsche, whose impact was so riveting that Bely abandoned a prospective career in science to become a poet, a defender of symbolist aesthetics, and eventually a novelist; later he would claim that he had studied *Zarathustra* no less than seven times.

In this spirit, the first volume of his autobiography is called *On the Border of Two Centuries,* a title that is true to its literal time frame leading up to 1900, but which in a larger sense evokes a Zarathustrian polarity of two eras.[5] As the youthful Bely struggles to make the transition from science to art, we sense that an age of decadence is giving way to renewal and creativity.

Over a decade later, when starting to write *Petersburg,* Bely was still preoccupied with Nietzsche. Indeed, despite a decline in Russian interest in the philosopher, Bely even chose to work on his novel near Basel because of the Swiss city's links with Nietzsche's early career as a university professor. The main issue raised by the book's intricate, even esoteric staging of Zarathustrian millennialism is precisely the problem noted at the beginning of this chapter—that this motif could prompt such superficial and mistaken responses among its readers. For Bely in *Petersburg* takes pains to distinguish between Nietzsche's true followers and his facile vulgarizers, a point made by Nietzsche himself when he warned against the "ape of Zarathustra" (*WDB* 2:425–28; *Z*:3 "On Passing By"). The rich expressive texture of *Petersburg*—with its musical prose, its subtly interwoven motifs, and its quick succession of short, abruptly shifting units—is the best demonstration of what sophisticated readers could learn from Nietzsche. One of the novel's three main characters, however, is a self-proclaimed "Nietzschean," the term that Bely applied to mere vulgarizers.[6]

This character is Alexander Ivanovich Dudkin, a veteran of underground politics in the old Russian Empire who has now joined a terrorist group plotting to assassinate a highly placed bureaucrat. It gradually becomes clear that the motives for this deed are most ambiguous; like some actual terrorists at the time, the head terrorist in Bely's novel may be a double agent who hopes to use the assassination to advance his own position in the secret police. Alongside this utter cynicism, whose roots (the novel suggests) lie deep in Russian history, perhaps with Peter the Great's ruthless execution of his own son, Dudkin comes to seem naive and pathetic. He does not suspect that his group is a tool of double agents, he does not realize that the plot will require a son to use a bomb against his own father, and he cannot stand the solitude and anxiety of living as a conspirator on the run. Nonetheless, in explaining why he has become a terrorist, he names Nietzsche as the decisive influence: "Don't imagine I acted in the name of utopias or in the name of your strait and narrow way of thinking. After all I was a Nietzschean."[7]

Yet this credo, which meshes with the philosopher's praise for creative destruction or even with his notorious dynamite metaphor for the impact of his teachings, soon turns delirious. Dudkin suffers from horrifying dreams that, he confesses, end with an ominous nonsense phrase:

> He felt actual attacks of persecution mania, which continued in his dreams. . . . But what was most surprising, at such times there would come to memory the meaningless word *enfranshish*, the devil knows from where. (58)

In a book with many mysteries, this enigmatic word is perhaps the leading riddle; and scholars have suggested several answers. On an empirical plane Dudkin's word probably comes from the French phrase *en franchise*, to be seen on boxes of insect powder in his cockroach-infested apartment. On a metaphysical plane, *enfranshish* read backward becomes Shishnarfne, the Persian terrorist who later drives Dudkin to insanity, in a situation that dramatizes Bely's occult belief in the power of mirror words.[8] In the context of Zarathustrian millennialism, however, Bely's language play is a coded attack on Dudkin as a Nietzschean vulgarizer. It gives a ridiculous new name to the philosopher's Persian hero, and recasts his general critique of morality as a deeply compromised terrorist plot. Even Nietzsche's penchant for French terms such as *ressentiment* or *décadence,* in whose context *en franchise* could sound like a slogan for liberation, is reduced to nonsense.

Alongside this scorn for vulgarizers, *Petersburg* repeatedly works to postpone the end-of-century transition when decadence yields to renewal. This tendency, to become even more prominent with later writers, is hardly surprising given the course of twentieth-century history. Here Bely's novel contrasts with his autobiography, which in stressing the border between centuries had reverted to more traditional chronology. But in *Petersburg,* set during the nation's defeat in the Russo-Japanese War and the abortive Revolution of 1905, the boundary date has been delayed by five years. Later, when Bely revised the novel during the teens and twenties, he introduced after-the-fact prophecies of intervening historical events that imply further postponements. Thus in the epilogue, which shows another main character studying Egyptian antiquities in 1913 (when the novel first came out), that character glimpses the millennial moment when decadence finally reaches an end: "He foresees the fate of Egypt in the twentieth century. Culture is a moldering head: everything in it has died; nothing has remained. There will be an explosion: everything will be swept away" (292). The last sentence, a product of Bely's revisions, pushes the date of the crucial transition ahead to either 1914 or 1917 while keeping prudently silent about the value of the Bolshevik Revolution. *Petersburg* thus begins the process of detaching Zarathustrian millennialism from its original fin-de-siècle framework.

III

Bely's *Petersburg* is not the only major twentieth-century novel whose basic structure involves a deliberate deferral of late-nineteenth-century fears and expectations. Thus the very title of Joyce's *Portrait of the Artist as a Young Man* (1916) raises questions about how the concerns of its youthful 1890s hero relate to the mature art of a later, more modern age, as shown by Joyce's own style and method in telling the story. Similar issues mark *The Guermantes Way* (1920–21), the third volume of Proust's *Remembrance of Things Past,* where another, more easily distracted artist-to-be ascends the Parisian social hierarchy at the time of the Dreyfus case. In a more straightforward biographical manner, Woolf's stream-of-consciousness narrative in *Mrs. Dalloway* (1925) keeps circling back from 1920s London to the heroine's life in the 1890s, when her mature identity was established. Even Gide's *Lafcadio's Adventures* (1914), praised by its avant-garde contemporaries as a "cubist novel" worthy of Picasso or Braque, looks back to France and Italy in the 1890s for its parodic plot.

Among the novels that in varied ways project the fin de siècle ahead into the twentieth century, the most strikingly Nietzschean is Mann's *Doctor Faustus* (1947). Mann ingeniously retells Nietzsche's life as the biography of a composer, imagining an entire career that culminates in two masterworks, the *Apocalypse* oratorio and *The Lamentation of Doctor Faustus.* Because these works both focus on situations of "Last Judgment," they reawaken one of the traditional grounds for millennial expectation. But even as the novel uses details of Nietzsche's life and writings to comment on German history, it moves the philosopher's life ahead by some forty-five years. Thus Mann's Nietzsche-like hero goes insane about when the Nazis come to power, in the early 1930s (not in 1889); and he dies when Hitler's defeat is already obvious, in the mid-forties (not in 1900). During this period, however, his works have not become wildly popular, as Nietzsche's did in the 1890s; instead, they have been ignored by the regime.

By pushing Nietzsche's fin-de-siècle years ahead into the period of Nazi ascendancy, Mann gives a typically many-sided and sardonic response to Zarathustrian millennialism. On the issue of Germany's millennial dreams of a thousand-year Third Reich, he postpones the fateful turning point to 1945, implying that Hitlerism meant terminal decadence rather than renewal. On Zarathustra's role in that politics, often debated by historians, he creates a Nietzsche figure whose millennial music gets no hearing from the Nazis. But as the prominence of "Last Judgment" situations in his hero's work suggests, Mann rejects the very notion of moving beyond a Christian era chronology in the manner of Zarathustra, much less the idea of launching some broad critique of morality. Elsewhere, in fact, he dismisses this character as a cheap rhetorician exhibiting "hopeless *grandezza*," [9] implying that Zarathustra was a creation unworthy of Nietzsche's literary talents.

Yeats's poem "Politics," deliberately placed last in his collected *Poems*, responds quite harshly to some words of Mann's; but years earlier, in adopting a fuller, more sympathetic attitude toward Zarathustrian millennialism, Yeats in effect had already positioned himself as a contrasting counterpart to the German novelist. This attitude becomes especially clear and influential at several moments in the complex compositional history of his famous poem "The Second Coming" (1920). In 1922, when Yeats was nearing sixty, he published "The Trembling of the Veil," a much-revised account of his life in the 1890s and by far the longest part of his autobiography.[10] His title, from the French poet Mallarmé, addresses the mood of expectancy that often accompanied the fin-de-siécle sense of decline. Yeats explains:

> Is it true that our air is disturbed, as Mallarmé said, by "the trembling of the veil of the temple," or "that our whole age is seeking to bring forth a sacred book"? Some of us thought that book near towards the end of the last century, but the tide sank again. (210)

Despite the dismissive attitude toward the past evinced in this passage, Yeats's autobiography elsewhere shows his awareness of strong affinities between the fin-de-siècle spirit and the 1920s.

Nowhere are these connections more palpable than when Yeats recalls encounters in the 1890s with apocalyptic moods and images that, even as he wrote the autobiography, were reappearing in his poetry of the 1920s. Thus he discusses the prophecies of his old comrade Macgregor Mathers, who "began to foresee changes in the world, announcing in 1893 or 1894, the imminence of immense wars" (225). After wondering if this talk inspired some lines that he wrote back then about "unknown perishing armies," Yeats shifts almost imperceptibly to the 1920s. For when he mentions another of Mathers's ideas, his "often-repeated statement that anarchy would follow and accompany war," the phrase chimes with Yeats's recently written and now-famous couplet from the first stanza of "The Second Coming": "Things fall apart; the centre cannot hold; / Mere anarchy is loosed upon the world." Yeats had in fact cited the entire stanza earlier in "The Trembling of the Veil," introducing it with the ringing comment, "One thing I did not foresee, not having the courage of my thought: the growing murderousness of the world" (130). In this passage he explictly identifies the years of war, revolution, and disorder before 1922 as at once a deferral and an intensification of his fin-de-siècle intimations.

A climactic passage summing up Yeats's own contacts with the culture of the nineties again parallels "The Second Coming." Recalling his sense of impending change that would sweep away a fin-de-siècle milieu of overrefined and often self-destructive poets and painters, he exclaims "after our own verse, after all our subtle color and nervous rhythm . . . what more is possible? After us the Savage God" (234). This "Savage God" anticipates the "rough beast" in the poem's second stanza, slowly advancing with "a gaze blank and pitiless as the sun."

Unlike Mann, however, who first absorbed Nietzsche in the 1890s and saw him as mainly an analyst of decadence, Yeats only encountered him in 1902. At once recognizing an escape from the impasse of the 1890s, he read him with such fascination that he strained his eyes.[11] By the 1920s Yeats would give Nietzsche the role of "The Forerunner" in the grand psychohistorical system of *A Vision*, written concurrently with both the autobiography and "The Second Coming." The preface to this book is dedicated to Ezra Pound in Rapallo and ends with a reference to Descartes. Yet when, in a final image, Yeats compares "the mountain road from Rapallo to Zoagli" to "something in my own mind," he must also intend a tribute to *Zarathustra*, whose first part Nietzsche composed on walks along this very road.[12]

Yeats remains vague about the details, but Zarathustrian millennialism could in fact have been a forerunner for the basic time-consciousness of *A Vision*, which analyzes culture in terms of contrasting two-thousand-year dispensations. The parallels become even more striking when one epoch gives way to another, at a transitional moment like the one shown in "The Second Coming," which is said to arrive after "twenty centuries of stony sleep." Indeed, since the title of Yeats's poem applies a traditional millennial motif to the imagined emergence of a new cultural era, it actually does fulfill that secularization of religious imagery which was only latent in Nietzsche's *The Antichrist*. A similar twist marks the poem's last line, when it asks what rough beast "slouches towards Bethlehem to be born?" Here Yeats's end-of-century expectations of a "Savage God" have been recast, with all the tentativeness implied by the question mark, to suggest a more explicit Zarathustrian millennialism. Crucial in this regard is the startling allusion to Bethlehem, which not only functions as the place where an alien new era will "take back" an old one but also conveys two other Nietzschean attitudes: the sense of a long temporal perspective and the ambivalent rejection-and-awareness of a Christian date line.

In broader terms, the irregular two-stanza form of "The Second Coming" expresses a slippage inherent to Zarathustrian millennialism as it moves through the twentieth century. At some point the deferral and intensification of fin-de-siècle pessimism must turn into a dawning sense of the real millennium, and this is where Yeats puts the stanza break. In the first stanza we witness a deferral of the fin-de-siècle mood, which in Yeats's career did not originally derive from Nietzsche, despite his honorific title "Forerunner" in *A Vision*. As a result, when readers would ask Yeats about "the centre cannot hold" and other ominous (and now famous) phrases in this stanza, he at first identified this revival of his friend Mathers's prophecies with the year 1919. He meant the postwar turmoil before Irish independence or, abroad, Russo-German conflict in Eastern Europe after Versailles. In the 1930s, however, he liked to say that he had foreseen the rise of Hitler, an event arguably linked to his earlier concern with troubles in Eastern Europe. Yet if the first stanza pushes an end-of-century mood ever farther into the new century, Yeats's second stanza offers a drastic shift in temporal perspective. Beginning with a prophetic sense that "some revelation is at hand," this stanza quickly raises the stakes by twice renaming the event as a Second Coming. Readers glimpse the possibility of an even grander transition, one to be measured on a millennial clock of "twenty centuries." Yet its full meaning remains inscrutable because, as the poem says, "the darkness drops again" before it can be disclosed.

IV

In the early 1940s, in the interval between France's doomed war with Hitler and the rise of the Resistance, Malraux wrote *The Walnut Trees of Altenburg*. Left unfinished, it would be his last novel. But because it was never reprinted between 1950 and 1996 (except for two limited editions), it has been neglected, even though it anticipates his important work as an unconventional autobiographer.[13] The book also signals other major changes on Malraux's part, from roving internationalism to commitment to France, from a Popular Front outlook to Gaullism, and from immersion in the present to awareness of the past. As we shall see, this hinge work draws heavily on Zarathustrian millennialism, and even brings new life to the motif.

Walnut Trees depicts three generations of an Alsatian family in a looped sequence of sharply separated scenes. After opening with the grandson Vincent Berger as a French prisoner of war in 1940, it goes back to his father, grandfather, and great-uncle before and during World War I, when the Alsace was German;[14] it ends by returning to the grandson at war, shortly before he was taken prisoner. This temporal loop directly links the early part of the century to the recent French defeat. More specifically, since some of the earliest scenes in historical terms refer to Nietzsche—indeed they apportion facets of Zarathustrian millennialism among the family members—the novel's convoluted form becomes yet another vehicle for deferring and intensifying this motif. In fact, since Malraux reworked most of these scenes in his semiautobiographies of the sixties and seventies,[15] the structure of deferral is extended yet again, to include France's changed circumstances a generation later.

All three of the earlier, German Bergers have close ties with Nietzsche in their background, but the nature and implied worth of their contacts differ. The grandfather is intuitive but insightful, the great-uncle is aesthetic but narrowly exclusive, and the father passes from a superficial political attitude to broader cultural insight. Thus the grandfather, though never directly linked with Nietzsche, upholds a credo of total life affirmation much like the one that the philosopher associated with eternal recurrence, the main doctrine in *Zarathustra*: "If I had to live another life again, I should want none other than Dietrich Berger's (658/65)" (cf. *WDB* 2:202–3; *GS* 341). He is also deeply ambivalent about Christianity, but much more clearly than Nietzsche he is anti-Christian without being anti-Christ. Thus, though he has quarreled bitterly with Rome, he still faithfully attends Mass by standing outside the church during services (633–34/30–31).

His brother Walter, however, has actually known Nietzsche personally. The founder of an international conference center, he is proud to have helped rescue Nietzsche when he went insane twenty-five years earlier. On the trip back to Basel, when he heard Nietzsche sing his poem "Venice," Walter had a revelation: "It was sublime. . . . [T]he millennia of the starlit sky seemed as completely wiped out by man as our own petty destinies are wiped out by the starlit sky" (663, 664/72, 73).[16] Without naming *Zarathustra*, this passage highlights the lyric impulse of that book; it further implies that the great-uncle, like Bely, has recognized the millennial mood in Nietzsche but chooses to identify it exclusively with art. Yet despite Walter's direct contact with the fin-de-siècle roots of Nietzsche's fame, the narrative undercuts his approach. Not only is it suggested that Nietzsche disliked the great-uncle (667/77), but his insistence on human pettiness outside the privileged realm of art troubles Victor Berger, the third member of the clan (664/73), who has already had to confront his own mistaken views of Nietzsche.

Victor has just returned from the Ottoman Empire, where he became an adviser to the young Turks after drawing notice with his lectures on Nietzsche. "The echo of the still almost occult voice of Zarathustra did much," says the narrator, "to amplify the taut eloquence of Professor Vincent Berger, which was all the more striking in Turkish in that it made use of slogans instead of the traditional arabesque style" (637–38/36). Again going back to the origins of Nietzsche's fame, Malraux now points up another, explicitly politicized response to *Zarathustra*, based on vividness, compactness, and immediacy of communication. The story soon shows that, like Bely versus the "Nietzscheans," this sloganeering "voice of Zarathustra" is meant to reveal the failures of superficiality; but the non-Western setting adds an interesting variation. For in disrupting "traditional arabesque style," Zarathustra evokes millennial vistas on a different calendar. At first *Walnut Trees* stresses potential new beginnings, as Victor Berger advises the young Turks and then tries to stir up Turkish nationalism in central Asia. But when this mission fails, his entire political outlook collapses as well; and all that Berger sees in central Asia are the decadent fragments of an ancient religious dispensation: "The skeleton of Islam was the only framework supporting these people" (651/55). He returns home, eager for a fresh start. But even as the episode implies that his political Nietzsche is as mistaken as the uncle's aesthetic one, it usefully asks what Zarathustrian millennialism might mean once it is shifted outside the Western context to which it keeps an ambivalent attachment.

Victor's new approach to Nietzsche, wakened by discomfort with his uncle, crystallizes after he witnesses a fiery debate at one of Walter's colloquia, devoted to "The Permanence and Metamorphosis of Man." The topic has interested Victor in spite of himself, perhaps in part because Zarathustrian millennialism is predicated on the possibility of meta-

morphic cultural change. But only when he goes outdoors after the debate and gazes at the walnut trees of the title does he define his own
point of view. The result is a rich meditation on the role and significance
of culture that is all the more suggestive because Malraux republished it
at a time when he was still de Gaulle's minister of culture.[17]

This passage bears on Zarathustrian millennialism in three ways.
One involves Victor's very shift from politics to culture, which already
suggests a broader sense of Nietzsche. The second is his resistance to
extreme cultural compartmentalization, which would eliminate cross-
cultural understanding and, in the metaphor of one conferee, would re-
duce people within their culture to the situation of fish enclosed by the
walls of their aquarium (686/105). Zarathustrian millennialism, though
it stresses sharp breaks in one cultural tradition over time, would seem
to share these assumptions;[18] hence the enigmatic inscrutability of the
new dispensation heralded by Yeats's "rough beast." Victor's vision of
the walnut trees responds to this radical separatism by focusing on the
key role of creative struggle in all cultures, however disparate their traditions. Thus he recalls the wooden figures in Walter's conference hall,
which had previously illustrated the sharp contrast between a Gothic
past and a commercial present (691/111): "Between the statues and the
logs there were the trees, and their design which was as mysterious as
that of life itself" (694/116). Attention to the artifacts, he realizes, has
displaced the creativity of the human beings who made them.

Beyond moving from product to process in assessing culture, Victor's
reflections also foreshadow a more nuanced reading of *Zarathustra*. His
first detailed reaction to the walnut trees is especially revealing.

> The sense of fullness that surrounded the age-old trees came from their great
> bulk, but the effort by which the twisted branches sprang from the enormous
> trunks, the way the dark leaves burst forth from this wood, so old and so
> heavy that it seemed to sink itself into the earth rather than to drag itself
> out, imposed at once the idea of a will and a metamorphosis without end.
> (693/115)

Along with the Nietzschean phrasing in "fullness" or in reflexive verbs
like "sink itself," this sentence exploits, and perhaps even outdoes, the
metaphoric/parabolic style of *Zarathustra*.[19] It also recalls several key
Zarathustrian motifs: the command to remain faithful to the earth
(which counters the transcendental drift of Walter's aestheticism), the
emblematic use of trees to express key ideas,[20] and especially the initial
definition of the will to power in "On the Thousand and One Goals."

In a spirit similar to Malraux's character, this speech of Zarathustra's addressed the issue of large cultural differences and the creative process that underlies them. But in framing these ideas Nietzsche coined a term that was open to political abuse; as if wary about controversy over the will to power, Victor no longer echoes the "voice of Zarathustra" quite so closely. For if millennial feelings persist in the initial adjective "age-old," [21] the sentence ends by avoiding Nietzsche's signature phrase. It speaks only of a "will," then invokes "metamorphosis" instead of "power" to denote the grand moment of revivifying change. In thus declining to view the will to power solely or even mainly as power politics, Victor has shown that his earlier sloganeering has indeed given way to fuller cultural understanding.

This moment of independence sets the stage for later episodes of Walnut Trees, where Zarathustrian millennialism undergoes further mutations. One result is that Victor's response to Zarathustra continues to become more searching. When he sees some German soldiers break ranks to rescue the Russian victims of a gas attack in 1915, he first interprets their motives as an "assault of pity" (737/177). But then he corrects himself, insisting that he has witnessed "a very different deep impulse" (742/184), giving the impression that he agrees with Zarathustra's critique of pity (WDB 2:481; Z:4 "The Cry of Distress"). When he goes on to specify that the soldiers were driven by "anguish and fraternity," however, Victor shows that he has integrated Nietzschean ethics into a moral scheme of his own—one that his language indicates would join a Pascalian sense of human misery and desperation with more recent French ideals of democratic solidarity.

In these later episodes members of the Berger family also continue to feel millennial moods, but these feelings lose some of their earlier Nietzschean imprint. When Victor thinks about the soldiers' action, he finds that it reveals a facet of human nature "come from very far away in time," so that he can then call it an "Apocalypse of Humanity" (742/185). This phrase, with its ambivalent secularization of a traditional millennial motif, still recalls Nietzsche; but it emphasizes humanity rather than a Zarathustrian "superhumanity." A similar shift in mood occurs in the last section of Walnut Trees, which jumps ahead to the French defeat in 1940. After a frantic struggle to escape a tank trap the previous night, Vincent Berger wakes up in a village almost deserted because of the war; he is dazzled by the signs of ordinary human activity, which take on millennial proportions. Everything before him (it seems) has emerged "from the depths of time," whether it evokes "the

Gothic Age" or "the wells of the Bible," whether it resounds with "a hum of centuries" or comes to him "across the millennia" (764–65/221–22). Once again, motifs of Christian revelation mingle confusedly with something else, in this case even more remote from Zarathustra—an evocation of ordinary humanity in the guise of perennial France.

Notably absent, of course, is any strident rhetoric about the "French" nature of the scene, which in fact the narrative is careful to identify as "Flemish." And yet this millennial vision of a farm village in defeat, which is poised nonetheless on the brink of renewal—sensed above all in the ironic smile of a peasant woman too old to flee (766/224), perhaps a superannuated Marianne waiting for a "Carnot of the Year II"[22]—anticipates Malraux's future as a French public figure. The author would confirm the link again and again, beginning in 1944 when "Berger" became his pseudonym in the Resistance. Then in the sixties, when he was closest to de Gaulle, he would rework this dazzled vision of an ordinary farm village for his semiautobiographical *Antimémoires;* and finally in the seventies, when enlarging this work to form *Le miroir des limbes,* he made the book's final words refer back to the old woman's ironic smile.[23] With the author's entry into the Pantheon in 1996, this reframing of Zarathustrian millennialism in terms of French defeat and renewal would gain official recognition.

Malraux thus offers the clearest and most elaborate example of an ambiguity basic to Zarathustrian millennialism: it both refers and does not refer to the Christian calendar. Initially energized by the nineteenth-century fin de siècle, then carried past that deadline by the various disasters of twentieth-century Western history, this mood of crisis can actually flourish at many different times and places—and certainly outside Germany, as the diverse origins of our three main writers indicate, and even, as Malraux suggests, outside the West. Nor does it have to be true to the basic tenor of Nietzsche's thought or to its many nuances, as shown in the repeated attempts (by Bely as well as Malraux) to fend off partial or mistaken interpretations, or to try to bring one's own work closer to Nietzsche's "real" or "most relevant" meaning. Lacking any necessary connection with the year 2001 (despite Kubrick/Clarke or Yeats's "twenty centuries"), it is—quite simply—a millennialism before the millennium. It might even be called, in an echo of Malraux's flirtation with Trotsky in the thirties, a state of "permanent" millennialism. Standing at the cusp between decadent and avant-garde modes of cultural innovation, Zarathustra exhorts his audiences to creativity by ask-

ing, "What if the thousands of years of recorded history were placed under erasure?" Like many other readers of Nietzsche's most popular, if
not his best, book, Bely, Yeats, and Malraux tried to meet this challenge,
whose power should continue to make itself felt as long as people face
rapid change—millennium or no millennium.

NOTES

All Nietzsche translations are by Walter Kaufmann. Several ideas in this chapter were first developed in "From Turin to St. Petersburg and Beyond: Nietzsche
as Philosopher of the Fin de Siècle," a lecture given at the Smithsonian Institution in Washington, D.C., for a course titled "Great European Cities of the Fin
de Siècle: Elegance and Decadence," organized by Richard Pettit, 29 January
1991.

1. Matei Calinescu, *Five Faces of Modernity: Modernism, Avant-Garde,
Decadence, Kitsch, Postmodernism* (Durham: Duke University Press, 1987). The
very title of this book reflects the modernity-postmodernity debate, as its first
edition (1977) was simply called *Faces of Modernity: Avant-Garde, Decadence,
Kitsch*. Calinescu discusses Nietzsche mainly under the heading of decadence.
   2. Cited in Kurt Wilhelm, *Richard Strauss: An Intimate Portrait*, trans. Mary
Whittall (New York: Rizzoli, 1989), 72.
   3. Clarke's sequel, *2010: Odyssey Two* (New York: Ballantine, 1982),
makes it clear that he intended something quite different (perhaps a digitaliza-
tion of the hero's memories and his rebirth as an electronic field), but the interplay
of the Richard Strauss music with the film's images (in the absence of words) creates its own, quite independent set of implied meanings.
   4. Bernice Glatzer Rosenthal, ed., *Nietzsche in Russia* (Princeton: Princeton
University Press, 1986), 241. For neo-Christianity, neopaganism, and Nietzschean Marxism, respectively, see Rosenthal's "Stages of Nietzscheanism: Me-
rezhkovsky's Intellectual Evolution," 69–94; Edith Clowes's "Literary Reception as Vulgarization: Nietzsche's Idea of the Superman in Neo-Realist Fiction,"
315–30; and George L. Kline's foreword, xi–xvi.
   5. Andrey Bely, *Na Rubezhe Dvukh Stoletij* (1930; reprint Letchworth,
U.K.: Bradda, 1966).
   6. Andrey Bely, "Fridrikh Nitsshe," *Arabeski* (1911; reprint Munich: Fink,
1969), 80. Bely originally wrote this essay in 1907.
   7. Andrey Bely, *Petersburg*, trans., introd., and annotations Robert A.
Maguire and John E. Malmstad (Bloomington: Indiana University Press, 1978),
57. All later references appear parenthetically in the text.
   8. Omry Ronen (cited in *Petersburg*, 346–47) established the link between
enfranshish and insect powder, noting as well that the Russian term for such
powder is "Persian powder," thus accounting for the Persian origins of Shishnarfne. Vladimir Alexandrov has shown Bely's interest in Rudolf Steiner's doc-

trine that mirror words reveal a spiritual absolute; Steiner was also an early-twentieth-century exegete of Nietzsche. See Alexandrov's "Unicorn Impaling a Knight: The Transcendent and Man in Andrei Belyi's *Petersburg*," *Canadian-American Slavic Studies* 16, no. 1 (Spring 1982): 20.

9. Thomas Mann, "Nietzsche's Philosophy in the Light of Recent History," in *Last Essays*, trans. Richard Winston, Clara Winston, Tania Stern, and James Stern (New York: Knopf, 1959), 149.

10. William Butler Yeats, *The Autobiography of William Butler Yeats* (1916, 1935; reprint New York: Macmillan, 1965); all later references appear parenthetically in the text. "The Trembling of the Veil" comprises almost half of a six-part book so diverse in style and date of composition that it was originally called *Autobiographies*. An earlier version, written in about 1915 and not meant for publication, has been edited by Dennis Donoghue and is included in *Memoirs* (New York: Macmillan, 1973), 19–134.

11. "To Lady Gregory," [26 September 1902?], *The Letters of W. B. Yeats*, ed. Allan Wade (New York: Macmillan, 1953), 379.

12. William Butler Yeats, *A Vision* (New York: Macmillan, 1938), 7. This introductory passage is dated 1928. Compare Yeats's reference to the Rapallo-Zoagli road with Nietzsche's account of how he wrote part 1 of *Zarathustra*, *WDB* 2:1129. For Nietzsche as "The Forerunner," see *A Vision*, 126–29.

13. The novel has been recently reissued and carefully edited in *André Malraux: Oeuvres complètes, tome II,* introd. Michel Autrand, ed. Marius-François Guyard, Maurice Larès, and François Trécourt with the participation of Noël Burchin (Paris: Pléiade, 1996). The English translation has also been reprinted as *The Walnut Trees of Altenburg*, trans. A. W. Fielding, foreword by Conor Cruise O'Brien (Chicago: University of Chicago Press, 1992). Unfortunately, this translation does not preserve some nuances of Malraux's French that are relevant to this chapter; I have revised it when necessary. All later references appear parenthetically in the text, with the Pléiade version first and then the English translation, in the following format: (683/22).

14. Malraux gave the name Berger to this family because it could be either French or German.

15. Eventually collected to form *Le miroir des limbes* (1976), these writings began with *Antimémoires* in 1967 and continued with *Les chênes qu'on abat* (1971), *La tête d'obsidienne* (1974), *Lazare* (1974), and *Hôtes de passage* (1975). For a critical edition of the entire work, see *André Malraux: Oeuvres complètes, tome III,* introd. Marius-François Guyard, ed. Marius-François Guyard with the participation of Jean-Claude Larrat and François Trécourt (Paris: Pléiade, 1996).

16. For this poem, see *WDB* 2:1093; *EH* "Clever" 7.

17. It was the first section of *Antimémoires,* placed directly after the introduction in a unit called "The Walnut Trees of Altenburg."

18. Seguin, a participant in the colloquium who argues against cultural compartmentalization, seems to make the same assumption: "The isolation of civilisations in the course of time, which was probable in face of the millennia, seemed relative, and even doubtful, when speaking about historical civilisations;

that he could not feel himself as different from a man of the twelfth century as from an Egyptian of the early dynasties" (688–89/108).

19. In discussing *Zarathustra*'s style, Nietzsche himself stressed the central role of the *Gleichnis,* a word that can mean either "metaphor" or "parable." Hence he gives the following description of the book's intellectual movement: "Here on every *Gleichnis* you ride to every truth" (*WDB* 2:1132; *EH* "Books" Z 3)

20. For the significance of tree imagery in Nietzsche, see Eva Geulen, "Nietzsche's Trees—and Where They Grow," in *Signs of Change: Premodern, Modern, Postmodern,* ed. Stephen Barker (Albany: SUNY Press, 1996), 97–108.

21. The French word here is *séculaire,* the adjective from *siècle,* or century, just as *millénaire* comes from the French word for "millennium." Malraux's association of both words with cultural compartmentalization surfaced earlier in the colloquium, where one participant objected to thinking in centuries as a way of avoiding the difficulties that a millennial outlook poses for cultural continuity: "Carving the millennia up into centuries does not affect Mr. Möllberg's argument" (689/108).

22. Marianne is a symbol of the French Republic, and Carnot was the member of the Committee of Public Safety who in 1794 organized the victory of Fleurus, near France's northern border in the same general area as Berger's Flemish village. The image of Carnot in the year II, which uses the republican calendar to introduce yet another time line with its associated dispensation, appears in Malraux's oration at the Pantheon for Jean Moulin, the official leader of the Resistance. He explicitly connects an old woman symbolizing the Republic with Fleurus when he describes de Gaulle's assumption of full powers in 1958. See *Le miroir des limbes, Oeuvres,* 3:453, 115.

23. *Le miroir des limbes, Oeuvres,* 3:219–40, 879.

PART TWO

Cultural Dramatics

CHAPTER 7

Circuits of Bad Conscience

Nietzsche and Freud

Judith Butler

Nietzsche offers a view of conscience as a mental activity that not only forms various psychic phenomena, but is itself *formed*, the consequence of a distinctive kind of internalization. In Nietzsche, who distinguishes conscience from bad conscience, the will is said to turn back upon itself. But what are we to make of this strange locution; how are we being asked to imagine a will such that it recoils and redoubles upon itself; and how, most pertinently, is this figure being offered as a way to articulate the kind of reflexivity central to the operation of bad conscience? Freud will use a similar language in writing of the formation of conscience, especially in relation to paranoia and narcissism. He describes conscience as the force of a desire—although sometimes a force of aggression—as it turns back on itself, and he understands prohibition, not as a law external to desire, but as the very operation of desire as it turns on its own possibility. What sense do we make of the figure that emerges in the context of both explanations, that of a will that turns back on itself, that of a desire that turns back on itself? We must ask not only how this figure of recoiling and redoubling becomes central to understanding bad conscience, but what this figure suggests about the bodily position or disposition encoded in the structure of reflexivity. Why does a body doubled over on itself figure what it means to be a self-conscious sort of being?

The notion that morality is predicated on a certain kind of violence is already familiar, but more surprising is that such violence founds the subject. Morality performs that violence again and again in cultivating the subject as a reflexive being. This is, in part, what led Nietzsche to reflect that morality is a kind of illness. If this turning on oneself can be called a kind of violence, it cannot simply be opposed in the name of nonviolence, for when and where it is opposed, it is opposed from a position that presupposes this very violence. I do not wish simply to underscore the aporetic structure involved in the assumption of morality, nor simply to affirm the generalized violence in any and all moral positioning, although both insights, furnished by deconstruction, form a point of departure for what I seek to do. Rather, I would suggest that the subject who would oppose violence, even violence to itself, is itself the effect of a prior violence without which the subject could not have emerged. Can that particular circle be broken? How and when does that breakage occur? And what emerges as a significant possibility in which the subject loses its closed contour, the circularity of its own reflexive closure? A pure will, ontologically intact prior to any articulation, does not suddenly emerge as a principle of self-augmentation and self-affirmation that exceeds the bounds of any and all regulatory schemas. Rather, the formative and fabricating dimension of psychic life, which travels under the name of the "will," and which is usually associated with a restrictively aesthetic domain, proves central to refashioning the normative shackles that no subject can do without, but which no subject is condemned to repeat in exactly the same way.

My inquiry concerns a persistent problem that emerges when we try to think the possibility of a will that takes itself as its own object and, through the formation of that kind of reflexivity, binds itself to itself, acquires its own identity through reflexivity. To what extent is this apparent self-bondage fully or exclusively self-imposed? Is this strange posture of the will in the service of a social regulation that requires the production of the subject a consequence or an expression of bad conscience? I suppose that those who seek to redeem Nietzsche by claiming that he can be invoked in the service of the ethical might think that the only alternative worse than bad conscience is its obliteration. But remember that Nietzsche not only distinguishes between the ethical and morality, but asks about the *value* of morality, thus instating a value by which morality might be assessed, but suggesting as well that this assessment, this valuation, may not be reducible to morality.

I take it that the juxtaposition of Nietzsche with the question of ethics is, indeed, a question because Nietzsche and various figures within the Continental tradition have been found guilty by association with irresponsible acts and events. What will be the response to these charges?

To take the side of the ethical, to relate each and every thinker to the ethical? Or will this be an occasion to think the problem a bit more carefully, to continue to pose the ethical as a question, one which cannot be freed of its complicity with what it most strongly opposes? Will this, paradoxically, become a time in which we reflect upon the more pervasive dimensions of complicity and what might be derived from such a vexed relation to power?

I understand the desire to resituate Nietzsche within the ethical domain as an effort to counter the caricature, within contemporary criticism, of Nietzsche as one who only destroys the domain of values (where that destruction is not itself a source of value, or a value in itself). I want instead to suggest that Nietzsche offers us a political insight into the formation of the psyche and the problem of subjection, understood paradoxically not merely as the subordination of a subject to a norm but as the constitution of a subject through precisely such a subordination. Indeed, to the extent that bad conscience involves a turning against oneself, a body in recoil upon itself, how does this figure serve the social regulation of the subject, and how might we understand this more fundamental subjection, without which no proper subject emerges? I want to suggest that, although there is no final undoing of the reflexive bind, that posture of the self bent against itself, a passionate deregulation of the subject may perhaps precipitate a tenuous unraveling of that constitutive knot. What emerges is not the unshackled will or a "beyond" to power, but another direction for what is most formative in passion, a formative power which is at once the condition of its violence against itself, its status as a necessary fiction, and the site of its enabling possibilities. This recasting of the "will" is not, properly speaking, the will of a subject, nor is it an effect fully cultivated by and through social norms; it is, I would suggest, the site at which the social implicates the psychic in its very formation—or, to be more precise, *as* its very formation and formativity.

Consider the general claim that the social regulation of the subject compels a passionate attachment to regulation, and that this formation of the will takes place in part through the action of a repression. Although one is tempted to claim that social regulation is simply internalized, taken from the outside and brought into the psyche, the problem is more complicated and, indeed, more insidious. For the boundary that divides the outside from the inside is in the process of being installed, precisely through the regulation of the subject. The repression is the very turning back on itself which the passionate attachment to subjection performs. How can a will be enticed to make such a turn? Are we to think that turn as an internal bending of the psyche against itself? If so, why is it figured as a body that turns on and against itself? Are the psychic and the somatic articulated through one another in such a way that the figuration of the first is implicated invariably in a chiastic relation to the second? Clearly, what is at stake is something more than and different from a relation between an external demand offered by regulatory power and an internal recoil registered as its secondary effect. If presupposed in the very notion of the subject is a passionate attachment to subjection, then the subject will not emerge save as an exemplification and effect of this attachment. I hope to show, first through a consideration of Nietzsche, then in relation to Freud, how the very notion of reflexivity, as an emergent structure of the subject, is the consequence of a "turning back on itself," a repeated self-beratement which comes to form the misnomer of "conscience," and that there is no formation of the subject without a passionate attachment to subjection.

Significantly, Nietzsche attributes a creative or formative power to conscience, and the act of turning back upon oneself is not only the condition of the possibility of the subject, but the condition of the possibility of fiction, fabrication, and transfiguration. Indeed, Nietzsche remarks that bad conscience *fabricates* the soul, that expanse of interior psychic space. If the subject is understood as a kind of necessary fiction, then it is also one of the first artistic accomplishments presupposed by morality. The artistic accomplishments of bad conscience exceed the purview of the subject; indeed, they will come to include "all ideal and imaginative phenomena," including conceptual thinking, figurative writing, and the conjectured fables and myths which compose the various retrospective imaginings of genealogy. In this sense, the condition of possibility of Nietzsche's own writing appears to be the bad conscience for which it seeks to give an account.

Nietzsche offers a narrative that seeks to account for this formation, but his narrative will be afflicted from the start by the very conscience that it seeks to uncover for us. The claim that conscience is a fiction is not to be confused with the claim that conscience is arbitrary or dispensable; on the contrary, it is a necessary fiction, one without which the grammatical and phenomenological subject cannot exist. But if its fictive status does not dispel its necessity, how are we to construe the sense of that necessity? More precisely, what does it mean to say that a subject emerges only through the action of turning back on itself? If this turning back on oneself is a trope, a movement which is always and only *figured* as a bodily movement but which no body literally performs, in what will the necessity of such a figuration consist? The trope appears to be the shadow of a body, a shadowing of that body's violence against itself, a body in spectral and linguistic form that is the signifying mark of the psyche's emergence.

Considered grammatically, it will seem that there must first be a subject who turns back on itself, yet I will argue that there is no subject except as a consequence of this very reflexivity. How can the subject be presumed at both ends of this process, especially when it is the very formation of the subject for which this process seeks to give an account?

If, in Freud, conscience is a passionate attachment to *prohibition,* an attachment which takes the form of a turning back on oneself, does the formation of the ego take place as the sedimented result of this peculiar form of reflexivity? The noun form *ego* will then reify and mask the iterated accumulation of this reflexive movement. Of what is this reflexivity composed? What is it that is said to turn back upon what? And what composes the action of "turning back upon"? I want to suggest that this logical circularity in which the subject appears at once to be presupposed and not yet formed, on the one hand, or formed and hence not presupposed, on the other, is ameliorated when one understands that in both Freud and Nietzsche this relationship of reflexivity is always and only figured, and that this figure makes no ontological claim. To refer to a "will," much less to its "turning back on itself," is a strange way to speak, strange because it figures a process which cannot be detached from or understood apart from that very figuration. Indeed, for Nietzsche, the writing of such figurations, and figuration in general, are part and parcel of the "ideal and imaginative phenomena" which are the consequences of bad conscience. Hence we do not come to know something about bad conscience when we consider the strange figure of reflexivity that Nietzsche offers us. We are, as it were, caught up in the luring effects of bad conscience at the very textual moment when we seek to know what, precisely, this bad conscience is. If it is credited with being the ground of figuration, yet can itself only be figured—indeed, figured *as* that ground—the circularity which might be lamented from a logical perspective concerned with establishing clear sequence becomes the constitutive feature of bad conscience, considered both as a figure and as the condition of possibility for figuration itself.

The apparent circularity of this account reappears in a related set of quandaries. What motivates the will to turn back on itself? Does it turn back on itself under the pressure of an external force or law, under the anticipated or recollected force of punishment? Or does this peculiar form of reflexivity take place prior to, or in some other form of complicity with, a set of externally imposed demands?

To clarify this last point it is important to reconsider the thesis that punishment precedes conscience and that conscience can be understood as the unproblematic internalization of punishment, its mnemonic trace. Although there are clearly textual moments in which Nietzsche appears to be arguing for such a temporal priority of punishment to conscience, there are also competing views in Nietzsche which call this sequential account into question.

If the will in Nietzsche is at its most productive—that is, its most conscientious—when it is turned back upon itself, then it appears that the severity of conscience is linked to the strength of the will of which it is composed. Similarly, for Freud, the strength of conscience is nourished precisely by the aggression that it forbids. In this sense, then, the strength of conscience correlates neither with the strength of a punishment received nor with the strength of a memory of a punishment received *but with the strength of one's own aggression,* one which is said to have vented itself externally but which now, under the rubric of bad conscience, is said to vent itself internally. This latter venting is also at the same time a fabricating: an internalization which is produced or fabricated as the effect of a sublimation.

This circularity appears to break the line of causality or internalization usually conjectured between an external or historical experience of punishment and an internalization of the mnemonic trace of that punishment in the form of conscience. But if conscience is self-derived in this way, and not derived unilaterally from an internalization of an external or historical punishment, is there some other way to understand its function in the process of social regulation? Is it possible to understand the force of punishment outside of the ways in which it exploits a narcissistic demand, or, to put it in a Nietzschean vein, is it possible to understand the force of punishment outside of the ways in which it exploits the will's attachment to itself?

To claim that there is a passionate attachment to subjection appears to presuppose that there is first a passion and that its aim is to attach to some kind of object. In Nietzsche, there will emerge a question of whether this primary passion, this will, precedes the attachments by which it is known, or whether its attachments precede its passions or acquire their passionate character only after an attachment is assumed. (It may invariably be both, participating in an incommensurable set of temporal trajectories. In some ways, we might see this question as pervading the debates between Lacanian and object-relations construals of Freud.)

NIETZSCHE'S ACCOUNT OF BAD CONSCIENCE

Nietzsche's consideration of bad conscience in *On the Genealogy of Morals* is introduced in section 16 of the second essay. At first the relation of this notion to the notion of conscience introduced earlier in the same essay is unclear. Conscience is introduced via the animal who is bred to keep promises, and in relation to the "sovereign" man. The one who makes and keeps his promise is one who "has bred in himself a . . . faculty" opposed to forgetfulness, namely, a memory, which becomes "a *memory of the will*" (*GM* II:1). Here Nietzsche refers to an "impression" that is actively sustained by a desire, one which is not forgotten but which, in being actively remembered, produces the protracted continuity of the will. But this impression is not specified. An impression from where? In the service of what? Nietzsche then insists that the one who makes promises will not allow anything to interrupt the process by which an original statement, "I will" or "I shall do this," culminates in the discharge of the designated act. The one who truly promises wields the power of the sovereign to enact what he says, to bring into being what he wills. In other words, the promising being establishes a continuity between a statement and an act, although the temporal disjunction between the two is acknowledged as an opportunity for the intervention of various competing circumstances and accidents. In the face of these circumstances and accidents, the will continues to produce itself, to labor on itself in the service of making of itself a continuity, where that continuity, that "long chain of will," as Nietzsche puts it, establishes its own temporality over and against any other which might seek to complicate or qualify its execution. This promising being is one who stands for himself through time and whose word continues through time, one "who gives [his] word as something that can be relied on because [h]e know[s] himself to be strong enough to maintain it in the face of accidents" (*GM* II:2). This protracted will, which is self-identical through time and which establishes its own time, constitutes the man of conscience. (Oddly enough, this ideal of the efficacious speech act presupposed by promising is undercut by Nietzsche's own notion of the sign chain, according to which a sign is bound to signify in ways that estrange the sign from the originating intentions by which it is mobilized. According to the historicity of the sign chain, it would be impossible to keep a promise, because it would be impossible to safeguard a sign from the various historical accidents by which its meaning is augmented in excess of its originating intentions.)

In section 3, which follows this discussion, Nietzsche reconsiders this idealization of the promising animal and asks how a memory can be created for a will. This returns us to the question concerning the status of the "impression" that is actively reanimated and relived, and which, in and through its reanimation, establishes the protracted continuity of the will. "If something is to stay in the memory, it must be burned in; only that which never ceases to *hurt* stays in the memory" (*GM* II:3). And we then learn of the "terror" that formerly attended all promises. Is this "terror," then, to be construed as the "impression" that works as the mnemonic device whereby the will makes itself regular and calculable? By section 4, Nietzsche poses the question of bad conscience explicitly but continues to treat it as if it were quite separate from conscience itself. He asks: How did "that other 'somber thing,' the consciousness of guilt, the 'bad conscience,' come into the world?" (*GM* II:4). But is it *other?* Is there a way for the will to become regular, to become the protracted continuity which underwrites the promise, without becoming subject to the logic of bad conscience?

Well-traveled discussions of the relation between debt and guilt follow (*GM* II:4), in which the failure to repay a loan awakens the desire for compensation in the creditor and injury is inflicted on the debtor. The attribution of moral accountability to the debtor thus rationalizes the desire of the creditor to punish the debtor. With that notion of "accountability" emerges a whole panoply of morally saturated psychic phenomena: intentionality, even certain versions of the will itself. But the desire to punish cannot be fully accounted for by the circumstances of the broken contract. Why does the creditor take pleasure in the infliction of injury, and what form does that pleasure take when injury is inflicted in the moralized action by which the creditor holds the debtor morally accountable and pronounces him guilty? What strange consummation of pleasure takes place in that attribution of guilt?

This account of how the attribution of guilt originates is not yet the formation of bad conscience (which would, of course, be the self-attribution or self-infliction of guilt). It presupposes that a contract has been broken, and the existence of the contract presupposes the institution of promising. Indeed, the debtor is one who fails to keep his promise, protract his will, and discharge his word in the execution of an act.

The punishment of the debtor thus presupposes the model or ideal of the promising animal, yet this promising animal could not come into being without the impressions of terror produced by punishment. The punishment of the debtor appears to emerge in response to an injury, the debt being cast as that injury, but the response takes on a meaning that exceeds the explicit purpose of achieving compensation. For the punishment is pleasurable, and the infliction of injury is construed as a seduction to life (*GM* II:6).

If this complicated scene animates the creditor, how do we understand the formation of bad conscience in the debtor? Nietzsche writes, "Punishment is supposed to have the value of awakening the *feeling of guilt* in the guilty person; one seeks in it the actual *instrumentum* of that psychical reaction called 'bad conscience,' 'sting of conscience' " (*GM* II:14).

But Nietzsche takes his distance from this formulation, since not merely psychic reactions but the psyche itself is the instrument of this punishment. The internalization of instinct—which takes place when the instinct does not immediately discharge as the deed—is understood to produce the soul or the psyche instead; the pressure exerted from the walls of society forces an internalization which culminates in the production of the soul, this production being understood as a primary artistic accomplishment, the fabrication of an ideal. This fabrication appears to take the place of the promise, the word actualized as deed, and to emerge on the condition that the promise has been broken. But recall that the execution of the deed was not without its fabrications: one effect of the promise is to produce an "I" which might stand for itself across time. Thus the fabrication of such an "I" is the paradoxical result of the promise. The "I" becomes continuous with its deed, but its deed is, paradoxically, to create the continuity of itself.

Bad conscience would be the fabrication of interiority that attends the breaking of a promise, the discontinuity of the will, but the "I" who would keep the promise is precisely the cultivated effect of this continuous fabrication of interiority. Can there even be a promising being, one who is able to discharge words into deeds, without the bad conscience which forms the very "I" who makes good his word through time, who has a memory of the will, and for whom the psyche has already been produced?

Nietzsche describes "bad conscience in its beginnings" as the "*instinct for freedom* forcibly made latent" (*GM* II:17). But where is the trace of this freedom in the self-shackling that Nietzsche describes? It is to be found in the pleasure taken in afflicting pain, a pleasure taken in afflicting pain on oneself in the service of, in the name of, morality. This pleasure in affliction, attributed earlier to the creditor, thus becomes, under the pressure of the social contract, an internalized pleasure, the joy of persecuting oneself. The origin of bad conscience is, thus, the joy taken in persecuting oneself, where the self persecuted does not exist outside the orbit of that persecution. But the internalization of punishment is the very production of the self, and it is in this production that pleasure and freedom are curiously located. Punishment is not merely productive of the self, but this very productivity of punishment is the site for the freedom and pleasure of the will, its fabricating activity.

As a peculiar deformation of artistry (which is, of course, indistinguishable from its primary formation), self-consciousness is the form the will takes when it is prevented from simple expression as a deed. But is the model by which an instinct or a will expresses or discharges itself in a deed in any sense prior to this self-thwarted expression of bad conscience? Can there be a model of promising that does not from the first presuppose bad conscience? The noble is described earlier as one for whom his work is "an instinctive creation and imposition of forms . . . the most involuntary and unconscious artists [that] there are" (*GM* II:17). The soul is precisely what a certain violent artistry produces when it takes itself as its own object. The soul, the psyche, is not there prior to this reflexive move, but this reflexive turning of the will against itself produces in its wake the metaphorics of psychic life.

If we understand the soul to be the effect of imposing a form upon oneself, where the form is taken to be equivalent to the soul, then there can be no protracted will, no "I" that stands for itself through time, without this self-imposition of form, this moral laboring on oneself. This fundamentally artistic production of bad conscience, the production of a "form" from and of the will, is described by Nietzsche as "the womb of all ideal and imaginative phenomena" (*GM* II:18). Bad conscience is fabricated, but it in turn is credited with the fabrication of all ideal and imaginative phenomena. Is there, then, any way to answer the question of whether artistry precedes bad conscience or is its result? Is there any way to postulate something before this "turning back upon itself" which is the tropic foundation of the subject and all artistry, including all imagination and conceptual life?

If bad conscience *originates* imaginative and ideal phenomena, then it is difficult to imagine which of Nietzsche's fabulous genealogical terms would not finally be attributable to this bad conscience. Indeed, his project of offering a genealogy of bad conscience appears to founder when the very terms he will use to account for this formation turn out to be the effect of this formation itself. Elsewhere he will refuse, for instance, to accept the notion of the will as a conceptual given. In *Beyond Good and Evil* he writes, "willing seems to me to be . . . something *complicated,* something that is a unit only as a word" (*BGE* 19). Once willing is elevated to the status of a philosophical concept, he writes, it is of necessity a kind of fiction. The same would clearly hold for the notion of "instinct," and also for the effort to account chronologically or sequentially for how anything can be derived from the will, or the will from anything else: "one should use 'cause' and 'effect' only as pure concepts, that is to say, as conventional fictions for the purpose of designation and communication—*not* for explanation" (*BGE* 21). In *On the Genealogy of Morals,* he reiterates that conceptualization emerges from the genealogy of torture as the promise of a certain escape: concepts, he writes, are an effort to gain release from a torture. Is the very conceptual apparatus of *On the Genealogy of Morals* implicated in this description, and is Nietzsche's text then an effort to escape from the tortures of bad conscience, although it owes its life, as it were, to that very source?

If all "imaginative phenomena" are the result of this violent interiorization, it follows that the genealogical account will be one of these phenomena, a narrative effect of the narrative it seeks to tell. The unmasking of the narrative is its remasking—inevitably. Indeed, it seems that the very creativity one seeks to oppose to the inhibition of strength is fundamentally dependent on that very inhibition. In this sense, repression appears to underwrite or guarantee both the being who promises and the writer of fiction, including conceptual fictions such as genealogy. The unity of will attributed to the promising is itself the *effect* of a repression, a forgetfulness, a not-remembering of the satisfactions which appear to precede repression and which repression makes sure will not appear again.

FREUD, NARCISSISM, AND REGULATION

In this final section, I would like to return to the problem of social regulation, not as acting on a psyche, but as complicitous in the formation of the psyche and its desire. To that end, I propose a detour through Freud; the Nietzschean resonances in his consideration of conscience will become clear.

The postulation of repression's primacy brings us directly to Freud, and to a reconsideration of the problem of punishment in relation to the formation of conscience and social subjection. If this subjection is not mechanistic, not the simple effect of an internalization, then how can we understand the psychic engagement with subjection in a way that does not disjoin the discourse of self-subjection from the problem of social regulation? How can cultivating a narcissistic attachment to punishment be the means by which the power of social regulation exploits a narcissistic demand for self-reflection which is indifferent to its occasion?

This suggestion of narcissism is, I would suggest, already at work in Nietzsche. The ascetic ideal, understood as a will to nothingness, is a way of interpreting all suffering as guilt. Whereas guilt works to deny a specific kind of object for human wants, it cannot obliterate the wanting character of humans. According to the dictates of guilt, then, "man had only to *want* something—and to begin with, it mattered not what, whereto, or how he wanted: *the will itself was saved*" (*GM* III:28).

In his analysis of neurosis, Freud understood this differently, as a kind of libidinal attachment to a prohibition which has as its purpose the thwarting of libidinal gratification. Where that thwarting constitutes a repression, the repression is sustained by the libido that it seeks to thwart. In neurosis, the ethical regulation of bodily impulse becomes the focus and aim of impulse itself. Here we are given to understand an attachment to subjection which is formative of the reflexive structure of subjection. The impulse which would be negated is inadvertently *preserved* by that very negating activity.

We can hear a resonance of Nietzsche when Freud describes the process by which libido comes under the censor of the law only to reemerge as the sustaining effect of that law. The repression of the libido is always to be understood as itself a libidinally invested repression. Hence the libido is not absolutely negated through repression but rather becomes the instrument of its own subjection. The repressive law is not external to the libido that it represses, but the repressive law represses to the extent that repression becomes a libidinal activity. Further, moral interdictions, especially those that are turned against the body, are themselves sustained by the bodily activity that they seek to curb.

The desire to desire is a willingness to desire precisely what would foreclose desire, if only for the possibility of continuing to desire. This desire for desire is exploited in the process of social regulation, for if the terms by which we gain social recognition for ourselves are those by which we are regulated *and* gain social existence, then to affirm one's existence is to capitulate to one's subordination—a sorry bind. How precisely this narcissistic attachment to attachment is exploited by mechanisms of social regulation is inadvertently made clear in a set of speculations that Freud offers on the repression of homosexuality and the formation of conscience and citizenship. In "On the Mechanism of Paranoia," he links the suppression of homosexual drives to the production of social feeling. At the end of that piece, he remarks that "homosexual drives" help to constitute "the social instincts, thus contributing an erotic factor to friendship and comradeship, to *esprit de corps* and to the love of mankind in general." [1] At the close of the essay "On Narcissism," he might be read as specifying the logic whereby this production of social feeling takes place. The "ego-ideal," he writes, has a social side: "it is also the common ideal of a family, a class or a nation. It not only binds the narcissistic libido, but also a considerable amount of the person's homosexual libido, which in this way becomes turned back into the ego. The dissatisfaction due to the non-fulfillment of the ideal liberates homosexual libido, which is transformed into sense of guilt (dread of the community)." [2] This transformation of homosexuality into guilt and, therefore, into the basis of social feeling takes place when the fear of parental punishment becomes generalized as the dread of losing the love of fellow men. Paranoia is the way in which that love is consistently reimagined as always almost withdrawn, and it is, paradoxically, fear of losing that love which motivates the sublimation or introversion of homosexuality. Indeed, this sublimation is not quite as instrumental as it may sound, for it is not that one disavows homosexuality in order to gain the love of fellow men but that a certain homosexuality can only be achieved and contained *through* this disavowal.

Another place in Freud where this becomes very clear is the discussion of the formation of conscience in *Civilization and Its Discontents,* where it turns out that the prohibition against homosexuality which conscience is said to enact or articulate founds and constitutes conscience itself as a psychic phenomenon. The prohibition against the desire is that desire as it turns back upon itself, and this turning back upon itself becomes the very inception, the very action of what is rendered entitative in through the term "conscience."

Freud writes in *Civilization and Its Discontents* "that conscience (or more correctly, the anxiety which later becomes conscience) is indeed the cause of instinctual renunciation to begin with, but that later the relationship is reversed. Every renunciation of instinct now becomes a dynamic source of conscience and every fresh renunciation increases the latter's severity and intolerance." [3]

According to Freud, then, the self-imposed imperatives that characterize the circular route of conscience are pursued and applied precisely because they are now the site of the very satisfaction that they seek to prohibit. In other words, prohibition becomes the occasion for reliving the instinct under the rubric of the condemning law. Prohibition reproduces the prohibited desire and becomes intensified through the renunciations it effects. The "afterlife" of prohibited desire takes place through the prohibition itself, where the prohibition not only sustains, but is *sustained by* the desire that it forces into renunciation. In this sense, then, renunciation takes place through the very desire that is renounced: the desire is *never* renounced but becomes preserved and reasserted in the very structure of renunciation.

This example leads us back to the trope with which we began, the figure of conscience as turning back on itself as if it were a body recoiled on itself, recoiled at the thought of its desire, for whom its desire is symptomatized as that posture of recoil. Conscience is thus figured as a body which takes itself as its object, forced into a permanent posture of negative narcissism, or, more precisely, a narcissistically nourished self-beratement (then, mistakenly, identified with a narcissistic *stage*).

Consider—as a parting shot—how the contemporary efforts to regulate homosexuality within the U.S. military are themselves the regulatory formation of the masculine subject, one who consecrates his identity through *renunciation* as an act of speech: to say "I am a homosexual" is fine as long as one also *promises* "and I don't intend to act." This, the suppression and sustaining of homosexuality in and through the circular posture by which a body utters its own renunciation, accedes to its regulation through the promise. But that performative utterance, however compelled, will be subject to infelicity, to speaking otherwise, to reciting only half the sentence, deforming the promise, reformulating the confession as defiance, remaining silent. This opposition will draw from and oppose the power by which it is compelled, and this short circuiting of regulatory power constitutes the possibility of a *postmoral* gesture toward a less regular freedom, one that from the perspective of a less codifiable set of values calls into question the values of morality.

NOTES

1. Sigmund Freud, "On the Mechanism of Paranoia," third section of "Psycho-Analytic Notes on an Autobiographical Account of a Case of Paranoia (Dementia Paranoides)," *The Standard Edition of the Complete Psychological*

Works of Sigmund Freud, ed. and trans. James Strachey, 24 vols. (London: Hogarth, 1953–74), 12:31.

2. Sigmund Freud, "On Narcissism: An Introduction," *Standard Edition,* 14:73–104.

3. Sigmund Freud, *Civilization and Its Discontents,* trans. James Strachey (New York: W. W. Norton, 1977), 84.

CHAPTER 8

Dramatis Personae

Nietzsche, Culture, and Human Types

David Owen and Aaron Ridley

I am still waiting for a philosophical *physician* in the
exceptional sense of that word—one who has to pursue
the problem of the total health of a people, time, race or of
humanity—to muster the courage to push my suspicion to its
limits and to risk the proposition: what was at stake in all
philosophizing hitherto was not at all "truth" but something
else—let us say, health, future, growth, power, life.
Friedrich Nietzsche, The Gay Science

One of the more striking features of Nietzsche's work is the frequency
with which he advances his philosophical arguments through the use of
human types. But precisely why he adopts this strategy and what its significance is for his concerns as a self-proclaimed cultural physician is not
so immediately clear. A standard interpretation of what is involved in this
use of human types is that Nietzsche holds the view that there are, as a
matter of scientific fact, certain subspecies of humanity and, thus, that
the cogency of any ethical or political argument is dependent on its being
predicated on the recognition of these natural subspecies. It is easy to see
why this interpretation is advanced given remarks such as the following:

> The *order of castes*, the supreme, the dominating law, is only the sanctioning
> of a *natural order*. . . . Nature . . . separates from one another the predomi-
> nantly spiritual type, the predominantly muscular and temperamental type,
> and the third type distinguished neither in the one nor the other, the mediocre
> type . . . [for whom] to be a public utility, a cog, a function, is a natural vo-
> cation. (*AC* 57)

However, in this chapter we argue that although there is some textual
support for this interpretation, the main thrust of Nietzsche's thought

directs us to an alternative account of human types and his use of them. Indeed, the standard account, we suggest, betrays Nietzsche's best insights and emasculates the challenge of his philosophy.

Our argument is presented in four stages. Section 1 makes plausible the claim that Nietzsche regards human types as expressions of various cultural relations. Section 2 situates Nietzsche's use of human types in the context of his activity as a cultural physician. Section 3 sets out Nietzsche's diagnosis of the condition of modern man. Section 4 presents his prognosis and prescription. We conclude that only a cultural understanding of human types can make sense of Nietzsche's conception of philosophy and of his therapeutic ambitions.

I

Supposing Nietzsche's thought is consistent, the way in which he conceptualizes human types must be compatible with his conceptualization of humanity as a type. In other words, an interpretation of Nietzsche's remarks on human types must be consonant with his general account of human subjectivity and agency. This section is therefore concerned with his ruminations about subjectivity and agency.

In *Beyond Good and Evil* Nietzsche describes the general economy of life as will to power:

> A living thing desires above all to *vent* its strength—life as such is will to power; self-preservation is only one of the indirect and most frequent *consequences* of it. (*BGE* 13)

This claim is reiterated in slightly different terms in the second essay of *On the Genealogy of Morals*. To define life as a matter of adaptation

> is to misunderstand the essence of life, its *will to power;* we overlook the prime importance which the spontaneous, aggressive, expansive, re-interpreting, re-directing and formative powers have, which "adaptation" follows only when they have had their effect. (*GM* II:12)

Nietzsche is not here offering an explanation of life but rather a characterization of it, a criterion for distinguishing life from matter. However, will to power as a criterion of life does not distinguish human life from other forms of life. To make this distinction, Nietzsche needs to specify the modality of will to power that characterizes human beings. Here is how he does it:

> Willing seems to me to be above all something *complicated,* something that is a unity only as a word. . . . [I]n all willing there is, first of all, a plurality of

sensations, namely the sensation of the condition we *leave,* the sensation of the condition towards which we *go,* the sensation of this "leaving" and "going" itself. . . . [A]s feelings and indeed many varieties of feeling, can therefore be recognized as an ingredient of will, so, in the second place can thinking: in every act of will there is a commanding thought—and do not imagine that this can be separated from the "willing," as though will would then remain over! Thirdly, will is not only a complex of feeling and thinking, but above all an *emotion:* and in fact the emotion of command. What is called "freedom of will" is essentially the emotion of superiority over him who must obey: "I am free, 'he' must obey"—this consciousness adheres to every will. . . . A man who *wills*—commands something in himself which obeys or which he believes obeys. (*BGE* 19)

In this phenomenal description of willing, Nietzsche is chiefly concerned to do three things. First, he is making the point that the willing in will to power is not the product of some simple unitary force, some "unknown x." This prevents his characterization from turning into a reductive or essentialist description. Second, he is noting that the modality of will to power that characterizes human being involves a *rapport à soi,* a relation of the self to itself. In other words, the feeling of power involved in this modality of will to power is necessarily mediated through consciousness. Third, insofar as human beings are both conscious and self-conscious, he is claiming that they have a reflective interest in experiencing themselves as agents.[1]

Consequently, and precisely because Nietzsche is not positing some "unknown x" as the underlying reality of human subjectivity, he must provide a naturalistic account of the emergence of this characteristically human modality of will to power. Such an account is set out in the second essay of the *Genealogy,* where Nietzsche describes the development of consciousness in terms of *bad conscience:*

I look on bad conscience as a serious illness to which man was forced to succumb by the pressure of the most fundamental of all changes which he experienced,—that change whereby he finally found himself imprisoned within the walls of society and peace. . . . All instincts which are not discharged outwardly *turn inwards*—this is what I call the *internalization* of man: with it there now evolves in man what will later be called his "soul." The whole inner world, originally stretched thinly as though between two layers of skin, was expanded and extended itself and gained depth, breadth and height in proportion to the degree that the external discharge of man's instincts was *obstructed.* . . . Lacking external enemies and obstacles, and forced into the oppressive narrowness and conformity of custom, man impatiently ripped himself apart, persecuted himself, gnawed at himself, gave himself no peace and abused himself, this animal who battered himself on the bars of his cage and who is supposed to be "tamed"; . . . this fool, this prisoner consumed with longing and despair, became the inventor of "bad conscience." (*GM* II:16)

Despite the somewhat lurid terms in which Nietzsche describes this phenomenon, he explicitly counsels us not to view it in a negative light:

> We must be wary of thinking disparagingly about this whole phenomenon because it is inherently ugly and painful. . . . This secret self-violation, this artist's cruelty, . . . this uncanny, terrible but joyous labor of a soul voluntarily split within itself[,] . . . this whole *active* "bad conscience" has finally— we have already guessed—as true womb of ideal and imaginative events, brought a wealth of novel, disconcerting beauty and affirmation to light, and perhaps for the first time, beauty itself. (*GM* II:18)

Far from construing this bad conscience as an unconditional calamity, then, Nietzsche regards it as—at least potentially—"pregnant with a future."

> Let us immediately add that . . . the prospect of an animal soul turning against itself . . . was something so new, profound, unheard-of, puzzling, contradictory and *momentous* on earth that the whole character of the world changed in an essential way. Indeed, a divine audience was needed to appreciate the spectacle which began then. . . . Since that time, man has been *included* among the most unexpected and exciting throws of dice played by Heraclitus' "great child," call him Zeus or fate,— . . . as though man were not an end but just a path, an episode, a bridge, a great promise. (*GM* II:16)

What is so momentous here is the emergence of consciousness. Nietzsche is describing the process whereby man acquires interiority, that is, the necessary condition of standing to himself in any relation whatever (good or bad). In other words, this process of interiorization, this process in which the "instinct for freedom (put into my language: the will to power)" (*GM* II:18) is turned inward, is the construction of the distinctively human modality of will to power. Man now necessarily stands in a relation to himself.

Given this account of how Nietzsche thinks about humanity as a type, what are its implications for how he thinks about human types? Is it the case, as the standard interpretation would have it, that the relations in which human beings stand to themselves are a function of biology? The naturalistic account of the genesis of consciousness would seem, after all, to be consistent with this thesis. Or is it, rather, that these relations are constituted in and through culture? Although Nietzsche occasionally suggests the former (e.g., *AC* 57), it seems clear that his primary concern is with the latter. This fact is illustrated by Nietzsche's

claim that it is a "rule that the concept of political superiority always resolves itself into the concept of psychological superiority" (*GM* I:6); so
that "everywhere 'noble'—'aristocratic' in social terms—is the basic
concept from which, necessarily, 'good' in the sense of 'spiritually noble,' 'aristocratic' . . . developed" (*GM* I:4). Indeed, this point is rein-
forced by the fact that Nietzsche's analysis of the emergence of both noble and slave morality is conducted entirely in terms of social conditions
and cultural relations and further by the fact that the eventual triumph
of slave morality over noble morality would be unintelligible if political
superiority were founded on biology. If this right, and it is difficult to see
how it might not be, we can conclude that Nietzsche's concern is, first,
with the way in which *rapports à soi* are constituted by and constitutive
of cultures (e.g., cultures in which noble rather than slave morality is
hegemonic) and, second, with the way in which typical configurations
of the self's relation to itself can be represented as human types (e.g.,
"noble" and "slave").

Our purpose in this section has simply been to make plausible the
claim that Nietzsche regards human types not in terms of genetic hard-
wiring but as expressions of cultural relations. We turn now to the implications of this point for Nietzsche's styles of philosophical argument.

II

Thus far we have been concerned with what Nietzsche means by a human type—that is, a particular configuration of internalized will to
power characterized by a specific mode of relation of the self to itself.
But this raises a related question: why does Nietzsche have recourse to
the idea of human types at all? Although, given our account of Nietzsche's notion of human types, it is relatively straightforward to see how
they may provide a tool for analyzing cultures, this does not by itself
take us very far. Rather, we need to situate Nietzsche's use of human
types in the context of his activity as a cultural physician. For Nietzsche
is concerned not merely to analyze cultures but to evaluate them—"and
so we need to know about the conditions and circumstances under
which the values grew up, developed and changed (morality as result, as
symptom, as mask, as tartuffery, as sickness, as misunderstanding; but
also morality as cause, remedy, stimulant, inhibition, poison)" (*GM* P6).
This evaluation takes the form of a diagnosis in which a symptomatology is combined with a pathology, a medical analogy that we suggest

makes clear Nietzsche's reasons for according such prominence to human types.

This medical analogy can be spelled out by considering what is involved in clinical judgment. As Albert R. Jonsen and Stephen Toulmin remark,

> With or without an explicit scientific foundation, then, the heart of clinical practice and training comprises a taxonomy of medical conditions. Medical students and interns in training are shown cases that exemplify the constellations of symptoms, or "syndromes," typical of these varied conditions. In this way they learn what to look for as indicative of any specific condition and so how to recognize it if it turns up again on a later occasion. The key element in diagnosis is thus "syndrome recognition": a capacity to *re*-identify, in fresh cases, a disability, disease, or injury one has encountered (or read about) in earlier instances.[2]

Thus what is involved in diagnosis is a capacity to recognize a cluster of symptoms as a syndrome with a distinct pathology. Notably,

> a description is clinically fruitful only when it is based on perceptive study of actual cases, and it is practically effective only if paradigmatic cases exist to *show* in actual fact what can otherwise only be *stated*: namely, the actual onset, syndromes, and course typical of the condition. Given this *taxonomy* of known conditions and the paradigmatic cases that exemplify the various types, diagnosis then becomes a kind of perception, and the reasons for justifying a diagnosis rest on appeals to analogy.[3]

This characterization of clinical judgment entails that the

> relations between a diagnostic conclusion and the evidence on which it is based (symptoms, onset, etc.) are precisely those typical of practical reasoning rather than theoretical proof. First, the conclusion is related to the evidence by *substantive* rather than formal connections. Second, the conclusion follows as a *rebuttable* presumption, not as a necessary entailment. Finally, the inference from the evidence to the conclusion is not timelessly valid, regardless of context, but thoroughly *circumstantial*: dependent on detailed facts about the circumstances and nature of the particular case.[4]

The relation between this model of clinical diagnosis and Nietzsche's use of human types is no doubt obvious but worth spelling out even so.

For physical symptom, read psychological symptom. For syndrome, read human type. For pathology (onset and course), read history. In other words, for Nietzsche, philosophical judgment, like clinical judgment, requires a taxonomy of (human) types so that distinct pathologies (of the soul) can be recognized in terms of particular constellations of (psychological) symptoms. But, of course, in order for this to be possible, an appropriate taxonomy must be constructed. How might such a taxonomy be constructed in the medical case? Any such construction must take place against the background of a general theoretical model of the human body, which specifies both a criterion of what sort of thing could count as a symptom (of health or disease) and a norm of physical health, which specifies a criterion of salience. It is only against such a background that certain recurring patterns of symptoms can actually achieve salience (i.e., can be identified as syndromes). The construction itself involves the identification of recurring patterns of symptoms across cases, synchronically and diachronically, through the reflective observation of a multiplicity of case histories. The same structure can be discerned in Nietzsche's project. Taking the place of a general theoretical model of the human body is Nietzsche's account of the distinctive modality of will to power characteristic of human being (see section 1): only particular expressions of this distinctive modality could count as symptoms (of health or disease) qua human subjectivity. Replacing the norm of physical health, which specifies a criterion of salience, is a norm of psychological health. Just as the norm of physical health is "life lived in the silence of the organs," [5] that is, the capacity to conduct one's physical conduct without the desire to be free of the limitations of one's body qua body, so Nietzsche's norm of psychological health is the capacity to conduct one's own psychological conduct (e.g., one's relationship to oneself) without the desire to be free of the limitations of one's self qua self. Thus Nietzsche suggests that psychological health (the "*noble soul*") is characterized by "*reverence for itself*" (*BGE* 287), while the sick man (e.g., the slave) "communes with himself" with a "glance which is a sigh. 'If only I were some other person!' is what this glance sighs: 'but there is no hope of that. I am who I am: how could I get away from myself? And oh—*I'm fed up with myself!*'" (*GM* III:14). Against this background, Nietzsche's construction of a taxonomy of human types involves the identification of constellations of psychological symptoms, synchronically and diachronically, through the reflective observation of a multiplicity of case histories of *rapports à soi,* of ways of living. This diagnostic technique is what Nietzsche calls "genealogy."

Human types, therefore, play an integral role in Nietzsche's philosophical project. Far from being merely ornamental or stylistic quirks, they are a condition of possibility of Nietzsche's activity as a cultural physician. But why—and how—does Nietzsche seek to practice his cultural therapy?

III

Nietzsche seeks to practice his cultural therapy, briefly, because he suspects that the best of his contemporaries (and indeed himself) are characterized and worn down by a half-conscious hatred of self and world and that the majority are characterized and worn down by an unconscious hatred of the same kind. This suspicion is grounded on Nietzsche's general conception of health. In place of creatures at ease with themselves, exercising and extending the range of their capacities, modern culture, Nietzsche observes, appears to cultivate "a shrunken, almost ludicrous species, a herd animal, something full of good will, sickly and mediocre . . . , the European of today" (BGE 62).

> Today we see nothing that wants to expand, we suspect that things will just continue to decline, getting thinner, better-natured, cleverer, more comfortable, more mediocre, more indifferent. . . . The sight of man now makes us tired—what is nihilism today if it is not *that?* . . . We are tired of *man.* (GM I:12)

Moreover, Nietzsche thinks that this condition is rarely recognized, not least because an essential aspect of it is "that the 'tame man,' who is incurably mediocre and unedifying, has already learnt to view himself as the aim and pinnacle, the meaning of history, the 'higher man'" (GM I:11). Thus the task Nietzsche sets himself is to develop a taxonomy in terms of which this general malaise can be more perspicuously diagnosed through a genealogical analysis of *rapports à soi*.

There are, crudely, two stages to Nietzsche's account. The first stage hangs on the existence of a social hierarchy. It will be recalled from the discussion in section 1 that Nietzsche describes the emergence of the distinctively human modality of will to power in terms of the repression of instinct engendered by enclosure "within the walls of society and peace." Such enclosure necessarily involves social hierarchy, for Nietzsche, because state formation is the product of violence.

> The shaping of a new population, which had up till now been unrestrained and shapeless, into a fixed form, as happened at the beginning with an act of violence, could only be concluded with acts of violence,—that consequently the oldest "state" emerged as a terrible tyranny, as a repressive and ruthless machinery, and continued working until the raw material of people and semi-animals had been finally not just kneaded and made compliant, but *shaped*. I used the word "state": it is obvious who is meant by this—some pack of blond beasts of prey, a conqueror and master race, which, organized on a war footing, and with the power to organize, unscrupulously lays its dreadful

> paws on a populace which, though it might be vastly greater in number, is still shapeless and shifting. In this way, the "state" began on earth. (*GM* II:17)

So the state consists of two classes of person: the conqueror and the conquered. The significance of this fact for Nietzsche is twofold. First, the conquerors are characterized by a lesser degree of internalization than the conquered, because the degree of instinctual repression is proportional to the degree of enclosure, and this itself is a function of position in the social hierarchy. Thus Nietzsche notes that those at the top of the social hierarchy are able to "compensate" themselves "for the tension which is caused by being closed in and fenced in by the peace of the community" by stepping outside of this enclosure and giving outward expression to the instinct for freedom (*GM* I:11). No such compensation is available to those at the bottom of the social hierarchy. Second, the conquerors are characterized by a feeling of power, because their position in the social hierarchy entails that they are able to command the conquered, while the conquered, for obvious reasons, are characterized by a feeling of powerlessness. These contrasting experiences result in two distinct patterns of self-relation, represented by Nietzsche as two distinct human types—the noble and the slave. The self-relation of the noble is characterized by a style of valuation in which the relationship of self to self and of self to world is affirmed: " 'the good' themselves, meaning the noble, the mighty, the high-placed and the high-minded, . . . saw and judged themselves and their actions as good, I mean first-rate, in contrast to everything lowly, low-minded, common and plebeian" (*GM* I:2). Thus noble morality is an expression of the feeling of power that attends being at the top of the social hierarchy, while its relatively unmediated character is a result of the low degree of internalization engendered by that position. The self-relation of the slave, by contrast, is characterized by a style of valuation in which the relationship of self to self and of self to world is one of opposition.

> Whereas all noble morality grows out of a triumphant saying "yes" to itself, slave morality says "no" on principle to everything that is "outside," "other," "non-self": and *this* "no" is its creative deed. (*GM* I:10)

The creativity comprised by this "no"—as a reflective expression of the "instinct of self-preservation and self-affirmation"—consists in drawing a distinction between doers and deeds, and in exploiting this distinction so that doers can be understood as choosing, as being accountable for, their deeds (see *GM* I:13 with II:10). This allows the slave to construe his suffering as the product of a choice on the part of the noble, for which the noble is guilty, and his own inability to act as the noble acts as a further choice, this latter being "the sublime self-deception that interprets weakness as freedom, and their being thus-and-thus as a *merit*" (*GM* I:13). Thus the slave conceives "of the 'evil enemy,' '*the evil one*' as the basic idea to which he now thinks up a copy and counterpart, the 'good one'—himself!" (*GM* I:10). In this way, slave morality expresses the feeling of powerless attending a position at the bottom of the social hierarchy, while its inventive, reflective character (which is made possible by the relatively high degree of internalization engendered by that position) consists in transforming the feeling of powerlessness into a feeling of power. Note that Nietzsche is not concerned here to blame or find fault with the slave but simply to provide a naturalistic account of how, under certain social circumstances, the sorts of moves that the slave makes become the only ones available if he is to experience himself as an agent in his own right.

So at the end of the first stage of his account, Nietzsche has constructed a taxonomy consisting of two human types—the type exhibiting the "noble" syndrome and the type exhibiting the "slave" syndrome. But now things become more complex. The second stage begins by subdividing the noble type into types exhibiting the "warrior" syndrome and the "priest" syndrome (*GM* I:7). This subdivision is motivated by Nietzsche's recognition of a division of labor within the ruling class, according to which one group affirms itself for its martial qualities and the other group for its spiritual qualities. Nietzsche speculates that this division of labor is rooted in two relationships constitutive of a conquering people: their warlike relation with other peoples and their spiritual relation with the gods (to whom their martial activities are offered as both tribute and entertainment—see *GM* II:7–10, 16, 19–20). But he is more interested in the significance of this division than in its origins, specifically insofar as the two subtypes represent different degrees of internalization within the noble class. The priest, unlike the warrior, does not find release from the tension of enclosure by engaging in military activity and is thus characterized by the feeling of powerfulness typical of the noble class combined, crucially, with a high degree of internalization. So the priest, like the slave, becomes clever but, not being an impotent victim of oppression, can be ingenious in the exercise of the (real) power that he has rather than ingenious, as the slave is, in the counterfeiting of power.[6]

The real significance of the priest, the genius of the priest, lies in his simultaneous solution of two problems. The first problem is his own: he is fed up with himself. Though a member of the ruling class, his non-participation in military activities prevents him from exorcizing feelings of tension through "murder, arson, rape, and torture" (*GM* I:11), and this leads him to "alternate between brooding and emotional explosions, habits which seem to have as their almost invariable consequence . . . intestinal morbidity and neurasthenia" (*GM* I:6). Therefore the priest has reason to envy the warrior. The second problem is the threat posed to sociality as such by slave morality. This threat is generated by the fact that, while the slaves can account for forms of suffering caused by the nobles (by blaming the nobles for it), they still need to account for all the other sources of human suffering. The problem, however, is that there is no one obvious to blame. Consequently, Nietzsche argues,

> the suffering are one and all dreadfully eager and inventive in discovering occasions for painful affects; they enjoy being mistrustful and dwelling on nasty deeds and imaginary slights; . . . they tear open their oldest wounds, they bleed from long-healed scars, they make evildoers out of their friends, wives, children, and whoever else stands closest to them. (*GM* III:15)

If this threat is to be dissolved, the slaves need to be given some less socially disruptive mechanism for accounting for their suffering. As the only member of the ruling order with the necessary resources of ingenuity, the priest

> fights with cunning and severity and in secret against anarchy and ever-threatening disintegration within the herd, in which the most dangerous of all explosives, *ressentiment,* is constantly accumulating. So to detonate this explosive that it does not blow up herd and herdsman is his essential art, as it is his supreme utility; if one wanted to express the value of the priestly existence in the briefest formula it would be: the priest *alters the direction of ressentiment.* . . . "I suffer: someone must be to blame for it"—thus thinks every sickly sheep. But his shepherd, the ascetic priest, tells him: "Quite so, my sheep! someone must be to blame for it: but you yourself are this someone, you alone are to blame for it—*you alone are to blame for yourself!*"—This is brazen and false enough: but one thing at least is achieved by it, the direction of *ressentiment* is *altered.* (*GM* III:15)

Thus the threat is defused. The slave is now provided with a single agent, that is, himself, who can be blamed for all of his suffering. Moreover, as the practitioner of this art of redirection, the priest also solves his own problem. He need no longer envy the warrior. The soul of the herd is now his: "*Dominion over the suffering* is his kingdom, that is where his instinct directs him, here he possesses his distinctive art, his mastery, his kind of happiness" (*GM* III:15).

So the priest establishes his spiritual dominion over the slave class (and, eventually, over the other nobles as well—see *TI* "Socrates" and *AC* 25–26) while the slave is now able to give meaning to forms of suffering not caused by the nobles. But it is the way in which this redirecting of *ressentiment* is accomplished that is most significant for Nietzsche. What the priest does, on Nietzsche's account, is to transcendentalize the doer/deed distinction exploited by slave morality so as to construct a dichotomy between the real and the apparent self (soul and flesh). The priest relates the apparent self

> (together with all that belongs to it, "nature," "the world," the whole sphere of what becomes and what passes away), to a quite different kind of existence which is opposed to it and excludes it unless it should turn against itself and deny itself: in this case, the case of the ascetic life, life counts as a bridge to that other existence. (GM III:11)

In other words, the priest turns life as such into an ascetic procedure. He constructs the ascetic ideal:

> The ascetic ideal has a goal,—which is so general, that all the interests of human existence appear petty and narrow when measured against it; it inexorably interprets epochs, peoples, man, all with reference to this one goal, it permits of no other interpretation, no other goal, and rejects, denies, affirms, confirms only with reference to its interpretation[;] . . . it believes there is nothing on earth of any power which does not first have to receive a meaning, a right to existence, a value from it, as a tool to its work, as a way and means to its goal, to one goal. (GM III:23)

What is this goal?

> It is absolutely impossible for us to conceal what was expressed by that whole willing, which was given direction by the ascetic ideal: this hatred of the human, and even more of the animalistic, even more of the material, . . . this longing to get away from appearance, transience, growth, death, wishing, longing itself—all that means, let us dare grasp it, a will to nothingness, an aversion to life, a rebellion against the most fundamental prerequisites of life. (GM III:28)

In other words, the goal of the ascetic ideal is to transcend the necessary limitations of being human and thus to refuse the tragic character of human existence by denying the role of chance and necessity as integral features of living a life. The success of this ideal derives from its capacity to heighten our feeling of power by presenting the individual as responsible both for his own suffering (i.e., sin) and for his own emancipation from suffering (i.e., salvation).

In terms of Nietzsche's typological investigations, the significance of the ascetic ideal is that it undercuts the distinction between noble and slave and seeks instead to establish a single, overarching human type, the ascetic individual—indeed seeks "to *exploit* the bad instincts of all sufferers for the purpose of self-discipline, self-surveillance, and self-overcoming" (*GM* III:16).

> That which constrains these men, however, this unconditional will to truth, is faith in the ascetic ideal itself, . . . it is the faith in a metaphysical value, the absolute value of truth, sanctioned and guaranteed by this ideal alone (it stands or falls with this ideal). (GM III:24)

Thus the general form of *rapport à soi* constituted here is an unconditional commitment to truthfulness driven by the desire for salvation. However, it is precisely this unconditional commitment to truthfulness that culminates in the self-overcoming of the ascetic ideal: "it is the awe-inspiring *catastrophe* of two thousand years of training in truthfulness that finally forbids itself the *lie involved in belief in God*," so that

> Christianity as dogma was destroyed by its own morality; in the same way Christianity as morality must now perish, too: we stand on the threshold of this event. After Christian truthfulness has drawn one inference after another, it must end by drawing its most striking inference, its inference against itself; this will happen, however, when it poses the question "what is the meaning of all will to truth?" (GM III:27)

In other words, the unconditional commitment to truthfulness culminates in the recognition that the value of truth cannot itself be unconditional, that is, that the dichotomy between "real" and "apparent" worlds cannot be sustained. And this, as the "unconditional will to truth" is "*faith in the ascetic ideal itself,*" is the recognition that faith in the ascetic ideal is no longer (truthfully) possible.

Thus, at the point at which the ascetic ideal is engaged in its own destruction, human beings have developed distinctive capacities for "self-discipline," "self-surveillance," and "self-overcoming" and a disposition to truthfulness, combined with (and predicated on) a thoroughly ascetic hatred of their this-worldly existence: a "hatred of the human," a "longing to get away from appearance, transience, growth, death, wishing, longing itself" (*GM* III:28). This is the condition of modern man as a human type, a condition that Nietzsche diagnoses and to which his therapy is directed.

IV

The modern condition offers both a threat and a promise. Nietzsche argues that the self-destruction of the ascetic ideal threatens to undermine our capacities for "self-discipline," "self-surveillance," and "self-overcoming" and our disposition to truthfulness precisely because we now lack an overarching goal in the service of which these capacities and this disposition are cultivated. But this undermining does not entail any diminution of our dissatisfaction with our this-worldly existence: the suffering endemic to life itself remains; all that has gone is the (ascetic) mode of valuing that rendered such suffering meaningful, and hence bearable. Thus Nietzsche discerns the outlines of a creature whose best capacities have atrophied and whose relationship to its own existence is one of perpetual dissatisfaction. The threat here is obvious:

> What is to be feared, what has a more calamitous effect than any other calamity, is that man should inspire not profound fear but profound *nausea*; also not great fear but great *pity*. Suppose these two were one day to unite, they would inevitably beget one of the uncanniest monsters: the "last will" of man, his will to nothingness, nihilism. And a great deal points to this union. (*GM* III:14)

So suicidal nihilism beckons. The one response to the situation that is absolutely ruled out is the one that has so far proved most successful at addressing problems of this sort, namely, adoption of the ascetic ideal, because the present crisis is caused by the self-destruction of that ideal. But Nietzsche argues that two plausible responses to the crisis are nonetheless possible for modern man. Both of these involve the construction of immanent ideals or goals: one response is represented by the type the Last Man, the other by the type the *Übermensch*.

The first response recognizes the reality of suffering and our (post-ascetic) inability to accord transcendental significance to it and concludes that the latter provides an overwhelming reason for abolishing the former to whatever extent is possible. This has the effect of elevating the abolition of suffering into a quasi-transcendental goal and brings with it a new table of virtues, on which prudence figures largest. In other words, this response takes the form of a *rapport a soi* characterized by a style of calculative rationality directed toward the avoidance of suffering at any cost, for example, of utilitarianism and any other account of human subjectivity that accords preeminence to maximizing preference satisfaction. In *Thus Spoke Zarathustra* Nietzsche portrays this type as follows:

> "What is love? What is creation? What is longing? What is a star?" thus asks the Last Man and blinks.
>
> The earth has become small, and upon it hops the Last Man, who makes everything small. His race is as inexterminable as the flea; the Last Man lives longest.
>
> "We have discovered happiness," say the Last Men and blink.
>
> They have left the places where living was hard: for one needs warmth. One still loves one's neighbor and rubs oneself against him: for one needs warmth.
>
> Sickness and mistrust count as sins with them: one should go about warily. He is a fool who still stumbles over stones or over men!
>
> A little poison now and then: that produces pleasant dreams. And a lot of poison at last, for a pleasant death.
>
> They still work, for work is entertainment. But they take care the entertainment does not exhaust them.
>
> Nobody grows rich or poor any more: both are too much of a burden. Who still wants to rule? Who obey? Both are too much of a burden.
>
> No herdsman and one herd. Everyone wants the same thing, everyone is the same: whoever thinks otherwise goes voluntarily into the madhouse
>
> "Formerly all the world was mad," say the most acute of them and blink.
>
> They are clever and know everything that has ever happened: so there is no end to their mockery. They still quarrel, but they soon make up—otherwise indigestion would result.
>
> They have their little pleasure for the day and their little pleasure for the night: but they respect health.
>
> "We have discovered happiness," say the Last Men and blink. (Z:1 "Prologue" 5)

Nietzsche's hostility to this first form of response is evident. His general objection to the Last Man is that the Last Man's ideal, like the ascetic ideal, is committed to the denial of chance and necessity as integral features of human existence. Whereas the ascetic ideal denies chance and necessity per se so that, while suffering remains real, what is objectionable about it is abolished, the Last Man's ideal is expressed as the practical imperative to abolish suffering, and hence, a fortiori, what is objectionable about it—that is, our exposure to chance and necessity. This general objection has two specific dimensions. The first is that the Last Man's ideal is unrealizable, insofar as human existence involves ineliminable sources of suffering—not least our consciousness that we come into being by chance and cease to be by necessity. Thus the Last Man's ideal is predicated on a neglect of truthfulness. The second dimension of Nietzsche's objection is that pursuit of the Last Man's ideal impoverishes and arbitrarily restricts our understanding of what we can be and, in doing so, forecloses our future possibilities of becoming otherwise than we are. Thus the Last Man's ideal entails an atrophying of the capacities (for self-overcoming, etc.) bequeathed by the ascetic ideal. Nietzsche brings these two dimensions together in *Beyond Good and Evil:* "You want, if possible—and there is no more insane 'if possible'—*to abolish suffering.* . . . Well-being as you understand it—that is no goal, that seems to us an *end,* a state that soon makes man ridiculous and contemptible—that makes his destruction *desirable*" (BGE 225).

The second response to the nihilistic threat posed by the self-destruction of the ascetic ideal is definitive of the *Übermensch* type. This response recognizes both the reality and the ineliminability of suffering and concludes that an affirmation of chance and necessity must therefore be built into the very conception of what it is for something to function as a (postascetic) ideal. So this response, insofar as it cultivates an affirmation of chance and necessity (i.e., *amor fati*), overcomes the (ascetic) hatred of or (modern) dissatisfaction with this-worldly existence. Yet the success of this overcoming is conditional on the exercise and development of the very capacities and disposition that are the bequest of the ascetic ideal. The disposition to truthfulness is a condition of recognizing the ineliminability of chance and necessity. But actually to recognize, let alone affirm, this awful fact about human existence requires the exercise of the capacities for self-surveillance (so that one can monitor oneself for the symptoms of self-deception in the face of this fact), self-discipline (so that one can resist the understandable temptation to deceive oneself about this fact), and self-overcoming (so that one can develop, in the face of this temptation, one's capacities for self-surveillance and self-discipline). Thus the ascetic ideal provides the tools required to overcome the crisis precipitated by its own self-destruction. In other words, the *Übermensch*'s ideal simply is the exercise and cultivation of the capacities and the disposition required to affirm the fact that chance and necessity are ineliminable. And because chance and necessity are ineliminable, and therefore require perpetually to be affirmed anew, such exercise and cultivation must itself be perpetual, a process without the slightest prospect of an end. The contrast with the Last Man's ideal is stark. Whereas the latter offers a feeling of power to its devotees by positing as realizable the unrealizable ideal of no more suffering—that is, of a fixed, final, *completed* state of being—the *Übermensch*'s ideal offers a feeling of power predicated only on the continual overcoming of the desire for any such state. What the Last Man longs for, in other words, the *Übermensch* distinguishes himself by unendingly and truthfully refusing to want.

It is of the first importance that the *Übermensch*'s ideal should represent a *process* as inherently valuable, rather than a product (such as the Last Man's completed state of life without suffering). There are two reasons for thinking this important. The first is the one mentioned above: given that chance and necessity are ineliminable features of living a life, a life oriented to the affirmation of this fact must recognize the ineliminably processual character of such an affirmation, and hence the ineliminably processual character of an ideal that serves rather than denies "the most fundamental prerequisites of life" (*GM* III:28). The other reason is that this ideal exhibits the form of practical reasoning that Nietzsche's genealogy itself deploys. By contrast with, say, Kant's conception of practical reasoning, which centers on an opposition between the real and the ideal (between the heteronomous and the autonomous), and so denies "the most fundamental prerequisites of life," Nietzsche's conception involves a continual process of movement from the attained to the attainable; and it is precisely this that the *rapport à soi* constitutive of the *Übermensch* exhibits. Thus, while Kant offers a juridical conception of practical reasoning structured in terms of the idea of *law,* Nietzsche offers a medical or therapeutic conception articulated through the idea of the type or exemplar. Which is to say, Nietzsche's genealogical investigation (at its best, i.e., its most self-consistent) exemplifies precisely that commitment to the affirmation of life which it recommends, that is, to an *Übermenschlich rapport à soi.* Process, not product; Dionysus, not Apollo.

V

The aim of this chapter has been to question the standard interpretation of Nietzsche's use of the idea of human types, according to which he holds that there are, as a matter of scientific fact, certain naturally occurring subspecies of humanity, and to propose an alternative understanding. If our account of the way in which human types typically figure in Nietzsche's thought is right—that is, if we are right to treat human types as exemplars of various *rapports à soi*—it is clear that any biologically based conception of human types must be simply incapable of making sense of Nietzsche's self-understanding as a cultural physician, his account of practical reasoning, his genealogical technique, his genealogy of morality, his critique of the ascetic ideal and of the Last Man, or, indeed, his recommendation of the *Übermensch* as an exemplar. Moreover, apart from making more sense of Nietzsche's philosophical activity, the account presented here also makes him a much more interesting philosopher, not least as an articulate proponent of the classical understanding of philosophy as medicine for the soul. For Nietzsche, as for Epicurus, "empty is the word of that philosopher by whom no affliction of men is cured. For as there is no benefit in medicine if it does not treat the diseases of the body, so with philosophy, if it does not drive out the affliction of the soul."[7]

NOTES

1. See Mark Warren, *Nietzsche and Political Thought* (Cambridge, Mass.: MIT Press, 1988).

2. Albert R. Jonsen and Stephen Toulmin, *The Abuse of Casuistry: A History of Moral Reasoning* (Berkeley: University of California Press, 1988), 41.

3. Ibid., 40.

4. Ibid., 42.

5. Georges Canguilhem, cited in Thomas Osborne, "Body Amnesia: Comments on Corporeality," in *Sociology after Postmodernism,* ed. David Owen (London: Sage, 1997), 188.

6. See Paul Patton, "Politics and the Concept of Power in Hobbes and Nietzsche," in *Nietzsche, Feminism and Political Theory,* ed. Paul Patton (London: Routledge, 1993), 144–61.

7. Epicurus, cited in R. W. Sharples, *Stoics, Epicureans and Sceptics* (London: Routledge, 1996), v.

CHAPTER 9

Satyrs and Centaurs

Miscegenation and the Master Race

Alphonso Lingis

THE MORAL COMMUNITY

When we go for a walk or a ride, we look at the rhythms of the green hills and the houses nestled among flowering bushes, at the shapes of gnarled pines clamped onto the edges of cliffs and the thousand-year-old barrel trunks of the boab trees in the Australian desert, at the blue hollows in the snowdrifts and the crimson depths of the skies at twilight. We look along the contours of things and down the spaces open between things.

When we go among people, when we leave our apartments to go to work, to go shopping, or to go for some relaxation and entertainment, we exercise a different kind of perception. We see people stationed at equipment, in the drivers' seats of buses, in barbers' chairs, at gas pumps, bank windows, computers, and cash registers. We see people moving down sidewalks, up and down escalators, along aisles. They are bustling about, agitated in every direction, but we sense a low-intensity fear among them. They are avoiding turning in certain directions, flailing their arms or poking their hands in certain ways, avoiding invisible barriers.

The pell-mell, heedless rush of people through the corridors and down the stairs in the subway station at rush hour can make us fear for our safety. Crowd press and panic does erupt sometimes, breaking the barriers and gates. Our perception of the movements of people around us being constrained by invisible cordons, ropes, barriers, and gates makes us feel safe among them, free to attend to our needs and concerns.

We feel that we ourselves, the bulk and mass of our bodies, are walls and barriers for them. As though afraid of us, they avoid colliding into us or entangling their limbs in ours. We feel safe in our workplaces when others treat us with respect, tact, and considerateness.

When we are sitting on the balcony of our hotel, on vacation, we can look out on the patterns and movements of people below like we look out on the forms and colors of a landscape. But when we are down among them, perceiving those invisible barriers, corridors, and gates continually gives rise to judgments—judgments that this one or that one is, that these people are acting or not acting the right way. The clerk in the drugstore located what we wanted, as one expects a clerk to do. We specifically said "No ice" and the waitress brought us orange juice with ice. Those people in the waiting room are shouting. That guy cut right in front of us. And we see moralizing judgments in all their looks turned our way, in a sternness momentarily fixing a glance when we zigzagged through the room full of people, in a knitting of the brow when we talked too loud, in an ostentatious turning away when we took a seat in our sweat-dank clothes.

Perceiving the invisible gates and corridors, sensing that people are, or are not, acting in the right way—this moralizing perception is not the same as perceiving the purpose and inner meaning of their behaviors. But the first, moralizing perception gives rise to the second, rationalizing perception. Seeing where those walking or running legs are heading, what these arms are reaching for, brings to flush another system of corridors, channels, and railings. People are not only keeping to the road because the muddy fields are slippery; this one is walking cautiously because she is carrying produce to sell in the market, that one is pushing through the crowd to catch the last bus home. This employee in the corridor of the supermarket is not only constraining his position and movements such that we can get by; we further see that he is putting price stickers on the sponges or taking the day's inventory of the stock. Perceiving the meaning of the agitations of the people around us is perceiving the goals ahead, the targets, and the stopping places, as well as the obstacles and pitfalls in their way.

The moralizing perception does not depend on this rationalizing perception. Rushing into the airport, we see that it is not choked with people milling around, there is order, there are invisible corridors and ropes and barriers about individuals; that is enough for us to see that we will be able to get done what we have to do. Out in the street we rarely look to see what individuals are doing and why—individuals in construction sites, individuals glimpsed behind windows bent over machines, individuals alone or gathered together on benches in parks. We only scan the scene to see that there are no dams broken, no fences being pushed over, no turnstiles being uprooted.

Catching sight of the goals of their movements, the purposes of their maneuvers, gives us a sharper sense of the ways clear for us. Because the two cars ahead have their turn signals flashing, that street is one-way the right way. Those running steps behind us in the dark merely signal the approach of a jogger. We feel an additional degree of assurance when we sense that the goals of our movements, the purposes of our operations, the reasons for our moves, are visible to those around us.

When, in response to our question, they tell us what they are doing and why, they formulate their account in words we can understand, in terms that make sense to us. When we do not interrupt them to ask, it is because the explanations they give to others make sense to us. Or it is because the invisible guardrails and turnstiles we perceive in their advance and the channels and partition walls we perceive around their operations make us think that they could give explanations that make sense to anyone.

They are constrained to be responsible, to be able to answer to us, to anyone, for what they are doing. They live and act under accusation—constrained in advance to do only what they can justify to anyone. This evidence of everyone held to be responsible, living under accusation, justifies our moralizing perception.

Down on the street, down among individuals of our species, our look scans the invisible walls, gates, and turnstiles around everybody. But our eyes are drawn to exemplary individuals. We perceive a decisive number of individuals as prone to do what is right, at cost to themselves. We perceive an inner force of conviction that prevents them from doing the wrong thing even if they would profit or obtain immediate gratification from doing it. We find assurance in the teller who gives us back the right change, pointing out that there was an extra ten-dollar bill in what we had handed her. We even find assurance in the adolescent who pauses a moment to hold the door for us while his companions are going on, joking among themselves.

We perceive also an inner force of courage in some individuals, which would drive them to prevent wrong being done to someone else even if to do so would result in disadvantage, injury, and even death to themselves. We count on such courage in anyone uniformed as a policeman or policewoman, but we know that police are ineffective unless a decisive percentage of the citizens are ready to risk harm to themselves to report felonious deeds and inform on suspects. The assurance that there is that quantum of courage in the bus driver who will take responsibility for the security of the passengers, in the shoppers in the store who would protect an old or infirm person like ourselves from a purse snatcher, is what our trust in the moral community rests on.

SPECIES INTERATTRACTION

We go among people, to attend to our needs and concerns, to relax and be entertained, Friedrich Nietzsche said, out of a herd instinct. Some human animals are as solitary as orangutans, some as gregarious as chimpanzees; some are as proud and beautiful as panthers, some as timorous and obedient as sheep. Humans have cultured themselves, cultivated themselves, domesticated themselves, confirming and institutionalizing the herd instinct in themselves.

Gregariousness, in Nietzsche's conception, is dependence. An individual is drawn to members of its own species for protection and support. Human animals have not become servile through the force of masters who have subjugated them. They are servile because they want to be servile; unable to direct themselves—unable to will to direct themselves—they scan the corridors and the streets to pick up directives from others. They acquire useful skills, acquiescent dispositions, and deferential postures and attitudes.

The herd instinct works through a specific recognition of protection and support. This recognition is the moralizing perception, which sees the walls, gates, and turnstiles through which people move, and the rationalizing perception, which sees the goals, targets, and stopping places to which their movements are subjugated.

Nietzsche's identification of gregariousness with weakness and dependence invokes an essential egoism, a will to power that is a will to ever more power, in every living organism. Nietzsche failed to recognize that there is a primary interattraction among individuals of a species. Terns, albatrosses, gulls, and boobies accept any member of their species on the isolated, predator-free rocky islands where they collect in vast numbers to lay eggs and raise their young. Prairie dogs, frogs, and many species of insects form undifferentiated multiplicities into which any individuals of these species are attracted. Specific vocalizations, which are not messages conveying warnings or signaling food, convey their species interattraction.

Nietzsche takes gregariousness to characterize species that are prey for other species. But there is an interattraction also among individuals of predatory species—leopards, falcons, and cobras—who hunt alone.

Among members of the human species, there is species interattraction more basic than the moralizing and rationalizing perception that seeks security and support. The most solitary of humans, like van Gogh, Gauguin, Beethoven, or Nietzsche, who flee the security and support of the moral community as domestication and devitalization, are attracted to their own kind, to one another.

The primary interattraction among individuals of the human species involves some sort of recognition. This recognition is not a cold intellectual act that identifies individuals as members of the same species on the basis of certain distinctive traits. It is not the sort of intellectual operation performed by a biologist who identifies species of frogs by the number and color of the spots. It is also not simply a recognition that what we perceive looks similar to us. The primary interattraction, the primary recognition, occurs in laughter and in sexual excitement. These occur as so many random occasions for the gratuitous release and contagion of excess energies.

Already by the age of ten days, when his eyes are not yet focused, an infant recognizes his mother. The infant smiles in response to his mother's smile. It is not that the infant sees the mother's smile, sees the upturned lips in visual space and interprets it as a sign of benevolence, because he knows that when he feels benevolence he smiles. He is not solving a four-term equation: $(my)S/B : (her)S/X$. There are in fact two unknowns: $(my)S = X/B : (her)S/B = X$. The infant has not seen his own smile.

Identification by perception of similar traits remains derivative when the infant grows up. We can see another person as a whole pattern in visual space; we can explore this pattern from all sides by walking about it. But we see only fragments of ourselves—the lower part of our front side only. In reality, we see and recognize another less by the outlines than by the inner lines of their bodies. We recognize our acquaintances at distances too great to discern their complexions and the shapes of their bodies, by the inner diagrams of their gaits and of their gestures. And we cannot see our own gait—not even in a mirror.

For an infant to recognize his mother as one like himself is to feel a current of benevolence invading him. This benevolence is not simply a state in the privacy of a mind; it acts as an attraction of mother to child and of child to mother that induces corresponding motor diagrams in each, induces the facial movement of the mother on the infant. In the attraction they become alike.

Laughter ripples from an infant during the absorption of nourishment or during a warm bath. The excess energy vibrates on itself in intensity, which is felt in the explosive exuberance of laughter. The mother who laughs with her infant also feels a surplus energy over and beyond what is necessary to hold the infant at her breast and produce the milk; she laughs and swings the baby back and forth, she gets up and dances as she rocks the baby. And the baby, looking at the mother's laughing face, laughs now in feeling the excess dancing energies of the mother being communicated to him.

Our perception of the individuals around us yields traits that mark difference, even opposition from us. You find yourself in an airport in Abu Dhabi, unable to leave the transit lounge, an American, when the television is showing the reports of America's bombing of Libya. You push to the back of the room and sit against the back wall, trying to be invisible. A mullah comes into the room, carrying a copy of the Koran and fingering his beads. He does not see your leg stretched out on the floor, trips, and catches hold of a bystander, but as he does so two bottles of Johnny Walker fall from his robes and smash on the floor, soaking you in an alcoholic puddle. Laughter breaks out, spreading wider as people get up to see what is going on. Laughter rises and falls and rises again as eyes meet eyes. The mullah himself and you are laughing when your eyes meet.

In each individual the laughter is now no longer pleasure over the unexpected, the incongruous, but pleasure over the boundaries, the clothing, the body armor of strangers in an airport being dissolved, pleasure over the evident pleasure of others. This laughter makes the object or event that unleashed laughter slip out from attention and sets into motion an intense human communication.

If the mullah had tripped and smashed his smuggled Johnny Walkers in the toilet, he would not have laughed. Awkwardness is transformed into clowning, distress into exuberance, in the transparency of each to the others. And the gratuitous release of energy in laughter gives even the mullah the sense of adolescent insouciance beyond what the bottles of Johnny Walker had promised. The energy of the laughter is felt by those who laugh as a surplus of energy that was in them despite the fatigue of the night, despite the new constraints of the international incident that will affect their lives and yours. We can feel and see all this surplus energy when, ten minutes later, the flight is announced and everybody grabs their bags and jumps up with adolescent gusto.

We recognize whoever laughs as one like us—even if we do not see what he or she is laughing at, do not see what is funny. And we are drawn to anyone who laughs by a primary movement of sensibility. Human interattraction is not at bottom a fearful and cautious alliance for purposes of mutual defense and mutual cooperation. Humans are transparent to one another in the exhilaration unleashed periodically by an awkwardness, an incongruity, an absurdity.

Erotic excitement is also the attraction in which we recognize members of our species. A bare-breasted woman is dancing voluptuously in the street in Salvador during Carnaval; we fix our fevered eyes on her and feel a current of complicity with the men and women around us, white or black, adolescent or aged. We find ourselves aroused by feeling the warm thigh of the dozing passenger next to us on the bus, as we are not aroused by the warm vinyl of the bus seat. During rush hour when we are standing in a packed subway car, we feel in a ripple of excitement someone's fingers lightly brush the inside of our thigh. Whether we are male or female, we feel aroused when, leaning over a gable, we see in the neighboring yard a woman sprawled on a towel spread over the summer grass, pleasuring herself. Whether we are straight or gay, we feel our penis pulsing when we look over some rocks in the summer beach and see a man writhing under a gleaming erection. In his *White Book* Jean Cocteau drew a picture of an aroused penis and labeled it "The part of a man that never lies." Whatever the educated, disciplined, decent mind may say, the penis stiffening, the labia and clitoris throbbing with blood and excitement and pleasure, affirm Yes I like that, yes he or she is my kind, yes I am attracted to him and her.

Philosophers have explained that the identification or recognition of others as members of one's own species is realized in language and in collaboration. We recognize as another human someone with whom we can speak; those whose tongue we do not or cannot learn are babblers and barbarians. But speaking with someone whose tongue we do understand comes to an end when he or she makes truth claims based on his or her tribal ruler, ancestor, or deity. The concept of "humanity" and of belongingness to humanity is then the correlate of the practice of a rational language that makes truth claims based on evidence open to all. Species interattraction depends on the development of the Esperanto of reason.

But if we begin to speak to another, it is because first we recognize him or her as one with whom we could laugh together, and we speak to him or her about what we laugh and weep over. Prior to the speech that is informative and imperative, the speech that directs and orders, there is the speech that articulates for those who were not there and articulates further for those who were what we laugh and weep over, what we bless and curse.

Martin Heidegger took practical behavior to be primary, and for him the primary *Mitsein,* the primary association among individuals of the human species, occurs when we recognize in another someone who deals with implements, obstacles, and goals that we can understand because we can put ourselves in his or her place. But do we not recognize as members of our species all sorts of individuals with whom we have no practical projects in common, who are not collaborators with us?

The kind of practical recognition that Heidegger isolates and analyzes indeed involves interattraction, but not species interattraction. In the measure that I recognize another as like myself because I can plant rice, operate a computer, or pilot an airplane, we team up to separate ourselves from the rest of the species. We seek to identify ourselves as farmers, computer literates, or pilots inasmuch as we set out to plant a row of rice in the paddy alongside the peasant woman, inasmuch as we set out to review what he has on the spreadsheet, inasmuch as, though only verbally, we go through all the names of functions of the dials on the instrument panel of the plane. It is when the computer programmer herself and the pilot himself stumbles and laughs over an operation or an instrument she does not know or he has forgotten that the recognition of common humanity and the attraction between us is suddenly felt.

THE EXOTIC ONES

In our workplace, while shopping, in the laundromat or in the bus, we are distracted by some individuals. The curve of a cheek or breast or torso, the robust harmony of the salient muscles, the richness of a complexion, and the splendor of a mane of hair draw our eyes irresistibly, on policewomen as on idlers, on the street kid knifed and being laid on a stretcher as on the paramedics themselves.

Of all the ways someone can be important to us—a socialized individual whose behavior we can count on, a source of information, a skill enlisted for our tasks, someone whose courage we can appeal to in case of need, a caring companion, someone who shares and appreciates our concerns and pleasures—it seems to us that physical splendor is incidental to all these, and is even a factor of fickleness and betrayal. Philosophers and thinkers concerned with how people interact and with how people could best interact have ended up sensing an opposition between the ethical and the aesthetic, between the ethical person and the beautiful body. We are timid about going up to someone strikingly handsome to ask for assistance or to offer our friendship, sensing that his or her awareness of his or her own physical splendor will make it impossible for him or her to look on our bodies without some level of distaste and disdain. We sense that people of striking physical beauty, peacocks among us poultry, are not the people we should marry, are not the ones who will be devoted to raising our children, are not the people with the most insight when we want to discuss our problems, are not going to be the best amateur or professional sociologists or mathematicians or theologians, and are not the best people to hire to get the job done.

Yet we cannot keep our eyes off them. We cannot stop dreaming of them. When someone of spectacular physical beauty appears, in the airport, in the restaurant, in the office, this apparition nowise fits in, is nowise justified by, the moralizing and justifying perception we have of the people at their posts and moving down invisible corridors. But these now appear somehow vulgar and mean.

Health, not the mere absence of deformity and disease but the evidence of a biological superabundance overflowing the discipline and training that restrains our forces, fascinates us. Our looks are vitalized by the hale and hearty look on laborers who after a full day of grueling toil run off in boisterous horseplay. Serene and assured in the vigor of our own well-being, we are nonetheless spellbound to watch from our hotel window in Rio the electric storm pounding the stranded cars and flooded streets of the city, and below us on the stormy beach, strobe-lit by the lightning, teams of Brazilians shouting hits and misses in a game of beach volleyball.

Beyond the health that we perceive in smooth and effective biological operations and applied work, we catch sight of a health beyond health, triumphant in the number and quantity of onslaughts, contaminations, and corruptions it passes through, admits into itself, and overcomes. Such is the health of vultures and condors. Such is the preposterous health of the young woman come back from trekking the length of Tibet, the brazen health of the young couple who climbed on bicycles at the Arctic Ocean and now, a year later, have reached Tierra del Fuego.

There is also a tropical vigor of the mind that beguiles us. This fascination is different from the assurance and pleasure we find in witnessing the competence, the mastery of the details of the situation, and the calm working out of the solution that we admire in a police officer, a doctor, and an administrator in a department of civic works. There is a kind of mind that fascinates us even when running on idle. We perceive a superabundant energy in that mind that contemplates depravities without flinching, without being contaminated, that rises over them with wisecracks, banter, and laughter. It is the health of mind of the cop who grew up in this neighborhood and who knows all the schemes and scams, betrayals and self-deceits of the punks, junkies, dealers, petty and major racketeers of the neighborhood, but still enjoys no one's company more than theirs in those disreputable bars and fronts. It is the health of mind of the whorehouse madam who has seen everything, believes nothing and no one, and still has a heart of gold and a good sense that social workers and psychotherapists in whose hands her cronies fall from time to time do not have.

We are fascinated by youth. Youth is insolent, impetuous, brash. Without cocky impulsiveness, youth is merely impotence. We are delighted by the shameless old woman who spent her widowhood indulging every whim and pleasure and who, the attorney discovers when she dies, had just spent the last franc of her savings.

Someone who buys up rubies, Persian rugs, and old masters and ensures them or puts them in a bank vault as an investment is scandalously abusing them. The production of luxury objects is destructive of labor that could have been devoted to something useful. Anyone who destroys his wealth, pouring out champagne like water to his visitors or filling the bathtub with it for a woman he has picked up for a one-night stand in a city he is visiting for a convention, understands luxury products. A man who works hard and uses his wealth to purchase jewelry to adorn himself with, suits tailored in London and shoes handmade in Rome, and a hundred-thousand-dollar sports car that he drives cautiously and keeps in meticulous repair will be viewed by everybody as a poor asshole who has a great deal of pathetic needs. How a surge of jubilation will pass through us when we see him take off his gold chain and put it on the throat of a waitress at a truck stop, when he drives his sports car at reckless speeds and can honestly boast one day of driving it into the river.

We who, in moving out among people, are on the lookout for the corridors, gates, and turnstiles that constrain them are reassured by every figure in whom power and direction are consolidated. Years after their downfall tyrants such as Somoza, Marcos, and Pinochet are revered and regretted by a third of the populace. We are also reassured by every David that stands before a Goliath, whether his stone fells or misses him. But the power consolidated in a ruler or in a rebel does not mesmerize us as does the power that exposes itself needlessly to the unforgiving strokes of fate, the fatalities of chance.

These are games in which what one loses, if one loses, is completely disproportionate to what one wins, if one wins. One stands to lose everything. The courage that we count on to maintain the corridors, gates, and turnstiles of the social arena fades before the blazing glory of the bravado that defies, provokes, and challenges death in a gratuitous and unrepeatable game. Is it not the intrinsic glory attached to bravado that accounts for the fact that if we find out that someone we know really has never lied, never cheated on a lover, never duped, never took advantage of a friend, never got shitfaced drunk, never fucked selfish as a beast, we feel a kind of indifference and even disdain for that person?

We watch fascinated a helicopter rescue operation, a mountaineer scaling a vertical cliff, a pair of martial artists performing actions intricate, skillful, and effective. But nothing so mesmerizes us as erotic activities. A woman bursting with erotic pride and decorated with brazen ostentation pumping her way down the corridor of a hospital draws our eyes shamelessly away from the meritorious and medically effective operations of the nurses and doctors. Not only our late capitalist, but every civilization has shamelessly pursued a double standard, honoring with its right hand with medals, parades, and statues women who have selflessly waged superhuman struggles to save their children from hard times or crack gangsters, who have saved the neighborhood from developers and the environment from nuclear pollutants, and also honoring with its left hand cabaret performers, vixens over whom diplomats and heads of state lost their heads, gypsies whose fickle hearts could not sustain a love more than six weeks and over whom an endless succession of men left their wives and children. Nothing a male does—a window washer in the wind sixty floors over the street, a fireman climbing a ladder to rescue an invalid from a blazing building, a champion boxer— so fevers the mind as a male flaunting all his virile voluptuousness. The corrida, where the bullfighter's supple, slender body is poised like a dancer, his genitals flaunted in jeweled splendor from his skintight garb, provocatively exposed to the horn of the ferocious bull, is the supreme theater for the glorification of erotic virility.

Our distracted attention abruptly focused on individuals of extravagant health, sumptuous beauty, smoldering eroticism, or reckless bravado is not surveying, comprehensive, but discontinuous, ecstatic. A wall has been smashed through, a gate torn open, a turnstile overturned. These aberrant, outlandish, exotic individuals are not the sort of landmarks exemplary individuals are. Whenever one of them makes an appearance, we abruptly no longer feel justified in our compulsion to judge, no longer feel that they have a responsibility to answer to and for what they do and say. Our fascination is an imprudent and unwise spasm in our quotidian sensible heads.

MISCEGENATION

Nietzsche saw in the exotics another morality, positive and preceding the morality of the servile. In European history he found the ethics the priests had formulated for the ranks of the feudal system, the serfs and merchants, but also the ethics of warriors and knights—the ethics of guilt and also the ethics of honor, a morality of discipline and a morality of breeding and taste. In the Renaissance the morality of warriors and knights had been instinctually taken up by the builders of cities and empires, the architects and artists, and creators of literature and music.

Nietzsche ranks these anomalous and spectacular individuals as both the first and the higher kind of humans. This ranking is intrinsic: Nietzsche will show in them positive, positing, upsurging forces of life that affirm themselves. Among the servile, not only are the dominant forces self-denying, life-denying, but the servile perception itself is reactive and rancorous; the servile values are constructed by reversing the noble values, the servile conscience is a will turned back on itself, willing willlessness.

But, in addition, there is in Nietzsche's ranking the superiority of creativity, of artistry. Above the truthful mind, accorded to record what is, is the mind that creates visions of what might be; above the body skilled and disciplined to adapt to its environment and to the tasks at hand is the body moving in its own free space, glorying in its multiplicity of rhythms, speeds, and melodic diagrams. The excesses of sentient power give rise to dreams, the power to see what the world does not lay out before our eyes—the individual nocturnal dreams and the daylight dreams of Apollonian artworks. The excesses of energy give rise to dances, non-teleological movements that take and give pleasure in their own rhythms and melodies. Nietzsche's valuation is intrinsic; artistry is not appreciated for what it contributes to the herds of the uncreative and philistine; the artistry of dreamers and dancers is a consecration and glorification of themselves.

Nietzsche's individualism is not tied to the concept of rational self-determination or self-legislation, but to that of an animal independence. Superior physical strength and skills and aggressive instincts are seated in some as individuals. The existence of two moralities, two cultures, was to Nietzsche evidence that, although self-domestication has made the masses of humans gregarious, there are some by nature who are as solitary as the beasts of prey. While Nietzsche sees the herd instinct of the gregarious as dependence, he sees these anomalous individuals as self-sufficient beyond all concern for self-preservation. Theirs is an overflowing, squandering independence.

Nietzsche's individualism, however, falsifies his conception of the existence of the noble animals, of lions, jaguars, eagles, falcons, and serpents. And it falsifies his conception of the relationship between the noble species of animals and the noble individuals within the human species.

Nietzsche's positivism excludes an adequate conception of the relationship of an animal species with its environment. Every species has evolved in an environment, an ecosystem, that supports and sustains it. And every organism inhabits its environment with other individuals of other species. It itself is an environment inhabited by other species. The relationship of an individual with other individuals of its species, and with individuals of other species, is not one of domination and subjugation.

Nietzsche's themes of individualism and creativity seated in the individual make him depict the nobles as drawing their distinctive forces out of a basic animality innate in themselves. But the diagrams of typical behavior a species of organism exhibits are not so many discharges of its reflex circuitry, so many actualizations of its own physiological potentialities.

If Zarathustra associates with lions and eagles, the association would only be one of analogy, of recognized kinship. The identification would be on the mental level: knights saw themselves as lions and tigers, stags and falcons; they decorated themselves with images of lions, tigers, stags, and falcons. But, in fact, did they not really acquire the beauty of their lean forms and swift movements from stallions and foxes? Did they not really acquire their courage from the bulls they faced in the corrida? It is in actually living among lions, stallions, eagles, and serpents that humans take on the noble traits of these species. As it is in actually living among sheep, poultry, and domestic dogs and cats that humans take on the servile traits of these domesticated species.

There is perhaps no species of life that does not live in symbiosis with another species. The microbiologist Lynn Margulis established that chloroplasts and mitochondria, the oxygen-processing cellular energy producers in plants and animals, were originally independent cyano-bacteria that came to live inside the cells of plants and animals. Colonies of microbes evolved separately and then formed the symbiotic systems that are the individual cells, whether of algae or of our bodies.

Human animals live in symbiosis with thousands of species of anaer-obic bacteria—six hundred species in our mouths, which neutralize the toxins all plants produce to ward off their enemies, four hundred species in our intestines, without which we could not digest and absorb the food we ingest. Some synthesize vitamins; others produce polysaccharides or sugars our bodies need. The number of microbes that colonize our bod-ies exceeds the number of cells in our bodies by up to a hundredfold. Macrophages in our bloodstreams hunt and devour trillions of bacteria and viruses entering our porous bodies continually. They replicate with their own DNA and RNA and not ours; they are the agents that main-tain our borders. They, not some Aristotelian form or dominating will, are true agencies of our individuation as organisms.

We also live in symbiosis with rice, wheat, and cornfields, with berry thickets and vegetable patches, and also with the nitrogen-fixing bacte-ria in the soil that their rootlets enter into symbiosis with in order to grow and feed the stalk, leaves, and seeds or fruit. We also move and feel in symbiosis with other mammals and with birds, reptiles, and fish.

During the Neolithic era, human animals began domesticating other animals—sheep and goats, cattle, camels and horses. They fenced them in certain pastures with their circumambulatory movements with whips, stones, and staves. They confined them in corrals, pens, and corridors from one pasture to the next. They drove them to the slaughtering block. They themselves moved within pens and corrals, down roads and corri-dors, through gates and turnstiles, and to stopping places. When they looked at one another, they saw fellow nomads, that is, fellow herdsmen moving with the right or wrong movements within a landscape of cor-rals, pens, and fenced corridors.

It can be argued that the State, as such, resulted from a kind of "chemical" fusion between herdsman and planter, once it was realized that the tech-niques of animal coercion could be applied to an inert peasant mass. Apart from their role as "Lords of the Fertilizing Waters," the first Dictators called themselves "Shepherds of the People." Indeed, all over the world, the words for "slave" and "domesticated animal" are the same. The masses are to be corralled, milked, penned in (to save them from the human wolves outside), and, if need be, lined up for slaughter. The City is thus a sheepfold superimposed over a Garden.[1]

Symbiosis is typically taken to be understood when the association is seen to be beneficial to both sides. This kind of explanation takes the movements issuing from an organism to be teleological, goal oriented. It takes them to issue from a lack or a need. Symbiosis would be interdependence.

But if needs and lacks arise within an organism, it is because an organism is a plenum, a material system that produces more energy than is transmitted into it and releases that energy in movements. So many of these movements are not predatory! Organisms do not move in an environment where everything is at rest; they move among other living organisms, some of which they inhabit, some of which inhabit them. The movements liberated from them do not block or hold those movements only; they compose their differentials, directions, rhythms, and speeds with those movements in the environment.

Nietzsche identified as the "virtues"—*virtus*—of the nobles physical splendor, a health that seeks out and consumes corruption, a tropical vigor of the mind, the cocky impulsiveness and insolence of youth, the compulsion to give away, to squander, the compulsion to play games where what one stands to lose is completely disproportionate to what one stands to win, the compulsion to play games with chance, bravado rather than courage—traits that have never been, cannot be, identified as virtues in ethics, in the ethics of the moral and rational community. They are in fact traits that humans acquire not by actualizing some potential in their natures, in their biologically predatory natures. They are instead traits that they acquire in entering into symbiosis with noble animals.

Nietzsche recognizes that the traits of the nobles are not virtues. The term "virtue" implies merit, acquired through effort and labor. He restores for them the Renaissance concept of *virtu,* which privileges the feature of strength. But Nietzsche thereby falsifies the traits of the nobles by his theory of will to power, which is a will to ever more power. In reality what he identified as features of the nobles unrecognized and unvalued in every rational morality we identify as "exotic traits." They are traits certain humans have acquired in their commerce with other species, and in particular the solitary species recognized from the times of the most ancient cultures as noble animals.

In these animals, their forms, their movements, and their external appearance lend themselves to the utilitarian explanations of biologists. But when a human animal comes to inhabit their territory with them, or even inhabit their bodies as they his, the movements released by the excess energies in his body compose with the differentials, directions, rhythms, and speeds of their bodies. It is then that his body contracts movements that are not acquisitive, stabilizing, or productive, that extend neither toward a sustenance nor a support nor a result. The woman who rides a horse lurches with the surges of its impulses, feeling the thrill of speed and the soothing decompression of retardation. While the speed of the horse serves it in the wild, the thrill of riding nowise serves the woman in the corridors, cubicles, and desks of the rationalized human community. Biologists will explain the immediate urge to attack in the bull as protective of his harem and of his own more vigorous genes, but in the confrontation the fearlessness the torero picks up from the bull no longer has this biological finality and becomes bravado.

Nietzsche does not itemize, among the virtus of the nobles, the unlimited elaboration of eroticism beyond sexual vigor. Indeed, it is hard to construe the erotic parading and swagger as power and will to power. But there is already an extravagance, a gratuity, and a toying with fate in the surface splendors of the other animals, an ostentation that makes them a temptation to their predators. We naked apes have become erotically seductive to one another only by acquiring the splendor of lion and stallion manes in our hair, exposing the splendor of mollusks in our eyes, the harmony of peacocks and cranes in our biped walking, the sleekness of eels and fish in our nakedness. And the gratuity, the bravado, the heedless expenditures, the throwing ourselves after the demonic grail of a flashing grin, a satiny breast, a hairy cock is a fate laid on us in our commerce with foxes and leopards covered with the springtime splendor of their fur, with quetzals in the high mountains, senderowasi birds of paradise in the rain forest, pheasants on the ground spraying in the sun their glittering plumes, with ocean mollusks exposing their nacreous colors and forms.

NOTES

1. Bruce Chatwin, *The Songlines* (London: Picador, 1988), 226.

CHAPTER 10

Nietzsche and the Problem of the Actor

Paul Patton

It is often argued that the modern self enjoys a freedom in relation to the social roles it can adopt that was absent in earlier periods. Thus Steven Lukes has described the modern individual as one who "confronting all possible roles . . . may in principle adopt, perform or abandon any at will (though not all, and probably not even many, at once)."[1] Such a conception of the modern self implies a distinction between the social roles available in a given period and the self that chooses between them. For this reason, social theorists frequently resort to the figure of the actor as a metaphor for the relation between the self and its social identity.

The metaphor provides a convenient means to represent particular social roles as contingent features of selfhood or subjectivity. However, it is a troublesome metaphor. On the one hand, the figure of the self as actor tends to sustain a conception of the essential self behind the social roles. Lukes's description of the modern self above illustrates the first horn of the resultant dilemma. On the other hand, for those who reject as fiction the idea of an indivisible self at the center of individual thought and action, the self seems to collapse into its roles. Erving Goffman's account of the self as a back projection from the roles performed illustrates the second horn. For Goffman, the self is no more than a dramatic effect, something imputed on the basis of performance: "a *product* of a correctly staged and performed scene, not its *cause*."[2] For those like Goffman who reject the idea of an essential self behind the roles, a further series of problems arise with regard to human agency: Who or what is it that acts through the available social roles? How might these roles change?

Alasdair MacIntyre illustrates one of these problems of agency when he argues that the loss of the capacity for moral judgment that is characteristic of modern society may be explained by reference to precisely this experience of selfhood. He presents an account of the modern subject of moral judgment as nothing more than the various moral scripts in terms of which judgments may be framed. Although it is tempting to regard as liberatory the experience of a self that is free to adopt any role, MacIntyre points out this can also lead to moral paralysis: "The specifically modern self . . . finds no limits set to that on which it may pass judgment. . . . Everything may be criticized from whatever standpoint the self has adopted, including the self's choice of standpoint to adopt." [3]

Judith Butler's account of gender as performance offers a further demonstration of some of the tensions inherent in the metaphor of self as actor. In *Gender Trouble,* she characterizes gender as a "performative accomplishment," by which she means that gender roles are achieved by means of the repeated reenactment of certain coded gestures, movements, and corporeal styles. As such, she argues, gender is "a constructed identity, a performative accomplishment which the mundane social audience, including the actors themselves, come to believe and to perform in the mode of belief." [4] Despite her insistence that enactment is constitutive of identity and that there is no true gender identity behind the roles, the metaphor of performativity led some critics to suppose that there must be a subject who chooses to "take on" the roles. To reject this voluntarist conception of gender, *Bodies That Matter* begins by repudiating the suggestion that gendered performance is an "act" in the theatrical sense, or that gender role is a mere artifice that can be taken on or off at will, as though "one woke in the morning, perused the closet or some more open space for the gender of choice, donned that gender for the day, then restored the garment to its place at night." [5]

Thus, against the tendency of the metaphorics of performance to reinstate a conception of the subject who decides to adopt a particular role, Butler argues that there is no subject independent of the norms that constitute gender identity. However, in doing so, she raises all the more starkly the question of agency in relation to gender roles. If gender is embodied by the enactment of norms, and if subjects are only constituted as masculine or feminine by virtue of such enactment, then how can these norms be contested? Butler's answer relies on the iterability of all performance: that repetition is always differential implies the constant possibility of displacement of those norms. Nonetheless, there remains a difference between enacting and being acted by new or different norms that is not yet explained. Some questions that arise in relation to the experiential conditions of agency are left in suspense by this answer.

Nietzsche's reflections on the nature of the self as actor may help to clarify the complex of issues that relate subjectivity to role and agency. He was, of course, among the first to reject the idea of the "soul-atom" and denounce the Christian conception of the will in favor of a conception of the self as multiplicity. At the same time, the actor is one of his principal metaphors for the modern European experience of self. Moreover, it is clear that actors are not his preferred type of "human flora and fauna" (*GS* 356). Zarathustra finds them a noisy species, all too common among the great mass of ordinary Europeans: "where the marketplace begins, there begins the uproar of the great actors" (*Z*:1 "Of the Flies in the Marketplace"). It is not immediately apparent why he should have been troubled by the metaphor of the self as actor. Nevertheless, section 361 of *The Gay Science* begins with his declaration, "The problem of the actor has troubled me for the longest time." The aim of this chapter is to explore Nietzsche's reasons for regarding the actor self as a problem and the relevance of this problem for contemporary questions about social role and agency.

First we need to understand the nature of Nietzsche's problem with regard to the figure of the self as actor. Nowhere in section 361 does Nietzsche explain just what is his problem, although he does provide a clue at the outset when he wonders whether it is not only from the angle of this problem "that one can get at the dangerous concept of the 'artist'—a concept that has so far been treated with unpardonable generosity." This generosity toward the artist is evident throughout *The Gay Science,* many passages of which are devoted to praise of art and artists. For example, in section 107 he argues that art as "the *good* will to appearance" is what enabled we humans to relate to ourselves with a degree of distance and freedom from all-too-human seriousness. In section 290 he argues for the need to "'give style' to one's character," thereby defending a form of relation to the self that treats it as a work of art. In section 78 the theatrical arts are singled out for special praise on the grounds that they, along with religion, have given us the capacity for an internal perspective on who and what we are: Nietzsche writes that artists, "especially those of the theater," have taught us "the art of staging and watching ourselves." The problem of the actor is therefore tied to Nietzsche's enthusiasm for and use of the concept of the artist. It offers him an "angle" from which to articulate doubts about the artistic relation of the self to the self that is otherwise recommended throughout *The Gay Science.*

In section 361 Nietzsche does not state expressly what these doubts are. Instead he outlines a genealogy of the virtues characteristic of the actor, some of which are shared with other kinds of artists. They include "falseness with a good conscience; the delight in simulation exploding as a power that pushes aside one's so-called 'character,' flooding in and at times extinguishing it; the inner craving for a role and mask, for *appearance.*" His suggestion is that these virtues are not peculiar to actors but common to all those whose lives unfold in situations of relative impoverishment or need. The actor's art would have developed among social groups that existed in relations of dependency, such as diplomats, Jews, or women: "Reflect on the whole history of women: do they not *have* to be first of all and above all else actresses?" (*GS* 361). In other words, the actor's instinct is one born out of relative weakness or impoverishment. It is an instinct not so much of slaves but of servants, one that would have developed most readily among families of lower classes who had to survive, as he says,

> in deep dependency, who had to cut their coat according to the cloth, always adapting themselves again to new circumstances, who always had to change their mien and posture, until they learned gradually to turn their coat with *every* wind and thus virtually to *become* a coat. (*GS* 361)

Insofar as this account derives the actor's instinct from the position of relative weakness, it parallels Nietzsche's genealogy of slave morality. However, the very similarity between the conditions of the emergence of slave morality and those of the actor's instinct gives us reason to doubt that this is all there is to the problem of the actor. After all, it is a principle of Nietzsche's genealogical analysis that the value of things is not determined by their origin. In *On the Genealogy of Morals,* he writes, "The cause and origin of a thing and its eventual utility, its actual employment and place in a system of purposes, lie worlds apart" (*GM* II:12). Thus the fact that a mode of being originated in response to dependency does not condition its value in the present. Nietzsche's problem of the actor cannot therefore be derived simply from this account of the origins of the actor's instinct. To fully appreciate this problem, we must turn to a nearby part of *The Gay Science,* section 356, titled "How things will become ever more 'artistic' in Europe." In this passage Nietzsche explores certain consequences of the idea that the actor subject is destined to collapse into its various roles, or that those who turn their coat with every wind end by becoming a coat.[6]

HOW APPEARANCE BECOMES BEING

The Gay Science 356, begins with an observation about Nietzsche's present: "Even today, in our time of transition, when so many factors cease to compel men, the care to make a living still compels almost all male Europeans to adopt a particular *role,* their so-called occupation." Although Nietzsche's ultimate concern in this section does indeed bear on the nature of modern European society, his sociological comment at the outset only serves to introduce a more immediate object of concern, namely, the manner in which social roles can affect the person who assumes them and the manner in which individuals relate to those roles. Over time, he argues, people forget the accidents, moods, or caprices that led them to take up a particular "vocation." They forget the contingency of the fact that they now play this role rather than that role. They forget how many other roles they might have played and confound themselves with the role: "Considered more deeply, the role has actually *become* character; and art, nature" (*GS* 356). Nietzsche is of course not the first philosopher to comment on this phenomenon. In book 3 of *The Republic,* Socrates asks, "Have you not observed that imitations, if continued from youth far into life, settle down into habits and second nature in the body, the speech and the thought?"[7] In the context of Plato's discussion of the appropriate education for the future rulers of the republic, this poses a problem with regard to acting. The phenomenon of role becoming character leads him to argue that the young guardians should not be allowed to play characters less noble than they were expected to become, for fear of corruption. The young men and women should only be allowed to impersonate the deeds of "good men," particularly when these are acting "steadfastly and sensibly."[8]

From the perspective of our own present, Nietzsche's reference to the occupations undertaken by male Europeans is an unnecessary limitation of the phenomenon of role becoming character in at least two respects: men assume roles other than those of occupation or profession, and women also assume a variety of social roles. Butler's account of gender roles as at once performance and an indispensable part of subjectivity or "character" shows that Nietzsche's concern with occupations may be extended to encompass the many kinds of roles involved in the construction of a social identity. It is no doubt true that the sexual politics of the latter part of the twentieth century has made us more aware of the contingency of gender roles than was common in Nietzsche's day. It has also made possible a degree of self-conscious experimentation with gender roles that would have been unthinkable in earlier periods. Conversely, it is more difficult for us late moderns to find convincing examples of the kind of identification of self with a single profession or occupation to which he refers. There is something anachronistic about the idea of such wholehearted identification with one's employment or profession alone: we more readily find examples of this phenomenon in literature or film that deals with the recent past.

Consider the principal character in Ishiguro's novel *The Remains of the Day,* an aging butler addressed only as Mr. Stevens who has spent his life employed in the service of one of the grand houses of the English landed gentry. Stevens's role has become so embedded in his character that he cannot relate to other people, or even to his own actions, except in terms of his conception of what is required of a butler. The novel relates his trip to visit a former housekeeper, Miss Kenton, long since married and moved to the other side of the country. Although there are indications that his visit to this woman has a personal and emotional motivation, Stevens justifies the journey to himself in terms of its potential to resolve a staff problem in the house. This manner of interpreting his own actions sums up Stevens's life and the nature of his relation to Miss Kenton while she was housekeeper under his authority. Despite an emotional attraction between them, he was never able to consider her or their relationship in other than professional terms. At one point, having just repelled an attempt by Miss Kenton to engage in social interaction outside the bounds of their respective roles, he says, "A butler of any quality must be seen to *inhabit* his role, utterly and fully; he cannot be seen casting it aside one moment simply to don it again the next as though it were nothing more than a pantomime costume." [9] A truly great butler thus exhibits the kind of dignity that entails never being induced to abandon the professional being he inhabits. We are given to believe that Stevens has personal opinions, but these he keeps entirely to himself. His ideal of dignity demands that he should never take off his role unless completely alone. On several occasions he displays such dignity: for example, when he continues to serve guests while his father dies, or when Miss Kenton announces her acceptance of another man's offer of marriage.

From a perspective outside that of the butler, it would be easy to see his life as a tragic waste. A familiar humanism would dictate that this was a life in which role had become character to such a degree that the butler is condemned to a life empty of the pleasures of human warmth and companionship. His devotion to his calling cuts him off from the possibility of an open and acknowledged emotional relationship with Miss Kenton. However, Stevens's life can be read as a tragedy only if we assume that there is a true self, an inner core of emotions and desires, that he was unable to express from within the confines of his role. Given the degree to which appearance has become being in his case, it is not clear that any such assumption is warranted. His ethic of service makes total immersion in the role a criterion of greatness as a butler. From the point of view of his own conception of himself, therefore, one cannot deny him a certain moral strength along with his dignity, as a result of his wholehearted commitment to his occupation. His role is a mask, but one that he never takes off, not even when his own happiness or his own grief are at stake. The dignity that he acquires thereby is not unlike that which Zarathustra attributes to the tightrope walker in the prologue. Zarathustra's place in the attention of the crowd in the marketplace is usurped by a tightrope walker, who falls and is about to die. Zarathustra comforts him with the thought that he has undertaken a dangerous occupation and dies in the pursuit of his calling, saying, "There is nothing in that to despise" (Z:1 "Prologue" 5). Stevens too apparently sacrifices his life in the service of his calling. "Apparently" because, in another sense, he only truly becomes who he is (a tightrope walker, a great butler) through the sacrifice of all that is extraneous to the role.

Stevens thus exemplifies the artistic relation to his own life and to himself that Nietzsche praises in *The Gay Science* 290, to the extent that he fashions himself in the service of an ideal. He does live his life as a role, for he allows that the butler persona is something he might shed, although never in front of others. Yet while he is conscious of himself as acting a part, Stevens does not for all that become a mere actor. He genuinely and utterly inhabits his role. Indeed, in the terms of his own definition of what makes a great butler, it is precisely the lesser butlers who are mere actors, for these "will abandon their professional being for their private one at the least provocation. For such persons, being a butler is like playing a pantomime role; a small push, a slight stumble, and the facade will drop off to reveal the actor underneath." [10]

ARTISTS AND ACTORS

The phenomenon of role becoming character is a precondition and a premise for the issue that really concerns Nietzsche in "How things will become ever more 'artistic' in Europe." This phenomenon serves as a prelude to the exposition of a further problem, namely, the prospect of a form of modern life in which acting becomes the predominant mode of relation to social roles and actors become "the real masters." He approaches this problem by contrasting periods of European history in terms of the different manner in which men (he confines his remarks here to male Europeans) experience their relation to their adopted or allotted occupation. First, there are periods in which "men believed with rigid confidence, even with piety, in their predestination for precisely this occupation, precisely this way of earning a living, and simply refused to acknowledge the element of accident, role, and caprice" (*GS* 356). In these periods, such as the Middle Ages, individuals' belief in their predestination for a particular role endows them with a particular "faith" that in turn sustains "classes, guilds, and hereditary trade privileges." Then there are those opposite ages of a more democratic temper, in which "the individual becomes convinced that he can do just about everything and *can manage almost any role*, and everybody experiments with himself, improvises, makes new experiments, enjoys his experiments; and all nature ceases and becomes art" (*GS* 356).

In these more democratic periods, a different kind of "*role faith*" characterizes people's relation to their occupations: "an artist's faith, if you will." This faith first emerged among the Athenians during the Periclean age, and Nietzsche believed that it was becoming more and more the faith of modern Europeans and Americans. Hence the suggestion in the title of this section that things will continue to become ever more "artistic" in Europe. But why should this pose a problem? Elsewhere, as he says in section 361, he has treated the concept of the artist with "unpardonable generosity." He has praised the artist as the figure from whom those who would contribute to the emergence of new values have most to learn, and he has often referred to his own kind as "we artists." Nietzsche's fear in section 356 is therefore not directed at the mode of relation to the self that he calls the artist's role faith. Rather, his fear relates specifically to the fact that this artist's faith is an inherently unstable mode of relating to one's roles. At this point he considers what happens when the phenomenon of appearance becoming being takes over the modern artistic subject: people who experience themselves as capable of managing almost any role tend to become actors "whenever a human being begins to discover how he is playing a role and how he *can* be an actor, he *becomes* an actor" (GS 356).

Nietzsche offers no further justification here for this principle of all-too-human psychology. In "On the Problem of the Actor," he suggests an explanation when he points to the *pleasure* involved in acting. He there refers to "the delight in simulation exploding as a power that pushes aside one's so-called 'character,' flooding in and at times extinguishing it" (GS 361). Whatever the reason, what does occur once individuals become conscious of their occupations as roles is here described as "a rather odd metamorphosis that does not merit imitation in all respects" (GS 356). In effect, what was hitherto a particular mode of relating to one's roles (consciously, artistically) expands to become the only role. What was initially a metarole, a mode of relating to the variety of roles one might have adopted, becomes a role like any other. The artist-self collapses into a single role, and the individual becomes just an actor. Goffman points to a plausible basis for this dynamic when he notes that the very obligation to appear as a socially acceptable character forces people to become "practiced in the ways of the stage." [11] According to Nietzsche, the phenomenon of artists becoming actors first appeared among the Greeks, whom he described in *Daybreak* as "actors incarnate" who "*play-acted before themselves*" (D 22). Modern individuals, he fears, are well advanced along this same road.

A WORLD OF ACTORS

Far from being an occasion for unqualified celebration, the suggestion that things will become ever more "artistic" is thus a cause for concern on Nietzsche's part. His worry relates to the fact that this process will lead to more and more people perceiving themselves as actors. The remainder of section 356 explores the social consequences of such a state of affairs. Nietzsche's attitude is clearly ambivalent. On the one hand, he favors the capacity for invention and experimentation that comes with the role faith of the artist and the fact that the artistic relation to the self allows individuals to "enjoy" their experiments in self-creation. For these reasons he welcomes those periods in which "the 'actors,' *all* kinds of actors, become the real masters" as among the "maddest and most interesting ages of history."

But, on the other hand, he worries that such periods are disadvantageous to the flourishing of another type, namely, the "great architects" endowed with the strength to build, those with the courage to make plans that encompass the distant future and those with a genius for organization. The state builders in *On the Genealogy of Morals* were artists of this sort, exemplifying that "terrible artists' egoism that has the look of bronze and knows itself justified to all eternity in its 'work'" (*GM* II:17). However, these were "involuntary and unconscious" artists, individuals who exemplified a premodern faith in their predestination for a particular way of life. Nietzsche believes not only that individuals of this type were the founders of society but also that they were the foundations on which rested the possibility of a durable social order. Premodern societies were built on the role faith of individuals who perceived their roles as destiny and who saw themselves as having value only insofar as they were like stones set *"in a great edifice"* (*GS* 356). The argument of *The Gay Science* 356 is that such unconscious artists will become an endangered species once actors become the dominant type of "human flora and fauna." When *"all* kinds of actors" become masters, what dies out is "the fundamental faith that would enable us to calculate, to promise, to anticipate the future."

Nietzsche's diagnosis of the way things are headed in modern society anticipates much that has been written about "postmodernity." He points to an important feature of modern social systems in noting that they are not "societies" in the old sense of the term. They do not rely on the role faith of earlier periods but are indeed compatible with the role faith of actors. In this sense, he argues, *"all of us are no longer material for a society; this a truth for which the time has come"* (*GS* 356). In other respects this diagnosis appears to be incomplete. Nietzsche's comments take no account of the extent to which, even in his own time, European society had become dependent on systems of production and consumption that generated their own mechanisms of calculation and anticipation of the future. He did not appreciate or foresee the development of global systems that regulate the movement of individuals, goods, and information and that embody their own immense "genius for organization." Modern societies are indeed "cynical" in the sense that the beliefs of individuals are no longer foundations of social order. The manner in which individuals relate to their occupations and roles is similarly irrelevant to the maintenance and reproduction of modern society.

Yet Nietzsche's diagnosis is also prescient in ways that he could not have foreseen. Twentieth-century developments in the technology of the image, along with the manner in which these have become central to the government of populations, have transformed the public sphere of modern social life into an electronic stage. There are unconscious as well as involuntary actors among the performers: some of them are genuine, but most of them are bad actors. The career of one of the most famous bad actors in recent times, Ronald Reagan, confirms Nietzsche's claim that we are no longer material for a society in the old sense of that word. Reagan's success as a politician turned precisely on the fact that he was an actor and that he was perceived to be acting his political roles. He stands as an emblem of a social world in which subjects have become actors and governing means "giving acceptable signs of credibility." Modern politics is driven by perceptions of reality, and political consensus "is like advertising and it is the same effect that is achieved—commitment to a scenario." [12]

There are several dangers associated with this self-conscious and experimental state of social being. One is that feelings of insecurity and *ressentiment* will lead some to attempt to reinstate the old form of society as an edifice made of stone.[13] Another is that attachment to any ideals other than the instrumental ones of good performance will be lost. Mere actors are not artists in the sense that Nietzsche values the artistic mode of relation to the self. His objection to actors is that they lack the wholehearted commitment to their occupations and roles that he considers to be a condition of the creation of new values. The problem is not just that in a society of actors we are unlikely to find many examples of the type of artist who possesses the capacity to consciously create new institutions or forms of life and thereby new values. For Nietzsche, new values are always embodied in new institutions and forms of social life, and it is not only those who consciously abandon the old who contribute to the creation of the new. One of the social conditions for the emergence of new types of human beings is the extreme embodiment of existing institutions and practices. Those who push a given form of life to its limits also contribute to the emergence of the new. At various points in *Thus Spoke Zarathustra*, Nietzsche points to virtues that are required if one is to contribute to the creation of new values. These include courage and commitment to a single virtue, even to the point that one lives or dies for one's virtue. They include the capacity to truly want a particular course of action: "Always do what you will—but first be such as *can will*" (Z:3 "On the Virtues That Make Small" 3). On Nietzsche's analysis, willing always involves the *affect* of command: there is something in the self that obeys, or that one believes obeys. Mere actors are those in whom this affect is absent. Consider Zarathustra's complaint against those he calls "the small men":

> Some of them will, but most of them are only willed. Some of them are gen-
> uine, but most of them are bad actors. There are unconscious actors among
> them and involuntary actors; the genuine are always rare, especially genuine
> actors. (Z:3 "On the Virtues That Make Small" 2)

As a rule it is genuine people rather than actors who are capable of willing. Throughout his writings he contrasts genuine persons with mere
actors. In *Twilight of the Idols* he asks: "Are you genuine? or only an actor? A representative? or that itself which is represented?" (*TI* "Maxims
and Arrows" 38). There are, of course, as the passage above suggests,
also "genuine actors." These are neither unconscious nor involuntary
actors but individuals who consciously and deliberately adopt certain
roles, and who pursue them even at the expense of their other desires,
like Mr. Stevens in *The Remains of the Day*. However, even genuine
actors are bound by the confines of the roles they have chosen to play.
Stevens's career demonstrates the limitations of this type, because as a
servant he willingly accepts limits to what he may say or do. The genuine artist is one whose will is not constrained in this way by the scripts
available to a given role at any given time.

   The problem with the actor subject thus turns out to be a problem of
agency, although not in precisely the same terms as those problems that
were identified at the outset above. Nietzsche's problem concerns the
possibility of willing where this involves the capacity to identify one's
self with certain roles and motives at the expense of others. It is only indirectly related to the possibility of change or variation in the roles available at any given time. It closely resembles the problem that MacIntyre
identifies as arising from the modern experience of selfhood, namely, the
loss of any strong identification with particular values, motives, or reasons for acting and thereby the capacity for moral judgment. Nietzsche
poses the problem somewhat differently in terms of the shift from the
role faith of the artist to that of the actor. His fear is that the role faith
of the artist can too easily become the role faith of the actor, when he
would prefer that it become more like the role faith of the unconscious
artist, the believer in destiny for whom the individual is solid, "and
above all not an actor!" (*GS* 356). His point is not that the modern self
lacks any culturally embedded character but that it risks acquiring the
superficial character of a mere actor. Both of these problems with regard
to agency express a common underlying difficulty facing modern indi-

viduals: that of being aware of the arbitrary character of the roles that one has assumed, and of the contingency of the fact that one has assumed these roles, but no less committed to some of them despite that awareness. The task, in other words, is to have an artistic relation to oneself and yet avoid becoming a mere actor with no commitment other than the faith in one's ability to assume any given role.

NOTES

An earlier version of this chapter, titled "Postmodern Subjectivity: The Problem of the Actor (Zarathustra and the Butler)," appeared in *Social Analysis*, no. 30 (1991): 32–41. For their comments and helpful discussion in the course of revision, I am indebted to Moira Gatens, William Connolly, Kathleen Higgins, and, particularly, Justine McGill.

1. Steven Lukes, conclusion to *The Category of the Person*, ed. M. Carrithers et al. (Cambridge: Cambridge University Press, 1985), 298.
2. Erving Goffman, *The Presentation of Self in Everyday Life* (London: Allen Lane and Penguin, 1969), 223.
3. Alasdair MacIntyre, *After Virtue* (Notre Dame: University of Notre Dame Press, 1981), 30.
4. Judith Butler, *Gender Trouble* (New York: Routledge, 1990), 141.
5. Judith Butler, *Bodies That Matter* (New York: Routledge, 1993), x.
6. This is not the first passage in which Nietzsche considers the phenomenon of appearance becoming being. Consider *Human, All-Too-Human* 51: "*How appearance becomes being*":

> Even when in the deepest distress, the actor ultimately cannot cease to think of the impression he and the whole scenic effect is making, even for example at the burial of his own child; he will weep over his own distress and the ways in which it expresses itself, as his own audience. The hypocrite who always plays one and the same role finally ceases to be a hypocrite; for example priests, who as young men are usually conscious or unconscious hypocrites, finally become natural and then really are priests without any affectation; or if the father fails to get that far then perhaps the son does so, employing his father's start and inheriting his habits. If someone obstinately and for a long time wants to *appear* something it is in the end hard for him to *be* anything else. The profession of almost every man, even that of the artist, begins with hypocrisy, with an imitation from without, with a copying of what is most effective. He who is always wearing a mask of friendly countenance must finally acquire a power over benevolent moods without which the impression of friendliness cannot be obtained—and finally these acquire power over him, he *is* benevolent.

7. Plato, *The Republic* 395d.
8. Ibid., 396d.

9. Kazuo Ishiguro, *The Remains of the Day* (London: Faber and Faber, 1989), 169. Emphasis in original.

10. Ibid., 42.

11. Goffman, *Presentation of Self,* 222.

12. Jean Baudrillard, *America,* trans. Chris Turner (London: Verso, 1988), 109; originally published as *Amerique* (Paris: Éditions Bernard Grasset, 1986). On Reagan, see Brian Massumi, "The Bleed: Where Body Meets Image," and the response by Paul Patton, "Reagan and the Problem of the Actor," in *Rethinking Borders,* ed. John C. Welchman (London: Macmillan, 1996), 18–50.

13. William Connolly points to this danger as the one realized in contemporary forms of fundamentalism, in "Reworking the Democratic Imagination," *Journal of Political Philosophy* 5, no. 2 (June 1997): 194–202.

CHAPTER 11

Nietzsche's Contest

Nietzsche and the Culture Wars

Alan D. Schrift

But as the youths to be educated were brought up to compete
with one another, their educators in their turn were in contest
with each other. Full of mistrust and jealousy, the great music
masters Pindar and Simonides took their places next to each
other; the sophist, the advanced teacher of antiquity, contested with his fellow sophist; even the most general way of
teaching, through drama, was only brought to the people in
the form of an immense struggle of great musicians and
dramatists. How wonderful! . . . What a problem reveals
itself to us when we enquire about the relationship of
competition to the conception of the work of art!—
        Friedrich Nietzsche, "Homers Wettkampf"

. . . I have been more a *battlefield* than a human being.
        Letter to Heinrich Köselitz, 25 July 1882

Nearly a half century ago, at the conclusion of his contribution to the
Festschrift honoring Ernst Jünger, Martin Heidegger observed that
"Nietzsche, in whose light and shadow everyone today, with their 'for
him' or 'against him,' thinks and reflects, heard a command which demands a preparation for taking over a dominion of the earth. He saw
and understood the conflict for domination about to be enkindled [and]
heard that command to reflect on the essence of a planetary domination." [1] That Heidegger sees Nietzsche heeding a command to reflect and
prepare for earthly domination is of less interest to me than his noting

that everyone thinks in terms of a position for or against Nietzsche. In particular, the gesture of setting up "Nietzsche" as a battlefield on which to take one's stand against or to enter into competition with the ideas of one's intellectual predecessors or rivals has happened quite frequently in the twentieth century. We see this gesture in Heidegger's own reading of Nietzsche as a response to the vitalist / racist readings of Nazi ideologues like Oehler and Bäumler; in Adorno and Horkheimer's reading as a leftist response to Heidegger and to fascism; in Deleuze's reading as a challenge to the French Hegelians; in the sixties / structuralist references to Nietzsche in the context of their social scientific and antiacademic challenge to Sorbonne philosophical orthodoxy; in Derrida's choice to make his first real departure from Heidegger through his reading of Nietzsche in *Spurs;* in Gadamer and Derrida choosing to debate the merits of dialogue versus deconstruction at the Paris Goethe House encounter in terms of their respective readings of Nietzsche vis-à-vis Heidegger; and so on. The list could continue, but the point should be clear: there is something about "Nietzsche" that makes him a desirable site for such polemics. In fact, perhaps more than any other philosopher in the twentieth century, Nietzsche brings us face-to-face with, to borrow a phrase from Derrida, *the politics of the proper name.*

As the twentieth century draws to a close, we see this polemical turn to Nietzsche again in the most recent philosophical developments in France. At roughly the same time that Jürgen Habermas, in *The Philosophical Discourse of Modernity,* was taking his stand on Nietzschean terrain against the French for following Nietzsche's anti-Enlightenment and antimodern itinerary, a new generation of French thinkers appeared who also set "Nietzsche" up as a primary site on which to specify their reasons for turning away from the views of their teachers—the "philosophers of the sixties"—those philosophers who in the English-speaking philosophical community have come to be called "poststructuralists." These reasons have much to do with what each generation saw to be the task of philosophy. But they have to do as well with the new generation's turn away from what they regard as the excessive and irresponsible political stances of their philosophical predecessors. Seeing the need both for a rejuvenated notion of the subject and for a notion of community grounded in liberal-democratic principles, they refuse to overlook the incommensurability of many of the assumptions and conclusions of French Nietzscheanism with this or any other notion of community.

Taking Nietzsche as the site of their stand against the "philosophers of the sixties" is certainly a part of what is going on in two of the better-known works to have been written by this new generation of French thinkers: Vincent Descombes's *Le même et l'autre: Quarante-cinq ans de philosophie française (1933–1978)*[2] and Luc Ferry and Alain Renaut's *La pensée 68: Essai sur l'anti-humanisme contemporain.*[3] If these works left any doubt concerning the role their authors thought Nietzsche played in the evolution of the French left avant-garde in the 1960s, their position on the Nietzschean tradition in France was made explicit in a work on which they and several others collaborated, a work whose polemical title states the matter clearly: *Pourquoi nous ne sommes pas nietzschéens.*[4] In this collection the authors put forward their objections both to Nietzsche and to those Nietzscheans (read "poststructuralists") who dominated the French academic world when these authors began their studies in the 1960s. These "master thinkers" of the sixties—Foucault, Deleuze, Derrida, Althusser, Lacan—taught them that the ideals of the Enlightenment were only "a bad joke, a somber mystification"; they turned them away from the humanism of Merleau-Ponty and Sartre, introducing them instead to "the philosophers of suspicion: Marx, Freud, and Heidegger of course, but above all, Nietzsche, the inventor of that 'genealogy' in the name of which [they] had to treat every discourse as a symptom."[5] Arguing against the basic precepts of poststructuralism, the essays in this collection call in one way or another for philosophy to refrain from its recent tendency toward "infinite deconstruction" and to return instead to its "ancestral desire for rationality, which the relativism of the modes of thought of difference" made too easy to renounce.[6]

The authors of these essays admit a certain indebtedness to Nietzsche, which is to say, they acknowledge that "no one today believes in Absolute Knowledge, in the meaning of history, or in the transparency of the Subject."[7] But while "thinking with Nietzsche," they make clear that they will also think against him—against his resistance to argumentation, against his repudiation of truth, against his objections to democracy and equality. And they make equally clear that they refuse to follow the philosophical itinerary that marks the Nietzschean*ism* of the generation of thinkers in France who immediately preceded them. In fact, in many of the essays it is as much the Nietzschean*ism* of their predecessors as Nietzsche's ideas themselves that becomes the focus of critique. Because the French Nietzscheans are seen to valorize Nietzsche's immoralism, elitism, and hierarchization—positions that, however philosophically interesting, the French anti-Nietzscheans claim must be challenged on realpolitikal grounds—they are in turn criticized for overlooking all that is politically problematic in Nietzsche's thinking. So, for example, we have André Comte-Sponville offering an extended reading of many of Nietzsche's more disturbing passages in which he finds Nietzsche articulating brutish, racist, elitist, sophistic, and aestheticized views that run against so much of what underpins the ideals of modern liberal democracy that he can only ask, in concluding, "why would we be Nietzschean?"[8] Or, taking another example, we find Descombes focusing on the contemporary French Nietzscheans conflating rhetoric and philosophy, denying rationality, and merely repeating Nietzsche's critique of modern philosophy without adding anything of philosophical merit to that critique. More troubling still, according to Descombes, is that when they do go beyond Nietzsche's own critique, the Nietzscheans make things worse, because while Nietzsche's critique was philosophical, their contributions—"philosophically incoherent," "badly conceived," and put forward in terms that are "desperately confused"—leave philosophy for a discourse whose rhetoric is morally irresponsible and politically dangerous.[9]

How should one respond to such critiques? Writing in the genre of polemic, these writers do not seek to understand the authors they are reading. Instead, they want to indict: like lawyers, they marshal the evidence in as damaging a way as possible in order to justify their political indictment of "neoconservatism," "irresponsibility," or "barbarism." Why do they choose to take this approach? Well, for one reason, because it sells. And not just in France. For clearly there is an audience for such "criticisms" on this side of the Atlantic, as can be seen in the appearance of the recent series from Princeton University Press, edited by Thomas Pavel and Mark Lilla, titled "New French Thought." Pavel and Lilla's editorial "mission statement" leaves little doubt as to their intentions: "The aim of this series is to bring to a cultivated public the best of recent French writing in the humanities in clear, accessible translations. The series focuses on the younger generation of philosophers, historians, and social commentators who represent the new, liberal, humanistic bent of French intellectual life." The perspective of the editors is made more clear, perhaps, in Lilla's introduction to one of their first publications, *New French Thought: Political Philosophy*, where he writes that "the almost universal abandonment of the Hegelian, Marxist, and structuralist dogmas" on the French intellectual scene in the last fifteen years has "also signaled the demise of a certain conception of the intellectual himself, as a 'master thinker' whose philosophy of history or theory of power licensed him to deliver ex cathedra judgments on the political events of the day. This image of the French *philosophe* may still have its admirers in certain airless corners of American and British universities, but it has virtually disappeared in France."[10]

Whether this last comment is wishful thinking on Lilla's part is worth questioning,[11] especially in light of Pierre Bourdieu's emergence as a dominant cultural force in France in the 1990s. Moreover, Lilla's conclusion that the presence of the philosophers known as "poststructuralist" has "virtually disappeared" in France is, to say the least, overstated. One need only look at the number of conferences, new books, and special journal issues addressing Deleuze's work that have recently appeared in France,[12] or take note of the attention paid to the publication of Foucault's four-volume *Dits et écrits*[13]—arguably the most significant publishing "event" in France in the past decade—to realize that it is not only the English-speaking world that is interested in the work of French poststructuralist philosophers.

But to repeat the question I raised a moment ago: how should one respond to the polemical attacks coming from these new *nouveaux philosophes?*[14] Several rejoinders are possible. Some will no doubt try to defend Nietzsche and the French Nietzscheans, answering the criticisms one by one and constructing a defense against the accusations raised. I, however, am not certain that such a defense is necessary. This is not to say that I agree with the criticisms raised by recent French (or German, for that matter)[15] anti-Nietzscheans against either Nietzsche or his French legacy. But it is to say that, in a sense, this line of defense has already been made, by Derrida among others, in response to the Nazi appropriation of Nietzsche, and Derrida's general rejoinder can be applied as well to readings like those of Comte-Sponville, Descombes, and Ferry and Renaut.[16] In particular, one of the points that emerges in Derrida's response is that Nietzsche wrote some things that lend themselves to the sort of use made of his works by the Nazis. Consider the following remark from *Otobiographies* in the context of a reading of Nietzsche's 1872 text, *On the Future of Our Educational Institutions.*

> Even if the intention of one of the signatories or shareholders in the huge "Nietzsche Corporation" had nothing to do with it, it cannot be entirely fortuitous that the discourse bearing his name in society, in accordance with civil laws and editorial norms, has served as a legitimating reference for ideologues. There is nothing absolutely contingent about the fact that the only political regime to have *effectively* brandished his name as a major and official banner was Nazi.[17]

Which is to say, it is not just the result of an unfortunate coincidence or Nietzsche's bad luck that his works, rather than the works of, say, Kant or Leibniz became linked as they did with National Socialism.

But does this make Nietzsche a Nazi? Of course not. It does, however, say something about his texts and the risks that all writers run when they allow their works to enter the sphere of public discourse; namely, when they make their writings public, they sanction de facto their work being appropriated and grafted onto other contexts. These risks become extreme when a writer chooses to write with the hyperbolic rhetoric that one finds in Nietzsche. And one finds this same rhetorical excess in much of the work of recent French philosophers, an excess that Ferry and Renaut in particular exploit constantly in their own often rhetorically excessive response to the "sixties philosophers." [18]

This response is not the one I wish to pursue here, however. For although I think that one can, and others perhaps will, defend Nietzsche and the French against their readings at the hands of Descombes or Ferry and Renaut, I have chosen to draw attention to the French anti-Nietzscheans not to refute their interpretations but because they have chosen to focus on Nietzsche and the Nietzscheanism of poststructuralist French philosophy to make what is fundamentally a *political* rejoinder to the writings of the philosophers who I have framed elsewhere as "Nietzsche's French legacy." [19] As such, their critiques represent what one might call a sign of the new times in France, and perhaps elsewhere.

But as several recent works have shown, Nietzsche's fortunes have played themselves out among both the left and the right almost since his texts first appeared.[20] The recent turn to the right in Europe and the United States, and the resurgence of nationalism often accompanying if not driving this turn, has led to new associations between Nietzsche and the right that should concern those leftist intellectuals, in the English-speaking world and elsewhere, who will continue to turn to Nietzsche as a philosophical resource. Left-leaning readers of Nietzsche have legitimately criticized those readings that make Nietzsche out to be a "simple" misogynist, or a straightforwardly anti-Semitic or anti-Enlightenment thinker. But at the same time, there are problems with many of those readings that seek to "save" Nietzsche from charges of misogyny or anti-Semitism or to make him compatible with a leftist or left-leaning liberal-democratic politics. Rather than directly confront and take account of Nietzsche's many crudely racist, sexist, or elitist remarks, those who attempt to package Nietzsche as a champion of the left often choose to overlook them as insignificant or momentary lapses. With a writer whose prose is both as nuanced and as excessive as Nietzsche's, a certain amount of selective inattention may be unavoidable. But as philosophical and political centers are shifting to the right, which appears to be the case as we approach this *fin de millennium,* we overlook the less progressive of Nietzsche's remarks at our peril.[21]

Does this mean one should give up on Nietzsche, turning to a "safer" thinker like Kant or Levinas? I do not believe it does. For many of the themes that first led the French to Nietzsche in the sixties are worth recalling today—themes like emphasizing perspective and interpretation; attending to power differentials and the links between relations of power, discursive practices, and knowledge relations; refusing to see the world as a series of binary, hierarchical oppositions; attending to the interconnections of philosophical, cultural, and political institutions; seeing the world in terms of relations and becoming rather than in terms of fixed identities; making judgments—political and ethical as well as aesthetic—without appealing to fixed, formal or given criteria. And other Nietzschean themes, in particular, the critique of nationalism and the critique of fixed notions of self-identity, while not necessarily a part of the sixties Parisian landscape, may be more relevant today than ever. This may in part explain why, at this historical moment, Nietzsche has become as important a resource, and as omnipresent a reference, for the cutting edge of critical scholarship in the *English*-speaking philosophical and critical worlds in the 1980s and 1990s as he was for the philosophical-literary avant-garde in Paris in the 1960s and 1970s.

Is this simply another case of the English-speaking scholarly community's operating twenty years behind the continental times? Or are we witnessing genuinely innovative American, British, and Australian developments of the poststructural themes that emerged from the French Nietzscheanism of the sixties and seventies? If, as I would like to suggest the essays collected in this volume indicate, the answer to this latter question is yes, then we will have to see whether the English-speaking critical world will be able to avoid the backlash against Nietzsche's influence that has emerged recently in France. But it bears noting that this backlash has already started in the United States, as Nietzsche's name, alone or in conjunction with many of the French Nietzscheans, has often been mentioned in politically motivated attacks on the "left's" supposed "control" of the American academy. The most widely discussed example has been, of course, Allan Bloom's *Closing of the American Mind.*[22] But one might also consider the rhetorical function Nietzsche plays in James Miller's *The Passion of Michel Foucault*.[23] Or how, in the popular press's reporting of "The Heidegger Affair" and "The DeMan Affair," it was not uncommon to loosely link Heidegger's or DeMan's reported Nazi sympathies backward to Nietzsche and forward to Derrida and deconstruction. Although these links usually are incapable of standing up to close critical scrutiny, they seem often to take hold in the imagination of the popular audience, as we can see, for example, in the following rhetorical ploy found in the work of one of the darlings of the intellectual right, Dinesh D'Souza, whose *Illiberal Education* moves on one page from J. Hillis Miller, Geoffrey Hartmann, and Jacques Derrida to DeMan's writings to *Mein Kampf* and back to *Allegories of Reading* before closing with a non sequitur misquote from Nietzsche: "men would rather believe in nothingness than believe in nothing."[24]

There is, however, reason to be optimistic about the future of Nietzsche's legacy, especially insofar as the identity politics that has produced ethnic nationalisms in Eastern Europe and Africa calls for a critical response in which the Nietzschean critiques of both identity and nationalism can be of value. For example, while much interpretive work is needed to show how Nietzsche can be used to support democratic pluralism, such work can be and is being done.[25] Consider, in this regard, the following comment from Ernesto Laclau:

> A democratic society is not one in which the "best" content dominates unchallenged but rather one in which nothing is definitely acquired and there is always the possibility of challenge. If we think, for instance, in [*sic*] the resurgence of nationalism and all kinds of ethnic identities in present-day Eastern Europe, then we can easily see that the danger for democracy lies in the closure of these groups around full-fledged identities that can reinforce their most reactionary tendencies and create the conditions for a permanent confrontation with other groups.[26]

This, I would argue, is precisely the sort of leftist political position that a Nietzschean account of—and critique of—nationalism and identity can be used to support.

In fact, one might begin such a Nietzschean account with an examination of section 475 of *Human, All-Too-Human,* where Nietzsche offers one of his most powerful indictments of nationalism. In the context of rejecting the artificial and perilous separation of Europe into distinct nations through the "production of *national* hostilities," Nietzsche suggests that it is not the interests of the many but the interests of a few—"certain princely dynasties and certain classes of business and society"—that "impel to this nationalism." It is precisely at this point that Nietzsche situates the origins of modern anti-Semitism: "The entire problem of the *Jews*," he writes, "exists only in national states." He continues, in a passage that should refute definitively the charge that Nietzsche is simply and straightforwardly anti-Semitic,

> It is here that their energy and higher intelligence, their capital in will and spirit accumulated from generation to generation in a long school of suffering, must come to preponderate to a degree calculated to arouse envy and hatred, so that in almost every nation—and the more so the more nationalist a posture the nation is again adopting—there is gaining ground the literary indecency of leading the Jews to the sacrificial slaughter as scapegoats for every possible public or private misfortune. (*HH* 475)

Whether Nietzsche himself may succumb to an identity politics at the level of culture or ethnicity that his philosophical critique of nationalism should have distanced him from is, of course, a matter worth addressing. But insofar as he here provides tools for a critique of national identity in favor of the *cosmopolitan* ideal of producing "the strongest possible European mixed race," there is still reason to look to his critique as a resource for criticizing a politics of ethnic or cultural identity.

Similarly, the Nietzschean critique of dogmatism, grounded as it is on a perspectivist position that calls for multiplying points of view and avoiding fixed and rigid posturings, may be an important voice to heed in constructing a politics that can challenge the panoply of emerging fundamentalisms. At the same time, a thoroughgoing perspectivism can accommodate a notion of radical contingency that seems both theoretically desirable and pragmatically necessary at the present moment to many who—from the perspectives of feminist and gender studies, queer theory, minoritarian studies, cultural studies, and, in general, from any oppositional perspective—hope to move from theory to action. In other words, to be able to see the world with more and different eyes (*GM* III:12) now appears to be a political necessity for those individuals who, by virtue of their membership in certain historically marginalized groups, find themselves in socially subordinated positions that result from traditional and/or essentialist judgments as to their diminished worth. By refusing to dogmatically maintain traditional group identifications as simply the objective and necessary recognition of "natural kinds," an appeal to the radical contingency of such groupings opens all sorts of avenues of resistance by those who have suffered from the traditional and oppressive distribution of powers, goods, and privileges.

In one of his earliest pieces, the unpublished "Homers Wettkampf," Nietzsche suggests that the Greeks knew that "competition is vital if the well-being of the state is to continue" (HC 191). Indeed, as the agonistic opposition between the Apollonian and Dionysian arts continually incited each other to new and more powerful creative productions (see *BT* 1), the Greek educational system was designed to cultivate respect for the *agon*. In fact, in contrast to what Nietzsche regarded as the modern ambitiousness that seeks the exclusive position of absolute dominance, the Greeks saw the ongoing contest of powers as necessary for cultural advancement. The kernel of the Hellenic idea of competition, he writes, is its loathing "a monopoly of dominance and fear[ing] the dangers of this, it desires, as *protective measure* against genius—a second genius" (HC 192; translation altered). The Greeks' hostility to the "'exclusivity' of genius in the modern sense" is born of their recognition that not only will several geniuses incite each other to action; they will also "keep each other within certain limits" (HC 191–92).

An absolute victory within the *agon* would thus mark the death of the *agon*, and Nietzsche acknowledges that to preserve freedom from dominance, one must be committed to maintaining the institution of the *agon* as a shared public space for open competition. It was, according to Nietzsche, through their healthy respect for competition that the Homeric Greeks were able to escape "that pre-Homeric abyss of a gruesome savagery of hatred and pleasure in destruction" (HC 193) that we learn about in Hesiod's *Works and Days*, "a world of myths in which Uranus, Kronos and Zeus and the struggles of the Titans would seem like a relief" (HC 188). And without that healthy and respectful competition, Greek culture could only deteriorate, as evidenced by the declines of Athens and Sparta following their respective rises to unrivaled cultural hegemony.

What Nietzsche's reading of the Greek *agon* shows us, and what I think Nietzsche's critiques of nationalism and the metaphysical assumptions underlying rigid identity politics should show us as well, is that a politics of difference is not only just; it is also good. The merits of such an agonal politics have been explored recently by several political theorists. Chantal Mouffe, for example, has made the "permanence of conflict and antagonism" a central feature in her articulation of a "radical and plural democracy." Contrary to liberal democratic theorists like John Rawls, for whom conflict and antagonism are "seen as disturbances that unfortunately cannot be completely eliminated, or as empirical impediments that render impossible the full realization of a good" that total social harmony would constitute, Mouffe argues that pluralism is necessary for democracy, and dissensus—conflict and contestation, diversity and disagreement—is a necessary condition of pluralism.[27] Rather than erase differences through the postulation of some imagined consensus yet to be achieved, Mouffe calls instead for the development of a positive attitude toward agonal differences that sees in a pluralism "whose objective is to reach harmony . . . ultimately a negation of the positive value of diversity and difference," not the life but the death of a democratic polity.[28]

Bonnie Honig has also argued for an agonistic politics that, drawing on the work of Hannah Arendt, comes close to a Nietzschean position on several points.[29] Bringing Judith Butler's account of performativity, an account I have discussed elsewhere as drawing heavily on Nietzsche,[30] together with Arendt's agonism, Honig sees in Arendt a politics that eschews the representation of "what" we are in favor of a performative politics that "agonistically generates 'who' we are by episodically producing new identities, identities whose 'newness' becomes 'the beginning of a new story, started—though unwittingly—by acting [wo]men [and] to be enacted further, to be augmented and spun out by their posterity.'"[31] She continues, in a passage with strong, albeit unacknowledged, Nietzschean overtones:

> Arendt's politics is always agonistic because it resists the attractions of expressivism for the sake of her view of the self as a complex site of multiplicity whose identities are always performatively produced. This agonism eschews the complacent familiarities of the what-ness of subjectivity and it rejects the seductive comforts of the social for the sake of action and its exhilarating capacity to generate new relations and new realities.
>
> From Arendt's perspective, a political community that constitutes itself on the basis of a prior, shared, and stable identity threatens to close the space of politics, to homogenize or repress the plurality and multiplicity that political action postulates.[32]

Such a perspective is, for Honig, particularly well suited for feminist political action insofar as an "agonistic feminism" will both accommodate the pluralism that should be a source of strength in women's movements and allow for strategies of political engagement that challenge the dominant sex/gender hierarchies.

Working from a more explicitly Nietzschean framework, William E. Connolly also focuses on Nietzsche's appeal to the contestatory nature of the *agon* while arguing for a reinvigorated democracy, understood not in terms of the drive for consensus but as a dynamic social space in which agonistic respect is folded into "the ambiguities, conflicts and interdependencies that constitute social relations."[33] Connolly makes agonism central to democratic practice as he takes the impossibility of arriving at a final and fixed identity—whether social or individual—as the basis for cultivating the "agonistic respect" necessary for democracy. For Connolly, as for Honig, Nietzsche's agonal dynamism operates both interpersonally and intrapersonally as Nietzsche's account of the multiple self—of the self as a struggle between competing drives and impulses—can likewise serve as a model for a dynamic and pluralistic polity. By attuning oneself to the "differences that continue to circulate through my or our identity [one] can engender a certain *empathy* for what we or I am not. Empathy, then, emerges from the ambiguous, relational character of identity itself, when this ambiguity is affirmed rather than denied or regretted." [34] Although human beings operating within modernity and the slavish morality of oppositional identity politics that it has fostered are no longer capable of exhibiting this empathy, such empathy for what we are not remains for Nietzsche a possibility for those sovereign individuals who will be able to overcome modernity. In fact, this is what Connolly takes Nietzsche to mean by the "pathos of distance":

> an attachment to that which differs from you growing out of glimmers of difference in you, an attachment that takes the form of forbearance in strife and generosity in interdependence rather than a quest to close up the distance between you through formation of a higher unity. . . . This ethos of agonistic respect amidst a world of dissonant interdependencies is crucial to the fabric of democratic politics: . . . it folds a pathos of distance into democratic relations of contestation, collaboration and hegemony. [35]

Connolly is aware of how un-Nietzschean this all will sound to those for whom the model executors of Nietzsche's "grand politics" were Hitler or Mussolini. But is it really so un-Nietzschean? For although Nietzsche was, to be sure, a critic of democracy, we should also recall that his criticisms here, as elsewhere, were *timely*, which is to say that his criticisms were directed toward "that which *now* calls itself democracy" (*WS* 293; emphasis added). Consider, in this context, Nietzsche's critique of liberal institutions in several of his "untimely" skirmishes in *Twilight of the Idols*. He opens "Skirmish" 39, titled "Critique of Modernity," by noting that everyone is now agreed that our institutions are no longer fit for anything, but quickly adds that the problem lies not in our institutions but in us. We moderns have lost all those instincts out of which institutions grow, instincts that Nietzsche describes as antiliberal to the point of malice: "the will to tradition, to authority, to centuries-long responsibility, to *solidarity* between succeeding generations backwards and forwards *in infinitum.*" Nietzsche then proceeds to develop the forward-looking dimension of this description: "The entire West has lost those instincts out of which institutions grow, out of which the *future* grows: perhaps nothing goes so much against the grain of its 'modern spirit' as this. One lives for today, one lives very fast—one lives very irresponsibly: it is precisely this which one calls 'freedom.'"

This section is immediately preceded by the equally interesting, and pertinent, section, "Skirmish" 38, titled "My Conception of Freedom," in which Nietzsche offers us an account of freedom in the context of a critique of liberalism. The value of a thing, he begins, lies not in what one attains with it but in what one must do to attain it. The example he gives is liberal institutions, which "cease to be liberal as soon as they are attained." As a result, there is in fact "nothing more thoroughly harmful to freedom than liberal institutions," because in their drive toward making everything equal, they undermine the will to power that is necessary for freedom to exert itself in the overcoming of resistances. War, Nietzsche says, is a training in freedom, and the free man, he claims, is a warrior.[36] But by war, does he mean anything other than what we have here been calling the *agon?* Nations, and individuals, which were worth something for Nietzsche, which "*became* worth something, never became so under liberal institutions: it was *great danger* which made of them something deserving reverence, danger which first teaches us to know our resources, our virtues, our shield and spear, our *spirit*—which *compels* us to be strong." Freedom, he concludes, should be understood "as something one has and does *not* have, something one *wants*, something one *conquers.*" And for this reason, and this is perhaps what is key here, it is not liberal institutions but the *struggle* for liberal institutions that is most likely to promote the freedom that will know itself as "the will to self-responsibility."

Nietzsche's thought here fits nicely with the idea of democracy as always "to come," always something that we are on the way toward, and toward which the agonal relations between us are not something to be regrettably put up with but are, in fact, the only means by which we will be able to engage in democratic political practices. Nietzsche himself noted as much when he wrote that this democracy yet to come "wants to create and guarantee as much *independence* as possible: independence of opinion, of mode of life [*Lebensart*] and of employment" (*WS* 293). And he observed—an observation as pertinent at the end of our century as it was at the end of his—that the three great enemies of this threefold sense of independence "are the indigent, the rich and the parties" (WS 293).

Connolly himself takes note of this Nietzschean sensibility, the same sensibility that admired the Greek *agon* while despairing over the Christian-dogmatic tendency to seek the elimination of difference because it has always and only understood difference as opposition. Following the famous opening section of *Twilight*'s "Morality as Anti-Nature," in which Nietzsche notes that the only way that the Church, and morality more generally, knows how to combat the passions is through their extermination, there comes this less famous statement of Nietzsche's alternative, which Connolly cites:

> The Church has at all times desired the destruction of its enemies: we, we immoralists and anti-Christians, see that it is to our advantage that the Church exists. . . . In politics, too, enmity has become much more spiritual—much more prudent, much more thoughtful, much more *forbearing*. . . . We adopt the same attitude toward the "enemy within"; there too we have spiritualized enmity, there too we have grasped its *value*. One is *fruitful* only at the cost of being rich in contradictions; one remains *young* only on condition the soul does not relax, does not long for peace. (*TI* "Morality" 3)

Thus at the end of his productive life, as at the beginning, Nietzsche continued to appeal to the idea that competition and contestation—the *agon*—is necessary for the continued well-being of the individual and the community. Although Nietzsche did not choose to link the *agon* with democracy, his oversight should not keep us from acknowledging that it is precisely *totalitarianism* that requires the elimination of competition and contestation in the political sphere. In fact, Nietzsche acknowledges this very point in *The Wanderer and His Shadow* (289), where he noted that democratic institutions serve to combat the "ancient pestilence, lust for tyranny." And, contrary to the right's tendency to desire an identity or unanimity that presumes the elimination of their antagonists, Nietzsche never tires of invoking the desirability of a "worthy enemy, against whom one can test one's strength" (*BT* P1), whose enduring presence is required for the *agon* to continue and for each of the agonal partners to proceed along the path of self-overcoming.[37]

To conclude, then, we need not leave Nietzsche to the right and their use of him to legitimate their identification of difference with discrimination and appeals to nationalistic or ethnic hegemony. For there are grounds for the left to look to Nietzsche as well as they explore the possibilities for democratic politics within a differential and agonistic public space, to the Nietzsche who saw in the ancient goal of agonistic education "not a boundless and indeterminate ambition like modern ambition," and who saw as the highest site on which the dramas of culture should be fought not the battlefields of Europe but the Athenian Dionysian festivals in which "the most general way of teaching, through drama, was only brought to the people in the form of an immense struggle of great musicians and dramatists" (HC 192). It was this Nietzsche who looked to the Homeric competitions to understand his own future; it is to this Nietzsche who speaks to the "cultivation of agonistic respect among interwoven and contending constituencies"[38] that we might still attend as we look to a new century with strategies for avoiding a recurrence of those undemocratic confrontations that have plagued this past century; and it is, in closing, this Nietzsche we invoke when we respond to today's anti-Nietzsche polemicists by affirming that there are still good reasons to be Nietzscheans.

NOTES

1. Martin Heidegger, *The Question of Being*, trans. W. Kluback and J. T. Wilde (New York: Twayne, 1958), 107. Translation altered.

2. Vincent Descombes, *Le même et l'autre: Quarante-cinq ans de philosophie française (1933–1978)* (Paris: Éditions de Minuit, 1979); English translation: *Modern French Philosophy*, trans. L. Scott-Fox and J. M. Harding (Cambridge: Cambridge University Press, 1980).

3. Luc Ferry and Alain Renaut, *La pensée 68: Essai sur l'anti-humanisme contemporain* (Paris: Gallimard, 1985); English translation: *French Philosophy of the Sixties: An Essay on Antihumanism*, trans. Mary Schnackenberg Cattani (Amherst: University of Massachusetts Press, 1990).

4. Alain Boyer et al., *Pourquoi nous ne sommes pas nietzschéens* (Paris: Éditions Grasset et Fasquelle, 1991); English translation: *Why We Are Not Nietzscheans*, trans. Robert de Loaiza, ed. Luc Ferry and Alain Renaut (Chicago: University of Chicago Press, 1997). In addition to essays by Descombes and by Ferry and Renaut, this collection includes essays by Alain Boyer, André Comte-Sponville, Robert Legros, Philippe Raynaud, and Pierre-André Taguieff. Somewhat curiously, while the French edition simply lists the authors in alphabetical order, the University of Chicago Press translation publishes the collection under the editorship of the two authors most well known and, I suppose, most marketable.

5. Luc Ferry and Alain Renaut, preface to *Pourquoi nous ne sommes pas nietzschéens*, 7; English translation, p. vii.

6. Ibid.

7. Ibid., 8; English translation, pp. vii–viii.

8. André Comte-Sponville, "The Brute, the Sophist and the Aesthete: 'Art in

the Service of Illusion,'" in Boyer, *Pourquoi nous ne sommes pas nietzschéens,* 91; English translation, p. 64.

9. Vincent Descombes, "Nietzsche's French Moment," in Boyer, *Pourquoi nous ne sommes pas nietzschéens,* 107; English translation, p. 75. For a more detailed and critical response to these essays, see my review in *New Nietzsche Studies* 2, nos. 3–4 (Summer 1998): 112–16.

10. Mark Lilla, "The Legitimacy of the Liberal Age," in *New French Thought: Political Philosophy,* ed. Mark Lilla (Princeton: Princeton University Press, 1994), 15.

11. See, for example, the recent Dossier on Pierre Bourdieu titled "L'Intellectuel dominant?" in *Magazine Littéraire* (October 1998). One might wonder what Lilla makes of Bourdieu's regular contributions to *Le Monde Diplomatique* and *Liberation* on current topics in politics, economics, and culture.

12. See, for example, Eric Alliez, *La signature du monde, ou, Qu'est-ce que la philosophie de Deleuze et Guattari?* (Paris: Éditions du Cerf, 1993); Alliez, *Deleuze: Philosophie virtuelle* (Paris: Synthelabo, 1996); Alain Badiou, *Deleuze: La clameur de l'être* (Paris: Hachette, 1997); Mireille Buydens, *Sahara: L'esthéthique de Gilles Deleuze* (Paris: Vrin, 1990); Jean-Claude Dumoncel, *Le symbole d'Hecate: Philosophie deleuzienne et roman proustien* (Paris: Éditions HYX, 1996); Dumoncel, *Le pendule du Docteur Deleuze: Une introduction à l'Anti-Oedipe* (Paris: EPEL, 1999); Alberto Gualandi, *Deleuze* (Paris: Belles Lettres, 1998); Guy Lardreau, *L'exercice différé de la philosophie à l'occasion de Deleuze* (Paris: Verdier, 1999); Thierry Lenain, *L'Image: Deleuze, Foucault, Lyotard* (Paris: Vrin, 1997); Jean-Clet Martin, *Variations: La philosophie de Gilles Deleuze* (Paris: Payot, 1993); Martin, *L'Image virtuelle: Essai sur la construction du monde* (Paris: Éditions Kime, 1996); Philippe Mengue, *Gilles Deleuze, ou, Le système du multiple* (Paris: Éditions Kime, 1994); René Scherer, *Regards sur Deleuze* (Paris: Éditions Kime, 1998); Jacques Serrano, ed., *Après Deleuze: Philosophie et esthétique du cinema* (Paris: Dis Voir, 1997); Juliette Simont, *Essai sur la quantité, la qualité, la relation chez Kant, Hegel, Deleuze: Les 'fleurs noire' de la logique philosophique* (Paris: L'Harmattan, 1997); Arnaud Villain, *La guêpe et l'orchidée: Essai sur Gilles Deleuze* (Paris: Belin, 1999); and François Zourabichvili, *Deleuze, une philosophie de l'événement* (Paris: Presses Universitaires de France, 1994). In addition, at least three major conferences on Deleuze have taken place in the past few years, the proceedings of each of which have been published in France: *Gilles Deleuze: Une vie philosophique: rencontres internationales Rio de Janeiro-Sao Paulo, 10–14 juin 1996,* ed. Eric Alliez (Paris: Synthelabo, 1998); *Gilles Deleuze: Annales de l'Université Libre de Bruxelles,* ed. Isabelle Stengers and Pierre Verstraeten (Paris: Vrin, 1998); and *Gilles Deleuze: Immanence et vie,* published in the journal *Rue Descartes: College International de Philosophie* 20 (May 1998), ed. Eric Alliez, Danielle Cohen-Levinas, Françoise Proust, and Lucien Vinciguerra.

13. Michel Foucault, *Dits et écrits,* 4 vols. (Paris: Gallimard, 1994).

14. It is perhaps worth recalling that André Glucksmann's manifesto of the "new philosophy," *Les maîtres penseurs* (Paris: Éditions Grasset and Fasquelle, 1977), also included an anti-Nietzsche polemic.

15. See, for example, Jürgen Habermas, *The Philosophical Discourse of*

Modernity, trans. Frederick G. Lawrence (Cambridge, Mass.: MIT Press, 1987);
and Manfred Frank, *What Is Neostructuralism?* trans. Sabine Wilke and Richard
Gray (Minneapolis: University of Minnesota Press, 1989).

16. While I do not want to suggest in the least that Comte-Sponville, Descombes, Ferry, or Renaut have any connections with or sympathies for Nazi ideology, I do want to note that their readings are very selective in terms of what
they attend to in Nietzsche and the French Nietzscheans. For that reason, Derrida's comments seem relevant to their reading practices.

17. Jacques Derrida, *"Otobiographies,"* in *The Ear of the Other: Otobiog-
raphy, Transference, Translation,* trans. Avital Ronell, ed. Christie V. McDonald (New York: Schocken Books, 1985), 30–31.

18. For example, in reaction to Lyotard's question in *Libidinal Economy,*
"What was Marx's left hand doing while he wrote *Capital?*" Ferry and Renaut
write: "We consider it fortunate that, in spite of the marginalization of philosophical activity by the ambient technopolitics of the '68 period, the discovery
of these traces of what passed for thought at the time means that the need for
historians to try to reconstruct texts that would otherwise have been regarded
as caricature can be permanently avoided" (*French Philosophy of the Sixties,*
17–18). Examples such as this litter their text.

19. While there are, to be sure, substantive issues involved here, one should
perhaps also note that complex issues concerning professional jealousies and
Parisian academic politics are also at work in the backlash against the French
Nietzscheans.

20. Nietzsche's cultural and political reception in France and Germany is
discussed in a number of recent works, including Douglas Smith, *Transvalua-
tions: Nietzsche in France, 1872–1972* (Oxford: Oxford University Press, 1997);
Steven E. Aschheim, *The Nietzsche Legacy in Germany, 1890–1990* (Berkeley:
University of California Press, 1992); and Seth Taylor, *Left-Wing Nietzscheans:
The Politics of German Expressionism, 1910–1920* (Berlin: Walter de Gruyter,
1990). An earlier and more narrowly focused discussion of Nietzsche's reception
by the German left is to be found in R. Hinton Thomas, *Nietzsche in German
Politics and Society, 1890–1918* (Manchester: Manchester University Press,
1983). A collection of writings highly critical of Nietzsche that were published
originally in the most influential literary review in France in the nineteenth and
early twentieth century, the *Revue des Deux Mondes,* has also recently appeared: Bruno de Cessole and Jeanne Causse, ed., *Nietzsche: 1982–1914* (Paris:
Maisonneuve et Larose: Éditions des Deux Mondes, 1997).

21. This and several of the following paragraphs are taken, with minor al-
terations, from the concluding pages of my *Nietzsche's French Legacy: A Genealogy of Poststructuralism* (New York: Routledge, 1995), parts of which also
appear in my "Kofman, Nietzsche, and the Jews," in *Enigmas: Essays on Sarah
Kofman,* ed. Penelope Deutscher and Kelly Oliver (Ithaca: Cornell University
Press, 1999).

22. Allan Bloom, *The Closing of the American Mind* (New York: Simon and
Schuster, 1987).

23. James Miller, *The Passion of Michel Foucault* (New York: Simon and
Schuster, 1993).

24. Dinesh D'Souza, *Illiberal Education: The Politics of Race and Sex on Campus* (New York: Macmillan, 1991), 192. This, quite remarkably, is how D'Souza apparently renders Nietzsche's closing remark from the *Genealogy:* "man would rather will *nothingness* than *not* will [lieber will noch der mensch *das Nichts* wollen, als *nicht* wollen . . .]."

25. In addition to the well-known work of Wendy Brown, Judith Butler, and William E. Connolly, see, as an example of the kind of interpretive work I am suggesting, Lawrence J. Hatab's *A Nietzschean Defense of Democracy: An Experiment in Postmodern Politics* (Chicago: Open Court, 1995).

26. Ernesto Laclau, "Power and Representation," in *Politics, Theory, and Contemporary Culture,* ed. Mark Poster (New York: Columbia University Press, 1993), 292.

27. Chantal Mouffe, "Democratic Politics and the Question of Identity," in *The Identity in Question,* ed. John Rajchman (New York: Routledge, 1995), 44.

28. Ibid.

29. This may explain in part why her "agonistic feminism" has met with such strong resistance from feminist political theorists and why Arendt herself has more than a few feminist critics.

30. See my *Nietzsche's French Legacy,* 54–58.

31. Hannah Arendt, *On Revolution* (New York: Penguin, 1963), 47; Bonnie Honig, "Toward an Agonistic Feminism: Hannah Arendt and the Politics of Identity," in *Feminist Interpretations of Hannah Arendt,* ed. Bonnie Honig (University Park: Pennsylvania State University Press, 1995), 149.

32. Honig, "Toward an Agonistic Feminism," 149. Honig does link Nietzsche with Arendt more directly in "The Politics of Agonism," *Political Theory* 21, no. 3 (August 1993): 528–33.

33. William E. Connolly, *Political Theory and Modernity* (Ithaca: Cornell University Press, 1993), 195.

34. Ibid.

35. Ibid.

36. One might here recall the etymology Nietzsche provides in *GM* I:5 of the Latin *bonus* (good), which when traced back to *duonus,* leads him to conclude that the "'goodness' of a man in ancient Rome" was understood as a "man of strife, of dissention (*duo*), as the man of war."

37. I thank Debra Bergoffen for suggesting that I recall Nietzsche's idea of the "worthy enemy" in this context.

38. Connolly, *Political Theory and Modernity,* 197.

PART 3

Culture and the Political

CHAPTER 12

Nietzsche for Politics

Wendy Brown

> Behold the good and the just! Whom do they hate most?
> The man who breaks their table of values, the breaker, the
> lawbreaker; yet he is the creator.
>
> *Friedrich Nietzsche,* Thus Spoke Zarathustra

We late moderns remain bound to a modernist habit of measuring the political worth of a thinker by his or her proximity to the political beliefs we want enacted, and this because of an infelicitous collapse of the political and the intellectual domains, a collapse itself pursuant to the radically insecure standing of each in modernity.[1] Conventionally, the "politics" of a thinker is identified either with his or her explicit political views and alliances, that is, with political biography, or with the political values expressed in the theory (democracy, socialism, individuality, community, etc.), that is, with political ideology. Meanwhile, the politics of theory itself is generally debated in terms of relevance, applicability, and accessibility, or in terms of the value of abstraction, universalism, and theorizing as such. In short, theory's value for politics is conventionally measured by its capacity to effect or explain political life, a capacity about which it is mostly defensive and almost always comes up short.

In proposing a different way of thinking about the relation of theory to politics, and about the political value of particular theories and theorists, I want to suggest that if we affirmed rather than denied the persistently untheoretical quality of politics—the resistance of political life to theory—we might then pursue an intercourse between politics and theory more productive than one of identity or application. If theory and politics consist of quite different, even conflicting, semiotic impulses and aims, perhaps we could conceive a usefully *agonistic* relationship between them to avoid the more conventional relations of mutual condemnation, inadequacy, or reproach. I further want to explore the possibility that democratic politics, the most untheoretical of all political forms, paradoxically requires theory, requires an antithesis to itself in both the form and the substance of theory, if it is to gratify its potential to produce a dynamic egalitarian order. I argue that democracy requires a nondemocratic element, which might be termed Nietzschean in part, both because democracy is not an end in itself and in order not to become the most damnable things that Plato, Nietzsche, and other philosophical critics of democracy say about it.

In some always partial fashion, theory makes an object of everyday life and practices and in that very gesture divests those practices of their everydayness, their lived and practical quality. In this simple sense, it is in the nature of *the relation* of politics and theory to distinguish themselves from each other: theory abstracts from political life and holds it up to examination and thus cannot at the same time be identical with or even mirrored by it. But politics is also "untheoretical" and theory "unpolitical" in another sense. Among human practices, politics is a particularly untheoretical practice because the bids for power that it comprises are necessarily at odds with the theoretical project of opening up meaning, of "making meaning slide" in Stuart Hall's words. Discursive power functions by concealing the terms of its fabrication and hence its malleability and contingency; discourse fixes meaning by naturalizing it, or else ceases to have sway as discourse.[2] This domain of fixing or naturalizing meanings is the venue, and the idiom, in which politics transpires. Even the politics of deconstructive displacement implicates such normativity, at least provisionally. Still more simply, pure critique, although of inestimable value as a theoretical practice, is politically ineffectual.

Theory, however, cannot fix meaning in this political fashion without ceasing to be theoretical, without sacrificing the very dynamic of theory, without falling into empiricism, positivism, or doctrine. For theory ("journeying in order to see," its Greek etymology reminds us) to live, it must keep moving, it must keep taking distance on, and hence undoing, the terms of its objects. At the moment that theory fixes meaning, at the moment that it defines definitively, it has made an object *in* the world, has invested itself in that object, and thus ceases to be theoretical. As politics does, theory undoes. But this does not mean that they are opposites. A far more interesting relation is conceivable.

As Tocqueville discerned, the relation of theory and politics in *democracy* is an especially vexed one: while democracy is more antagonistic to theory than are other regimes, consequent to its attachment to "common sense" and its nervousness about elite knowledges, democracy also needs theory more, consequent to the democratic citizen's "readiness to believe the multitude," such that mere "opinion is more than ever mistress of the world." [3] But there is another paradox of democracy that further complicates its relationship with theory. Spinoza, Etienne Balibar suggests, portrays democracy as unable "to find its own principle" [4] even as democracy functions as an essential stabilizing element in other regimes. According to Balibar, Spinoza can only define democracy itself as "a perfect aristocracy[,] . . . an intrinsically contradictory concept." [5] This paradox results from the tension Spinoza posits at the core of all regimes between state and mass (*imperium / multitudo*); true democracy lacks this tension (insofar as state and mass are one) and thus negates itself as a regime.

Spinoza's argument about democracy's stabilizing function in non-democracies issues from his conviction that the tension between state and mass must be relaxed via some accord between them, precisely the accord that a democratic element offers. The value of democracy for Spinoza pertains to its equilibrating force in nondemocratic regimes that cannot themselves manage the economy of energy and fear circulating between state and mass. [6] Balibar does not say that Spinoza denies democracy's existence, only that he cannot locate a principle that defines, animates, and binds it as a regime; democracy thus becomes literally impossible for Spinoza to theorize. In Balibar's account of the unfinished character of the *Tractatus Politicus,* "we see [Spinoza] finally bogged down in a search for the 'natural' criteria of citizenship . . . and, if I dare say it, we watch him die before this blank page." [7]

Leaving aside the specifics of Spinoza's argument about the state-mass relationship as well as the question of the relationship between Spinoza's terminal illness and his unfinished treatise on politics, I want to consider the thesis that Spinoza's inability to theorize democracy is rooted in its lack of a principle of its own, and its consequent lack of material *for* theory. What if democracy does in fact lack what other regimes have in principles such as excellence, *raison d'état,* imperial right, or property? Must democracy then be supplied a principle or purpose from without, must it be attached to a principle other than itself, or else face being an amorphous and aimless rather than politically purposive entity, and face as well severe vulnerability to insurgency from within and conquest from without?

Again, Tocqueville's challenge would seem to parallel Spinoza's. Fol-

lowing his discussion of America's valorization of "individual understanding," Tocqueville describes the limit of this inclination for a body
politic: "without . . . common belief no society can prosper; say, rather,
no society can exist; for without ideas held in common there is no common action, and without common action there may still be men, but
there is no social body." [8] Yet because democracies *do* harbor social bodies, because they are not generally aimless, vulnerable, or even especially
unstable, perhaps there is a vacuum in democracy that will inevitably
attach to a historically available principle—nationalism, racism, xenophobia, cultural chauvinism, market values, Christianity, imperialism,
individualism, rights as ends—if some other principle is not more deliberately developed and pursued. Perhaps it is also the case that while
the principles to which democracy inadvertently attaches are not inherently dangerous and unsavory ones, they are likely to be so *if* they are not
formulated reflectively given the tendency in democracies toward both
popular self-aggrandizement and the instrumentalist sensibility figured
by rights and the market. Especially consequent to its imbrication with
capitalism, contemporary democracy may be said to tend toward both
narcissistic decadence and technocracy, which in very different ways introduce markedly undemocratic forces into democracy.

The task of conceiving Nietzsche's value for democratic politics in this
chapter, then, will wind around two related themes: the value of antidemocratic critique for democracy and the value of theory for politics
in terms other than those of application, method, ideology, or critique.

Theoretical self-consciousness may be deployed to interrupt democracy's relatively automatic cathexis onto undemocratic principles—it
may serve both as a means of enlightenment about this cathexis and as
a source of alternative principles. Thus theory may be a vehicle through
which democracy can overcome itself without sacrificing itself, without
turning against itself. Yet this use of theory does not resolve the basic
paradox about democracy discerned by Spinoza and Tocqueville. If
democracy inherently lacks a principle of its own, then any principle
brought to it necessarily will be antidemocratic. If democracy and principle are antithetical, democracy therefore attaches to principles that are
at least partially at odds with it. This suggests that the antidote for democracy's degenerative tendencies is homeopathic—it requires installing
another antidemocratic element in democracy's heart. This is the paradox that brings theory and politics into specific relation in democracy,
and the one for which Nietzsche's critique of democracy, as well as his
more general critique of the political, may be rendered most useful.

The task of conceiving Nietzsche's value for democratic politics in this
chapter, then, will wind around two related themes: the value of antidemocratic critique for democracy and the value of theory for politics
in terms other than those of application, method, ideology, or critique.

Through Nietzsche, I will speculate about the value of theory for politics as a source of diagnosis, unlivable critique, and unreachable ideals rather than as a source of models, positions, causes, or origins. In so doing, I want to argue for a significant character distinction between politics and theory, which does not mean that there are no theoretical moments in politics and no politics in theory. It is rather to say that the prospect for a relationship useful to both may depend crucially on keeping their respective identities aloof and intact in the course of such a relationship.

Conventional ways of locating Nietzsche's politics include examining the convergence of his thought with Nazi doctrine; his reduction of all demands for justice to envy; his misogyny and racism; his heroic ethic and esteem for ancient Athenian culture; his opprobrium toward the masses, democracy, socialism, liberalism, and especially the sacred cow of modernity, political equality. Nietzsche has been variously character-ized as antipolitical, apolitical, and engaged in a "politics of transfigu-ration" (Strong). He has been cast as deadly to politics; as a "haunt" or "conscience" to political thought and political life; as providing the ethos for a liberal ironism (Rorty), for a recovery of moral-political re-sponsibility (Honig), and for an agonistic liberal radicalism (Connolly); and as a "way out" of Marxism, phenomenology, and existentialism in the twentieth century (Foucault). Most politically sympathetic treat-ments of Nietzsche try to draw a politics *out of* his thought, even as they recognize that there is much in Nietzsche that cannot be redeemed for democratic practice. But what if we conceive Nietzsche's thought in-stead as a knife to a raiment that is the cover for the ideals and prac-tices constitutive of political life? What if Nietzsche's thought does not guide but only exposes and challenges, functioning to strengthen democratic culture by disturbing and provoking it? Affirming Foucault's Nietzschean dictum, that "knowledge is made for cutting," perhaps Nietzschean critiques and genealogies can cut into politics, productively interrupting, violating, or disturbing political formations rather than be-ing applied to, merged, or identified with them. The importance of this work would seem to be especially great for democratic politics, if what I have been suggesting through Spinoza is true, that democracy inevitably attaches to undemocratic elements and is also inhospitable to theory, in-cluding the theoretical self-consciousness required to grasp and redress the Spinozist point about democracy's hollow center.

To pursue these possibilities, I want to consider first Nietzsche the ge-nealogical "psychologist," the thinker who deploys speculative genealogies to probe the psychological production of values such as justice, equality, or Christian morality. What is the significance of Nietzsche's diagnostic pose and genealogical approach for reconceiving a relationship of theory to politics? How does genealogy itself refigure the relation between the intellectual and the political? How does genealogy's crossing of philosophy and history open up the political present without itself taking the place of politics?

"We are unknown to ourselves, we men of knowledge," Nietzsche begins *On the Genealogy of Morals*, "and with good reason. We have never sought ourselves" (*GM* P1). It is this ignorance that Nietzsche seeks to redress with his genealogical tracings of the desires (not only the unmediated will to power but also its thwarted forms—envy, resentment, jealousy, and revenge) that materialize into the moral and political formations of equality, liberal justice, and the state. Unlike other genres of philosophical or historical criticism, including those delineated in his own "Advantages and Disadvantages of History for Life," genealogy permits an examination of our condition that interrogates its very terms and construction. Genealogy reveals the terms by which we live by rupturing them, by doing violence to their ordinary ordering and situation. In this, genealogy paradoxically aims to dislocate that which is both its starting point and its object: the present. And in that dislocation, it also dislocates the conventions of politics, morality, and epistemology constitutive of the present.

Nietzsche's intentions with genealogy can also be figured as calling into question the familiar through a complex of *strategic reversals*. Consider section 6 of the preface to *On the Genealogy of Morals,* which begins,

> This problem of the *value* of pity and of the morality of pity . . . seems at first to be merely something detached, an isolated question mark; but whoever sticks with it and *learns* how to ask questions here will experience what I experienced—a tremendous new prospect opens up for him, a new possibility comes over him like a vertigo, every kind of mistrust, suspicion, fear leaps up, his belief in morality, in all morality, falters—finally a new demand becomes audible. (*GM* P6)

In this account of genealogical movement, Nietzsche reminds us that genealogy is, at bottom, a form of artful questioning, a way of asking "what really happened there" about a commonplace. He reminds us too that when this question truly grips the questioner, it disturbs a much larger nest of beliefs than that with which the genealogist begins. One might think here not only of Nietzsche's *Genealogy of Morals* but of

Foucault's *History of Sexuality* and the way that each calls into question the *structure* and *function* of conventional beliefs and standard histories about their subject—and not only the beliefs and histories themselves.

The questioning Nietzsche recommends is necessarily of a historical kind, specified in the next portion of the passage quoted above:

> Let us articulate this *new demand* [that has become audible by virtue of questioning the value of the morality of pity]: we need a *critique* of moral values, *the value of these values themselves must first be called in question*—and for that there is needed a *knowledge of the conditions and circumstances in which they grew, under which they evolved and changed* (morality as consequence, as symptom, as mask, as tartufferie, as illness, as misunderstanding; but also morality as cause, as remedy, as stimulant, as restraint, as poison), *a knowledge of a kind that has never yet existed or even been desired.* (GM P6; latter two emphases added)

Calling into question a commonplace (in this case the value of the morality of pity) produces a new political possibility (a critique of morality as such), which in turn produces a need for a new kind of knowledge (a particular kind of history of morality). A radical critique of moral values requires knowing the history of how they were occasioned, the conditions under which they grew, changed, and took hold—precisely the history that must be buried by values that naturalize themselves as universal and transhistorical. But there is something else highlighted by this passage: the movement between knowledge and politics, between questioning and demand, consists of an *oscillation* that does not collapse these terms into one another. Questioning produces an experience of vertigo; the vertigo produces a demand; the demand requires new knowledge; and the new knowledge can materialize into a new worldview. The questioning and the political demand *incite* each other, but the chain of incitation would be aborted if the movement collapsed through direct politicization of knowledge or a reduction of politics to questioning.

Nietzsche continues:

> One has taken the *value* of these "values" as given, as factual, as beyond all question; one has hitherto never doubted or hesitated in the slightest degree in supposing "the good man" to be of greater value than "the evil man," of greater value in the sense of furthering the advancement and prosperity of man in general. . . . But what if the reverse were true? What if a symptom of regression were inherent in the "good," likewise a danger, a seduction, a poison, a narcotic, through which the present was possibly living *at the expense of the future?* . . . So that precisely morality would be to blame if the *highest power and splendor* actually possible to the type man was never in fact attained? So that precisely morality was the danger of dangers? (GM P6)

Three different instances of genealogy's strategy of reversal emerge in this passage. Nietzsche reverses the givenness of everyday values, upsetting their unchallengeable status in an effort to disclose the power this status carries and covers. Whatever has been accepted "as factual, as beyond all question," shall now be posed as a question, as a fiction, as utterly dubious because utterly contingent. But if reversals function as a form of questioning, they also emerge as part of the answer to the question. Hence the morally good is made to appear regressive and dangerous, rather than progressive and valuable, while morality itself appears as that which might inhibit rather than foment or express the "power and splendor" of man. Finally, genealogy also conjures a reversal in the accepted course of history—it challenges progressive accounts with intimations of regression, as in suggesting that the present may be "living off the future" rather than paving that future.

If Nietzsche in this preface articulates some of the critical workings of genealogy and especially its refiguration of the relation between knowledge and politics, such moments of self-consciousness about this relation are relatively rare. Foucault renders much more explicit the aims and effects of genealogy in this regard.[9] He characterizes the project of genealogy he adapts from Nietzsche as one of discerning the political "ontology of the present."[10] Such discernment is expressly contrasted with "an analytics of truth"—philosophical criticism—a contrast achieved largely through a postmetaphysical historical, but not historicist, orientation. A political ontology of the present, which Foucault sometimes also describes in the terms of 'diagnosis,' "does not consist in a simple characterization of what we are but, instead—by following lines of fragility in the present—in managing to grasp why and how that-which-is might no longer be that-which-is."[11] A political ontology of the present, in short, requires that form of questioning that unsettles the present's givenness, that is "made in accordance with these kinds of virtual fracture which open up the space of freedom understood as a space of concrete freedom, i.e., of possible transformation."[12]

Foucault's endeavor of a "diagnosis" or "ontology" of the present entails reconfiguring both the relationship of philosophy to history and the relation of philosophy and history to politics. The task of philosophy becomes curiously historical: apprehending the nature of ourselves in the present, philosophy must recognize us as historical beings and our time as a time in history. Conversely, history is subjected to philosophical critique insofar as it must be divested of reason and direction at the same time that it is tethered to conventionally philosophical questions: how can we know our time and ourselves when we cannot move beyond or outside of them? While never fully resolvable, Foucault responds to this problem on genealogy's behalf: "Effective history studies what is closest, but in an abrupt dispossession, so as to seize it at a distance." [13]

Because even genealogical "histories" cannot be divested of projects by which they are inevitably inflected, philosophical self-consciousness is required to keep track of such projects. These histories also require philosophy to interrogate the terms of objects of historical study, even as philosophy requires genealogy—a radical historicization of its terms— to do the same. Genealogy or "effective history," Foucault reminds us, "differs from traditional history in being without constants." [14] It "emphatically excludes the 'rediscovery of ourselves'" and "becomes 'effective' to the degree that it introduces discontinuity into our very being." [15] History bound to the task of creating an ontology of the present is thus consonant with the Socratic charge to philosophy to expose the familiar as an illness: "its task is to become a curative science." [16]

In the strange locution of mixed genres figured by the phrase "political ontology of the present," genealogy not only crosses "being" and "politics" in counterintuitive fashion, but also philosophy and history, undercutting the premises by which each ordinarily excludes the other in its self-definition. At the same time, in posing the diagnostic question, Who are we? genealogy attaches both history and philosophy to a political task, that of knowing our ill body and bodies. Thus, for example, in his genealogy of contemporary "governmentality," Foucault traces the unlikely imbrication of "pastoral power" and *raison d'etat* to bring into view the contemporary political rationality that not only governs but also produces us: "Our civilization has developed the most complex system of knowledge, the most sophisticated structures of power: what has this kind of knowledge, this type of power *made of us?*" [17] Again the notion of subjects produced by knowledge and power confounds boundaries conventionally drawn between philosophy and history, being and politics, as well as governance and production.

Importantly, however, if genealogy is concerned with the apprehension of political conditions, it does not thereby politicize intellectual inquiry. Rather, genealogy's refiguring of philosophy and history extends to a refiguring of the political in a manner that directly opposes this term to conventional understandings of politicization on one side and policy on the other.[18] While genealogy is saturated by a political animus, while it is deployed to replace "laws of history" with exposures of mechanisms of power and relations of force, while it is carried out in the name of denaturalizing the present to highlight its malleability, genealogy neither prescribes political positions nor specifies desirable futures. Rather, it aims to make visible why particular values, positions, and visions of the good occur to us as they do, and especially to reveal when and where those formulations turn out to operate in the same register of what Foucault calls "political rationality" as those we criticize or presume to escape.[19]

In genealogy's challenge to the purity of origins and linear, teleological development, the corporeality of history as well as the history of the body are brought into relief. "The search for descent is not the erecting of foundations: on the contrary, it disturbs what was . . . considered immobile; it fragments what was thought unified; it shows the heterogeneity of what was imagined consistent with itself."[20] In a similar fashion, genealogy reveals the historicity of feelings and the extent to which history is composed of feelings—suffering, revenge, and so forth—as mutually constitutive. In tracing political formations as both the effect of and producing desire, desire itself is historicized. Shedding its immutable and timeless quality, desire is both given a place in history and grasped as a critical element of human history.

The aim of genealogy's displacements and revaluations, according to Foucault, is a "dissociation of the self[,] . . . its recognition and displacement as an empty synthesis."[21] The task of genealogy "is to expose a body totally imprinted by history and the process of history's destruction of the body."[22] As Nietzsche spoke of a certain vertigo in genealogical inquiry, Foucault writes,

> History becomes "effective" to the degree that it introduces discontinuity into our very being—as it divides our emotions, dramatizes our instincts, multiplies our body and sets it against itself. "Effective" history deprives the self of the reassuring stability of life and nature, and it will not permit itself to be transported by a voiceless obstinacy toward a millennial ending.[23]

The measure of genealogy's success is its disruption of conventional accounts of our identities, values, origins, and futures. Genealogical accounts disturb our habits of self-recognition, pose an "us" that is foreign: this is the disconcerting effect of Nietzsche's *Genealogy of Morals* and *Thus Spoke Zarathustra* as well as Foucault's *Madness and Civilization, History of Sexuality,* and *Discipline and Punish.* Each begins with a story by which we commonly recognize ourselves—as morally "good," enlightened, intrinsically reasonable, sexually liberated, politically humane—and asks not only whether these stories are "really true" but also what function of power each purported "truth" serves, what each fiction conceals, regulates, or mobilizes. Thus the project of deconstructing the inevitability, the naturalness, and the intractability of a time or a thing converges with the project of deconstructing the present as a culmination of the progress of the past, as well as with the exposure of power's operation in maintaining this present. Neither of these is equivalent to politics; it could even be argued that they are antipolitical endeavors insofar as each destabilizes meaning without proposing alternative codes or institutions. Yet both may also be essential in sustaining by rejuvenating an existing democratic regime. For the vertigo genealogy aims to achieve may amount to the very measure of collective or individual identity dissolution that can disrupt without destroying, that can offer the possibility of resolving into another story.

Why would identity dissolution or destabilization be actively sought for democracies? If, as I suggested in the opening pages, democracies tend toward cathexis onto principles antithetical to democracy, then critical scrutiny of these principles, and challenges to the political formations that ensue, is crucial to the project of refounding or recovering democracy. What Machiavelli classically cast as the "return of a republic to its beginnings" might here be supplemented with the notion of a theoretical endeavor, genealogy, that continuously examines and reworks even the very foundations of a polity. Identity dissolution, achieved theoretically, is thus a means of asking whether we are who we want to be, of choosing principles by which to order ourselves, in short, of interrupting that tendency in democracy to adhere to nondemocratic principles in an unreflective fashion. Importantly, the challenge to identity that genealogy offers is not equivalent to political dissolution—it is a calling into question that is not the same as destroying or prohibiting a particular formation of identity. Genealogy is not politics but a register of reflection on it; its effect is to disturb political space and political formations rather than claim such space or create such formations on its own.

Thus far I have considered the way Nietzsche's genealogical work refigures the relations among history, philosophy, and politics and, in so doing, offers a basis for refiguring the meeting point between theory and politics as a point of incitation or provocation. A more familiar Nietzsche, however, establishes philosophy and politics as flatly rejecting one another and describes democracy in wholly unflattering terms. I want to consider these dimensions of Nietzsche's thought as a means of reflecting further on both the relationship of theory and politics and the possibilities of using Nietzsche's critique of democracy as a means of invigorating democracy.

In *Twilight of the Idols,* Nietzsche polemicizes against philosophers and philosophy as "antilife." The philosophical inquiries of Socrates and Plato are condemned as "symptoms of degeneration or decay" in Greek life, as to "judge the value of life" itself constitutes a negation of life (*TI* "Socrates" 2). Dialectics is characterized as poor manners—the revenge of the rabble—and specious thought: "honest things . . . do not carry their reasons exposed in this fashion" (*TI* "Socrates" 5, 7). More generally, Socratic philosophy is portrayed as an expression of *ressentiment* that *devitalizes* its opponents. "As long as life is *ascending,* happiness equals instinct" (*TI* "Socrates" 11), whereas philosophy reproaches the senses, the body, the instincts, and history as deceivers about the "true world," the world of becoming, and draws us into the world of appearance (*TI* "Reason" 6). Greek philosophy waged this reproach, Nietzsche argues, out of a pathological response to the "anarchy of the instincts" accompanying Athens's decline:

> If one needs to make a tyrant of *reason,* as Socrates did, then there must exist no little danger of something else playing the tyrant. . . . The fanaticism with which the whole of Greek thought throws itself at rationality betrays a state of emergency. . . . The moralism of the Greek philosophers from Plato downwards is pathologically conditioned. . . . Reason = virtue = happiness means merely: one must imitate Socrates and counter the dark desires by producing a permanent *daylight*—the daylight of reason. (*TI* "Socrates" 10)

For Nietzsche, the decadence of the Greek philosophers is a *symptom* of the decline of Greece's greatness: "the philosophers are the *decadents* of Hellenism, the counter-movement against the old, the noble taste (—against the agonal instinct, against the *polis,* against the value of the race, against the authority of tradition)" (*TI* "Ancients" 3). In the decline of Athens, Nietzsche discerns the more general tendency of philosophy toward revenge and *ressentiment,* its assault on that before which it feels small and humiliated. Out of its experience of impotence or injury vis-à-vis public life or culture, philosophy seeks to substitute for them, to displace and replace rather than engage them. (Plato would seem to be the exemplar here.)

Although Nietzsche frequently generalizes from this depiction of philosophy in Greek culture to insist that philosophy as such is antilife, Nietzschean philosophy, often masquerading as allegory or psychological maxims, also aims to provoke the spirit of overcoming that affirms humanity. Hence Nietzsche's polemic against philosophy is at the same time a call for philosophy of a different sort. His critique of philosophy centers on the will to power in it that potentially vanquishes its object— man—in an effort to dominate that object, but this same will to power makes it a potent instrument of other values as well.

If Nietzsche bears some ambivalence toward philosophy in the name of life, there is no such ambiguity in his open hostility toward politics, where the latter encompasses moral doctrines such as equality, institutions such as the state and political parties, politicians, righteous position taking, and policy making. Nietzsche's objections to moral political doctrine, especially liberalism, include his notorious disdain for the rabble and for the "little men" whose envious, petty, and poisonous nature he believes sap all strength from a culture.[24] Nietzsche's critique of political solutions to unfairness and injustice and their origins in resentment and revenge is distilled in his forthright claim, "'Men are not equal' . . . life wants to climb and overcome itself climbing" (Z:2 "On the Tarantulas"). If liberal doctrine thus inevitably partakes of slave morality, when this critique is compounded by Nietzsche's despisal of the state—"coldest of all cold monsters . . . where the slow suicide of all is called 'life'"—then all state-centered political formations, whether socialist, democratic, or totalitarian, appear even more antagonistic than philosophy to "life" and culture (Z:1 "On the New Idol"). "The better the state is established," Nietzsche polemicizes, "the fainter is humanity."[25]

Even these critiques do not plumb the depths of Nietzsche's hostility to politics, a hostility many have termed aesthetic but that might be better understood as an intense *anti-institutionalism* rooted in his critique of slave morality. "'The will to power' is so hated in democratic ages," he argues, "that their entire psychology seems directed towards belittling and defaming it" (WP 751). In *Twilight of the Idols*, Nietzsche emphasizes the massified, deindividualizing character of democratic institutions, the way in which they lose "man" in a regime putatively designed to protect "everyman":

> "Equality" . . . belongs essentially to decline: the chasm between man and man, class and class, the multiplicity of types, the will to be oneself, to stand out—that which I call *pathos of distance*—characterizes every *strong* age. The tension, the range between the extremes is today growing less and less— the extremes themselves are finally obliterated to the point of similarity. (*TI* "Skirmishes" 37)

This appreciation of distance—not simply hierarchy—as culturally invigorating emerges in Nietzsche's characterization of freedom as "the will to self-responsibility" that "preserves the distance which divides us" (*TI* "Skirmishes" 38). Thus, like Foucault, Nietzsche's complaint against modern politics is that it excessively organizes and institutionalizes human relations: it dissolves our separateness even as it fabricates us as "individuals"; it throws us into proximity in a fashion that mutes our own capacity to express responsibility, creativity, and hence freedom. Like Rousseau, Nietzsche regards mass social intercourse and the institutions that perpetuate it as the enemy of discerning sensibility. In this regard, tolerance, one of democracy's proudest virtues, emerges as a symptom of its baseness.

> To put up with men, to keep open house in one's heart—this is liberal, but no more than liberal. One knows hearts which are capable of *noble* hospitality, which have curtained windows and closed shutters: they keep their best rooms empty . . . because they await guests with whom one does *not* have to "put up." (*TI* "Skirmishes" 25)

In short, Nietzsche regards political life, especially modern political life, as harboring values and spawning institutions that displace and discourage individual and collective aspiration, creativity, distinction, and culture. The state is "organized immorality," a "tremendous machine" that "overpowers the individual" and substitutes for it a mechanical individualism in which all are reduced to units (*WP* 717, 718). Parties are for unthinking followers—"whoever thinks much is not suitable as a party member: he soon thinks himself right through the party" (*HH* 579). And political doctrines are mostly justifications of and for the weak against the strong but also of the rational against the Dionysian, in either case issuing from *ressentiment* (*TI* "Ancients" 4).

While Nietzsche concedes a potentially synergistic relation between politics and culture when the former itself partakes of "greatness" (Periclean Athens is the ambivalent example to which he frequently recurs), politics is more often cast as the enemy of culture. Insisting that all justice is born of "envy" or other elements of slave morality, and that nationalism and anarchy draw on the basest human instincts and desires, war is the only element of political life that Nietzsche celebrates as ennobling for the collective spirit (*HH* 477). The antagonism of politics to culture pertains not only to the former's mobilization of herd morality but also to its ethos of static domination, its tendency to fix or stabilize its domain via enervating institutions:

> Like every organizational political power, the Greek *polis* spurned and distrusted the increase of culture among its citizens; its powerful natural impulse was to do almost nothing but cripple and obstruct it. The polis did not want to permit to culture any history or evolution; the education determined by the law of the land was intended to bind all generations and keep them at *one* level. . . . So culture developed *in spite* of the *polis*. (*HH* 474)

Nietzsche's negative view of institutions generally, like that of his twentieth-century student, Foucault, pertains to his conviction that they contain and constrain life, dominating through excessive control and devitalization of their subjects. Institutions also endure over time, and in this too are contrary to a cultural ethos of creativity and struggle. Thus, Nietzsche jokes, "the overthrow of beliefs is not immediately followed by the overthrow of institutions; rather the new beliefs live for a long time in the now desolate and eerie house of their predecessors, which they themselves preserve, because of the housing shortage" (*HH* 466). In short, for Nietzsche, modern political institutions aim to fix and stabilize, they aim to achieve a kind of static domination, as well as to invest the world with the *ressentiment* of justice born of envy. Culture, by contrast, represents the prospect of innovation, aspiration, and creative effort. Like theory, culture climbs, slides, and functions to undo meaning, conventional practices, and, above all, institutions.

Nietzsche's critique of democracy is largely unlivable. No matter what its form—socialist, liberal, or communitarian—modern democratic life in state societies cannot be conducted with shuttered rooms and aristocratic practices that disregard most of humanity, with contempt for the many or the reduction of all democratic doctrine to envy and resentment. So what would it mean to inject a noble sensibility that discriminates and discerns, that aspires to greatness and shuns petty ambition and petty injury, into democratic institutions and practices? Indeed, how might democracy harbor antidemocracy not as a practice of tolerance but as a means of preventing itself from sliding into technocracy, on one side, and base attachments or principles, on the other? What is the *force* of theory as "antipolitics" in renewing decayed democratic political life?

Another way of putting the problem: What use for a discussion about the relation of theory and politics is a philosopher who is hostile to both in the name of something called "life" or culture? Nietzsche's insistence on the limiting force of both theory and politics does not prevent their productive intercourse to produce an illness, "as pregnancy is an illness." Although it was not his purpose, Nietzsche offers the basis for an agonistic interlocution between theory and politics, especially in democracies, which are inherently antitheoretical and inherently lack a binding principle. Politics and theory can question each another without having to answer to each other—without being either identical or accountable.[26] I am further suggesting that politics, which fervently fixes meanings and generates their consolidation in institutions, requires theory's antipolitical rupture of these meanings and institutions in order not to become the nightmare of human sociality that politics is persistently, almost inevitably, capable of becoming. The realm of politics needs to be cut through by counterforces both to incite its virtues and, in a technocratic age, to abet its slide into a historically unprecedented machinery of domination.

A productive relation between theory and politics might be conceived on the model of Nietzschean friendship. "In a friend one should still honor the enemy. Can you go close to your friend without going over to him? You should be closest to him with your heart when you resist him" (Z:1 "On the Friend"). Can theory and politics manage such *amour?* It would require affirming the autonomy, value, and strength of each, *believing* in them, restoring good faith in them, and for that, both would have to be transformed. But this kind of relation also calls forth from democracy what does not come easily to it, namely, *effort,* the struggle to overcome itself that is also the means by which it can save itself from turning into its opposite. Indeed, democracy's lack of a principle means that it risks "having nothing that is difficult," and what is difficult for the spirit, Nietzsche insists in *Zarathustra,* is "what the spirit's *strength* demands" (Z:1 "On the Three Metamorphoses"). This does not mean that democracy must have a difficult principle at its heart in order to have a strong spirit but that the struggle between democratic and antidemocratic impulses, between political imperatives and antidemocratic theoretical disruptions, is less likely to be dangerous than invigorating for democracy if platitudes are not deployed to quickly quell this struggle.

Genealogy may be a particularly important practice for democratic renewal insofar as it is uniquely suited to bring to light a specific democracy's historical attachments to and imbrications with nondemocratic principles. Genealogy challenges conceits of purity: through it, particular democracies are revealed as enfolded with histories of imperialism or slavery or punishment and as bearing a present saturated with those histories. In this, genealogy also challenges the institutions of democracies, indeed, the institutionalization of democracy, precisely the institutionalization that Nietzsche abhors as antilife and that others have critically interrogated as incompatible with democracy understood as the perpetual sovereignty of the people, as the continuous practice of freedom.[27]

But Nietzsche's theoretical challenges to democracy also become important in another way, serving as challenges to democratic values themselves. Particularly in late modernity, when liberal democracy is all that is left standing in a history of tried-and-failed regimes, liberal democracy risks more than ever a laconic, self-satisfied tendency, avoiding "what is difficult" both because its antitheoretical nature produces no internal questioning and because it faces no challenges from without. Democracy lives its many paradoxes today without featuring the struggle over them as its potential life force, its potential greatness. Liberal democracy rarely submits to interrogation its cardinal values of mass equality and tolerance without dismissing such challenges as antidemocratic, nor does it engage critiques of its subordination of culture to political equality and the market. Consequently, we gaze across a seemingly unbridgeable chasm to the art and monuments of previous centuries, without asking whether what Nietzsche designated as culture's antipathy to the democratic sentiment could be made a productive interlocutor of democracy, offering precisely the challenge that might lead democracy to "climb" in the manner Nietzsche insisted was the sole purview of culture.

In this spirit let me make a final return to a theme raised earlier, by way of Tocqueville and of Balibar's reading of Spinoza. If democracy is governance by the people, and a people is the opposite of the state, yet no modern democracy can persist without the state form, perhaps it is this paradox that Nietzschean philosophy helps us stage as political possibility rather than entrapment. Permanent resistance to the state that both limits and ensures the democratic form becomes a means of sustaining democracy insofar as it is the state form that dissolves democracy. Only through the state are the people constituted as a people; only in resistance to the state do the people remain a people. Thus, just as democracy requires antidemocratic critique in order to remain democratic, the democratic state requires resistance rather than fealty in order not to become the death of democracy. Similarly, democracy requires theory's provision of unlivable critiques and unreachable ideals—it requires incitement to efforts, principles, and aims that it cannot provide for itself or fulfill without losing itself yet must be incited by in order not to become profoundly undemocratic. It is this array of difficult paradoxes that compose Nietzsche's bouquet to democratic aspirations.

NOTES

1. The autonomy of each has been eroded by a range of forces—politics by bureaucracy, political economy, technology, mass media, and privatized functions of the state, and theory by a variety of other interpretive practices including ethnography, all manner of social science, journalism, and most recently literary criticism. Thus, even as the relationship between theory and politics has been stabilized by certain modernist conventions, the figure of each has grown uncertain and insecure.

2. In Foucault's phraseology, "power is tolerable only on condition that it mask a substantial part of itself. Its success is proportional to its ability to hide its own mechanisms" (Michel Foucault, *The History of Sexuality*, vol. 1, trans. Richard Hurley [New York: Vintage, 1978], 86).

3. Alexis de Tocqueville, *Democracy in America*, trans. Henry Reeve (New York: Schocken Books, 1961), 2:10.

4. Etienne Balibar, "Spinoza, The Anti-Orwell," in *Masses, Classes, Ideas: Studies in Philosophy Before and After Marx*, trans. J. Swenson (New York: Routledge, 1994), 24.

5. Ibid., 25.

6. Benedict de Spinoza, *The Political Works*, ed. and trans. A. G. Wernham (Oxford: Clarendon Press, 1958).

7. Balibar, "Spinoza, The Anti-Orwell," 26.

8. Tocqueville, *Democracy in America*, 8.

9. See especially Michel Foucault, "Nietzsche, Genealogy, History," in *The Foucault Reader*, ed. Paul Rabinow (New York: Pantheon, 1984); an interview titled "Critical Theory / Intellectual History" and a lecture, "The Art of Telling the Truth," both in *Michel Foucault: Politics, Philosophy, Culture: Interviews and Other Writings, 1977–1984*, ed. L. Kritzman (New York: Routledge, 1988).

10. Foucault, "The Art of Telling the Truth," 95.

11. Foucault, "Critical Theory / Intellectual History," 36.

12. Ibid.

13. Foucault, "Nietzsche, Genealogy, History," 89.

14. Ibid., 87.

15. Ibid., 88.

16. Ibid., 90.

17. Michel Foucault, "Politics and Reason," in *Michel Foucault: Politics, Philosophy, Culture*, 71.

18. Colin Gordon, "Governmental Rationality: An Introduction," in *The Foucault Effect*, ed. Colin Gordon (Chicago: University of Chicago Press, 1991), 10.

19. Foucault, "Politics and Reason," 83–85.

20. Foucault, "Nietzsche, Genealogy, History," 82.

21. Ibid., 81.

22. Ibid., 83.

23. Ibid., 88.

24. In *Twilight of the Idols*, this disdain is expressed as "liberalism: in plain

words, *reduction to the herd animal*" (*TI* "Skirmishes" 38). In *Thus Spoke Zarathustra*, it is captured in the parable "On the Flies of the Marketplace" (*Z:*1).

25. "Notes" (1875), in *The Portable Nietzsche,* ed. and trans. W. Kaufmann (New York: Penguin, 1954), 50.

26. "*No one* is accountable for existing at all, or for being constituted as he is. . . . *We* invented the concept 'purpose': in reality purpose is *lacking.* . . . We deny God; in denying God, we deny accountability: only by doing *that* do we redeem the world" (*TI* "Errors" 8).

27. Political thinkers as diverse as Rousseau, Arendt, Foucault, and Wolin contribute to this perspective.

CHAPTER 13

Democratizing the *Agon*

Nietzsche, Arendt, and the Agonistic
Tendency in Recent Political Theory

Dana R. Villa

It seems to me that those who criticize the conflicts between
the nobles and the plebeians condemn the very things which
were the primary cause of Roman liberty, and that they pay
more attention to the noises and cries raised by such quarrels
than to the good effects that they brought forth; nor do they
consider that in every republic there are two different inclina-
tions: that of the people and that of the upper class, and that
all the laws which are made in favor of liberty are born of the
conflict between the two.

Machiavelli, The Discourses

Every talent must unfold itself in fighting.
Friedrich Nietzsche, "Homer's Contest"

Politics means conflict.
Max Weber, Parliament and Government

To speak of an agonistic politics in a liberal-democratic context invites
skepticism, given the traditional liberal fear of stirring up the moral passions and conflicting visions of the good that divide citizens of a pluralist society. To speak of a "democratic agonism" is, perhaps, to push this
skepticism to outright disbelief, given the heroic/aristocratic virtues associated with the agonal ideal articulated by both Friedrich Nietzsche
and Hannah Arendt. Yet many contemporary political theorists (Sheldon
Wolin, William E. Connolly, Chantal Mouffe, and Bonnie Honig among

them) have turned to a broadly agonistic model of politics as *the* way of advancing a radical democratic agenda. These theorists worry that modern democracies are hardly democratic at all; that the bureaucratic edifice of the state has usurped the space of the political, rendering citizens the passive recipients of policy decisions; that, finally, liberal theory has contributed to this state of affairs by promoting a conception of politics that is essentially juridical /administrative, one that seeks ways of diminishing, if not eradicating, the contest and debate that is the lifeblood of a robust democratic politics.[1]

With regard to the last point, agonistic democrats worry that John Rawls and other advocates of proceduralist liberalism are so anxious to avoid conflict that they construct a set of public institutions, and a code of public argument and public justification, that leaves precious little space for initiatory or expressive modes of political action.[2] What Rawls calls the "domain of the political" is seen as so strictly circumscribed that it marginalizes not only substantive moral argument but also essential questions of economic power and political identity. Agonistic democrats share Michael Sandel's fear that "fundamentalists rush in where liberals fear to tread" and his suspicion of the hard distinction between public and private that Rawls's political liberalism is (apparently) built on.[3] While skeptical of Sandel's civic republican remedy (and his call for a frankly moralistic public discourse), agonistic democrats tend to agree with his basic point that political liberalism has been all too successful in separating the *homme* (or *femme)* from the *citoyen*.[4]

Viewed against the background of a liberalism that desires, above all, to remain neutral with respect to controversial views of the good life, agonism appears to provide a much-needed life- and reality-restoring corrective to political theory. Contemporary agonists remind us that the public sphere is as much a stage for conflict and expression as it is a set of procedures or institutions designed to preserve peace, promote fairness, or achieve consensus. They also (contra Rawls) insist that politics and culture form a continuum, where ultimate values are always already in play; where the content of basic rights and the purposes of political association are not the objects of a frictionless "overlapping consensus" but are contested every day, in a dizzying array of venues. With its battle cry of "incessant contestation," political agonism seems to provide a welcome return to the repressed essence of democratic politics: conflict.

The political agonist is, however, open to an array of equally compelling liberal objections. Isn't a politics of rules, interests, and accommodation infinitely preferable to a politics of action, passions, and ideological conflict? Doesn't a more expansive and expressive public sphere, one in which ultimate values and questions of group identity are actively engaged, exacerbate the divisions within society, threatening to burst the fragile integument of liberal secularism asunder? Finally, doesn't an agonistic politics, even a "radically democratic" one, make the friend / enemy distinction the core of political life? Doesn't it threaten to turn us all, if not into Carl Schmitts, into Rush Limbaughs?[5]

One need not be a Rawls or a Madison to worry about the consequences of an "incessantly contestatory" (and presumably more ideological) politics, even if one shares the sense that Americans, at least, are deeply alienated from political life. Indeed, the trouble with recent formulations of an agonistic politics is that they have tended to celebrate conflict, and individual and group political expression, a bit too unselectively. One can agree with their diagnosis of some of the ills of liberal theory and practice (the tendency to overvalue consensus, order, and rational deliberation, for example) without being entirely persuaded by their cure. Making citizens more expressive, and demanding that their expressions be heard in the public realm, may not, in the end, make them any less subservient to the rule or any more resistant to "normalization" (so much, at least, is suggested by the analyses of Richard Sennett and Michel Foucault).[6] Moreover, it is hardly the case that liberalism itself has been free of the worry that citizens of a constitutional order, democratic or otherwise, will gradually come to think and act as docile subjects of that order rather than as vigilant watchers over political authority (think of Locke in the *Second Treatise,* Thoreau in "Civil Disobedience," or Mill in *On Liberty*). This suggests that the real problem is not how to encourage and make room for expression, unruly or otherwise. Rather, it is how to promote an ethos of independent thought and action, one that is sufficiently impersonal to be both morally serious and publicly oriented.

As Honig has argued, one can learn much from Nietzsche in this regard. But one can learn even more, I would argue, from the selective appropriation of Nietzsche performed by Arendt. More than any other theorist, Arendt demonstrates the political relevance of Nietzsche's agonistic stance. At the same time, her reading of Greek political experience, along with her appreciation of the lessons of Socrates and Kant, made her acutely aware of the need to set limits, both institutional and characterological, to the *agon* that *is* political life. If Arendt goes much further than any liberal would go in her advocacy of an agonistic ethos in politics, she distinguishes herself from contemporary agonists by her emphasis on the impersonal dimensions of such an ethos. Impersonality does not denote the effacement of the individual under his civic mask or persona (Arendt is not the champion of an unvarnished civic republicanism that many have made her out to be). Her agonism, like Nietzsche's, is surprisingly individualistic in character. But, unlike his, it is not particularly expressive. This creates an instructive tension with the formulations of contemporary agonists. In my view, the impersonality of Arendt's agonistic ethos makes it preferable to these more recent formulations.

In what follows I present Arendt's selective appropriation of Nietzsche in light of current debates. First, I sketch the concerns that inform Nietzsche's agonism and Arendt's. I then turn to consider the difference between her appropriation of Nietzsche and that of the advocates of "incessant contestation." [7] I conclude with some reflections on the limits of the agonistic strand in contemporary political theory.

AGONISM IN NIETZSCHE AND ARENDT

Throughout his work, Nietzsche addresses the problem of a modern, "democratic" culture that has inherited the prejudice of "slave morality" against individualizing action. While *Beyond Good and Evil* (1886) and *On the Genealogy of Morals* (1887) provide the most profound meditations on this theme, the broad problematic is already established in *On the Use and Disadvantage of History for Life* (1874). Nietzsche's critique of historicism—his insistence that great action demands a protective, partly closed horizon—prefigures his later polemics against philosophical skepticism and religious and scientific versions of the "ascetic ideal." Indeed, the theme that "knowledge kills action" goes back to *The Birth of Tragedy*. From the beginning, "Socratism," understood as a will to truth that dissolves life-sustaining illusions, is under indictment.[8] What makes the later texts interesting, however, is Nietzsche's specification of what constitutes a "healthy," action-promoting moral horizon. In *Beyond Good and Evil* and *On the Genealogy of Morals*, Nietzsche leaves the exhortatory rhetoric of *Lebensphilosophie* behind, focusing instead on those structures that inhibit independent action and that stand in the way of fashioning the self as a work of art.

In *On the Genealogy of Morals* Nietzsche argues that the *moral epistemology* set in place by the "slave revolt in morality" is one that is intrinsically hostile to action and the active life. If the aristocratic Greeks lacked a developed distinction between an actor and his acts, a subject and his "effects," it was because they could not conceive of the noble man as *other* from his deeds. To be and to act were, from their perspective, the same (*GM* I:10). It is only the reactive man, the "slave," the man who *cannot* act, who needs the comforting fiction of a subject entirely separate from its actions or "effects." Thus, in his famous parable of the lamb and the bird of prey (*GM* I:13), Nietzsche writes that "to demand of strength that it should *not* express itself as strength, that it should *not* be a desire to overcome, a desire to throw down, a desire to become master, a thirst for enemies and resistances and triumphs, is just as absurd as to demand of weakness that it should express itself as strength."

Yet despite the absurdity, this is how we, "masters" and "slaves" alike, come to think of the relation between the doer and his deed. Thanks to the "fiction" of a neutral subject "behind" the actions of the "strong man" or the reactions of the "weak," human agents are rendered morally accountable for *all* their actions. Such accountability is a lighter burden for those who abstain from action; indeed, it turns their abstention into a kind of virtue. For the man predisposed to manifest his virtues in action, to individualize himself through the *performance* of great or noble deeds, such accountability shifts the standard of judgment of action away from its beauty or greatness and toward its presumably disruptive consequences for the social whole. Through the "fiction" of the subject—the moral epistemology of "slave morality"—action is moralized and the actor rendered subservient to a code of conduct that applies universally to society as a whole. "Active," agonistic agents cease to compete with their peers in order to demonstrate their excellence. They become, like the rest of us, "responsible" subjects, self-surveilling and slow to initiate anything, ever conscious of the code of conduct of the "herd."

Nietzsche does not hold out the possibility, or even the desirability, of re-creating the state of almost animal-like health that he ascribes to the Homeric Greeks. The bulk of *On the Genealogy of Morals* is devoted to telling the long, bloody story of how responsibility originated. And despite all the gruesomeness of the "morality of mores" and the "social straitjacket," Nietzsche leaves no doubt that what he calls the moralization and internalization of man is the price paid for creating an "interesting" animal, an animal capable of autonomy and self-legislation (*GM* II:2). The problem is that so many of us get stuck in the intermediate stage of bad conscience, the stage of an internalized social code that en-

courages continual self-monitoring and condemnation of the strong passions essential to initiatory action. To frame what is typically considered
the moral life as a transitional phase, one all too dependent on the myth
of a divine surveillance apparatus in the sky, is one aim of the *Genealogy*'s materialist history of morals.

Of course, liberal democracy sees itself as making enormous contributions to the project of autonomy, to the creation of a social space in
which more and more individuals not only live the life they please but
also attain a degree of moral maturity and independence of judgment
previously undreamed of. The goal of the second and third essays of *On
the Genealogy of Morals,* and of much of *Beyond Good and Evil,* is to
shatter this self-conception. If the morality of mores had to make men
"to a certain degree necessary, uniform, like among like, regular, and
consequently calculable" in order for responsibility to emerge, the democratic age accelerates rather than reverses this process. Democracy does
not create the conditions for the "sovereign individual"; on the contrary,
it represents the triumph of *ressentiment* and the will to sameness and
unconditionality that characterizes slave morality. As Nietzsche writes
in *Beyond Good and Evil:*

> *Morality in Europe today is herd animal morality*—in other words, as we un-
> derstand it, merely *one* type of human morality beside which, before which,
> and after which many other types, above all *higher* moralities, are, or ought
> to be, possible. But this morality resists such a "possibility," such an "ought"
> with all its power: it says stubbornly and inexorably, "I am morality itself,
> and nothing besides is morality." Indeed, with the help of a religion which in-
> dulged and flattered the most sublime herd-animal desires, we have reached
> the point where we find even in political and social institutions an ever more
> visible expression of this morality: the *democratic* movement is the heir of the
> Christian movement. (*BGE* 202)

The democratic subject is, according to Nietzsche, the herd animal
par excellence, the living embodiment of the "morality of timidity." His
virtues—the virtues of "public spirit, benevolence, consideration, indus-
triousness, moderation, modesty, indulgence and pity"—stand in direct
opposition to the virtues manifest in the masters' agonal striving. Indeed, these latter virtues (and the passions that underlie them) are seen
as the greatest threat to the democratic community (*BGE* 199).[9]

When we ask how Nietzsche envisions nonslavish, nonconformist
virtues (the virtues of the "sovereign individual"), the answer does little
to soothe democratic sensibilities. Nietzsche's ethos of self-overcoming

and his hostility to universalizing moral codes lead him to laud not simply action over passivity but all those characteristics that distinguish the "healthy" from the "sick." Great passions, great energies, the will to command oneself and others, the willingness to sacrifice oneself and others—these, together with an intense appreciation of the Greek valuation of "struggle and the joy of victory," delineate a masculine aestheticism that stands in the greatest possible tension with the democratic repudiation of rulership (see *TI* "Skirmish" 38; also *BGE* 199, 203; *GM* III:14). For Nietzsche, the affirmation of life requires the affirmation of rule, of rank and "the pathos of distance" (*GM* I:2). One must rule oneself by focusing one's energies with the severest discipline; one can achieve greatness in politics only insofar as one is willing to *command*. Whether discussing the self or the polity, Nietzsche invariably deploys the metaphor of the work of art, with its implication of violence toward the "raw materials" (internal or external) that need shaping (see *GS* 290). His examples of "sovereign individuals," those who are "autonomous and supramoral," tend either to be virtuosic artists (like Goethe or Beethoven) or political actors of great, but ruthless, *virtu* (Cesare Borgia, Napoleon).

Given Nietzsche's coupling of the "herd animal" with democracy, and his aristocratic conception of the agonistic virtues, it is hardly surprising that his critique of the "responsible subject" fell on deaf ears for so long. Foucault's *Discipline and Punish* changed all that by showing how the modern state produced "docile subjects" through the proliferation of "microtechniques of power." Quite self-consciously, Foucault provided a *Genealogy of Morals* for the democratic age, one that attempted to demonstrate that rights and disciplines are two sides of the same coin.[10] From a Foucauldian point of view, our ostensibly greater freedom masks an ever more profound internalization of norms; indeed, it is possible only on the basis of our becoming "self-surveilling" subjects.

Foucault's analysis provides an essential touchstone for most contemporary agonists. Their calls for "resistance" and "excess" presuppose that liberal democracy has been all too successful in "taming" its citizens, diminishing or diverting their potentially political energies. Again, the general theme is hardly new: recall Machiavelli's and Rousseau's civic republican critiques of Christian passivity, or Mill's and Tocqueville's prescient analyses of democratic conformity (it was, after all, Mill who called for a strong dose of "pagan self-assertion" to balance the inherited burden of "Christian self-denial").[11] Foucault's unique contribution to this thematic was to suggest not only that power permeated everyday life (in the form of the disciplines) but also that the very process of producing "docile subjects" created resistances and multiple sites of struggle in places hitherto relegated to the extreme margins of political life (hospitals, schools, factories, prisons). Thus, precisely at the moment when the *agon* seemed like the most ancient of history, it reemerged in the interstices of the welfare state itself.[12] Agonistic subjectivity—the subjectivity of Nietzsche's "masters" and his elite of "sovereign individuals"—returned in the democratized form of the politics of resistance.

But Foucault's updating of Nietzsche remained insufficient from the standpoint of the radical democratic project. While generating a "politics of everyday life," its center of gravity was, in fact, ethical rather than political; its foremost concern, resisting the imposition of identities on groups and individuals. And it is for this reason that "radical democrats" have turned to Arendt's expressly *political* reformulation of Nietzsche's agonism. What is it that attracts them to Arendt?

First, there is the central place she gives to action in her conception of the political. This sets her at odds with the liberal focus on institutions, procedures, interests, and "negative freedom" (the freedom *from* politics).[13] But Arendt goes far beyond the affirmation of "public freedom" and "public happiness" that we encounter in the civic republican tradition. Like Nietzsche, she affirms the initiatory dimension of all genuine action, its radically innovative character.[14] And, like Nietzsche, she affirms the contingency of human (and especially political) affairs, disdaining all teleological orderings and utilitarian criteria. For Arendt, the freedom of action is manifest in its capacity to transcend both the needs of life and the supposed necessity of history. The Nietzschean formula "the deed is everything" holds for her, as it is through deeds—through initiatory political speech and action—that human beings tear themselves away from the everyday, the repetitive, the merely reactive (*GM* I:13). *Unlike* Nietzsche, however, she insists that action properly occurs only in a public sphere characterized by relations of equality. Citing the Greek polis, she goes so far as to identify freedom and equality.[15] Human plurality—the existence of diverse equals—is for her the sine qua non of political action. Indeed, all genuinely political action is, in fact, an "acting together."[16] Contra Nietzsche, rulership signals the end of political action, its dissolution into the instrumental and fundamentally unfree activity of command and obedience.[17]

Second, radical democrats are attracted by Arendt's endorsement of

the "fiercely agonal spirit," which she sees as animating all genuine political action. Again like Nietzsche, Arendt turns to the Greeks to isolate
the "immortalizing impulse," the passion for greatness, as *the* specifically political passion.[18] The impulse to distinguish oneself, to prove oneself the best of all, lies at the heart of action's tremendous individualizing power. But whereas Nietzsche's agonistic stance culminates in a
heroic individualism, Arendt's expressly political version dovetails with
what she calls the "revolutionary spirit" and the spirit of resistance.[19]
Her examples are not virtuosic statesmen but the spontaneous heroic action manifest in the American Revolution, the Paris Commune of 1871,
the 1905 Russian Revolution, French Resistance fighters, and the Hun-
garian revolt of 1956. This makes it possible and plausible for contemporary agonists to assimilate her to "an activist, democratic politics of
contest, resistance, and amendment."[20] And while radical democrats
are generally quite skeptical of Arendt's Nietzsche-inspired distinction
between the social and the political, viewing it as an aristocratic excres-
cence, they applaud the spirit behind pronouncements such as the following (from *The Human Condition*):

> It is decisive that society, on all its levels, excludes the possibility of action,
> which formerly was excluded from the household. Instead, society expects
> from each of its members a certain kind of behavior, imposing innumerable
> and various rules, all of which tend to "normalize" its members, to make
> them behave to exclude spontaneous action or outstanding achievement.[21]

Here Arendt mediates between Nietzsche's critique of the ascetic regimes
through which individuals are "tamed" and made useful to the "herd"
and Max Weber's savage depiction of the *Ordnungsmensch* fostered by
the bureaucratic penetration of everyday life. And, of course, she prefigures Foucault's basic theme in *Discipline and Punish*.

Third, Arendt draws out the specifically political consequences of
Nietzsche's antifoundationalism, showing how the will to an extrapoliti-
cal ground in the modern age can only be nihilistic, antipolitical, and
antidemocratic.[22] The will to find a transcendent ground for politics is a
will to escape the irreducible relativity of human agreements and opinions; it is the will to discover an immovable authority that will put an
end to the incessant debate and contestation that *is* democratic politics.
Arendt gives Nietzsche's anti-Platonism a political (and democratic) spin
by arguing for a groundless "politics of opinion," one that recognizes
the human need for stability but eschews (in Honig's words) a "law of

laws that is immune to contestation and amendment."[23] What makes Arendt's conception of an agonistic public sphere so attractive to radical democrats is not that it puts everything up for grabs (a viable public sphere depends on relatively firm laws and lasting institutions) but that the meaning and authoritativeness of its founding and basic institutions are a function of the clash of conflicting interpretations. So conceived, the public sphere is, above all, an institutionally articulated site of perpetual debate and contestation.

If we add to Arendt's focus on action, praise of the spirit of resistance, and political "postfoundationalism" her ingenious adaptation of Nietzsche's perspectivism for demands of a democratic public sphere,[24] it is easy to see why the proponents of a politics of "incessant contestation" turn to her just as often as to Nietzsche for inspiration. This is not to say, however, that they believe that Arendt succeeds in stripping agonism of its aristocratic trappings. On the contrary, Wolin, Connolly, and Honig take her to task for maintaining distinctions that they view as either unjustifiably elitist or essentialist. Thus Wolin attacks Arendt's distinction between the social and the political, charging that her desire for a "pure politics" unsullied by economic concerns and the needs of the "masses" is, at base, deeply antidemocratic. An Arendtian politics of memorable deeds performed by virtuosic actors is, according to Wolin, scarcely compatible with democratic politics, the primary thrust of which is to "extend the broad egalitarianism of ordinary lives into public life."[25] Similarly, Connolly charges her with maintaining a "political purism" parallel to Kant's moral purism, one that purges "the social question and the body" from the public realm, leaving a "bleached and aristocratic" version of human plurality, one deprived of important "dimensions of diversity which might otherwise enrich and fortify it."[26]

From a somewhat different angle, Honig attacks Arendt's apparently hard and fast distinction between public and private, which she views as both arbitrary and self-defeating.[27] Arendt's conception of the public sphere is, according to Honig, overly formalistic; it is also deeply conservative insofar as it naturalizes the public/private distinction. It thereby seals off inherited race, class, gender, and ethnic identities from contest and reformulation.[28] Whereas Wolin sees Arendt's conception of agonistic action as entailing the social/political distinction, Honig suggests that action as theorized by Arendt is essentially destabilizing, boundless, and unpredictable. It mirrors the movement of Derridean *différance*. Hence the public/private distinction as deployed by Arendt arbitrarily confines the unconfineable: it seeks to put the genie (disruptive, "excessive" action) back in the bottle. Arendt is blind to her own insight. Radical democrats must save her from herself.

ETHOS AND LIMITS OF THE POLITICAL *AGON*

These critiques and emendations of Arendt's agonism will strike a chord with all serious readers of her work. In the end, however, I think the criticisms are too easy; they turn a deaf ear to the underlying concerns that shape her political appropriation of Nietzsche. Arendt's distinctions between the social and the political, or the public and the private, are not motivated by a Nietzschean desire to keep the healthy, active few separate from the "sick," resentful masses; nor are they designed to erect a "non-negotiable" barrier that confines and emasculates her account of "disruptive" action. Rather, these distinctions (and the dramaturgical conception of action and the public sphere they underwrite) serve to focus our attention on the central role that impersonality and self-distance play in the preservation of a (genuinely) agonistic ethos. What matters for her is less *where* political action takes place and *what* it concerns than the spirit in which it is undertaken. Let me explain.

To *act,* for Arendt, means appearing on a public stage, before diverse equals. In so doing, we leave behind the private self of needs, drives, and a diffuse interiority. We take on a public persona, create a public self, one whose words and deeds are judged by the "audience" of our civic peers. Arendt's insistence on the social / political and public / private distinctions highlights the discipline, stylization, and conventionality assumed by the virtuosic political actor in the presentation of such a self. Only if actor and audience are adept at distinguishing between their civic / political selves and the self driven by material and psychological needs can something like a relatively autonomous political sphere exist at all. Arendt's distinctions are designed not to exclude groups of agents from the political sphere but to point out the dangers inherent in certain mentalities or approaches to the public realm. Insofar as action is driven by the immediacy of unbearable oppression or material want, it cannot hope to attain the degree of impersonality that is the hallmark of *political* action. The passions and needs that drive such desperate, often violent action have little to do with what Arendt calls "care for the world," by which she means concern for the artificial "home" that a political association provides for human beings. It is concern for this "in-between," for the structure of institutions and terms of association it sets, that marks the *political* actor.

Another way of putting this is to say that action must have a constitutional referent for it to qualify as political for Arendt. If we are to be fair to her, we must understand "constitutional" broadly, in the Greek rather than the more restricted American sense. "Constitutional" in the former sense denotes a whole way of life, the way of life of the democratic, oligarchic, or aristocratic regime.[29] Political action in a constitutional democracy would, in Arendt's understanding, be citizenly action aimed against the state and other forces that threaten to restrict or overturn the pluralist and (politically) egalitarian terms of association the constitution sets out. Of course, the precise nature of these terms and their moral implications are the stuff of ongoing, open-ended debate and contestation.[30] The democratic political life, as Arendt understands it, is agonistic, often raucous, and passionate in its moral commitments; it is neither narrowly legalistic nor top down in its functioning. It is, however, importantly limited to *public* issues and terms of discourse. It is also more interested in playing the game than winning (this is Arendt's definition of a *public-spirited* agonism, what she calls the "joy of action"). Of course, *public* issues are not set in stone, and much of the content of democratic politics is debate over what issues are, in fact, of public (and constitutional) concern.[31] From an Arendtian point of view, however, Wolin's identification of democratic politics with grassroots struggles for social justice is far too restrictive in its redefinition of the "public," just as Honig's Derrida-inspired "radicalization" of action as the boundary-blurring force par excellence is far too indefinite.

This serves to highlight an Arendtian departure from Nietzsche, one that also distinguishes her from contemporary agonists. Arendt's understanding of institutions and law as marking out the boundaries of the public realm (an understanding equally indebted to the Greeks and the American founders) and her emphasis on the artificiality and relative fragility of this "man-made realm" offer a marked contrast to the celebrations of democratic flux found in Wolin and Honig. For Wolin, democratic action is essentially transgressive and revolutionary. By its very nature, it stands in extreme tension with any "settled constitution." Indeed, democracy is "reduced" and "devitalized" by form; it is not a form of government at all but "a mode of being," an "experience" of common action that can be, at best, episodic, momentary.[32] Honig does not go nearly as far down this vitalist path, stressing as she does Nietzsche's and

Arendt's shared "reverence for institutions." Nevertheless, her voluntarist assertion that Arendt relies on the practice of promising to create
"fragile stabilities" amid the contingent, flux-filled realm of politics dramatically underplays the extent to which Arendt envisions agonistic
politics as a function of a "relatively permanent" public sphere.[33]

Arendt also departs radically from Nietzsche in her reliance on the
Renaissance and eighteenth-century tradition of *theatrum mundi,* a tradition she traces back to her beloved Greeks. It is her appreciation of the
theatrical dimensions of political action—of the artificiality and conventionality that make it possible for the self to don a public mask and to
be judged by criteria appropriate to their public role—that underlies her
fierce critique of both voluntarism and romantic expressivism in politics.
Both, she thinks, read the common public world back into the self, destroying its autonomy and relative permanence.[34] It is because she wants
to combat expressivism and the "worldlessness" it promotes that she
identifies freedom with *virtù,* that is, with the virtuosity of the performing actor:

> Freedom as inherent in action is perhaps best illustrated by Machiavelli's
> concept of *virtù,* the excellence with which man answers the opportunities
> the world opens up before him in the guise of *fortuna.* Its meaning is best ren-
> dered by "virtuosity," that is, an excellence we attribute to the performing
> arts (as distinguished from the creative arts of making), where the accom-
> plishment lies in the performance itself and not in an end product which out-
> lasts the activity that brought it into existence and becomes independent of
> it. The virtuoso-ship of Machiavelli's *virtù* somehow reminds us of the fact,
> although Machiavelli hardly knew it, that the Greeks always used such meta-
> phors as flute-playing, dancing, healing, and seafaring to distinguish politi-
> cal from other activities, that is, that they drew their analogies from those
> arts in which virtuosity of performance is decisive.[35]

The explicitness of this passage notwithstanding, Arendt's critics have
uniformly ignored the worldly thrust of her theatrical model of political
action, of action as *performance.*[36] Without exception, they dismiss her
conception of the public sphere as a theatrical space where such (distanced, impersonal) freedom can dwell, the better to bring agonistic action in line with some version of the expressivist model. Thus Wolin insists that moments of genuine democratic politics arise as expressions of
"the common being of human beings," while both Connolly and Honig
argue that agonistic action flows from the energies of "multiple selves."[37]
While the emphases on "common being" and "the subject as multiplicity" are themselves in tension (one suited to the project of reviving the

demos, the other to identity politics broadly construed), they share a profound devaluation of the *worldliness* of political action, its impersonal or theatrical character. For Wolin, Connolly, and Honig, democratizing the *agon* is inseparable from making agonistic action *expressive* action.

Why is this such a sin? What could possibly be wrong with overcoming the constricting conventionality assumed by Arendt's theatrical model in favor of a more transgressive, Nietzschean, conception? What do we lose by detaching the *agon* from Arendt's strong notion of a public world and a public self?

For one thing, we lose the ground of a "care for the world," which, in Arendt's view, animates all genuinely political action. In its stead we find the demands for social justice and recognition of emergent identities. Such demands are not to be taken lightly. The problem is that they do little to promote an agonistic ethos that rises above interest group politics. This problem has not gone unnoticed by contemporary agonists, who point out the need for "an ethos of engagement" and an attitude of "agonistic respect." Connolly, for one, argues against both Arendt and Rawls by calling for a politicized form of pluralism, a pluralism freed from the myth of a single common good and from the split between *homme* and *citoyen*.

> In such a culture, participants are not called upon either to leave their meta-physical presumptions at home when they enter the public realm nor to pursue a single common good to be acknowledged by all parties in the same state. Such a public plurality of religious / metaphysical perspectives fosters a democracy appropriate to the intercultural diversity of the late-modern world if and when an *ethos of engagement* is forged between numerous constituencies honoring different metaphysical assumptions and moral sources.[38]

Connolly thinks he can evade the charges that agonism is either (a) dangerously irresponsible in its glorification of conflict or (b) merely a dressed-up version of interest group politics by imagining a political culture that fosters such an ethos, a democratized version of the eristic virtues celebrated by Nietzsche. By deploying Foucauldian "arts of the self" to therapeutically dissolve our inner sources of envy and resentment, we are free to enlarge the political domain beyond the boundaries envisaged by the "aristocrat" Arendt and the liberal Rawls, without fear of exacerbating the latent conflict between our incompatible religious, moral, and philosophical views.[39]

The problem is that this version of agonistic politics presupposes a culture in which no individual's or group's "fundamental metaphysical position" is *fundamental* in the sense that it is a truth that stands in irreconcilable conflict with other ultimate values. The pathos of the agonistic actor—his consciousness of the tragic dimension of value conflict, of his own "here I stand, I can do no other"—is replaced by an *agnostic* willingness to suspend the truth claim implicit in his own ultimate values. Connolly suggests that through "work on the self" the encumbered self can take on a new lightness of being, one untainted by the "will to the unconditional" and *ressentiment*. Thus what Rawls calls the starting point of political liberalism, namely, the "absolute depth of that irreconcilable latent conflict" between controversial views of the good life, ceases to be a problem.[40]

Simply put, this is presuming a lot. Connolly's vision of an "impure" agonistic politics, one that no longer depends on a "hard" public/private distinction of the sort deployed by Arendt or Rawls, rests on the idea of a citizen body in which a sizable proportion of individuals have "overcome" themselves in the Nietzschean sense.[41] "Work on the self" replaces the classical concern with political education. Connolly suggests that the root of seemingly ineradicable moral and political conflict is in fact a psychologically rooted disgust at one's own materiality, a disgust that is then projected onto an anathematized "other."

Such an analysis illuminates one of the basic mechanisms of prejudice, to be sure, but it provides scant resources for recovering a sense of the public or cultivating a *civic* agonism. Indeed, the most striking thing about it is its poststructuralist assumption that all potentially violent conflict is a function of an overly bounded, substantialist conception of identity. As an abstract thesis, this may well be correct. However, the conclusion Connolly draws—that our most urgent political need is "work on the self"—fits all too well with the subjectivist assumptions of a therapeutic age.

Arendt's version of an agonistic politics is predicated on a completely different diagnosis of the pathologies of contemporary politics. For her, the identifying mark of the modern age is the loss of a robust sense of the public realm. In attempting to recover such a sense, she does not (contra Connolly) insist on a singular conception of the public good. Rather, she adapts Nietzsche's aestheticism and perspectivism for her own *political* purposes, suggesting ways we might think of the public world and political deliberation that break free of the civic republican tradition's focus on a univocal "common good." In *The Human Condition* she writes,

> The reality of the public realm relies on the simultaneous presence of innu-
> merable perspectives and aspects in which the common world presents itself
> and for which no common measurement or denominator can ever be devised.
> For though the common world is the common meeting ground of all, those
> who are present have different locations in it, and the location of one can no
> more coincide with the location of another than the location of two objects.
> Being seen and heard by others derive their significance from the fact that
> everyone sees and hears from a different position. *This is the meaning of pub-
> lic life,* compared to which even the richest and most satisfying family life can
> offer only the prolongation or multiplication of one's own position with its at-
> tending aspects and perspectives. . . . Only where things can be seen by many
> in a variety of aspects without changing their identity, so that those who are
> gathered around them know they see sameness in utter diversity, can worldly
> reality truly and reliably appear.[42]

It is not, in other words, a question of fostering an ethos of a unitary
"common good" in opposition to the "corruption" represented by a
multitude of interests, of juxtaposing a singular and abstract universal
to myriad concrete particulars. Rather, what Arendt strives to impart is
the need for distance and a certain minimum amount of self-alienation
if the "public world" is to have any reality for us. It is the agonistic play
of perspectives on *this* world, and the competing interpretations of the
public good that inform and animate it, that Arendt wants to encourage.
But in order to be "free for the world"—in order to appreciate and value
the play of perspectives for its own sake—one must, to some degree, be
free of the most pressing concerns of life. Arendt's distinction between
the social and the political, the object of so much critical fire, is intended to reinforce *this* point. One cannot value the "play of the game"
if winning the game is crucial to the sheer survival of oneself or one's
group; nor can one value this play of perspectives if the question of basic
material subsistence looms larger than all others. For Arendt, an agonistic politics ends where violence, or the most basic demands of the
body, intrudes.

This brings us to what Arendt viewed as the "other side" of agonistic political action, namely, the capacity for disinterested, independent
judgment. If the conflict of opinions that *is* political life is not to devolve
into a struggle defined by Schmitt's friend/enemy distinction, it is imperative that action be informed by a faculty of judgment that is sensitive to particulars, that is not bound by a set of rules or an ideology.
What contemporary agonists fail to appreciate is that although Arendt
worries about the broad phenomenon of depoliticization, she is (never-

theless) hostile to all modes of civic engagement predicated on ideological mobilization or subscription to a Weltanschauung.[43] The formation of an opinion (and opinions, not interests, are the stuff of genuine politics for Arendt) presumes the capacity for what she calls representative thought, which is blocked by adherence to an ideology.

> I form an opinion by considering a given issue from different viewpoints, by making present to my mind the standpoints of those who are absent; that is, I represent them. This process of representation does not blindly adopt the actual views of those who stand somewhere else, and hence look upon the world from a different perspective; this is a question neither of empathy, as though I tried to be or to feel like somebody else, nor of counting noses and joining a majority but of being and thinking in my own identity where actually I am not. The more people's standpoints I have present in my mind while I am pondering a given issue, and the better I can imagine how I would feel and think if I were in their place, the stronger will be my capacity for representative thinking and the more valid my final conclusions, my opinion.[44]

This is Arendt's gloss on Kant's notion of an "enlarged mentality" (*eine erweiterte Denkungsart*) found in the *Critique of Judgment*. Like Kant, Arendt considers the capacity for an enlarged mentality, for representative thought, essential to opinion formation and judgment. And, also like Kant, she insists that disinterestedness—the liberation from one's own private interests—is the crucial precondition for the kind of imaginative exercise we find in representative thinking.[45] Thus Arendt's political actor displays not only initiatory energy but also detached judgment (what Weber, in his lecture "Politics as a Vocation," calls "a sense of proportion"). Similarly, the specific *meaning* of his or her actions—their justice or injustice, glory or baseness, beauty or ugliness— appears only to those capable of detached judgment.

Arendt's emphasis on detached judgment as a crucial component of any morally defensible agonistic politics seems to take us far from the Nietzschean focus on action and energy (the "will to power"), approximating instead the stateliness of Aristotelian prudence (*phronesis*). And this is how many commentators on her theory of judgment have, in fact, read her. Consider, however, Nietzsche's definition of a praiseworthy, life-enhancing form of intellectual "objectivity" as "the ability *to control* one's Pro and Con and to dispose of them, so that one knows how to employ a *variety* of perspectives and affective interpretations in the service of knowledge" (*GM* III:12). Arendt wants to pose a parallel norm for political judgment. And, as with her emphasis on the theatrical dimensions of political action, the focus on the distanced or disinterested quality of political judgment throws the expressivism underlying contemporary formulations of the agonistic ideal into sharp relief.

Arendt's conception of an agonistic politics thus stands at a crucial remove from the versions proposed by contemporary (Nietzsche-inspired) agonists. As I have tried to show, this difference has little to do with Arendt's admiration for the Homeric Greeks. Rather, it has to do with her stipulation that action and contestation must be informed by both judgment and a sense of the public if they are to be praiseworthy. The mere expression of energy in the form of political commitment fails to impress her. Of course, some will find this version of the agonistic ethos still too selective, still too aristocratic in its demand for "disinterestedness." How can victims of injustice and oppression be expected to rise to her standard, to forget their rage at what they have suffered? The answer is that Arendt does not expect them to, nor does she want them excluded from the public realm. What she emphasizes is the possibility, open to virtually everyone, that political action—debate and deliberation—will cultivate a public-spiritedness that is not limited by group affiliation or interest; that genuinely values a plurality of opinions on the same issue; and that is characterized by an independence of mind not typically celebrated by the civic republican tradition. That interest-driven politics encourages none of these effects indicates that little is to be gained by stripping the agonistic ethos of its impersonal dimensions and making the self, multiple or otherwise, the center of politics.

CONCLUSION

Contemporary agonists applaud Arendt's politicization of Nietzsche's agonistic ideal; they decry the narrow set of boundaries they see her imposing on the public realm. The self, they argue, must be drawn in, in all its gendered, racial, and class-based concreteness. To fail to do so is to indulge in the aristocratic fantasy of a pure politics, a politics without substance and without relevance. If Arendt points the way to a politicization of Nietzsche, this politicization can be completed only by further "Nietzscheanizing" Arendt, that is, by stressing the boundary-blurring force of "boundless" political action. Only then will contemporary struggles for justice be given their due in an agonistic politics.

At one level, one cannot but agree with these general points. But, as I have tried to indicate, there is reason for disquiet also. "Incessant contestation," like Foucauldian "resistance," is essentially reactive. What is contested or resisted are the "normalizing," identity-imposing practices of the bureaucratized welfare state, or of cultural representation. This is, in its own way, a remarkably constricted view of politics and political contestation. Moreover, its reactive quality ensures that, disclaimers aside, there will not be much "agonistic respect" for different views of the public good. A genuinely agonistic ethos presumes not merely pluralism but plurality in Arendt's sense: a diversity of (distanced) views on the same object or issue. An agonistic politics that fails to sufficiently appreciate the specificity of the public sphere more or less ensures that its claims to justice will be read by opponents as sheer ideological dogma. Politics, then, is merely fighting—as both Machiavelli and Weber suggested in their respective versions of Realpolitik.

Contemporary agonists are to be applauded insofar as they remind us, with Arendt, that action is at the heart of politics. From an American perspective, this means recognizing daily that the Constitution is not a machine that "runs by itself." They are also to be applauded for reminding us (again with Arendt) that deliberation and consensus are *parts* of political action but by no means its totality. Finally, they deserve praise for their attempts to prod a radically underpoliticized culture in a more political, and indeed more progressive, direction.

It is, however, the *localness* of their prescription that gives one pause, and which should prompt us to question whether their criticisms of Arendt really hit the mark. One often has the sense when reading contemporary agonists that they are rewriting the young Nietzsche. However, instead of worries about the life-dissipating effects of an excess of history, we get variations of the theme of the "use and abuse of legalism (or constitutionalism) for politics." The sense pervading their work is of a law- or rule-induced sclerosis that has depleted the agonal energies of politics. Rawls serves as a handy theoretical manifestation of what the neo-Nietzscheans view as *our* "sickness." Anything that serves to loosen or question norms, inspire "resistance," empower historically oppressed groups, or build "more slack into the system" is given a warm welcome in the face of a liberalism that is perceived as increasingly "regularian." This is merely to point out that the agonistic strand in contemporary political theory is of a particular time and an even more particular place. As such, it rebels against the very idea of boundary drawing and an overly stabilized distinction between public and private. In its more extreme forms, it even rebels against the "constitutionalization" of democracy.[46] However, unlike Arendt (and, indeed, unlike the mature Nietzsche), it takes the broad constitutionalist separation of public and private completely for granted. Like deconstruction, it is necessarily parasitic on its "texts."

Arendt's agonism, informed by the experience of totalitarianism, transcends this problematic. It exercises greater caution because it takes correspondingly greater risks. Her theory of political action operates without a safety net of the sort her more "radical" critics assume. Hence her agonism focuses on public-spiritedness, independent judgment, and self-distance in addition to initiatory action. The limits and qualifications she attaches to the agonistic ethos remind us not only of the risks of politics but also of the centrality of a care for the world—a care for the public realm—to any humane politics. Where such care is present, the world is indeed humanized by the "incessant and continual discourse" generated by a plurality of political opinions.[47] Where such care is absent— where the concerns of the self or the group dominate—politics is *simply* conflict. This is why Arendt, like the antiagonist Rawls, wants to maintain a distinction between *homme* and *citoyen*. These two radically dissimilar theorists strictly delineate the "domain of the political" not out of a passion to exclude or homogenize but precisely because they take difference so seriously. For it is only when differences are mediated politically, through shared institutions and shared citizenship, that they can be, as Machiavelli insisted, the "cause" of liberty.

NOTES

1. See Sheldon Wolin, "Fugitive Democracy," and Chantal Mouffe, "Democracy, Power, and the Political," both in *Democracy and Difference*, ed. Seyla Benhabib (Princeton: Princeton University Press, 1996); Bonnie Honig, *Political Theory and the Displacement of Politics* (Ithaca: Cornell University Press, 1993); and William E. Connolly, "A Critique of Pure Politics," *Philosophy and Social Criticism* 23, no. 5 (Fall 1997). I should note that Wolin is the most expressly critical of Arendt's agonism and Nietzsche's influence on her, whereas the others tend to wish that she was consistently Nietzschean. See Wolin's essay, "Hannah Arendt: Democracy and the Political," in *Hannah Arendt: Critical Essays*, ed. Lewis P. Hinchman and Sandra K. Hinchman (Albany: SUNY Press, 1994). However, as "Fugitive Democracy" and his essay "What Revolutionary Action Means Today" (in *Dimensions of Radical Democracy*, ed. Chantal Mouffe [New York: Verso, 1992]) demonstrate, Wolin's participatory stance is quite consistent with a democratized (antiaristocratic) agonism.

2. See John Rawls, *Political Liberalism* (New York: Columbia University Press, 1993); and Charles Larmore, "Political Liberalism," in Larmore, *The Morals of Modernity* (New York: Cambridge University Press, 1996).

3. Michael Sandel, *Democracy's Discontent* (Cambridge, Mass.: Harvard University Press, 1996).

4. These are not Sandel's terms, but it is helpful to be reminded of the classical liberal divide so fiercely attacked by Rousseau and Marx. For a defense of political (Rawlsian) liberalism's continued insistence on some form of this distinction, see Larmore's essay, "Political Liberalism."

5. See Martin Jay's afterword to *Hannah Arendt and the Meaning of Politics*, ed. Craig Calhoun and John McGowan (Minneapolis: University of Minnesota Press, 1997), 348.

6. See Richard Sennett, *The Fall of Public Man* (New York: W. W. Norton, 1992); and Michel Foucault, *The History of Sexuality, Volume I,* trans. Robert Hurley (New York: Vintage, 1976).

7. I borrow the latter phrase from Seyla Benhabib. See her introduction to *Democracy and Difference, 9.*

8. Of course, Nietzsche recognizes his own participation in the "will to truth" and the Socratic project, broadly conceived. The pertinent reflections are in *GM* III. For a sophisticated account of the seeming paradox, see Alexander Nehamas, *Nietzsche: Life as Literature* (Cambridge, Mass.: Harvard University Press, 1985).

9. This theme is central to Hobbes and Kant, both of whom viewed political discord as arising from competitive "vainglory."

10. Michel Foucault, *Discipline and Punish,* trans. Alan Sheridan (New York: Vintage, 1979).

11. John Stuart Mill, *On Liberty,* ed. David Spitz (New York: W. W. Norton, 1975), 59.

12. See Michel Foucault, "The Subject and Power," afterword to Hubert Dreyfus and Paul Rabinow, *Michel Foucault: Beyond Structuralism and Hermeneutics* (Chicago: University of Chicago Press, 1983).

13. See Benjamin Barber, *Strong Democracy* (Berkeley: University of California Press, 1984), for a defense of action as the central political problem.

14. Hannah Arendt, *Between Past and Future* (New York: Penguin, 1968), 151 (hereafter cited as *BPF*); *The Human Condition* (Chicago: University of Chicago Press, 1958), 177 (hereafter cited as *THC*); *On Revolution* (New York: Penguin, 1962), 21 (hereafter cited as *OR*). Cf. Nietzsche, *HL* 1, 2.

15. Arendt, *OR,* 30–31. Of course, Arendt follows the Greeks in viewing equality as a political status accorded to citizens rather than as an attribute of human beings as such, or as a broader social ideal.

16. Arendt, *THC,* 188–89.

17. Arendt, *OR,* 30.

18. Arendt, *THC,* 17–18.

19. See Arendt, *OR,* chap. 6, and *BPF,* preface.

20. Honig, *Political Theory and the Displacement of Politics,* 77. See also my essay "Postmodernism and the Public Sphere," *American Political Science Review* 86, no. 3 (September 1992): 712–21.

21. Arendt, *THC,* 40.

22. See especially Arendt's discussions in "What Is Authority?" (in *BPF*) and *OR,* chap. 5. I discuss Arendt's antifoundationalism at length in Dana R. Villa,

Arendt and Heidegger: The Fate of the Political (Princeton: Princeton University Press, 1996).

23. Honig, *Political Theory and the Displacement of Politics,* 116. See also Chantal Mouffe, *The Return of the Political* (New York: Verso, 1993), 14.

24. See Arendt, *THC,* 57–58.

25. Wolin, "Hannah Arendt: Democracy and the Political," 290. Wolin specifically attacks Arendt's Nietzschean inheritance, viewing it as the source of her disdain for the "masses" and her aristocratic preference for a politics of "lofty ambition, glory, and honor" rather than one essentially concerned with questions of social justice.

26. Connolly, "A Critique of Pure Politics," 17.

27. This has been a frequent charge in the critical literature generated by Arendt. See, for example, Hanna Pitkin's essay, "Justice: On Relating Public and Private," in *Hannah Arendt: Critical Essays.*

28. Honig, *Political Theory and the Displacement of Politics,* 118–23.

29. See Aristotle, *The Politics,* bk. 3, chaps. 6, 7. See also George Kateb's discussion in his *Hannah Arendt: Politics, Conscience, Evil* (Totowa, N.J.: Rowman and Allanheld, 1983), 18–19.

30. One genuine problem with political liberalism is that it frames constitutional essentials or basic principles as beyond argument. There is an extremely broad sense in which this must be true (e.g., the principle of equal rights under the law); however, the tendency of political liberals is to pack the maximum possible content under the rubric "constitutional essentials." See, for example, Larmore's discussion in "Political Liberalism," 135–36.

31. For reasons set out below, I think Honig's assertion that Arendt sets up a "public-private distinction that is beyond contestation" misses the point of Arendt's insistence on the distinction (*Political Theory and the Displacement of Politics,* 119).

32. Wolin, "Fugitive Democracy," 37, 43.

33. Honig, *Political Theory and the Displacement of Politics,* 85–86, 103. There is an uncontroversial sense in which Honig's interpretation is correct, for like Hobbes and the social contract tradition generally, Arendt sees agreement, rather than tradition, nature, or the Deity, setting the terms of political association. But Honig wants to go further than this, insisting that nothing but a *practice* or performative speech act underlies the establishment of an arena for agonistic *praxis*. Arendt's suspicions concerning the will in politics (and particularly Rousseau's formulation of its fundamental or grounding role) should make us somewhat skeptical of this reading. For her, promising creates a binding web of obligation, artificial but permanent, a worldly structure that stands independent of continued willing or nilling. See Arendt, *BPF,* 163–64.

34. See Arendt, *THC,* 55–77.

35. Arendt, *BPF,* 153.

36. Honig emphasizes action as a *performative* in Arendt, drawing on J. L. Austin's work to conceptualize speech that is also a deed. She ignores, however, the explicitly theatrical dimension of Arendt's theory of political action.

37. Wolin, "Hannah Arendt: Democracy and the Political," 303; Honig, *Political Theory and the Displacement of Politics,* 77–84; Connolly, "A Critique

of Pure Politics," passim. I should note that whereas Honig thinks that Arendt celebrates a Nietzschean "multiple self," Connolly sees her denial of the body as placing her in the mainstream of Western philosophical thought.

38. Connolly, "A Critique of Pure Politics," 21. See also William E. Connolly, *The Ethos of Pluralization* (Minneapolis: University of Minnesota Press, 1995).

39. Rawls, *Political Liberalism*, xxiv–xxvi.

40. Ibid., xxvi.

41. Honig proposes a similar strategy, arguing that the Nietzschean idea of the "subject as multiplicity" enables a democratization of the overman, in which the latter is seen not as a peculiar and rare subject or caste but as a part of the self—indeed, of all selves. See Honig, *Political Theory and the Displacement of Politics,* 65.

42. Arendt, *THC,* 57; emphasis added.

43. This, obviously, was the result of her experience and analysis of totalitarianism. See especially her essay "Ideology and Terror" included in Hannah Arendt, *The Origins of Totalitarianism* (New York: Harcourt Brace Jovanovich, 1975).

44. Arendt, *BPF,* 241.

45. Ibid., 242. Cf. pp. 219–22 and Hannah Arendt, *Lectures on Kant's Political Philosophy,* ed. Ronald Beiner (Chicago: University of Chicago Press, 1982).

46. See Wolin, "Fugitive Democracy," along with the essays in Sheldon Wolin, *The Presence of the Past: Essays on the State and Constitution* (Baltimore: Johns Hopkins University Press, 1989).

47. Hannah Arendt, *Men in Dark Times* (New York: Harcourt Brace Jovanovich, 1968), 30.

CHAPTER 14

"A Nietzschean Breed"

Feminism, Victimology, Ressentiment

Rebecca Stringer

Is it hunger or superabundance that has here become creative?

> *Friedrich Nietzsche,* The Gay Science

In *The Gay Science* Nietzsche writes that his assessment of the aesthetic values of any given creative enterprise will begin with the question, noted above, as to whether "hunger" or "superabundance" can be discerned as the motivating force of the given enterprise, the "need" that compels it. But this does not mean that the art of either impulse will follow the same respective patterns of aesthetic expression. Nietzsche further explains that hunger and superabundance do not neatly and respectively correspond to the immortalizing "desire for *being*" and the tumultuous "desire for *becoming*" (GS 370). An art of hunger cannot always be discerned by its expression of a desire for fixity, or an art of superabundance for its desire for change. Instead, "fixity" and "change" deserve "dual interpretation": both can be expressions of either art. The creative deeds of *ressentiment* that Nietzsche delineates throughout his work with historical, biological, epistemological and (always) psychological examples can be understood as the art of hunger.[1] This chapter preserves something of the ambiguity in Nietzsche's method of interpretation as it considers feminism's art of hunger by way of a range of recent accounts of "victim feminism" and feminist *ressentiment*.[2]

I take as a given feminism's status as a largely, but not singularly, reactive political project with an appetite for the redistribution of power in society that is expressed in a variety of ways, or through a variety of creative enterprises. The writings on feminist victimology and *ressentiment* discussed here critique either feminism in general or a particular feminism on the grounds that the politico-moral values that are enshrined in its creative enterprises are at the very least no longer workable, their political efficacy expired. The accounts are quite varied (it is, after all, a matter of interpretation) and are drawn from two distinct arenas of feminist writing: the popular press—Rene Denfeld, Katie Roiphe, and Naomi Wolf; and the academy, in particular feminist political theory— Wendy Brown, Marion Tapper, and Anna Yeatman.[3] One of the more consistent themes within this body of work is the presence of Nietzsche, who figures in all but one account.

That the accounts are varied is telling. To illustrate by way of analogy, if the range of examples of victimology and *ressentiment* were added together to form an index, the index would create the impression that the only nonvictimological or *ressentiment*-free positions available are occupied by the critics themselves. The index would, in a sense, be deceiving, because each writer offers, implicitly or explicitly, a counterimage of the phenomena they criticize. However, given the wide range of examples that have accumulated, it is clear that victimology and *ressentiment* in feminism are altogether more pervasive and more "mobile" than any single account admits. Victimology and *ressentiment* are, it seems, less than immovable keystones of feminist thought, more than passing or past phases, and not necessarily the attributes of any one particular feminism.

In dealing with a wide range of salient accounts of feminist victimology and *ressentiment,* it is my general aim to consolidate the existing debate. This consolidation, around which this chapter is structured, entails delineating the major themes and inner conflicts of the debate, although not in a neutral fashion. The first section, in which I deal with the popular press accounts, acts quite consciously as a corrective to the more problematic aspects of these accounts while preserving their valuable insights. It is my particular aim to contribute an alternative interpretation of Nietzsche's concept of *ressentiment* to the feminist political theory end of the debate. This alternative interpretation will lead us to view the concept not only as a means of diagnosis but also as a concept that delineates a process of refinement in which politically motivating "negative emotions" become creative and eventually serve as the condition of possibility for superabundant, or "positive," creativity—not just the art of hunger.

If we begin with the idea that feminism can and should resist the politics of reactivity and relinquish its art of hunger, it follows that images of what "active" feminism looks like, and where it comes from, are required. My suggestion is that, rather than depart from Nietzsche when it comes to the second task, we can instead continue to think with his concept of *ressentiment* as a part of it. It will argued, with reference to William E. Connolly's notion of "agonistic indebtedness," that while Nietzsche's problematic association of *ressentiment* with femininity and emasculation should continue to be contested, with the task of coming to grips with feminist *ressentiment*, feminists can also afford to *expand* their indebtedness to Nietzsche.

FEMINIST VICTIMOLOGY

There is nothing wrong with identifying one's
victimization. The act is critical. There is a lot
wrong with molding it into an identity.
          Naomi Wolf, Fire with Fire

Feminist debate about victimology is not new, but its appearance in the feminist popular press is. That discourse about feminist victimology has attracted substantial contributions from popular press feminists is an indication of this discourse's significance to feminism's appeal as a social movement, indeed to feminism's "marketability" as a cultural formation. For these contributions aim precisely to revitalize feminism's appeal, to rewire its "marketing strategy," in order to overcome the "alienation" of "ordinary" women from feminism that, they argue, victimology has brought into effect. Although Denfeld, Wolf, and Roiphe have been vocal about their disagreements with one another, their accounts of "the victim problem in current feminism" have more substantive similarities than differences, with Wolf having produced the most generous and systematic account. The manner in which they deal with victim feminism follows the same line, and both Denfeld and Wolf exhibit the same desire to cure feminism of victimology and charge inexorably toward an alternative.

What, then, is feminist victimology, or victim feminism? It can be understood in general terms as an attitude fueled by the belief that women are victims of power, where power is understood *exclusively* as man's capacity to dominate—a capacity given a fixed and central place in a social order (patriarchy) that fosters its systematic and repeated expression. In short, and to exemplify, relations between the sexes are understood as "a system of sexism in which men as a group have access to power and privilege that women do not have." [4] This understanding of the sexed distribution of power is posited as an *exhaustive* account of power and, as such, breathes life into an elaborate feminist morality.

Feminist victimology is, on all accounts, a morally righteous kind of feminism. The experience of powerlessness (women's experience, whether they "realize" it or not), as the inverse and opposite of power, is the raw material from which the injurious effects of domination can be tabled. As Wolf writes, victim feminism proffers definitive judgment on good and evil with reference to sexual difference and thereby "casts women *themselves* as good and men *themselves* as wrong."[5] A mantle of virtue is bestowed on women and their distinctive ways of doing things, on account of their radical subjection to power, while men "as a group" take on the suits of evil as they are cast as the source of harm.

Under the auspice of victim feminism, resistance to domination begins with the process of articulating and tabling its effects to produce an undistorted view of how domination really works, where the responsibility for it really lies, and who stands outside of it—who can, at the end of the day, be evacuated to a position that is, morally speaking, "above" domination and outside of power. Wolf's criticism of situating feminism's constituency outside of power is that it "urges women to identify with powerlessness even at the expense of taking responsibility for the power they do possess."[6] It follows from this that adherents to a victimological line of thinking would avoid registering the figure of the consciously and deliberately powerful woman—who is not, and does not desire to be, above or outside of power—much less the workings of power within its own auspice. The possibility that women and feminists might themselves practice and participate in domination, that not all men have or use the capacity to dominate, that power expresses itself in forms other than domination, is rendered unthinkable if power is conflated with male domination.

This much is noted by Denfeld, who argues that victimology makes some women's conscious participation in "racism, sexism, and violence" at most invisible and at least excusable.[7] For Denfeld, under the auspice of victim feminism women are cast not only as victims but also as dupes. This casting serves a dual purpose. First, some women's participation in regimes of domination can be excused as "manipulated by negative male ideas."[8] Second, anointing patriarchy with great powers of deception is an effective means of defending feminism against negative criticism. Denfeld writes, "If you don't agree with current feminists about the enemy, that's only another sign that he exists."[9] Victimology, on Denfeld's account, embraces a hopeful purity of position and registers anything less as contaminated compromise. We can add to Denfeld's complaint that a victimological perspective will evade the idea that not all experiences of powerlessness are the same and should not, therefore, be collapsed under a single moral claim and that the experience of powerlessness offers no less distorted a view than does the "power-infused" view with which it competes politically.

Wolf argues that victimology is especially impoverished in the respect that it inhibits the registration and representation of women's capacities to assume positive relationships to power. It dwells exclusively on powerlessness, "molding it into an identity," ratifying and regenerating, rather than transforming, socially derived stereotypes of female weakness and vulnerability. Moreover, having granted victimhood the status of a grand category into which women as a group can be herded, feminists effectively eschew the conceptual strategies at their disposal for overcoming victim identity. As Sandra Harding has commented, "Victimology . . . often hide[s] the ways in which women have struggled against misogyny and exploitation."[10] Harding's comment indicates that even as a victimological perspective can have a dramatic reversal of the social order in mind—for men must be made to repent for the injuries they have caused by relinquishing the values, ideals, and sociocultural configurations that secure their power—the very logic through which relations of power are conceived from this perspective works against registration of struggle (successful and otherwise) with these values, ideals, and sociocultural configurations.

It is in this sense that victimology can be understood as an impasse, indeed a kind of paralysis. If the powerless (women) desire to fight power (men) but cannot themselves consciously assume power, how could they hope to attain any measure of efficacy without spiraling into the dogmatic pursuit of politico-moral purity that is revolutionary only in the sense that it circulates around the task of laying blame and seeking retribution? Denfeld, Wolf, and Roiphe would answer this question by pointing out that victimology credits its exponents with a grave contradiction made possible, and acceptable, through the use of "moral force." For, they argue, even as victimology dwells on powerlessness, its exponents are anything but lacking in political, intellectual, and ultimately institutional power. The power of victimology is shored up by moralism, and the configuration is contradictory given that this moralism is in turn founded on a claim to powerlessness. This claim to powerlessness is described by Wolf as a "misuse of the reality of women's victimization"—the claim is made on behalf of women in general but ultimately serves to benefit those making the claim in particular.[11]

So Wolf, Denfeld, and Roiphe take feminist victimology to task on two fronts. First, they claim that victimological assumptions about the nature of power, and women's relationships to power, are partial and deceptive in a way that has proved fatal to feminism's ability to deliver and sustain faithful representation of "ordinary" women, in both senses of the phrase. In other words, victim feminism is like a government radically out of touch with this population, its real constituency. Second, they indicate that victimology has what I will call "negative political efficacy"—for despite their will to delegitimate victimology on the grounds that it is not an effective feminist politics, the analyses of Wolf, Denfeld, and Roiphe demonstrate, if nothing else, that victimology is a remarkably "effective" political program. Negative political efficacy in this case is the ability to yield a considerable degree of institutional power and in so doing assume the appearance of benefiting all women, although this power is achieved through "illegitimate" means, on the basis of a profound misrepresentation of women's capacities, and ultimately to the advantage of relatively few—namely, the victim feminists themselves.

Not surprisingly, none of these writers has anything positive to say about victimology. Victimology cannot, on their accounts, be understood, or consciously salvaged, as a useful political ruse. Rather, for Wolf, victim feminism must be overthrown from its position of dominance, and for Denfeld, it must be jettisoned altogether. Wolf maintains that feminism has always been composed of "two traditions": victim feminism and power feminism. She sketches the characteristics of each, saying that victim feminism is prone to "resentment" while power feminism is "without resentment," and argues that a renaissance of the latter is crucial.[12] Denfeld joins Wolf insofar as she would also like to see "ordinary" women reclaim and reshape feminism in accordance with their own, individually determined needs and wants. However, her strategy for achieving this evinces less tolerance than does that of Wolf. Denfeld advocates "get[ting] rid of those who are driving women away [from the women's movement]."[13] That Denfeld takes a tone remarkably similar to the one she attributes to her "politically pure" victimological opponents is not insignificant.

While the kind of feminism Denfeld, Wolf, and Roiphe describe is most certainly in evidence, they borrow its tactics in order to critique it.

They defend "ordinary" women against an alienating and self-serving feminism in much the same way as this feminism is said to defend all women against an alienating and self-serving patriarchy. This point teases out an idea that follows implicitly from the accounts of Wolf and Denfeld: that feminism has come to *mimic* patriarchy insofar as its oppressiveness is similarly configured. That critiques of feminist victimology might themselves assume victimological tactics is not, in light of this point, difficult to imagine. Feminist victimology can be considered as an effect of *ressentiment,* but this does not mean that critical accounts of victimology cannot themselves be seen as motivated by *ressentiment.*

Without discussion of or reference to the feminist critique of liberalism, Denfeld and Wolf argue that feminism's political future should be relatively restricted, that its role should be pared down to equality seeking in the courts and issue-based campaigning. In addition, feminist consciousness should take the form of an individually determined set of principles such that there might be as many feminisms as there are women. Their suggestions for the future of feminism, or more specifically for a feminist future in which victimology will not figure, take the form of a negative imprint of victim feminism. They take the conditions of possibility and the characteristics of victim feminism and advocate the opposite conditions and characteristics. As I describe the primary divisions they reference in mounting this opposition to victim feminism, the most disagreeable aspects of their otherwise valuable accounts will emerge.

Denfeld, Roiphe, and Wolf all argue that victim feminism has been breeding in the academy since the late 1970s, that it reaches the status of an intellectual infection in women's studies departments and is expressed most potently in academic feminist writings on pornography, sex, and rape. A particular victim feminist "type" emerges from their writings. It is the figure of the feminist intellectual/philosopher/academic who promulgates victim feminism and alone benefits from it.[14] Rather than a removable aspect of their definition of victim feminism, the denigration of this figure forms an integral part of the definition. Rescuing feminism from its regrettable capitulation to the "obscurantism" of the academy would, for all three writers, free it from the quagmire of victimology and clear the way for the term "feminism" to become a more appealing and usable shorthand for "female power." The possibility of "power feminism," it seems, resides with the termination of feminist intellectual endeavor. Wolf quotes a passage "taken at random" from Luce Irigaray's *Speculum of the Other Woman* to demonstrate the irrelevance of her thinking, and that of others of her ilk, to genuine feminist imperatives.[15] Similarly, Denfeld denigrates women's studies by claiming that, in most North American universities, it revolves around the politically irrelevant practice of "goddess worship."[16] Roiphe's scathing critique of on-campus feminist culture places feminist theory, as it is currently taught in the academy, as responsible for the production of this culture. In taking academic feminism to task in this way, these writers make the issue of victimology cut across a divide between academic and nonacademic feminism, between academic feminists and "ordinary" women. Adopting the tactics of victimology—this time the virtues of ordinary women outweigh the evils of academic feminists—adds a further twist to the problematic of feminist victimology, and this same twist informs the other primary divide that operates particularly in Denfeld's account.

The other primary divide is the generational divide, which is often used to oversimplify a diverse and shifting complex of feminisms that has existed over time in order to account for, and defend, the reluctant feminism of a new generation of young women. A divide certainly exists, but it is not as reliable a source of contrast as Denfeld has assumed. For Denfeld, the feminist label has also to be rescued from older, embittered feminists by women such as herself—she is, we are told, "a good example of the young New Woman."[17] The "New Woman" finds the high moralism of victim feminism repugnant on account of its Victorian emphasis on women's sexual passivity and guilelessness. For Denfeld, the conflation of heterosexual sex with rape is the driving force behind separatist "new Victorian" perspectives on the staple feminist issues of rape, pornography, sexual harassment, and heterosexuality. This conflation, she argues, has produced a decidedly antisexual, and antiheterosexual, feminism. Thus the new Victorians manage to alienate young, libidinous, heterosexual women from feminism. Essentially, Denfeld is reiterating a familiar argument against Andrea Dworkin and Catherine MacKinnon and mounting an offensive on radical feminism. But in Denfeld's book, unconstrained as it is by the rigor of the academic press, these figures and their radicalism form a deceptive synecdoche for the entire field of contemporary feminism. Denfeld would argue that she has appropriated this deception, that the new Victorians already are the public face of feminism in North America, and that she is taking issue with them as such. But this does not explain why she has built her portrait of this separatist league around very broad brush strokes, and by

eliding the existence of other feminist perspectives on sex and rape in order to take issue with one of those perspectives.[18]

Denfeld's point that feminists should acknowledge women's strengths
rather than simply dwell on their vulnerabilities is well made, and it is
the case that sexual moralism of the kind that she describes emanates
from certain feminists. But it is nonetheless disturbing that, for Denfeld,
the relevance of a challenge to these problems is guaranteed through
its having *youthful* (and presumably heterosexual) proponents who are
rallied against their antecedents—as though the challenge to victimology has only been, and can only be, played out in accordance with a generational divide. It would be reasonable to argue that part of the effec-
tivity of victimology has been its ability to disseminate itself in many
directions—including being pulled through from older to younger generations of feminists—and to argue further that themes like the conflation of heterosexual sex with rape conduct victimology as metal con-
ducts electricity. But it is quite a different thing to argue, as Denfeld
does, that an entire generation of feminists are attempting to charge the
waters of the next generation's "freedom" with an outmoded and oppressive sexual moralism.

Wolf's, Roiphe's, and Denfeld's respective arguments that victimology has played a significant part in the academic imaginary of Western feminism are certainly valid. However, they are mistaken in their
assumption that feminist victimology has thrived unabated in the academic headquarters of this imaginary, and Denfeld is mistaken in thinking that young women are thereby best positioned to challenge it. Victimology is not entirely nebulous, but "locating" victimology in feminism
is simply not this easy. Rather than exemplify my claim by listing contemporary "academic" feminists who have taken issue with feminist
victimology directly—the next set of writers I will discuss should suf-
fice in this regard—I will use an older example that can in many respects
be read as betraying a victimological position but that in one important respect resists this position. The example is the late 1970s piece
by Sandra Lee Bartky titled "Towards a Phenomenology of Feminist
Consciousness."[19]

In her article Bartky places a struggle between a "consciousness of
weakness" and a "consciousness of strength" at the center of her meditation on the phenomenology of feminist consciousness.[20] For Bartky,
the consciousness of weakness—the domain of victimology—harbors
the memory of past injuries and an awareness of exposure to injury. It is

a blaming consciousness that identifies "men, society, and the system" as the guilty party for injuries suffered at the hand of their domination. Yet the paralyzing effects of the consciousness of weakness can, according to Bartky, be countered by the consciousness of strength. The latter is portrayed as an awareness of the skills and capabilities one has in spite of and as a result of victimization.[21] As such it is a means by which one might transcend the ensnaring circuit of negative emotions, blame, and retribution characteristic of victimology. While Bartky does not question the assumptions that underlie the consciousness of weakness, she clearly sees it as an impasse that is overcome through the consciousness of strength. Together, these twin consciousnesses are "enabling." So her account, in which the feminist is understood as a figure constantly negotiating the contrary states and conflicting effects of "weakness" and "strength," betrays an awareness of the dangers of victimology that Denfeld would view as highly uncharacteristic given Bartky's time of writing and social location. In addition, what we get from Bartky and what is lacking in Wolf is the idea that "power feminism" and "victim feminism" are not mutually exclusive categories into which the entire field of feminists and feminisms can be easily and conveniently divided, with or without reference to divisions between generations or social positioning ("academic" and "ordinary"). Rather, for Bartky, strength, power, weakness, and powerlessness *converge* at all points in the feminist spectrum, indeed within the very idea of "feminism."

If Bartky exemplifies that second wave academic feminists do not necessarily and automatically possess a penchant for victimology, then Roiphe's critical indictment of victim feminism demonstrates further that young women are not necessarily and automatically antivictimological. Roiphe, whose account further complicates Denfeld's generational divide, is entirely complicit in the denigration of feminist intellectual endeavor that is central to Wolf's and Denfeld's definitions of victim feminism, and she makes the most of the idea that feminist victimology is an intellectual infection that is transmitted pedagogically. However, her account can be used to illustrate *and* counter Denfeld's claim that victimology's alienating effects are played out along generational lines. For Roiphe's book is in itself testimony to the author's own alienation from feminism; yet the book contains abundant evidence of a broad population that does not suffer from this alienation. As I noted earlier, Wolf and Denfeld criticize victim feminists for having misused "the reality of women's victimization" to gain institutional power: Roiphe is leveling the same argument at her peers. According to Roiphe, far from fleeing the outmoded ideas of their antecedents and having it as their ambition to wrest feminism from the academic victimologists, young female and male students uncritically absorb victim feminist ideas at university. They willingly participate in an on-campus culture wherein the identification of oneself as powerless delivers a particular kind of power. Roiphe argues that her feminist peers eagerly identify themselves as oppressed subjects because the university has built a system of rewards around identity politics of this kind.[22] In other words, in the culture that Roiphe describes, one's incentive for identifying oneself as powerless is, paradoxically, power and status in the academy. Roiphe dubs those who embrace this paradox "with their will to power" a "Nietzschean breed."[23]

Roiphe's image of this Nietzschean breed is highly charged and profoundly dystopic. The finer points of Denfeld's indictment of the new Victorians notwithstanding, Roiphe's image stands as one of the most potent and least "sympathetic" illustrations of victim feminism in the debate so far. She writes,

> In the end, what is interesting about these feminists is not their hypocrisy, but their paradox. . . . They take status where they can get it. Socially and intellectually, the university rewards women for being sexy and rewards them for being oppressed. . . . Contradictory as these sources of strength may seem, these women draw from both. They are not about to surrender the opportunities and benefits offered to the flirt or the militant feminist.[24]

Roiphe's image of this "breed" captures well the paradoxical relationship to power endemic to a victimological position, yet it nonetheless calls up a significant danger to which critical indictments of victim feminism are prey. The image, which is exemplary of Roiphe's whole analysis, intimates that powerlessness *does not exist,* that victimology does not respond to victimization, but rather wholly creates the phenomena of victimization for itself.[25] This suggestion is peculiar to her account and obviously problematic: denying the existence of powerlessness is in no way necessary to the task of taking issue with the manner in which some feminists have elaborated powerlessness into a politico-moral position. Owing to Roiphe's intense disillusionment with feminism and potent resentment of her peers, her analysis comes close to joining hands with antifeminism. Denfeld makes it clear that if feminism were to follow her own prescriptions, it would be set on a path toward conclusion, the end of feminism, the "final wave." Roiphe, however, seems to think that feminism is for the most part already over. All that remains is a store of useful fictions to which power-seeking women and men can feign commitment.

In what sense, then, is Roiphe's breed "Nietzschean"? Given that the paradox that makes powerlessness an identity one assumes to eventually gain a position endowed with moral power has been correctly interpreted by others as an effect of *ressentiment,* precisely the opposite adjective—un-Nietzschean—would be a more appropriate term to use. As Wendy Brown notes, *ressentiment* is indeed an "expression" of will to power, but this expression is "far from the sort Nietzsche savors or respects: power born of weakness and resentment fashions a culture whose values and ambitions mirror the pettiness of its motivating force." [26] Alternatively, after the fashion of "dual interpretation," if we tackle the question as to the Nietzscheanism of this breed with reference to one of Nietzsche's more famous images, the parable of lambs and birds of prey in *On the Genealogy of Morals,* it is equally apparent that Roiphe's breed does not strictly conform to either creature (*GM* I:13). It is, rather, a collective of birds of prey parading as virtuous flock. Indeed, in light of the "twist" noted earlier wherein the critique of victimology runs the risk of producing yet another victimology, Roiphe herself is more suited to the position of the lamb, prey as she is to the plethoric display of strength, power, and status gaining in her milieu.

Wolf, Denfeld, and Roiphe are right to take issue with feminism's representation of women as victims, but victimology will not evaporate on the termination of feminist intellectual endeavor or the editing out of a "generation" of feminists. This is so for at least three reasons. First, as Roiphe and Bartky demonstrate, these feminist "types"—older, academic—are not wholly or singularly accountable for the advent and promulgation of victim feminism. Second, when Roiphe's "Nietzschean breed" is read against Denfeld's "New Women," it is clear that young women both contest and invest in victim feminism and are themselves "divided" on the issue. Third, the critical indictments of feminist victimology produced by Roiphe and Denfeld in particular have appropriated the tactics and affective drive of victimology and have thereby reproduced it.[27]

As the accounts of Wolf, Denfeld, and Roiphe reveal, the issue of feminist victimology is about the effects of negative emotions (anger, resentment, and hatred) on feminism and the fact that these emotions have been both enabling and paralyzing. Kathleen Woodward, who uses Freud's concept of anger to discuss this emotion in feminism, argues that anger was "once very enabling for feminism," but has now outlived

its efficacy and legitimacy.[28] The next set of accounts I address follow
Woodward insofar as they make similar arguments, appropriating not
Freud but Nietzsche, as a part of a critique of feminist affectivity. Nietzsche offers a sophisticated and elaborate conceptualization of resentment, and with this the debate about feminist victimology is taken to another level. However, unlike Woodward, who assesses the gendering of
Freud's concept of anger, these accounts do not explicitly think through
the gendering of the concept of *ressentiment*. For this reason a brief detour into the presence of Nietzsche in this feminist debate is required,
and the customary question will be addressed: What is Nietzsche, a famously misogynist philosopher, doing helping feminists think through
their politics?

NIETZSCHE AND "FEMINISM"

All "feminism," too—also in men—closes the door:
it will never permit entrance into this labyrinth of
audacious insights.
                    Friedrich Nietzsche, Ecce Homo

When speaking of the relationship between Nietzsche and feminism
one could very well be referencing both English meanings of the latter
term: the first, dominant *Oxford English Dictionary* meaning, "advocacy of women's rights"; or the second, now less common meaning, "the
development of female characteristics in a man" (also "feminization"
and, less synonymously, "emasculation"). At various times in his work
Nietzsche uses the term "feminism" (*Feminismus*) to denote weakness,
cowardice, mendacity, and "rule of feeling," describing it as something to which not just women but also men (notably Rousseau) were
prone (*WP* 95; see also *GM* III:27). He opposes this "feminism" to the
courageous process of self-overcoming, cheerfulness, and the will to
truth, and in *Ecce Homo* he writes that a feminist reader, male or female, will necessarily be shut off from the "labyrinth of audacious insights" that his books offer (*EH* "Books" 3). The dual meaning of
"feminism / *Feminismus*," and the subsequently ambivalent presence of
this term in Nietzsche's work, neatly encapsulates the two primary
proofs on which many feminists have relied when speaking of Nietzsche's misogyny: his denigration of both feminism and "the feminine."

These points of denigration coalesce in the concept of *ressentiment*
in a few respects. The most obvious is that feminism, the advocacy of

women's rights, is for Nietzsche an effect of a grandiose *ressentiment* at large in the creation of modern democratic states. The less obvious respect is the idea that for Nietzsche femininity—that which threatens to bring "feminism" into being—is a state into which men of *ressentiment* fall. It follows from this that femininity and *ressentiment* are strongly, and metaphorically, connected in Nietzsche's texts. The connection is called up by Max Scheler who, in his discussion of Nietzsche's concept of *ressentiment,* places "woman" at the top of his list of certain "typically recurrent 'situations'" in social life that are "*charged* with the danger of *ressentiment.*"²⁹ He writes,

> *Woman* is generally in such a situation. . . . The danger of feminine *ressentiment* is extraordinarily intensified because both nature and custom impose upon woman a reactive and passive role in love, the domain of her most vital interest. Feelings of revenge born from rejection in the erotic sphere are always particularly subject to repression. . . . [W]omen are forced to great reserve by stronger barriers of convention and modesty.³⁰

On Scheler's account, at the level of the social, femininity is marked by a predisposition to *ressentiment.* Masculinity, in contrast—or rather, a particular kind of masculinity, that of the noble—is marked by its ability to resist *ressentiment.* Of this resistance, Nietzsche writes, "*Ressentiment* itself, if it should appear in the nobleman, consummates and exhausts itself in an immediate reaction, and therefore does not *poison:* on the other hand, it fails to appear at all on countless occasions on which it inevitably appears in the weak and impotent" (*GM* I:10). Nietzsche's "countless occasions" are like Scheler's "typically recurrent 'situations'" in social life where the danger of *ressentiment* presents itself. Unlike women, the nobleman does not have to submit to those barriers of social convention that would bar his recourse to "immediate reaction." The reaction of the nobleman corresponds to the type of revenge that Nietzsche valorizes: that of immediate, self-defensive counterblow in response to perceived harm. This type of revenge stands in contrast to the vengeful ruse adopted by the slave, that of delayed, calculated revenge on a specific opponent—tactics that for Nietzsche are well suited to women, who with their "rapier-sharp minds" are "well-practiced in finding sore spots" (*HH* 414).

The presence of sexual difference in the division between creatures who are with and without *ressentiment* suggests it is no accident that Nietzsche describes *ressentiment* as the "shameful emasculation of feeling" (*GM* III:14). *Ressentiment* will delimit the strength and integrity of the nobleman by building a popular morality on the belief that "*the strong man is free* to be weak": a morality that makes the strong man accountable for the effects of his strength and places social constraints on his "desire to become a master." To what degree, then, is this noble's strength separable from his masculinity, his manliness? For perhaps it is also no accident that the ability of *ressentiment* to separate the strong man from his capacities and make him accountable for his actions is described by Gilles Deleuze as "the dreadful feminine power of *ressentiment*." [31] On my reading, Nietzsche's concept of *ressentiment* is, among many other things, a delineation of the way in which masculinity is threatened by "feminism"—in both senses of the term.

Thus Ellen Kennedy, who unequivocally labels Nietzsche a misogynist with whom no feminist should deal, argues that Nietzsche's portrayal of women as the weaker sex is a constitutive part of his critique of morality. She writes that "all the virtues [his] philosophy will 'transvalue'—pity, love, caution—are in a particular way 'feminine' and life-denying." [32] Although Kennedy is wrong to argue that Nietzsche denigrated women and femininity consistently throughout his work, there is little doubt that for Nietzsche *ressentiment* is an unhealthily feminizing force for men, and "man" per se. [33] In light of this, the use of Nietzsche's concept of *ressentiment* to diagnose certain aspects of feminist theory and practice is extraordinary: Nietzsche is used to critique feminism, rather than the other way around. Discourse on feminist *ressentiment* is not so much feminist Nietzsche scholarship but rather feminist scholarship that makes use of Nietzsche. The parameters of the latter do not at present include an exploration of the degree to which Nietzsche's concept of *ressentiment* might be said to connote a particular configuration of gender, or denote, on the plane of the sociological, a set of circumstances in which women generally find themselves. Although a comprehensive version of such an exploration is beyond the scope of this chapter, my cursory demonstration of one way in which women, femininity, and *ressentiment* are related in Nietzsche's texts has nonetheless begged the question as to what effect this might have on the critique of feminist *ressentiment*.

When we speak of feminist *ressentiment,* do we run the risk of reaffirming the critique of *ressentiment* as a project to rescue a particular kind of masculinity from "feminism"? Are the two kinds of scholarship noted above—feminist Nietzsche scholarship and feminist scholarship that appropriates Nietzsche—mutually exclusive? Connolly's term "agonistic indebtedness" is instructive for going some way toward answer-

ing these questions.[34] Simply put, on the one hand, Connolly contests
the darker sides of Nietzsche's philosophy and politics, and here we can
list as examples his misogyny, his flights of aristocratism, and the degree
to which his protean philosophy might be ultimately interpreted as so-
cioeugenicism. On the other hand, Connolly's project of "reworking the
democratic imagination" is strongly indebted to Nietzsche, to his poly-
theism, his recognition of and taste for diversity and multiplicity, and his
salient concepts of free spirithood and generosity. Following Connolly,
it is clear that one can do better than "close the door" and, in the fashion of Kennedy, argue that there can be no legitimate appropriation of
Nietzsche for feminism (or, for Connolly's purposes, democratic thinking). The next accounts are testimony to this: Nietzsche's concept of
ressentiment is extremely useful for coming to grips with what I have
been calling feminist victimology. Indeed, a further instance of "indebtedness" to Nietzsche in these accounts is their adaptation, deliberate or
otherwise, of Nietzsche's tactic of "performative critique." The argument, forwarded most recently by Richard White, that the manner in
which Nietzsche's books are written represents a conscious attempt to
stimulate the mode of being he most valorizes can be applied to these accounts. They each assume the genealogy's at once admonishing and hor-
tatory tone, and, following White again, we can say that these accounts
go some way toward "revising" Nietzsche's genealogy of morals by producing another chapter on *ressentiment*'s most recent workings.[35] Furthermore, in the case of feminist *ressentiment,* it is not Nietzsche's but
feminism's representation of women as the "weaker sex" that is to be
rebuffed.

Finally, although there is no reason why the discourse on feminist
ressentiment cannot be said to appropriately negotiate the sexist metaphorics of the concept itself in order to conceptualize a certain femininity that is without or beyond *ressentiment,* this alteration would confront yet another feminine metaphor. In allowing for what White calls a
"transformation of types"—that is, in allowing for the idea that the
master and slave types designate neither pure nor immutable states or
configurations of force—Nietzsche calls on yet another feminine metaphor, that of the "womb."[36] Simply put, this metaphor serves an important role not so much for theorizing how *ressentiment* might be resisted or overcome as for understanding *ressentiment* as a process of
refinement that delivers certain skills and can make certain forms of creative enterprise possible. The "achievement" of *ressentiment,* although
it is not a cheerful one, is that it has served as the condition of possibil-

ity for the bad conscience. The bad conscience is, in turn, an "illness . . . but an illness as pregnancy is an illness" (*GM* II:19). From the bad conscience an "animal with the ability to make promises" is "bred": the sovereign individual (*GM* II:1). The question as to what this means for the discourse on feminist *ressentiment* will be addressed when, in the next section, I argue that the discourse on feminist *ressentiment* can afford to increase its "indebtedness" to Nietzsche by thinking of *ressentiment* not so much as an eradicable "state" in which certain aspects of feminism are presently caught but as the condition of possibility for an ongoing and creative process through which feminism is formed and earns the capacity to form itself.

FEMINIST *RESSENTIMENT*

No wonder if the submerged, darkly glowering
emotions of vengefulness and hatred exploit this belief
for their own ends and in fact maintain no belief more
ardently than the belief that *the strong man is free* to
be weak and the bird of prey to be a lamb—for thus
they gain the right to make the bird of prey *account-*
able for being a bird of prey.
　　Friedrich Nietzsche, On the Genealogy of Morals

One recognizes the superiority of the Greek man or the
Renaissance man—but one would like to have them
without the causes and conditions that made them
possible.
　　Friedrich Nietzsche, Will to Power

We are reminded by Deleuze that Nietzsche's concept of *ressentiment* is at once "biological, sociological, historical, and political." [37] It is primarily on the plane of the political that theorists of feminist *ressentiment* use the concept, arguing as they do that certain feminist theories, practices, and political ruses are implicated in a "politics of *ressentiment*." [38] The concept presents the political theorist with a set of psychopolitical characteristics and epistemological moves that, where relevant, can be grafted onto the political attitude in question in order to "diagnose" it. A review of the etymology and meaning of the word *resentment* will help to reveal the two primary points made in the case against feminist political *ressentiment*: first, that it is nontransformative; second, that it in fact resuscitates and appropriates the relations of power it also ostensibly opposes. As we have seen, these points also appear in the discourse on feminist victimology, although there they are differently expressed, defended, and exemplified.

The French word *ressentiment,* from which the English *resentment* was derived, commonly denotes a state of vengeful rancor produced as an effect of an injurious encounter. The word *resent* conjugates the prefix *re-,* which designates both repetition and backward motion, with *sent,* which comes from the Latin verb *sentire,* "to feel." Thus *ressentiment* pertains to reactive feelings repeatedly felt and designates a psychological state that is always and only relational: resentment is always the product of "interaction" between injured forces and injuring forces (from the harmful actions of a tyrannical person to the more general condition of human suffering), and it always produces in turn a reactive desire on the part of the injured to exact retribution from the injuring (their assailant, "life"). As Anna Yeatman notes, *ressentiment* "makes sense to a subject who is systematically brutalized and exploited by more powerful forces."[39] *Ressentiment* is an *economy* of negative affect rather than an affect in itself: it is a configuration of emotions wherein pain is constantly remembered and revisited, and in which hatred and the desire for revenge are constantly renewed. What is most important for our purposes is the point at which *ressentiment* becomes "creative": that is, the point at which it becomes a "condition of possibility" and ceases to be simply a "condition."

Ressentiment gives birth to morals at the same time that it comes to serve as a means of identity formation, and on the plane of the political the concept can be used to discern the process through which negative and nontransformative political identities are achieved. The feeling of powerlessness and the experience of suffering are always at the root of *ressentiment*—whether incurred as a result of a loss of power (the noble forced to slavery) or a perpetual state of powerlessness (the "original" slave). In the case of feminism, the "danger" of *ressentiment* presents itself with the desire to counter the forces that have caused women's oppression historically. *Ressentiment* feminism can be understood, to use Yeatman's term, as a "reactive project of survival."[40] As such, this feminism forms its political identity in accordance with the tactic of inversion, and its opposition to the sociocultural configurations that have proved injurious to women is motivated by the will to reverse these configurations. This reversal occurs, at an imagined or discursive level— which is not to say that it does not have "real" effects—at the birth of feminist morals or, more specifically, when this feminism comes to equate women's powerlessness with women's goodness. As Yeatman describes, echoing the concerns of the popular press feminists dealt with above, "Such a feminism is committed to discovering what is good in women's distinctive ways of relating and doing things [and] ends up celebrating as virtues all those aspects of the identity of the oppressed which are associated with strategic self-preservation in a condition of weakness."[41] Similarly, Brown comments that this feminism maneuvers toward attaining "singular purchase on 'the good.'"[42]

For this feminism, patriarchy assumes the appearance of a system that enjoys the privilege of unhindered activity: patriarchy is a "force which does not separate itself from its effect or its manifestations."[43] This feminism will attempt to forge such a separation by casting the activity of patriarchy as the blameworthy cause of injury, as a force that must be separated from its manifestations (the doer posited beyond the deed) and be made accountable for its effects. With the introduction of accountability through accusation, this feminism casts itself and its constituency as the deserving creditors. However, the less obvious companion of this credit claim is an investment in, or indebtedness to, the power relationship from which it is elaborated. Nietzsche notes that the creature of *ressentiment* "requires a hostile world in order to exist": here this means that the evils of patriarchy *buttress* this feminism's moral identity and serve as a necessary resource for its "survival" (*GM* I:10). In this sense, this feminism is indebted to the configuration of power against which it is situated, an indebtedness that has two effects: for Yeatman, it "preserv[es] the identity of the oppressed subject"; for Brown, it "inadvertently redraw[s] the very configurations and effects of power that [it] seek[s] to vanquish."[44] As with the previous set of writers I discussed, Brown, Yeatman, and Tapper share the concern that the politics of *ressentiment* leads feminists to position themselves "politically" in a morally superior realm outside of power. In this realm—the margins, the bottom of the hierarchy—participating in power is admonished as an unfeminist act that is equated with "undemocratic domination."[45] One of the primary points found in each of their critiques is that this realm is no less implicated in a will to power and no less prone to the desire to dominate than is the center, the top of the hierarchy.

For Yeatman, whose analysis is concerned with feminism's turn to the state, a feminism motivated by *ressentiment* fails to discern the points at which "power as capacity" and "undemocratic domination" are separable. Yeatman advises that feminists can recognize and deploy, rather than evade or demonize, the positive aspects of power as used by those with greater factual power: namely, the "project of self-government" and Nietzschean "triumphant self-affirmation."[46] Although less optimistic than Yeatman about Nietzsche's currency for thinking through feminist politics "without *ressentiment*," Brown's concerns are similar. Her account turns on the politico-epistemological ramifications of *ressentiment* for feminism, and she focuses on modernist feminists.[47] She argues that the terms on which modernist feminists play out their rejection of the discourse of postmodernism are consistent with the "epistemological spirit and political structure of *ressentiment*."[48] Through its unsettling exposure of the truth / power nexus, the discourse of postmodernism has threatened to delegitimate and displace the linchpin of modernist feminist politico-morality: "our subject that harbors truth, and our truth that opposes power."[49] Tapper's account is quite different and bears the greatest relation to the accounts of the popular press feminists insofar as she focuses on feminism in the academy. However, unlike these writers, she does not end up rejecting feminist intellectualism, nor does she locate feminism's salvation, or demise, with an emergent new generation.

Tapper sees *ressentiment* as a motivating force shaping feminist institutional practices, arguing that the laudable feminist goal to make a space for feminism in the academy was usurped at some point by a problematic desire for power over. Feminism's "will to dominate" is manifest in what Tapper calls a "specific feminist configuration of power / knowledge" that comes as an effect of hard-won battles for affirmative action.[50] At the same time that she registers things like the emergence of women's studies, gender-inclusive curricula, equal opportunity legislation, and sexual harassment procedures as positive testimony to feminist success, Tapper argues that it is at precisely these points that feminists have lapsed into "unreflective complicity [with] modern forms of power."[51] She notes as an example the production of "feminist experts" deployed to detect the wrongdoings of men and goes on to warn of the danger of feminist "intellectual authoritarianism."[52] Although there is little or no mention of the bad conscience in the accounts of Yeatman, Brown, and Tapper, it should be added that the bad conscience is the first of many "products" of *ressentiment*'s creative enterprise. On my reading of feminist *ressentiment*, the feminist "success" of which Tapper speaks can be understood as a measure of the degree to which feminism has been able to instill a bad conscience in its adversaries, and in so doing attain a level of triumph over them.

As with the popular press feminists, Yeatman, Brown, and Tapper differ with regard to the way in which they locate and exemplify feminist *ressentiment,* and for this reason they cannot simply be unified under one banner. But the respect in which their accounts differ is in itself significant. The problem with Wolf, Denfeld, and Roiphe is that their examples tend to rely on overstated divisions, so much so that Denfeld's account is quite radically contradicted by Roiphe's. Here, with Yeatman, Brown, and Tapper, we have a sophisticated plurality of examples that tend to coalesce. But put together these accounts offer much less in the way of reflection on the greater relationship between feminism and *ressentiment,* or, more specifically, on the idea that an economy of negative emotions (resentment, hatred, anger, the desire for revenge) has to some degree served to constitute the feminist "impulse" and that one can *use* Nietzsche to argue against this being an entirely negative or indeed preventable state of affairs for feminism.[53] What I am suggesting is that in the same way as Nietzsche sees the bad conscience as an illness man was "bound to contract," we should understand *ressentiment* as an inevitable and potentially positive force in feminism. Of course, we should continue to critique those theories and practices that seem so freshly engulfed by *ressentiment,* but we should not think of the force of *ressentiment* as something we can isolate in and jettison from feminism. It is Brown who asks the crucial question, "Can we develop a feminist politics without *ressentiment?*" But the strategy of formulating *ressentiment*'s counterimage for feminism—a strategy of which Brown's question is expressive—sidesteps two equally important questions: Can we *imagine* feminism without *ressentiment?* and, Would feminism have been *possible* without *ressentiment?* In what remains I will address Brown's question, but with a view to reformulate the goal it posits in accordance with a different interpretation of the meaning of *ressentiment* than that employed in her analysis.

We are used to thinking of *ressentiment* as a negative and derogatory term that denotes a "terminal" condition rife in individuals, collectives, entire cultures, particular periods of history, and indeed "civilized" humanity as a whole. *Ressentiment* is a taming, disciplining, forming, negating, and falsifying configuration of forces that brings the "internalization of man" into effect through the means of repression, displacement, and separation. But if *ressentiment* is a "poison," it is also a "flower"; if it is a "sickness," it is also a "soil"; and if it breeds impotence, then it also fosters creativity. For *ressentiment* does not always and only denote an abiding, pure or static condition: the "state" of *ressentiment* is not in itself a "destiny." Three insights into the concept of *ressentiment* will serve to illustrate this.

First, Claudia Crawford's analysis of *ressentiment* is instructive insofar as it emphasizes *ressentiment*'s status as a process and identifies the six stages in the productive life of *ressentiment* that can be discerned in Nietzsche's texts—from slave revolt through to the appearance of the sovereign individual. As Crawford notes, this sixth stage "must be superseded by an infinity of others."[54] For the abundant range of traits to which *ressentiment,* as the precondition for the bad conscience, has given rise—intelligence, memory, self-reflection, calculability, autonomy, agency, and responsibility—will have their own, negative and affirmative, creative efficacies. Second, the figure of the sovereign individual emerges from the arboreal workings of *ressentiment* and stands beyond the master and slave types to realize the capacity to "creatively posit goals" and to sustain "autonomous agency."[55] Nietzsche casts the sovereign individual in the same light that he casts Greek and Renaissance men: of the latter two, he writes that "one would like to have them without the conditions that made them possible" (*WP* 882). Extending this, the third insight pertains to the role played by the "master" in Nietzsche's *Genealogy.* Unlike the sovereign individual, the master is not a product of *ressentiment* but rather is decidedly without *ressentiment.* That Nietzsche denigrates the *ressentiment*-riven slave is clear, but it does not follow from this that the "master" or "strong man" receives entirely affirmative treatment from Nietzsche. As Richard White has elucidated,

> While the noble master is an attractive and compelling figure in many respects, it also seems clear that Nietzsche deliberately *destroys* the possibility of our identification with him, by stressing his most horrible aspect as a murderous "beast of prey." Similarly, though the servility of the slave invites our contempt, Nietzsche also reminds us that without the slave, man would have remained an entirely stupid creature, and that all the achievements of our culture actually derive from the internalization of his suffering.[56]

Taken together, these insights into the concept of *ressentiment* problematize the goal of being "without *ressentiment*" to the same extent that they illuminate the many ways in which we live *with ressentiment.* Most important, however, they demonstrate that the concept of *ressentiment* itself deserves "dual interpretation": on the one hand, this force carries with it the weight of all negation; on the other, it provides a condition of possibility for forms of affirmation. Furthermore, let us not forget that when Nietzsche first presents his thesis on master and slave morality, he adds a range of qualifications, including that these moralities can coexist "within a *single* soul" (*BGE* 260).

As noted above, Yeatman argues that feminism should embrace the triumphant self-affirmation Nietzsche associates with nobility and in so doing develop a "reflexive relationship to its own history and contradictions"—a process that she thinks is already under way.[57] Having reviewed an interpretation of *ressentiment* that extends that employed by Yeatman, we can affirm her emphasis on self-reflexivity with the qualification that this trait is characteristic of Nietzsche's sovereign individual rather than his prereflective noble. Unlike Yeatman, Brown casts Nietzschean "alternatives" to *ressentiment* as "excessively individualized," choosing to part company with him on thinking through what feminism without *ressentiment* might look like. She goes on to note that for feminists to overcome *ressentiment* they must "assume responsibility for [their] situations."[58] Therefore, we can also affirm Brown's emphasis on responsibility, given first that responsibility—the "ability to make promises"—is precisely the trait to which *ressentiment* has given rise in the sovereign individual and second that Nietzsche's genealogy of *ressentiment* is "precisely the long story of how *responsibility* originated" (*GM* II:2).

For as long as *ressentiment* is seen as a terminally negative psycho-political state for feminism, its extirpation or subtraction from feminism will be advocated. One of the consequences of discerning the presence of *ressentiment* solely in "negative" feminist practices, such as those critiqued by Yeatman, Brown, and Tapper, is that it leaves no room for the perception of *ressentiment*'s positive effects for feminism: the reflexive desire for strength over weakness, the ability to posit goals and assume politicized agency, the ability to assume responsibility for power, the ability to generate ethics. For this reason, it is important that our understanding of *ressentiment* take the less often cited aspects of this concept into account: namely, its status as a process that will beget "an abundance of strange new beauty and affirmation" (*GM* II:18) and that promises the birth of "new, active power."[59]

NOTES

I would like to express my gratitude to Alan Schrift for his thoughtful and insightful editorial advice and to Sue Best, Heather Brook, William Connolly, Penny Deutscher, Barry Hindess, Barbara Sullivan, and James Tully for their generous and helpful comments on this or earlier versions of this chapter. Very special thanks to the invaluable Brian S. Roper.

1. This term "art of hunger" comes from David Owen's valuable analysis of Nietzsche's concept of *ressentiment* in his *Maturity and Modernity: Nietzsche, Weber, Foucault and the Ambivalence of Reason* (London: Routledge, 1994), 40.

2. "Victim feminism" is Naomi Wolf's term. I refer to this kind of feminism throughout the chapter as "victimology," not strictly in the criminological sense of the term, but rather in the sense that I elucidate below.

3. Rene Denfeld, *The New Victorians: A Young Woman's Challenge to the Old Feminist Order* (Sydney: Allen & Unwin, 1995); Katie Roiphe, *The Morning After: Sex, Fear and Feminism* (London: Hamish Hamilton, 1993); Naomi Wolf, *Fire with Fire: The New Female Power and How It Will Change the 21st Century* (New York: Chatto & Windus, 1993); Wendy Brown, *States of Injury: Power and Freedom in Late Modernity* (Princeton: Princeton University Press, 1995); Marion Tapper, "*Ressentiment* and Power: Some Reflections on Feminist Practices," in *Nietzsche, Feminism and Political Theory,* ed. Paul Patton (Sydney: Allen & Unwin, 1993) (also relevant from this volume is Daniel Conway's "*Das Weib an sich:* The Slave Revolt in Epistemology"); Anna Yeatman, "Feminism and Power," in *Reconstructing Political Theory: Feminist Perspectives,* ed. U. Narayan and M. Shanley (London: Polity Press, 1993).

4. Campaign against Pornography and Censorship, "Policy Statement" (1989); cited in Anne Marie Smith, "What Is Pornography? An Analysis of the Policy Statement of the Campaign against Pornography and Censorship," *Feminist Review,* no. 43 (Spring 1993): 72.

5. Wolf, *Fire with Fire,* 149; emphasis in original.

6. Ibid., 148.

7. Denfeld, *The New Victorians,* 161.

8. Ibid., 164.

9. Ibid.

10. Sandra Harding, *The Science Question in Feminism* (Ithaca: Cornell University Press, 1986), 31.

11. Wolf, *Fire with Fire,* 147.

12. I would wager that Wolf has Nietzsche in mind here, given that his *Genealogy of Morals* appears in her bibliography in *Fire with Fire* and that in addition to characterizing "power feminism" as "without resentment" (150), she writes that it should seek to preserve women's "will to power" (333).

13. Denfeld, *The New Victorians,* 277.

14. A more detailed version of this argument has recently been forwarded by Jean Curthoys in *Feminist Amnesia: The Wake of Women's Liberation* (New York: Routledge, 1997). She argues, I think problematically, that contemporary feminist preoccupation with "obscurantist" ideas (binary oppositions in particular) is an effect of a feminist retreat from politics.

15. Wolf, *Fire with Fire,* 136.

16. Denfeld, *The New Victorians,* 127–53.

17. Beatrice Faust, foreword to Denfeld, *The New Victorians,* ix. (Faust's foreword appeared only in the Allen & Unwin Sydney edition of Denfeld's book.)

18. For example, for Denfeld's purposes the work of either Sharon Marcus or Lynne Segal would have provided excellent counterexamples. See Marcus's "Fighting Bodies, Fighting Words: Towards a Feminist Theory and Strategy for Rape Prevention," in *Feminists Theorize the Political,* ed. Joan Scott and Judith Butler (New York: Routledge, 1992); and Segal's *Slow Motion: Changing Masculinity, Changing Men* (London: Virago, 1990).

19. Sandra Lee Bartky, "Towards a Phenomenology of Feminist Consciousness," in *Femininity and Domination* (New York: Routledge, 1994). This text was originally published in 1976.

20. Ibid., 211.

21. Although she arrives at this point from a very different direction, the following comment from Elizabeth Grosz—which has contributed significantly to my thinking on Bartky's article—shares something with Bartky's "consciousness of strength." Grosz writes, "The position of subordination, while it requires the loss or absence of many of the rights and privileges of the dominant position, also produces certain skills and modes of resourcefulness, the capacity precisely for self-sustenance and creativity that are lost for the dominator" (*Space, Time and Perversion* [Sydney: Allen & Unwin, 1995], 209).

22. Wolf also comments on this. She writes, "I've heard middle-class college students scramble to identify downward, thinking they have to pretend to *be* oppressed in order to *champion* the oppressed; in the process they yield their responsibility for using the power and resources they have" (*Fire with Fire,* 125). For Wolf, assuming the identity of the oppressed amounts to renouncing responsibility for power. For Roiphe, it more importantly means consciously gaining power.

23. Roiphe, *The Morning After,* 125.

24. Ibid.

25. Wolf also comments on this aspect of Roiphe's analysis; see *Fire with Fire,* 147.

26. Brown, *States of Injury,* 44.

27. I have found the following comment of Derrida's useful here. He writes:
Can one not say, in Nietzsche's language, that there is a "reactive" feminism, and that a certain historical necessity often puts this form of feminism in power in today's organized struggles? It is this kind of "reactive" feminism that Nietzsche mocks, and not woman or women. Perhaps one should not so much combat it head on—other interests would be at stake in such a move—as prevent its occupying the entire terrain. (Jacques Derrida and Christie V. McDonald, "Choreographies," *diacritics* 12 [Summer 1982]: 68).
On my reading, one of the "other interests" to which Derrida refers is precisely the problem of producing another victimology from the critique of victimology—a critique that, for Denfeld and Roiphe, has indeed taken the form of oppositional "combat."

28. Kathleen Woodward, "Anger . . . and Anger: From Freud to Feminism," in *Freud and the Passions,* ed. John O'Neill (University Park: Pennsylvania State University Press, 1996), 92.

29. Max Scheler, *Ressentiment,* trans. William W. Holdheim (New York: Free Press, 1961), 60–61.

30. Ibid., 61; emphasis in original.

31. Gilles Deleuze, *Nietzsche and Philosophy,* trans. Hugh Tomlinson (New York: Columbia University Press, 1983), 119.

32. Ellen Kennedy, "Nietzsche: Women as *Untermensch,*" in *Women in Western Political Philosophy: Kant To Nietzsche,* ed. Ellen Kennedy and Susan Mendus (New York: St. Martin's, 1987), 183.

33. Kennedy writes, "The outline of Nietzsche's view of women appeared first in *Menschliches Allzumenschliches* (1878) and remained constant throughout his other works" ("Nietzsche," 185). For substantive arguments to the contrary, see Ruth Abbey, "Beyond Misogyny and Metaphor: Women in Nietzsche's Middle Period," *Journal of the History of Philosophy* 34, no. 2 (April 1996): 233–56; and Lawrence J. Hatab, "Nietzsche on Woman," *Southern Journal of Philosophy* 19 (Fall 1981): 333–45.

34. William E. Connolly, "Reworking the Democratic Imagination," *Journal of Political Philosophy* 5, no. 2 (June 1997): 194.

35. Richard White, "The Return of the Master: An Interpretation of Nietzsche's *Genealogy of Morals,*" in *Nietzsche, Genealogy, Morality: Essays on Nietzsche's Genealogy of Morals,* ed. Richard Schacht (Berkeley: University of California Press, 1994), 71.

36. Nietzsche writes, "This secret self-ravishment, this artists' cruelty . . . eventually this entire *active* 'bad conscience'—you will have guessed it—as the womb of all ideal and imaginative phenomena, also brought to light an abundance of strange new beauty and affirmation, and perhaps beauty itself" (*GM* II:18).

37. Deleuze, *Nietzsche and Philosophy,* 145.

38. Yeatman, "Feminism and Power," 147.

39. Ibid.

40. Ibid. In the same way, Nietzsche writes of *ressentiment* in Jewish culture as the product of this culture having been "placed in impossible circumstances" (*AC* 24).

41. Yeatman, "Feminism and Power," 148.

42. Brown, *States of Injury,* 47.

43. Deleuze, *Nietzsche and Philosophy,* 122–23.

44. Yeatman, "Feminism and Power," 148; Brown, *States of Injury,* ix.

45. Yeatman, "Feminism and Power," 146.

46. Ibid., 147.

47. Brown, *States of Injury,* 47.

48. Ibid., 45.

49. Ibid., 47.

50. Tapper, "*Ressentiment* and Power," 130.

51. Ibid., 139.

52. Ibid.

53. Perhaps the view that the politics of *ressentiment* is not "preventable" for feminism would be shared by Yeatman. In the conclusion to her article she notes that her analysis of feminism's problematic relationship to power is not geared toward suggesting that this relationship "could [have been] otherwise" (155).

54. Claudia Crawford, "Nietzsche's Mnemotechnics, the Theory of *Ressentiment,* and Freud's Topographies of the Psychical Apparatus," *Nietzsche-Studien,* Band 14 (1985): 296.

55. Owen, *Maturity and Modernity,* 37.

56. White, "The Return of the Master," 66; emphasis in original.

57. Yeatman, "Feminism and Power," 155.

58. Brown, *States of Injury,* 51.

59. Crawford, "Nietzsche's Mnemotechnics," 296.

Performing Resentment

White Male Anger; or, "Lack" and Nietzschean Political Theory

Jeffrey T. Nealon

> To the psychologists first of all, presuming they would like to
> study *ressentiment* close up for once, I would say: this plant
> blooms best today among anarchists and anti-Semites—
> where it has always bloomed, in hidden places, like the violet,
> though with a different odor.
>
> *Friedrich Nietzsche*, On the Genealogy of Morals

White men are *angry* these days, and this chapter presents a Nietzschean reading of the performative subject known as the "white, angry male" (hereafter, WAM) in contemporary American political discourse. I am also, however, interested in possible diagnoses of this phenomenon that are available to us in current Nietzsche-inspired political theory— represented here by William E. Connolly and Judith Butler. I will try to end, in fact, by making some contentious connections between WAM discourse and these, which I take to be the most productive and influential of current Nietzschean political theories.

Of course, as we begin to look at WAM discourse, we need to recognize that a certain bastardized version of Nietzsche is already at play. The frontline performers of this anger—Pat Buchanan, G. Gordon Liddy, and Rush Limbaugh—take themselves to be a certain type of popularized Nietzschean:[1] unwilling to hear anything about "victims" (other than themselves), they perform their rhetoric of self-overcoming in front of a growing audience of angry followers.

Of course, on further examination, this WAM discourse shows its pedigree not in Nietzsche but precisely in that which Nietzsche set out to analyze in *On the Genealogy of Morals* and so much of his other work: resentment. Because white men are now overtly marked as a group, they find themselves besieged by the double consciousness that other groups have long had to manage within American culture, and they are deeply resentful about this.[2] The white male has been marked with its own difference, and the performers of resentment take this as their own special brand of victimization. While the WAMs take themselves to be Nietzschean "great birds of prey," in the end they show themselves to be closer cousins to his "little lambs," bleating the refrain "you are evil; therefore, I am good" (see *GM* I:13).

As Gilles Deleuze writes in *Nietzsche and Philosophy,* such a resentful subject "makes the object responsible for [the subject's] own powerlessness. . . . It is venomous and depreciative because it blames the object in order to compensate for its own inability to escape from the traces of the corresponding excitation. This is why *ressentiment*'s revenge, even when it is realized, remains 'spiritual,' imaginary, and symbolic in principle."[3] From Pat Buchanan's new *Kulturkampf* to Rush Limbaugh's demonization of the welfare mother; from the various "independent republics" set up in the western United States to Tim McVeigh's symbolic reasons for bombing the federal building in Oklahoma City,[4] the purveyors of WAM discourse are first and foremost resentful purveyors of anger-as-revenge, artists of resentment who constantly construct a symbolic metaphorization out of what they take to be a wounding or expropriating act.

This is, of course, *not* to say that the economy of resentment is somehow unreal, or that killing federal workers is *merely* a symbolic act. It is, rather, to insist that WAM resentment creates effects on the sociopolitical level through a pernicious symbolic economy of othering, creating enemies solely to bolster the WAM's own sense of inherent goodness. As Nietzsche writes, "Picture 'the enemy' as the man of *ressentiment* conceives him—and here precisely is his deed, his creation: he has conceived 'the evil enemy,' '*the Evil One,*' and this in fact is his basic concept, from which [the man of *ressentiment*] then evolves, as an afterthought and pendant, a 'good one'—himself" (*GM* I:10). The resentful person has an identity only insofar as he or she is angry at someone else, an "Evil One."

So why even bother to reopen a discourse about *anger?* Why not just cede the field to the rancorous chorus of whiners and moaners and try to perform another mode of comportment toward the other— communicative rationality, the ethical face-to-face, the openness to alterity stressed in leftist political, feminist, and postcolonial discourses? Indeed, can there really be any kind of ethically or politically productive anger, insofar as anger seems intimately associated with the renunciation of alterity? Isn't "anger" as a category of political analysis irrevocably tainted by a kind of reprehensible xenophobia?

To take up these questions, we would first need to make a distinction between resentment and anger. Resentment, as Nietzsche shows in *On the Genealogy of Morals,* is the first and last safe harbor for the stable subject, who, as Nietzsche writes, "from the outset says No to what is 'outside,' what is 'different,' what is 'not itself'" (*GM* I:10). Such subjective resentment is different from anger because resentment never properly sets out from itself: the rancorous subject's "No" to alterity is assured "from the outset" (or, really, from *before* the outset). Rancor admits of no alterity and gives rise to nothing other than self-assured smugness. As Nietzsche shows throughout the *Genealogy,* resentment preeminently produces more reified, effective, and pernicious versions of resentment. It cannot, in Nietzschean parlance, create *affirmative* values.

Anger, however, can be deterritorializing at certain sites—it can produce something other, a line of flight. Anger does not accrue quite so easily to an assured movement of subjective appropriation and control. It is in this sense that Jean-Luc Nancy writes,

> Anger is the political sentiment par excellence. It brings out the qualities of the inadmissible, the intolerable. It is a refusal and a resistance that with one step goes beyond all that can be accomplished reasonably—in order to open possible paths for a new negotiation of the reasonable but also paths of uncompromising vigilance. Without anger, politics is accommodation and trade in influence; writing without anger [merely] traffics in . . . seductions.[5]

Perhaps one could say that resentment is being angry at-the-other, for the sake of the self. Nancy's Nietzschean anger as a "political sentiment," however, is precisely anger for-the-other: political anger does not merely say no to difference but precisely "brings out the qualities of the inadmissible, the intolerable." In short, anger can produce a response that is more than a repetition of the same: anger is perhaps another of the myriad names for a movement outside the self that does not merely return to the self.

To put it slightly differently, resentment necessarily presupposes and reifies existing categories of recognition; it judges injury by the failure to attain a phantasmatic ideal. Resentment, then, is always a metaphoric or *representational* type of anger, which protects an interior space from interrogation and contamination; for Nietzsche, resentment brings about the reinterpretation of bodily suffering as "*orgies of feeling*" (*GM* III:20). As Gilles Deleuze expands on this claim, "The word *ressentiment* gives a definite clue: *reaction ceases to be acted in order to be something felt (senti)."* [6] *Ressentiment,* then, is the (non)reaction that characterizes the victimized bourgeois subject, the one who consistently translates exterior provocations—opportunities to respond—into interior states or representational "feelings," slights to be felt and remembered, each new trauma a metaphor for all the others that have robbed him of his autonomy and happiness.

In contradistinction, what we might call the political anger of transformation introduces a metonymic movement that calls for(th) an attention and response to alterity. The metaphoric speech act "feel my pain" is in this way at considerable odds with the angrier speech act "do something about pain." Anger produces or gestures toward new categories, rather than pleading in the name of existing ones; and a political anger would thereby open a space for us to respond to subjective or communal expropriation in other than resentful ways. To paraphrase Deleuze and Guattari, I am trying to suggest in this chapter that anger can be a factory (a site of *production*) for subjectivities rather than primarily a theater (a site of *representation* or *recognition*) for the staging of an already-reified drama of subjectivity. In a Nietzschean vocabulary, perhaps the subject we know as the *angry* white male is in fact better described as the *resentful* white male.[7]

To further sharpen the distinction between anger and resentment within a Nietzschean frame, resentment is always based on or in some notion of *failure, absence,* or *lack:* I resent the other because the other has something that I do not; or, in more properly Hegelian or Lacanian language, I always desire or derive *recognition* from the other. I both desire and lack completeness, and I resent the social fact that I must submit to the other in order to attain a measure of this completeness. Of course, it is precisely the continual refinement of such subjective lacks that one can read in the *Genealogy*'s three essays—the movement from resentment proper to the bad conscience to the ascetic priest (cannily shadowing the *Phenomenology of Spirit*'s opening movement from consciousness to self-consciousness to Reason). Each step of the way, Nietzsche demonstrates, a subjective lack is made more precious—more productive of reactive effects.[8]

And, as Nietzsche shows us throughout the *Genealogy,* resentment and its lack-inspired kin are poisonous because they always separate the subject from what it can do—always downplay the affirmative *acts* of subjective performativity and subordinate them to the conceptual language of recognition. As he writes, "The slave revolt in morality begins when *ressentiment* itself becomes creative and gives birth to values: the *ressentiment* of natures that are denied the true reaction, that of deeds, and compensate themselves with an imaginary revenge" (*GM* I:10). The resentful subject who is the WAM, for example, ignores the angry affirmation of the sociopolitical dice throw and tries instead to argue that someone else has rigged the table before the game even started. Immigrants, Affirmative Action Recipients, FemiNazis, Liberal Media Moguls, the UN: they supposedly rule the field, and refuse recognition of the WAM's expropriation. For example, William Pierce, founder of the National Alliance and Cosmotheist Church (after he splintered from the National Socialist White People's party in 1970) and author of the infamous *Turner Diaries*,[9] writes that there are several ways to get "free money" in America: "be an 80-IQ welfare mom having illegitimate children every nine months; be a homosexual 'performance artist'; a foreign dictator in the good graces of New World Order elitists; someone who burns their own neighborhood."[10] As Kathy Marks goes on to explain, Pierce holds "that this 'free money' is not available to working white Americans because their job is to provide this 'free money.'"[11]

Of course, this is not to deny that the much-ballyhooed return of the resentful white male in American political discourse has its phantasmatic and material roots in a kind of righteous anger—in the majority of such men's very real exclusion from a white, middle-class male ideal of power and privilege. When Norm from Scranton calls Rush Limbaugh to complain of his expropriation, he appeals to the same sense of need, exclusion, and frustration that drives more obviously righteous claims to discrimination. Indeed, there has been much recent discourse from the American left concerning alternative ways to harness this failure, to transform the WAM's resentment against women, immigrants, and minorities into a political anger aimed at the likelier causes of their expropriation: transnational corporations, the Republican upward redistribution of wealth carried out during the 1980s and 1990s, corporate welfare, union busting through so-called right-to-work legislation, and so on. Certainly there is no simple solution to the WAM phenomenon, but any productive intervention would first have to redirect this anger, make it productive of something other than resentment.[12] As Deleuze writes, within a Nietzschean frame, "the possibilities of a cure will be subordinated to the transformation of types."[13]

For the purposes of the present argument, then, I am—following Nietzsche's metaphorics of sickness and health—most interested in a *diagnosis* of the WAM phenomenon. Most specifically, I am interested in exploring the theme of lack that runs through both the resentful, right-wing WAM discourse and the more radical, left-wing discourse that would attempt to redirect or redeploy the WAM's ire. Both right and left seem to agree that the system has *failed* these people, and WAMs need to respond to their expropriation by re-representing themselves to the public at large. However, the telling point in this return of the WAM is that a discourse of identity's lack—failure to attain the ideal of white male autonomy—tends to level all identity "failures" onto the same plane, and thereby to homogenize the very specific interpellative conditions that produce a particular subjectivity. Norm-from-Scranton's anger, while very real, is simply not of the same order as other brands of social interpellation. Likewise, discriminations based on age, weight, race, style of dress, and physical challenge are obviously not of the same category, and getting a lousy table in a restaurant is not in any meaningful way akin to being denied employment—even if both events take place due to the same discriminatory reason.

At its strongest, however, an identity politics of exclusion (whether it be "conservative" or "radical") attempts to conflate these specific injuries around the common theme of lack or expropriation: any specific lack or failure becomes a symptom of a more generalized lack; likewise, what we have in common is that we all lack in some way. The consensus in political theory seems to be that we meet on the common ground of intersubjective impasse. The difference between right and left is that a conservative discourse finds resentment lying on the common ground, whereas a liberal one argues for the possibility of expanded recognition or subversion of the norm.

But this is where the birds of prey who are progressive or liberal political theorists meet up again with the newly born little lambs of angry white maledom, where the theorized identity discourse of the left meets the WAM: both share this notion that lack is the inevitable state of things in the political world. And this is also where Nietzsche-inspired social theory meets its own brand of resentment, its own fetishization of *failure*. William Connolly, for example, overtly thematizes his political theory as a Nietzschean end run around the debilitating political effects of resentment. "The Nietzsche / Foucault ideals of self as work of art," he writes, are an important component of the "drive to move the subject of desire away from *ressentiment*";[14] as he clarifies, such performative models "begin to subdue subterranean resentment of the *absence of wholeness* in what one is, treating the *absence as a source of possibility* for experimental engagement."[15] Here we see the Hegelian shell game of negativity (the very *engine* of resentment) oddly reintroduced by Connolly as its own cure: it is a matter of learning to live with "absence of wholeness," learning to tolerate difference, representing your own expropriation for the other to recognize in him-, her-, or itself. While Connolly thematizes his project as the Nietzschean "introduction of a new possibility of being out of old injuries and differences,"[16] it seems that on another reading his theory reproduces and reifies the very lack-inspired economy that gives rise to resentment in the first place: in other words, the recognition or reinscription of *absence* or *failure* only reifies the privilege of presence or wholeness.[17]

Even Judith Butler's Nietzschean political discourse, which, like Connolly's, I admire greatly,[18] is unfailing in its commitment to the productivity of failure. In "Burning Acts" Butler articulates very persuasively the questions that Nietzsche's *On the Genealogy of Morals* poses to contemporary political debates about hate speech and responsibility. Specifically, she analyzes Nietzsche's famous dictum "there is no 'being' behind doing, effecting, becoming; 'the doer' is merely a fiction added to the deed—the deed is everything" (*GM* I:13), emphasizing particularly the juridical notions buried within this theory of performative subjection. As Butler writes, "In a sense, for Nietzsche, the subject comes to be only within the requirements of a moral discourse of accountability. The requirements of blame figure the subject as the 'cause' of an act."[19] She goes on, then, to pose a question to Nietzsche's discourse: "If there is an institution of punishment within which the subject is formed, is there not also a figure of the law who performatively sentences the subject into being? Is this not, in some sense, the conjecturing by Nietzsche of a prior and more powerful subject?"[20]

Indeed, it is in and around this prior performative "law" of interpellation that Butler will locate both the subjection of the subject and its opportunities for response. To be sure, she argues, the law constitutes the subject as accountability; but it is precisely in the *failure* of the law to suture or enforce accountability—the failure fully to configure the subject in accordance with a representation of juridical norms—that subjective *response* and *subversion* of the law is made possible. As Butler writes, such a "failure" of the law is productive insofar as it "is the occasion for an allegory . . . that concedes the unrealizability of that [cultural] imperative from the start, and which, finally, cannot overcome the unreality that is its condition and its lure."[21] Or, as she puts it a bit more straightforwardly in her discussion of performative identity in *Bodies That Matter*: "Since the law must be repeated to remain an authoritative law, the law perpetually reinstitutes the possibility of its own failure."[22] The totalized configuration of identity, accountability, and the law inexorably *fails*, and that is why subjectivity can always be reinscribed or redescribed: as Butler writes, "The name fails to sustain the identity of the body within the terms of cultural intelligibility."[23] And it is precisely this *failure* that is then the engine of performativity's productivity and its political project; as she writes about Laclau and Mouffe, "Lack or negativity is central to the project of radical democracy precisely because it constitutes within discourse the resistance to all essentialism and descriptivism."[24]

Of course, Butler's readings of Lacan, Žižek, and Laclau and Mouffe also bring out her critique of lack—she exposes the *ahistorical* nature of failure in psychoanalysis, its resentful reduction of all laws to the transhistorical law of castration. She consistently asks, in other words, after the *historical construction* of practices and subjectivities; she asks after the ways in which lack is installed and made concrete at specific sites and in specific practices, rather than insist on or point out a transhistorical law. As she argues concerning psychoanalysis and social theory,

> That there is always an "outside" and, indeed, a "constitutive antagonism" seems right, but to supply the character and content to a law that secures the borders between the "inside" and the "outside" of symbolic intelligibility is to preempt the specific social and historical analysis that is required, to conflate into "one" law the effect of a convergence of many, and to preclude the very possibility of a future rearticulation of that boundary.[25]

Surely, as Butler argues, a specific analysis of historical expropriations is a linchpin of political engagement, and such a historical or contextual emphasis is especially crucial in psychoanalytic frames, as a guard against coming to the same tautological, difference-erasing conclusion in every historical moment and epoch.

But, at the same time, I think we would have to ask whether a historicized version of this law of failure is any less prone to function as an engine to erase difference? Does historicizing exclusion open the way to a becoming-angry, or does it primarily offer a more reified way to represent cultural resentments? Does arguing that the ubiquity of lack is socially constructed and enforced (rather than essentially found) somehow make the problem of tautology disappear?[26] Are Rush's listeners' "kudos and dittoes" any more or less resentful just because the lacks they reference can be fairly specifically historicized?

The expropriating work of the negative has certainly been valuable to a political ethics, because lack is both revelatory and dangerous to the smugly humanist subject, who is exposed to the hazards of alterity by its recognition of the lacks within itself. We may, however, need to hesitate here and ask a question much like Steven Shaviro's question to Lacanian film theory: "But is it really *lack*," he asks, that the subject finds "so dangerous and disturbing?"[27] Is it really *lack* that opens or keeps open ethical relations? Isn't it more likely that the inevitability of *lack* leads to an equally inevitable *resentment*—the reification of the imaginary desiring link to what is (supposedly) lacking? As Shaviro points out, discourses of failure—lack of totalization, lack of identity, lack of completeness—inexorably protect the "conservative, conformist assumption . . . that our desires are primarily ones for possession, plenitude, stability, and reassurance."[28] It seems, as Shaviro writes, that "even at its ostensibly most critical," tarrying with the negative "does nothing but reinscribe a universal history of lack and oppression";[29] and in the process such a tarrying protects the horizon of wholeness, if only as that which we can never attain.

In more properly Nietzschean parlance, lack or failure could hardly be inevitable insofar as "whatever exists, having somehow come into being, is again and again reinterpreted to new ends, taken over, transformed" (*GM* II:12). If there is an allegory of anything in Nietzsche, it seems to be an allegory of immanence and production rather than (or at least in addition to) an allegory of inexorable loss.

Indeed, it seems that the inevitability of lack—what Butler calls "the unrealizability of that [cultural] imperative from the start"—leads to an inevitability of resentment, an allegory of inexorable failure that quickly mutates from resentment ("it's your fault") into its cousin, bad conscience ("it's my fault"). But the problem with such an allegorical reading of Nietzsche is that it makes or leaves only certain paths available for transformational *anger*, especially something like white male anger. Certainly, one of the greatest successes of the new social movements and their theorized politics of identity has been the mobilization of anger-as-lack: women, minorities, and queers, for example, can mobilize around a critique of the completely unjustified and unjustifiable privilege of the straight-white-male norm in American society. For some, perhaps for everyone, normativity inexorably fails; one is never fully sutured to one's subaltern subject position, and the angry demand for recognition that comes from outside the norm—"We're here and we're queer!"—will necessarily disrupt and reconfigure that norm. The norm fails to account for or recognize otherness; and under a Nietzschean topological reading of forces, which always asks after the *effects* of an intervention rather than some inherent meaning, an anger based in normativity's lack and its re-inscription certainly can do productive work in many political contexts.

But what if one *is* the supposed norm—the white male—and one is nevertheless stuck with a certain kind of inevitable "failure"? How does one deploy or redeploy that anger, that failure, that normativity? At oneself? At other versions of one's subject position? And how can this happen without transmuting resentment's effects inexorably into the poisonous effects of Nietzschean bad conscience—with bad conscience itself functioning only as a rest stop on the highway to ascetic priest-hood? Is Nietzsche offering us an *inevitable* story in the *Genealogy*? Are there not differing effects and differing deployments of force? Can *all* force be understood as a reaction to failure? Is all anger territorializable as anger over loss? Within a political discourse of normativity's lack, is there a subject position available to the WAM other than xenophobia or self-flagellation, the twin towers of *ressentiment*? [30]

I suppose the question I am trying to pose goes something like this: just as queer theorists like Eve Sedgwick argue that conclusions from es-sentialism/constructionism debates in feminism cannot be simply im-ported into queer politics (where essentialism does substantially differ-ent work in responding to those who would thematize queerness merely as the perverted social construction of a "lifestyle"),[31] it is not at all clear that subjective lack or failure as a theoretical engine of political analysis and response leaves any other-than-resentful response available to the WAM subject position. This is *not*, I hasten to add, to say that this dis-course doesn't do a *tremendous* amount of work in analyzing and re-deploying political angers in other contexts. But the overarching reach of the theoretical frame itself—the fact, as Butler puts it, that "con-science doth make subjects of us all" through an allegory of loss—seems a bit suspicious, and not because it does not do *enough* work; rather, I would suggest that perhaps this frame does *too much* work, because it seems to explain virtually everything on the political horizon in terms of representing and recognizing the subject's lacks and failures.

For Butler, of course, there is no subject at all without this failure;

and she argues, based on this reading, that all consciousness in Nietz-sche is besieged by bad conscience.[32] As she argues in *The Psychic Life of Power,*

> Considered along Nietzschean and Hegelian lines, the subject engages in its own self-thwarting, accomplishes its own subjection, desires and crafts its own shackles, and so turns against a desire that it knows to be—or knew to be—its own. For a loss to predate the subject, to make it possible (and im-possible), we must consider the part that loss plays in subject formation. Is there a loss that cannot be thought, cannot be owned or grieved, which forms the condition of possibility for the subject?[33]

As Butler shows, it is clear that Nietzsche insists on a "subjection, with-out which no proper subject emerges";[34] Nietzsche shows time and again how the doer is backloaded from the deed as the action's supposed "cause." But what is not so clear in Nietzsche is how you get from this notion of inevitable subjection to the notion that subjection is the in-evitable installation of "loss." Loss of what? If, as Butler argues, there is no subject in Nietzsche but for the recoil of an act, where does this "pre-date[d]" loss come from?

As Butler writes, "The address that inaugurates the possibility of agency, in a single stroke, forecloses the possibility of radical auton-omy."[35] Surely, there is always subjection where there is subjectivity; but, I wonder, how do we know the subject wants "radical autonomy," and wants it enough to recognize each time autonomy's failure? Where does that desire for wholeness come from? Butler insists that "Nietzsche offers us a political insight into the formation of the psyche and the problem of subjection, understood paradoxically not merely as the sub-ordination of a subject to a norm, but as the constitution of a subject through precisely such a subordination."[36] Again, this insight seems ir-reducible, but that simultaneity of subject and subjection being the case, it would seem to follow that the pathos of loss or lack cannot exist al-ways and everywhere.

If, as Butler argues, "loss inaugurates the subject and threatens it with dissolution,"[37] it seems that a kind of transcendental desire for whole-ness—and its subsequent lack—does quite a lot of unthematized work within the social drama of subject formation. The diagnostic Nietz-schean topology of subjectivities—how much and what kind of force is manifest in a particular situation?—seems territorialized on one kind of force and hence one kind of subjectivity: the one who lacks. In Nietz-sche, while it seems clear that there is always subjection—the subject is never simply in control of its itinerary—such subjections call forth responses, and not all response is territorializable as response to loss. All action in Nietzsche is not necessarily resentful, and all consciousness does not take the form of bad conscience. One would always need to do an analysis—a Nietzschean diagnosis or interpretation—to find out what forces were at work in a particular economy. While, strictly speaking, there is no purely active (i.e., unconstrained) force in Nietzsche— all subjective force is deployed in response to subjection—this does not evacuate the diagnostic distinction between active (for Nietzsche, "noble") and reactive ("base") forces (see esp. *GM* I:10).

Following Nietzsche, I would argue that the work of the negative does not comprise the privileged horizon for diagnosing or enacting transformation in a postmodern society, where totalization or representation has given way to the proliferating intensity of production. Strictly speaking, the *Genealogy* shows us that the ubiquity of "lack" is impossible, insofar as even the most reactive of forces *produces* something as response: even the most poisonous internalizing forces produce a certain kind of nihilism or will-to-nothingness that may offer the opportunity to open the subject out.[38] Nietzsche consistently warns against prescriptive or transcendentalizing understandings of power and argues for diagnostic or immanent ones:

> Henceforth, my dear philosophers, let us be on guard against the dangerous old conceptual fiction that posited a "pure, will-less, painless, timeless knowing subject"; let us guard against the snares of such contradictory concepts as "pure reason," "absolute spirituality [*Geistigkeit*]," "knowledge in itself": these things demand that we should think of an eye that is *completely unthinkable*, an eye turned in no particular direction, in which *the active and interpretive forces*, through which alone seeing becomes seeing *something*, are supposed to be lacking. (*GM* III:12; emphasis added)

There is, for Nietzsche, no moment in which active force is "lacking" or "incomplete": even the force that turns on itself—the forces of resentment and bad conscience—*produces* things. Unfortunately, resentment and bad conscience have produced ascetic priesthood, but they produce nevertheless: "bad conscience is an illness, there is no doubt about that, but an illness as pregnancy is an illness" (*GM* II:19). "Bad conscience" is like "pregnancy" insofar as it is an effect that brings other effects into being; it gives birth to something. For Nietzsche, there is always production, immanence. Cathexis onto the state where things "are supposed to be lacking" is the misdiagnosis of the nihilist and the philosopher.

The ethical force of what I am calling a political anger comes about in the *emergence of* and *response to* the other, not in an inexorable allegory of subjectivity's failure to comprehend or assimilate otherness, or its failure to be recognized in and for its lacks. Certainly, the subject-as-lack also produces "a play of affects and effects," but preeminent among them seem to be resentment and reification rather than some kind of opening to alterity, and the WAM is par excellence this style of "failing" subject: the WAM *knows* that it has been expropriated, denied recognition; the WAM knows the norm has failed and that it itself is nothing but this failure. But, at least in the case of the WAM, that "failure" only makes sense within an impossible imaginary link to "success": failure, in other words, only reifies the impossible normativity of totalization. And, in the case of the WAM, such an allegory of necessary failure leads to the inevitability of resentment: the WAM already lives within an understanding of subjectivity as failure to approximate the norm, and he responds with the symbolic violence that we have all come to know and fear. The WAM is the man of *ressentiment,* but it seems the only thing available to him under a system that would understand subjectivity as an allegory of failed normativity. Because he "is" this phantasmatic norm, the WAM's failed anger has no productive place to go.

The angry political subject, to put it bluntly, is—or needs to be—angry over something more than its losses or failures. If failure is indeed the only engine of subjectivity, then the resentful anger of the WAM is both well founded and here to stay, the paradigm of subjectivity itself. In the end, it seems that an ethics or politics of originary lack knows too well how to be angry; it too quickly thematizes the other as somehow like the self in its identity. The subject is angered when it is seemingly expropriated by the other or the others. According to such a politics of expropriation, we are all symptoms; we are the way we lack. But, as Nietzsche teaches us, to hold that a specific identity is a symptom of an originary or socially common lack is always to separate an identity or a body from what it can do—from the ways in which angry subjects can *respond* to the specificities of subjection within the very terms of that subjection. Nietzsche writes, "All instincts that do not discharge themselves outwardly *turn inward*—that is what I call the *internalization* of man: thus it was that man first developed what was later called his 'soul'" (*GM* II:16). As Butler persuasively points out, this claim about the soul-producing reactive effects of power is both necessary and undeniably productive in Nietzsche, who calls the reflexivity that gives rise to bad conscience "the womb of all ideal and imaginative phenomena" (*GM* II:18). Reflexivity—what Nietzsche calls "*active* 'bad conscience'"

(*GM* II:18)—is the performative action that, given a certain reading or channeled in a certain way, can bring forth the constative effect of bad conscience.

But within this Nietzschean emphasis on action, if the founding of the subject is always already figured as a loss that gives rise to a lacking "soul," response to that lack is assured from before the fact: one responds by trying to make up for the loss and suture the gap. And whether that gap is thematized historically contingent or metaphysically primary seems to me to be of secondary consequence; the problem remains the same. In its angry attempts to close the gap, the subject continues to protect the normativity of what was supposedly lost: wholeness. This is the predicament of the WAM, lacking a privilege that was never really there, consistently reconstituting and reifying his phantasmatic links to that (non)lost (non)privilege with each resentful phone call to G. Gordon Liddy: "Norm, are you there?"

The primary relation in Butler's Nietzschean political discourse remains an imaginary relation of expropriation: revelation comes from incompleteness, lack, slippage. But to term this noncenter of the social or the subject a "failure" presupposes the normativity of a state that is somehow not constituted by interpellative social conditions—a state where the nation or the subject would or could be undivided. In a discourse like Butler's, which strives to highlight the constitutive social conditions of the subject's emergence, it seems odd to talk in terms of failure or lack. It seems that Butler's analysis would, as one of its founding premises, want to expose the promise of complete subjective freedom as an ideological or transcendental chimera founded by and in hegemonic normative narratives.

Finally, in taking into account the social interpellations of the subject, it seems that one would be obliged to account for *not-free* as otherwise than a *lack or failure of freedom*. The difficult effect of the politics of lack is that difference is thought symptomatically—in terms of its relation to a normative wholeness and its subsequent absence. As Nietzsche writes in the final section of the *Genealogy*, "*This* is precisely what the ascetic ideal means: that something was *lacking*, that man was surrounded by a fearful *void*—he did not know how to justify, to account for, to affirm himself; he *suffered* from the problem of his meaning" (*GM* III:28). Throughout the *Genealogy*, the Nietzschean question is not "what does it *mean*?" but rather "what does it *do*?": following from the action—the reflexivity or recoil—that is the subjectivization of the subject, certainly there can be lacking or negative or failing *effects*, but an allegorical installation of those effects as a founding interpellative moment tends to territorialize all production of subjective effects around the production of losses.

And as long as identity is thematized as an act conditioned by a prior lack, we will not be able to deploy a certain kind of Nietzschean productivity within subjectivity—an understanding of the subject as a verb rather than a noun, a multiple becoming rather than a monological symptom, a deployment of force rather than an assured process of mourning, a productive subjection that calls for(th) response rather than the revelation of an assured lack of wholeness. The lacking subject seems destined to remain a locus for resentment, naming itself always in terms of its failure to attain an ideal that it cannot ever hope—and does not even wish—to attain.[39] As Deleuze writes polemically, "Those who bear the negative know not what they do." [40] In other words, while its proponents take the process of loss and mourning to be an ethical *expropriation* of the subject, for Deleuze, this process is actually the assured movement of resentful subjectivity. Those who tarry with the negative, he suggests, know all too well what they do:[41] they know that totalization will fail, the subject will be frustrated, promises will inexorably be broken, black-helicopter conspiracy theories will continue to occupy much radio talk show airtime. And it is precisely because of this *success*—because lack surreptitiously returns the horizon of wholeness to the subject—that ethical and political anger, like cultural and sexual difference, must be reinscribed outside the realm of loss, lack, or failure.

This is not to say that there is some simple or obvious cure for the WAM diagnosis. One way or the other, it seems like we are destined to see more WAM deployment of what Nietzsche calls "the most dangerous of all explosives, *ressentiment*" (GM III:15). But a Nietzschean diagnosis of the WAM phenomenon can at least direct our attention toward the anger in a different way. As Molly Ivins writes, "O.K., the U.N. and the black helicopters are not the problem. But don't underestimate the anger itself." [42]

NOTES

Sections of this chapter have been incorporated into chapter 7 of my book *Alterity Politics* (1998).

1. For example, recall Limbaugh's self-generated intellectual genealogy,

"Kierkegaard, Nietzsche, Limbaugh," and the Nietzschean title of Liddy's auto-biography, *Will*. Buchanan, for his part, was a philosophy major at Georgetown.

2. See Michael Omi and Howard Winant, "Response to Stanley Arono-witz," *Socialist Review* 23, no. 3 (1994): 131, for a powerful analysis of white male anger:

These folks are now experiencing an "identity deficit": formerly, whiteness and maleness constituted cultural norms, and were thus invisible, transparent. Now, this unquestioned identity is being re-placed by a kind of "double consciousness." Whites and males must now manage their racial and gender identities to some degree, just as nonwhites and women have always done. Does this mean that they must necessarily identify with reactionary racial or gender politics?

3. Gilles Deleuze, *Nietzsche and Philosophy,* trans. Hugh Tomlinson (New York: Columbia University Press, 1983), 116.

4. As became clear at his trial, McVeigh was convinced that the order to at-tack the Branch Davidian compound in Waco was given from the Federal Build-ing in Oklahoma City (which, it turns out, is not the case). In an act fraught with symbolism, exactly two years later, on 19 April 1995, McVeigh blew up the build-ing as revenge. As Marks points out, 19 April remains a highly symbolic date for the WAM: in addition to the Waco Raid on that date in 1993 (which, in a nice symbolic touch, McVeigh used as the date of issue for his forged South Dakota driver's license), 19 April is also the anniversary of the 1775 Battle of Lexington ("the shot heard round the world" that began the American Revolutionary War) and the execution of Richard Wayne Snell—a member of the Covenant, the Sword and the Arm of the Lord—for the murder of a Jewish businessman and a black police officer. See Kathy Marks, *Faces of Right-Wing Extremism* (Bos-ton: Branden, 1996), 101. Hitler's birthday, we should note, is 20 April.

5. Jean-Luc Nancy, "The Compearance: From the Existence of 'Commu-nism' to the Community of 'Existence,'" trans. Tracy B. Strong, *Political The-ory* 20, no.3 (1992): 375.

6. Deleuze, *Nietzsche and Philosophy,* 111.

7. Nietzsche, of course, had little patience for the resentful white men of his own day: "I also do not like these latest speculators in idealism, the anti-Semites, who today roll their eyes in a Christian-Aryan-bourgeois manner and exhaust one's patience by trying to rouse up all the horned-beast elements in the people by a brazen abuse of the cheapest of all agitator's tricks, moral attitudi-nizing" (*GM* III:26).

8. See Deleuze's *Nietzsche and Philosophy,* 8–10, and all of chapter 5, "The Overman: Against the Dialectic."

9. *The Turner Diaries* (written by Pierce under the name Andrew Macdon-ald) is a right-wing fiction about the coming race war in America, and has been taken by many extreme WAMs as a kind of blueprint. Pierce's novel, for ex-ample, portrays the destruction of a federal building—FBI Headquarters—by an ammonium nitrate fertilizer bomb packed into a delivery truck, the strategy later used by *Turner* fan McVeigh in Oklahoma City. Likewise, the extremist group the Order—responsible for the murder of Jewish talk show host Alan

Berg and a $3.6 million armored car heist used to finance Aryan movements—
overtly took its inspiration from *Turner's* portrayal of "'the Organization,' a
right-wing group that starts a race war against the System, including extreme
violence to eliminate Jews, blacks and passive whites" (Marks, *Faces of Right-
Wing Extremism,* 86).

10. Summarized in Marks, *Faces of Right-Wing Extremism,* 59.

11. Ibid.

12. For suggestions on deploying this anger otherwise, see, in addition to
Omi and Winant, Molly Ivins, who writes, "Working-class people are getting
screwed by their own government. Its latest start is to cut the capital gains tax
and the estate tax that kicks in after a person leaves more than $600,000. More
tax breaks for the rich mean a larger share of the tax burden for everybody else.
What we have here is just a little case of misdirected anger" ("Lone Star Republic," *Nation* 264, no. 20 [26 May 1997]: 5.). See also groups like the Oakland-
based "Angry White Guys *for* Affirmative Action" (http://www.cts.com/browse/
publish/rocka.html).

13. Deleuze, *Nietzsche and Philosophy,* 116.

14. William E. Connolly, *The Ethos of Pluralization* (Minneapolis: University of Minnesota Press, 1995), 55.

15. Ibid., 69; emphasis added.

16. Ibid., xv.

17. For Connolly, of course, it is a matter of thematizing this absence as *excess* rather than *lack* (see p. 55), but it seems to me that one cannot so easily play
excess off against lack, insofar as both depend on some chimeric notion of normative wholeness.

18. Lest this seem merely a platitude, see my "Between Emergence and Possibility: Foucault, Derrida and Judith Butler on Performative Identity," *Philosophy Today* 40, nos. 3–4 (1996): 430–39, and "Theory That Matters," an en-
thusiastic review of *Bodies* published in *Postmodern Culture* 5, no. 1 (1994):
http://jefferson.village.virginia.edu/pmc/. The present argument grows, in fact,
out of a question posed in the final footnote of the review, where I suggest that
one might "open a dialogue with Butler concerning the problematic Hegelian
legacy of this notion of lack" in her work. Butler herself voices a similar reser-
vation in an exchange with Ernesto Laclau published in *diacritics* 27, no. 1
(1997): 10: "But I do wonder whether failure, for both of us, does not become
a kind of universal condition (and limit) of subject formation; a way in which
we still seek to assert a common condition which assumes a transcendental status in relation to particular differences."

19. Judith Butler, "Burning Acts: Injurious Speech," in *Performativity and
Performance,* ed. Eve Kosofsky Sedgwick and Andrew Parker (New York: Routledge, 1994), 220; see also *GM* II:3.

20. Butler, "Burning Acts," 200.

21. Ibid., 223.

22. Judith Butler, *Bodies That Matter: On the Discursive Limits of "Sex"*
(New York: Routledge, 1993), 108.

23. Ibid., 140.

24. Ibid., 195.

25. Ibid., 206; emphasis removed.

26. One is reminded here of Nietzsche's "On Truth and Lying in an Extra-Moral Sense" (in *Friedrich Nietzsche on Rhetoric and Language,* transs. and eds. Sander L. Gilman, Carole Blair, and David J. Parent [Oxford: Oxford University Press, 1989], 251), where he discusses the "finding of 'truth' within the rational sphere": "If someone hides an object behind a bush, and then seeks and finds it there, that seeking and finding is not very laudable." It seems that the proleptic Nietzschean critique of psychoanalysis would proceed along similar lines: if you install lack as the engine of subjectivity's desire, it should not surprise you when you find it everywhere, in "history" as well as in "theory."

27. Steven Shaviro, *The Cinematic Body* (Minneapolis: University of Minnesota Press, 1993), 16; emphasis in original.

28. Ibid., 53.

29. Ibid., 66.

30. Recent critics have argued that male subjectivity is nothing other than the combination of xenophobia *and* self-flagellation. See, for example, David Savran's "The Sadomasochist in the Closet: White Masculinity and the Culture of Victimization," *differences* 8, no. 2 (1996): 127–52. Taking his cue from Kaja Silverman's *Male Subjectivity at the Margins* (New York: Routledge, 1993), Savran argues that the contemporary male subject is a "reflexive sadomasochist," "the man whose violent instincts are turned not only against others, but also against the self" (130). While this diagnostic distinction does valuable work in describing specific effects, it hardly seems that one could territorialize *all* male subjectivity on this axis, or that all "reflexivity" is inherently "reactive" or "masochistic." Again, in a Nietzschean parlance, the quality and direction of any force is decided by its effects, not by the supposed nature of the force itself.

31. See "Axiomatic," the introduction to Sedgwick's *Epistemology of the Closet* (Berkeley: University of California Press, 1990). As an example of social constructionism used against queers, see conservative columnist Linda Bowles, writing after the "coming out" episode of television's "Ellen": "Homosexuals are made, not born. They recruit . . . using the public-school classrooms to indoctrinate our children. . . . They aren't trying to get into the Boy Scouts because they want to learn to tie knots!" (quoted in Tom Tomorrow, "Culture Wars Cartoon," *Nation* 264, no. 24 [23 June 1997]: 2).

32. See Judith Butler's *The Psychic Life of Power: Theories in Subjection* (Stanford: Stanford University Press, 1997) on the inevitability of bad conscience in Nietzsche's *GM:*

> The internalization of instinct—which takes place when the instinct
> does not immediately discharge as the deed—is understood to pro-
> duce the soul or the psyche instead; the pressure exerted from the
> walls of society forces an internalization which culminates in the
> production of the soul, this production being understood as a primary
> artistic accomplishment, the fabrication of an ideal. (74)

While this necessary reflexivity is certainly present in Nietzsche, there is nevertheless a topology of forces that one can diagnose, and not all of those forces are inherently "reactive"; there are, in other words, *effects* of reflexivity that are not merely resentful or internalizing.

33. Ibid., 24.

34. Ibid., 66.

35. Judith Butler, *Excitable Speech: A Politics of the Performative* (New York: Routledge, 1997), 26.

36. Butler, *The Psychic Life of Power,* 66.

37. Ibid., 23.

38. At the end of the *Genealogy,* the reflexivity that gives rise to the ascetic will to truth has itself called the will to truth into question, thereby inaugurating what *might* be the overcoming of nihilism, a line of flight for active forces: "All great things bring about their own destruction through an act of self-overcoming. . . . After Christian truthfulness has drawn one inference after another, it must end by drawing its *most striking inference,* its inference *against* itself; this will happen, however, when it poses the question *'what is the meaning of all will to truth?'*" (*GM* III:27).

39. As Wendy Brown argues in "Wounded Attachments," *Political Theory* 21, no. 3 (1993): 390–410, insofar as identity politics measures subjective injury in terms of exclusion from a kind of white male normativity of self-determination, such a politics inexorably harbors the ideal along with a resentment toward it; she writes, "Like all resentments, [identity politics] retains the real or imagined holdings of its reviled subject—in this case, bourgeois male privileges—as objects of desire" (394). Brown goes on to argue that because identity politics' productive moment consists in the "politicization of *exclusion* from an ostensible universal," it thereby remains "a protest that reinstalls the humanist ideal—and a specific white, middle-class, masculinist expression of this ideal—insofar as it premises itself on exclusion from it" (398).

40. Gilles Deleuze, *Difference and Repetition,* trans. Paul Patton (New York: Columbia University Press, 1994), 55.

41. Compare Nietzsche, *GM* I:14, where "Mr. Rash and Curious" agrees with our humble narrator that "weakness is being lied into something *meritorious*": "'for *they* know not what they do—we alone know what *they* do!'"

42. Ivins, "Lone Star Republic," 5.

Contributors

DAVID B. ALLISON teaches philosophy at the State University of New York at Stony Brook. He has published widely on Nietzsche, continental philosophy, and psychoanalysis, has edited several volumes, including most recently *Sade and the Narrative of Transgression* (1995), and has written (with Mark Roberts) *Disordered Mother or Disordered Diagnosis? Munchausen by Proxy Syndrome* (1999). He is currently completing a manuscript titled *Rereading the New Nietzsche*.

DEBRA B. BERGOFFEN is professor of philosophy and director of the Research and Resource Center and the women's studies program at George Mason University. Her areas of interest are continental philosophy and feminist theory. Her most recent work on marriage and desire pursues the implications of her book, *The Philosophy of Simone de Beauvoir: Gendered Phenomenologies, Erotic Generosities* (1997).

WENDY BROWN teaches women's studies and legal studies at the University of California, Santa Cruz, and political theory at the University of California, Berkeley. Her most recent book is *States of Injury: Power and Freedom in Late Modernity* (1995). She is currently completing a work provisionally titled *Liberalism Out of History*.

JUDITH BUTLER is the Maxine Elliot Chair in the Departments of Rhetoric and Comparative Literature at the University of California, Berkeley. Her most recent books are *The Psychic Life of Power: Theories in Subjection* (1997) and *Excitable Speech: A Politics of the Performative* (1997).

DANIEL W. CONWAY is professor of philosophy at The Pennsylvania State University. He has published widely on topics in nineteenth-century philosophy, contemporary continental philosophy, and political theory. His most recent publications include *Nietzsche and the Political* (1997) and *Nietzsche's Dangerous Game: Philosophy in the Twilight of the Idols* (1997).

JOHN BURT FOSTER, JR., is professor of English and cultural studies at George Mason University and editor of *The Comparatist*. In addition to numerous publications in the transnational study of nineteenth- and twentieth-century fiction, autobiography, and culture, he is the author of *Heirs to Dionysus: A Nietzschean Current in Literary Modernism* (1981).

DUNCAN LARGE is lecturer in German at the University of Wales, Swansea, and chairman of the Friedrich Nietzsche Society (U.K.). He has published various articles on Nietzsche and translations of Nietzsche's *Twilight of the Idols* and Sarah Kofman's *Nietzsche and Metaphor*.

ALPHONSO LINGIS is professor of philosophy at The Pennsylvania State University. Widely published in continental philosophy, his most recent books include *The Community of Those Who Have Nothing in Common* (1994), *Sensation* (1996), *The Imperative* (1997) and *Dangerous Emotions* (California, 2000).

JEFFREY T. NEALON is associate professor of English at The Pennsylvania State University. He is the author of *Double Reading: Postmodernism after Deconstruction* (1993) and *Alterity Politics: Ethics and Performative Subjectivity* (1998).

DAVID OWEN is lecturer in political theory and assistant director of the Centre for Post-Analytic Philosophy at the University of Southampton, U.K. He is the author of *Maturity and Modernity: Nietzsche, Weber, Foucault and the Ambivalence of Reason* (1994) and *Nietzsche, Politics and Modernity* (1995) and is currently working on philosophical conceptions of enlightenment.

PAUL PATTON is associate professor of philosophy at the University of Sydney. He edited *Nietzsche, Feminism and Political Theory* (1993) and *Deleuze: A Critical Reader* (1996) and is the author of *Deleuze and the Political* (forthcoming).

AARON RIDLEY is senior lecturer in philosophy and associate director of the Centre for Post-Analytic Philosophy at the University of Southampton, U.K. He is the co-editor of *Arguing about Art: Contemporary Philosophical Debates* and *The Philosophy of Art: Readings Ancient and Modern* (1995) and the author of *Music, Value and Passions* (1995) and *Nietzsche's Conscience: Six Character Studies from the Genealogy* (1998).

ALAN D. SCHRIFT is professor of philosophy at Grinnell College. He is the author of *Nietzsche's French Legacy: A Genealogy of Poststructuralism* (1995) and *Nietzsche and the Question of Interpretation* (1990), editor of *The Logic of the*

Gift: Toward an Ethic of Generosity (1997), and co-editor (with Gayle L. Ormiston) of *The Hermeneutic Tradition: From Ast to Ricoeur* (1990) and *Transforming the Hermeneutic Context: From Nietzsche to Nancy* (1990). He is currently working on a comprehensive anthology of twentieth-century French philosophy.

GARY SHAPIRO is Tucker-Boatwright Professor in the Humanities and professor of philosophy at the University of Richmond. He is the author of *Nietzschean Narratives* (1989), *Alcyone: Nietzsche on Gifts, Noise, and Women* (1991), and *Earthwards: Robert Smithson and Art after Babel* (1995).

REBECCA STRINGER is writing a doctoral dissertation on Nietzsche and feminism in the Political Science Program at the Australian National University.

DANA R. VILLA teaches political theory at the University of California, Santa Barbara. He is the author of *Arendt and Heidegger: The Fate of the Political* (1996) and *Politics, Philosophy, Terror: Essays on the Thought of Hannah Arendt* (1999) and the editor of the *Cambridge Companion to Hannah Arendt* (2000). He is currently completing a manuscript titled *Socratic Citizenship*.

Index

Text:	10/13 Sabon
Display:	Sabon
Composition:	G & S Typesetters
Printing and binding:	Edwards Brothers, Inc.

9236